Sigrid Norris and Carmen Daniela Maier (Eds.)
Interactions, Images and Texts

Trends in Applied Linguistics

Edited by
Ulrike Jessner
Claire Kramsch

Volume 11

Interactions, Images and Texts

A Reader in Multimodality

Edited by
Sigrid Norris and Carmen Daniela Maier

DE GRUYTER
MOUTON

ISBN 978-1-61451-164-9
e-ISBN (ePub) 978-1-61451-813-6
e-ISBN (PDF) 978-1-61451-117-5
ISSN 1868-6362

Library of Congress Cataloging-in-Publication Data
A CIP catalog record for this book has been applied for at the Library of Congress.

Bibliographic information published by the Deutsche Nationalbibliothek
The Deutsche Nationalbibliothek lists this publication in the Deutsche Nationalbibliografie;
detailed bibliographic data are available in the Internet at http://dnb.dnb.de.

© 2015 Walter de Gruyter, Inc., Boston/Berlin
Cover image: Roswitha Schacht/morguefile.com
Typesetting: RoyalStandard, Hong Kong
Printing and binding: CPI books GmbH, Leck
♾ Printed on acid-free paper
Printed in Germanyy

www.degruyter.com

Table of contents

Contributors —— ix

Sigrid Norris and Carmen Daniela Maier
1 Introduction —— 1

I Multimodal theory and methodology: How are they developed?

Suzie Wong Scollon
2 From mediated discourse and nexus analysis to geosemiotics:
   A personal account —— 7

Sigrid Norris
3 Developing multimodal (inter)action analysis: A personal account —— 13

Theo Van Leeuwen
4 About images and multimodality: A personal account —— 19

John Bateman
5 Developing a GeM (genre and multimodality) model —— 25

II Multimodal theory and methodology: What are their facets?

Rodney Jones
6 Mediated discourse analysis —— 39

Yuling Pan
7 Nexus analysis —— 53

Najma Al Zydjaly
8 Geosemiotics: Discourses in place —— 63

Jesse Pirini
9 Introduction to multimodal (inter)action analysis —— 77

Carmen Daniela Maier
10 Multimodal analysis of new corporate genres —— 93

Tuomo Hiippala
11 Multimodal genre analysis —— 111

III Conducting multimodal research

Carey Jewitt
12 Multimodal approaches —— 127

Kay O'Halloran and Victor Lim Fei
13 Systemic functional multimodal discourse analysis —— 137

Jeff Bezemer
14 Multimodal transcription: A case study —— 155

Emilia Djonov and John Knox
15 How-to-analyze webpages —— 171

Rick Iedema
16 A participatory approach to 'analysing' visual data: Involving practitioners in visual feedback —— 195

Sigrid Norris, Jarret Geenen, Thomas Metten and Jesse Pirini
17 Collecting video data: Role of the researcher —— 213

Jesse Pirini, Sigrid Norris, Jarret Geenen and Tui Matelau
18 Studying social actors: Some thoughts on ethics —— 233

IV Sample analyses

Jarret Geenen
19 Mediation as interrelationship: Example as kitesurfing —— 245

Tui Matelau
20 Vertical identity production and Māori identity —— 255

Arianna Maiorani
21 The Matrix phenomenon —— 267

Hartmut Stöckl
22 Typography —— 281

Sabine Tan
23 Multimodal constructions of factuality and authenticity in TV-news bulletins —— 297

Volker Eisenlauer
24　Facebook: A multimodal discourse analysis of (semi-)automated communicative modes —— 311

Gill Abousnnouga and David Machin
25　3-D realisation of discourse: The case of war monuments —— 323

Paul White
26　Multimodality and space exploration: Communicative space in action —— 335

Ingrid de Saint-Georges
27　Mediated discourse analysis, 'embodied learning' and emerging social and professional identities —— 347

Maria Jesus Pinar
28　Comic books —— 357

Alison Gibbons
29　Multimodality in literature: An analysis of Jonathan Safran Foer's *A Primer for the Punctuation of Heart Disease* —— 371

Sigrid Norris and Carmen Daniela Maier
30　Concluding remarks —— 381

Glossary —— 383
Index —— 399

Contributors

Gill Abousnnouga is a researcher in the Department of Media and Communication at Örebro University, Sweden. She has published numerous journal papers on war monuments along with a book, The Language of War Monuments (2013).

Najma Al Zidjaly is Associate Professor of Sociolinguistics in the Department of English at Sultan Qaboos University, Oman. She is the editor of Building Bridges: Integrating Language. Linguistics, Literature, and Translation in English Studies (CSP, 2012). Her other publications include articles in Multimodal Communication, Language in Society, Multilingua, Visual Communication, Communication & Medicine, IMQ, and Disability Studies Quarterly. Al Zidjaly is on the Editorial Board of Multimodal Communication. Her research interests include multimodality; geosemiotics; agency; disability, discourse, art and technology; social media and Arab (Omani) identity.

John Bateman is professor of Applied Linguistics at Bremen University where he has been researching issues of multimodality in various media for several years. He has published widely in the area, with recent books focusing on annotation methods for static page-based documents and the application of functional semiotics to the audiovisual moving image. He is currently head of the Bremen Institute for transmedial Textuality Research (BItT) and is developing multimodal semiotics further for film, illustrated documents and comics.

Jeff Bezemer is Senior Research Fellow at the Institute of Education, University of London and Deputy Director of MODE, a node of the National Centre for Research Methods that is focused on developing multimodal methodologies for researching digital data and environments (mode.ioe.ac.uk). He has published in the areas of workplace learning and professional communication; multimodality, literacy and pedagogy; multilingualism and education; and multimodal research methods.

Ingrid de Saint-Georges is an Associate Professor at the Faculty for Language and Literature, Humanities, Arts and Education at the University of Luxembourg. Her main research area is workplace learning and communication, usually approached from an ethnographic, multimodal and mediated discourse analytical perspective. Recent edited volumes and special issues include Multilingualism and Multimodality: Current Challenges for Educational Studies (2013, with J-J. Weber), Les compétences langagières dans la formation et dans la vie professionnelle – Transitions et transformations (2011, with Wyss, et al.), Les objets dans la formation et les apprentissage (2010, with D. Adé).

Emilia Djonov is a Lecturer in multiliteracies at the Institute of Early Childhood, Macquarie University, Australia. Her research interests and publications are in the areas of multimodal and hypermedia discourse analysis, visual communication, social semiotics, systemic functional theory, and multiliteracies.

Volker Eisenlauer is a Postdoctoral Scholar at the University of Salzburg. His areas of interest include Computer-Mediated Communication, Multimodal Discourse Analysis, Pragmatics, and Language Education. He received his Master's degree in Applied Linguistics from Macquarie University Sydney in 2002, his M.A. in German Philology from the University of Augsburg in 2004 and his PhD in English Linguistics from the University of Augsburg in 2012. He presented his findings at various major conferences and published in established volumes on language and media.

Jarret Geenen's doctoral research has been focused on the actions, interactions and learning trajectories which manifest in the sport of kitesurfing. Empirical interests also include the sociocultural construction of space/place and the ways in which cultural tools and/or mediational means affect perception, interpretation and knowledge construction.

Alison Gibbons is Senior Lecturer in Stylistics, Language and Literature at De Montfort University in Leicester (UK). She is the author of Multimodality, Cognition, and Experimental Literature (Routledge 2012) and co-editor of Mark Z. Danielewski (Manchester University Press 2011; with Joe Bray) and the Routledge Companion to Experimental Literature (Routledge 2012; with Joe Bray and Brian McHale).

Tuomo Hiippala is a doctoral student at the Department of Modern Languages, University of Helsinki. His research interests include genre, multimodality and functional linguistics. Previously, his work has been published in Journal of Pragmatics and Literary & Linguistic Computing.

Rick Iedema is Professor and Director of the Centre for Health Communication at the University of Technology, Sydney. He is also Fellow of the Academy of Social Sciences of Australia (FASSA). His research explores how communication impacts on the organization, quality and safety of care. His most recent work focuses on clinical handover, incident disclosure and professional communication around infection control. His most recent book (co-authored with Jessica Mesman and Katherine Carroll) came out with Radcliffe Oxford in 2013, titled Visualising health care improvement: Innovation from within.

Carey Jewitt is Professor of Learning and Technology and Head of the Culture, Communication and Media Department at the Institute of Education, University of London. Her research interests are the development of visual and multimodal research methods, video-based research, and researching technology-mediated interaction. She is Director of MODE – Multimodal Methods for Researching Digital Data and Environments, a NCRM Node, funded by the ESRC (Mode.ioe.ac.uk) and Crossing Boundaries, an ESRC funded project that explores the synergies between research methods in the arts and social sciences. Carey is a founding editor of the Sage journal Visual Communication, and her recent publications include The Sage Handbook of Researching Digital Technologies (2013) with Sara Price and Barry Brown, The Routledge Handbook of Multimodal Analysis, Second edition (2013) and Technology, Literacy and Learning: A multimodal approach (Routledge, 2008).

Rodney H. Jones is an Associate Professor in the Department of English at City University of Hong Kong. His research interests include health communication and digital literacies. He is co-editor (with Sigrid Norris) of Discourse in action: Introducing mediated discourse analysis (Routledge, 2005) and author of Health and risk communication: An applied linguistic perspective (Routledge, 2013).

John Knox is a Lecturer in the Department of Linguistics, Macquarie University, Australia. His research interests include multimodality, media discourse, language in education, and systemic functional theory.

Victor Lim Fei is Senior Curriculum Specialist and Senior Head for Technologies for Learning, Educational Technology Division, Ministry of Education, Singapore. He has been researching in the field of multimodality over a decade. Victor's publications include invited book chapters, articles, as well as papers in top-tier journals such as the Cambridge Journal of Education.

David Machin is Professor of Media and Communication at Örebro University, Sweden. He has published numerous books and journal papers mostly in the field of Critical Discourse Analysis, looking at text, sound, images and 3-D objects such as Introduction to Multimodal Analysis (2007), Analysing Popular Music (2010), Language of Crime and Deviance (2012) and How to do Critical Discourse Analysis: A Multimodal Introduction (2012). He is Editor of the international peer reviewed journal Social Semiotics.

Carmen Daniela Maier is Associate Professor, member of the Knowledge Communication Research Group and of Center for Corporate Communication at School of Business and Social Sciences, Aarhus University, Denmark. Among her latest publications are "Visual Evaluation in Film Trailers" in Visual Communication and "Communicating Business Greening and Greenwashing in Global Media" in The International Communication Gazette. In her current research, she focuses on the challenges of knowledge communication in the new multimodal context of research genres. Her research interests include social semiotics, multimodal discourse analysis, knowledge communication, environmental communication and corporate communication.

Arianna Maiorani is a Senior Lecturer in Linguistics in the Department of English and Drama, Loughborough University. She has published extensively in the field of Multimodality with a specific focus on films and Internet as cultural phenomena. Her research interests include multimodal discourse analysis of on line environments and SFL applied to literary texts.

Tui Matelau is a lecturer at Bridgepoint, Foundation Education at Unitec New Zealand. She is interested in researching Maori identity.

Thomas Metten works as a Lecturer in the Department of German Language and Literature Studies as well as in the Department for Cultural Studies at the University of Koblenz-Landau.

Sigrid Norris is Associate Professor of Communication Studies and Director of the Multimodal Research Centre at Auckland University of Technology. She is the author of Analyzing multimodal interaction: A methodological framework (2004), rosarot und schwarz. Gedichte (2008), and Identity in (inter)action: Introducing multimodal interaction analysis (2011). Further, she is the co-editor of Discourse in Action: Introducing mediated discourse analysis (2005) and editor of Multimdoality in practice: Investigating theory-in-practice-through-methodology (2011). Besides these books, Sigrid has published on multimodality and on identity production in a great variety of Journals and edited volumes. Her main research interests are the theoretical/methodological development of multimodality and multimodal identity production; and she is the founding editor and editor-in-chief for the international journal Multimodal Communication.

Kay L. O'Halloran is Director of the Multimodal Analysis Lab, Deputy Director of the Interactive Digital Media Institute (IDMI) and Associate Professor in the Department of English Language and Literature at the National University of Singapore. Her areas of research include multimodal analysis, social semiotics, mathematics discourse, and the development of interactive digital media technologies and mathematical and scientific visualization techniques for multimodal and socio-cultural analytics.

Yuling Pan is Sociolinguist and Principal Researcher at the U.S. Census Bureau. Her research areas include linguistic politeness, intercultural communication, and cross-cultural studies. Her numerous publications include Politeness in Chinese

Face-to-face Interaction (Ablex), Professional Communication in International Settings (with Suzanne Scollon and Ron Scollon, Blackwell Publishing), Politeness in Historical and Contemporary Chinese (with Dániel Z. Kádár, Continuum), and Chinese Discourse and Interaction: Theory and Practice (co-edited with Dániel Z. Kádár, Equinox).

María Jesús Pinar Sanz is a lecturer in Linguistics and Discourse Analysis at the University of Castilla-La Mancha (Spain). Her research interests are in multimodal discourse analysis. Within this field she has explored a variety of genres, ranging from comic books to political billboards and children picturebooks from a cognitive and/or systemic functional linguistics perspectives. She has published several articles on the generic structure of political ads and the relationship between the visual and verbal elements not only in political billboards but also in comic books and children's narratives.

Jesse Pirini is a PhD Candidate at AUT University in Auckland, New Zealand, and a member of the Multimodal Research Centre. He applies multimodal research approaches to social action. His current research focuses on heart disease and lifestyle. He is especially interested in how people who have experienced a heart event express agency within their social and physical environments.

Suzie Wong Scollon is an independent researcher based in Seattle. Her latest book is Intercultural Communication: A Discourse Approach, Third edition, co-authored with Ron Scollon and Rodney Jones.

Hartmut Stöckl is professor of English and Applied Linguistics at Salzburg University. His main research areas are in semiotics, text linguistics/stylistics, pragmatics and multimodal communication. He is particularly interested in the linkage of language and image in modern media and an aesthetic appreciation of advertising. His latest edited volumes are: Bildlinguistik (2011), Medientheorien und Multimodalität (2011), and Werbung – Keine Kunst!? (2012).

Sabine Tan is a Research Associate at the Multimodal Analysis Lab, Interactive Digital Media (IDMI) at National University of Singapore. Her primary research interests include (critical) multimodal discourse analysis, visual communication, and social semiotics.

Theo van Leeuwen worked as a film and television producer in his native Holland and Australia. Later he studied linguistics in Sydney and Paris, and variously taught film production, media studies and semiotics at Macquarie University, the London College of Printing and Cardiff University. Currently he is Professor of Media and Communication and Dean of the Faculty of Arts and Social Sciences at the University of Technology, Sydney. He has published widely in the areas of social semiotics, critical discourse analysis and multimodality. His books include Reading Images – The Grammar of Visual Design (with Gunther Kress); Speech, Music, Sound; Introducing Social Semiotics; Global Media Discourse (with David Machin); and Discourse and Practice – New Tools for Critical Discourse Analysis and The Language of Colour. He is a founding editor of the international journal Visual Communication.

Paul White is senior lecturer in Advertising Creativity at Auckland University of Technology and programme leader of New Zealand's only university ad school. He is also a founder member of the Multimodal Research Centre.

Sigrid Norris and Carmen Daniela Maier
1 Introduction

We are seeing a fast increase of interest in multimodal communication in various departments from business and design, communication studies and linguistics, psychology and sociology to health. This rise of interest also brings with it an interest in teaching multimodality in the undergraduate and the graduate classroom.

At the 2010 international conference titled *Multimodality, Mediation and Practice* held by the Multimodal Research Centre at Auckland University of Technology in New Zealand, scholars from a variety of approaches to multimodality attended. Due to the breadth and depth of presentations, a lively discussion about the emerging field of multimodality resulted and a number of lecturers and researchers lamented the fact that there is no Reader that can trace and encompass the increasing variety of approaches.

Discussing the need for such a book further after the conference, we decided to write/edit one that would give a taste of the breadth of theoretical, methodological and analytical issues in the area of multimodality. Thus, *Interactions, Images and Texts: A Reader in Multimodality* was conceived. It has taken some time to bring together all of the various authors and to actually put this Reader together, but we hope that it will prove useful for the undergraduate and postgraduate classroom, as well as to emergent researchers and researchers new to the field of multimodality. You will find the book equipped with key terms for each chapter that are defined in the alphabetised glossary for a quick reference. The terms were listed and defined by the particular authors and the names of the ones who defined them are listed in the glossary. We have decided to explicate exactly who defined a particular term as we find more and more examples in the literature where the seemingly *same terms are used differently* by different authors. This way, we hope to have alleviated some terminology confusion and enable the reader to understand the terms as the author(s) intended.

There is a short list of further readings at the end of each chapter. These readings are suggested by the author(s) who wrote the particular chapter, and are therefore, very useful suggestions when you become interested in reading more about specific topics. After these reading suggestions, each author has provided the reader with a project idea. These project ideas allow the book to be easily used as a teaching tool or as a guide for self-study. With these further readings, possible projects and an alphabetic glossary at the end of the book, we hope to have made the book useful for the various levels.

We have structured the book into four sections: I. *Multimodal theory and methodology: How are they developed?* Here, the reader will find personal accounts of some leading figures in the field of multimodality. These chapters are written in different styles, recounting some aspects of how, when, or why these theories or methodologies came about. We believe that it will be an interesting and varied read, where the reader will gain an insight into these authors' personal stories. In this section, the readers can discover the personal accounts of Suzie Wong Scollon about developing mediated discourse and nexus analysis, of Sigrid Norris about developing multimodal (inter)action analysis, of Theo Van Leeuwen about developing social semiotics, and of John Bateman about developing multimodal genre analysis.

In section II, *Multimodal theory and methodology: What are their facets?* we offer theoretically and methodologically focused chapters using and/or explaining the theories/methodologies developed by the scholars from the first section. These chapters are structured in the way discussed above, with key terms listed after the introduction of each chapter, further readings following the conclusion, and project ideas following the further readings. In this section, Rodney Jones explains and exemplifies in detail how mediated discourse analysis can be performed. Nexus analysis is the focus of Yuling Pan's chapter, while Najma Al Zydjaly introduces the main aspects of geosemiotics, and Jesse Pirini addresses multimodal (inter)action analysis. Carmen Daniela Maier investigates a new genre of corporate videos using a social semiotic approach, while Tuomo Hiippala closes this section with a multimodal genre analysis using the GEM model.

In section III, *Conducting multimodal research*, we present chapters that go into more depth in how-to do multimodal analyses and that illustrate the practical side of multimodal research. This section opens with Carey Jewitt's chapter on aspects of multimodal research. Kay O'Halloran and Victor Lim Fei elaborate in their chapter on the systemic functional approach, presenting in detail the primary methodological tools needed for this type of analysis. Acknowledging the challenges of multimodal transcription, Jeff Bezemer concentrates on explaining how he dealt with transcription in his case study. How to analyse webpages is the question posed by John Knox and Emilia Djonov in their chapter. Rick Iedema familiarizes the reader with a participatory approach to sensemaking of visual data, illustrating the consequences of involving practitioners in video-based research. This section of the book closes with two chapters co-written by Sigrid Norris, Jarret Geenen, Thomas Metten, Tui Matelau and Jesse Pirini who investigate the role of the researcher and aspects of ethics when collecting video data.

Then, in section IV, *Sample analyses*, we showcase smaller analysis chapters that give the reader a good understanding of the breadth of uses of multimodal research methodologies. Jarret Geenen offers an analysis of extreme sports, Tui Matelau analyses Maori woman identity, while Arianna Maiorani provides the reader with an example for the study of film advertising posters in her chapter. Hartmut Stöckl presents specific guiding principles needed for the multimodal analysis of typography. Sabine Tan turns to the analysis of news, while Volker Eisenlauer approaches Facebook, explaining the disempowering effects of the standardized options of the online environment upon its users. The communicative aspects of space in action are described by Paul White, while Gill Abousnnouga and David Machin focus on monuments. Ingrid de Saint-Georges addresses mediated discourse analysis referring to embodied learning and emerging social and professional identities. In Maria Jesus Pinar's chapter, the focus is on comic books, while Alison Gibbons elaborates on aspects of multimodality in literature in the section's last chapter.

In this section, we, the editors, introduce each chapter briefly, giving the reader a quick overview of the thematic orientation, the theoretical or methodological orientation, and the linkages to other similar chapters. Here, too, we provide key terms, further readings and a project idea.

The book can be read in various ways so that you can, as with any book begin to read from the first to the last section. But you may also, for example, begin working with one analysis chapter, find the links to other similar chapters and then move from there to the linked methodology in section two or the practical chapters in section three and read the personal accounts of those authors whose framework you are most interested in. Thus you may well be skipping back and forth between sections. We structured the book in this way on purpose, as we wanted this Reader to be a useful book that is adoptable by as many kinds of ways of teaching/learning as possible; allowing the teacher/student to decide which way is best for them.

As mentioned in the beginning, the idea and the content of this book were inspired by the insights that we gained during our discussions at a conference with other fellow researchers interested in teaching and working with various aspects of multimodality. It is our hope that this Reader will stimulate more discussions at conferences as well as in journals and classrooms across disciplines and geographical borders, driving multimodality research forward.

I Multimodal theory and methodology: How are they developed?

Suzie Wong Scollon
2 From mediated discourse and nexus analysis to geosemiotics: A personal account

Introduction

Mediated discourse analysis emerged at the turn of the millennium as Ron Scollon and colleagues combined discourse analysis with mediated action in an effort to develop activist sociolinguistics, to analyze discourse mediated by different means with an eye to effective social action. Ron returned to his dissertation done in the 70s to develop an ontogentic view of social practice, linking a one year-old's handing and speech in a nexus of practice (Scollon 2001). MDA has been used to examine such issues as immigration, unemployment, genetically modified corn, anthropogenic climate change and tar sands extraction and transport. Ron asked what an actor was doing, and how their speech/action arose out of a nexus of practice including narrative, first spoken then printed.

Narrative in MDA

Ron began paying attention to narratives in the early 70s as he developed mediated discourse analysis. In December 1972 we witnessed actions leading to escalation of the Vietnam war with a massive bombing of Hanoi and Haiphong in the secret "Operation Linebacker II". Though everyone in Honolulu could have observed the escalation of heavy tankers flying low to fuel B52 bombers in Guam, no protest action was possible because protest leaders became agents only in response to what they read in print, and there was a delay before an account appeared in *I.F. Stone's Weekly*, which made Ron's report a vain endeavor.

This early work in narrative fell under the rubric of the ethnography of communication, as he thought through ways in which stories were told in relation to participants and events. For example, when he was visiting my cousin Brenda in order to record her speech development, Brenda's mother told him a story and repeated it with embellishment when I appeared. He hypothesized that she did that to retain his interest as he had already heard the basic story. He looked at motives after Burke and continued to look at narratives as explanatory framings of self, role, etc. after Goffman, asking how and why narratives were told. He noted a kind of magnetism, with himself as analyst getting lost in the actions of the tales he was analyzing.

After our daughter was born, Ron recorded our speech around her (e.g. when she fell down and he tried to suggest a narrative to transform Rachel's crying into speech). Did she trip? I suggested an alternative explanation. Perhaps she was tired or dizzy. He told me a long narrative over coffee after breakfast, displaying his current work on Athabaskan, the only long narrative all day while Rachel was awake and the recorder was running. Did it inform me? Was it intended to? It was a habit developed before Rachel was born, as we walked the four miles from our downtown apartment to the university campus where he discussed Brenda's speech at a child language seminar.

The question Ron asked was: What makes a story a narrative? He noted a tendency to hear all past tenses or perfectives as narrative, and past tense transitive clauses as narrative clauses. He found the uses of narrative changing, with narrative becoming a style of telling that relies on temporally sequencing events whether real, imaginary, or mental, a kind of word form object or genre. He read Uspensky, who had been at Berkeley at the same time as Goffman. An associate of Bakhtin, Uspensky wrote on point of view in citation.

Looking at narrative use in newspapers, Ron found himself mostly just following stories, so he decided to trace a story from its first appearance on the radio news through newspaper and TV, comparing versions against each other. The bombing of LaGuardia airport at the end of 1975 captured his attention for days during the winter semester break. He noted:

The bomb explosion itself caused a change of frame, a group of frame breaks.... The story is
1) we were sitting around waiting
2) the explosion happened
3) we were casualties

He listened to the news on another radio station at 8am. The Dec. 31 Advertiser had a "screaming red headline" with 9 paragraphs adding only that the airport is open again and a reward has been announced. It was this headline that caught his eye as he walked past a news stand that holiday morning.

Questioning Labov's definition of narrative as recapitulating an event, he writes, "The _event_ exists only as an interpretation of physical and behavioral phenomena." ... "Activities do not become events until organized and that organization is an embedding. The structure _is_ the embedding."

Nexus analysis in Alaska

Nexus analysis as a tool for unifying micro-analysis of social interaction and broader socio-political-cultural analysis started in Alaska more than three decades ago as Ron and I conducted projects directed toward improving the access of Alaska Native people to public institutions from which they were being systematically excluded largely because of communicative technologies and practices. The institutions were educational, medical, legal, and economic.

An early activity was a booklet 'How to do beadwork' for children in a bilingual education program that led us to an analysis of text, images and interactions. The first page was a picture of a standing moose with text in Ahtna Athabaskan and English translation below. The last page showed a pair of feet covered by beautifully beaded moccasin tongues (Scollon and Scollon 2004). What the authors showed was the context, the reasons for doing beadwork, rather than the beadwork itself. Children would learn how to do that by watching their mothers.

The bilingual education program for Ahtna children was part of a nexus of legal pressures for such services mandated by the US Supreme Court in Lau vs. Nichols in 1974. Nothing happens in a social vacuum but rather in a nexus of historical trajectories of people, places, discourses including texts, images and interactions, ideas, and objects. In 1968 oil was discovered at Prudhoe Bay on the Arctic coast of Alaska. The Natives of the state sued the US government claiming ownership of all the land in the state, which resulted in a cash settlement, title to large portions of land, and health and social services. The world oil trade and the Alaska Native Claims Settlement Act formed two cycles in the nexus we were involved in. Both were subsumed by the world system then dominated by Cold War tensions between the US and the Soviet Union.

While Ron flew around the state, which has an area of 1,500,000 square kilometers, consulting and giving workshops to Alaska Natives and legal, educational and medical professionals, I taught Alaska Native students who wanted to become teachers while living at home instead of moving to Fairbanks where the University of Alaska is located. They were scattered across the state, 800 miles from east to west and 900 miles from north to south. I tried tape recorded audio lectures, videotapes, telephone conferencing and mail correspondence before stumbling on computer mediated communication. From earlier research on interaction between Athabaskans and ourselves as well as other outsiders, we posited that the asynchronous nature of computer communication would facilitate the teaching and learning of students who spoke or heard their elders speaking Athabaskan languages. It turned out that Athabaskan and other students who did not easily speak in class or visit professors' offices used this medium readily.

Whether discourse was mediated by computer terminals, telephones and microphones, or books and printed paper made a difference to people distantly related to an elder who refused to be tape recorded saying, "Separating the word from the body is death." We began to pay attention to mediation by machines as well as Goffman's interaction order as we noted that Athabaskans preferred narrative to conversation, and traced these interactive preferences in their historical bodies.

Geosemiotics

The landscape changed as we went from being students and impoverished researchers in Honolulu to faculty in a state newly enriched by oil. Instead of pedaling our bicycles in the mainstream traffic to get to classes, we flew and drove around a state more than twice the size of Texas, the next largest state. Not only were we navigating small icy landing strips and snow-covered roads, bicycle lanes appeared in Fairbanks as well as Honolulu as we tried to read the signs and listen to the sounds of Alaska Native languages.

Our first project in Alaska, before moving the family there, was to find a one year-old to compare with the subject of Ron's PhD dissertation. Unlike Brenda's milieu with books, TV, automobiles, shopping malls and street signs, the community where we located ourselves had only one gravel road from the airport to the village and one small store which sold no books. People spent more time on boats on the river than on wheels, and signs were not lettered but signs of wear where branches were broken and bushes trampled on.

That was the beginning of widening the circumference of study in time and space as we tried to account for differences in functions of language. We gathered blueberries, hunted caribou and heard more buzzing mosquitoes than words of Gwich'in. I learned to sew beads and watched women tan moosehide. The ecology of language in Arctic Village in the Brooks Range could not have been more different than that in Pearl City, Oahu where Brenda lived with her family. The discourses, material and ephemeral, were different, the historical bodies were different, and the interaction orders were different. We did not hear mothers speaking to babies or reading to toddlers. The only reading we observed took place at the post office and at church.

Signs as multimodal objects

Twenty years later we found ourselves in yet another ecology, that of ultra-urban Hong Kong, where forests of signs hang out over streets. Though there was a plethora of bilingual signs, we discovered that our students pretty much ignored the English portions just as we ignored the Chinese unless we forced ourselves to pay attention. We undertook an ethnography of communication centering on newspaper texts and readers, and marveled at how our students spoke to each other in Cantonese while creating English language texts.

We often traveled to China, where we heard Chinese languages that were not Cantonese and saw signs posted in simplified characters. I picked up a book about different fonts, and we began photographing street and shop signs, analyzing the placement of these multimodal objects in relation to the character sets, fonts, colors and other material characteristics such as whether they were to be read from left to right or from right to left.

We found to our surprise that our students were at least as disoriented in a city just a short distance from Hong Kong as we were. Though they spoke Cantonese, the language of Guangzhou, due to differences in their historical bodies, interaction orders and media use they felt lost. Their mobile phones did not work and they were accustomed to tracking each other using their phones from shop to shop in Hong Kong. They could not read the simplified characters on signs or even the pinyin used to spell words with roman letters, and they habitually mixed English with their Cantonese, which was disapproved of in China.

Though our students were dependent on traditional characters on signs to find their way around Hong Kong, they could not write many characters with a pen, having used the computer keyboard to call up characters they needed to write. Furthermore, their education in Hong Kong public schools provided little Chinese language, literature or history. Their historical bodies were colonized by the British rulers in Hong Kong. While they could not speak fluent English and wrote it with difficulty, neither could they write Chinese. The 500-year war on the vernacular that began with Nebrija's advice to Queen Isabella to create Castilian Spanish, standardize it, and outlaw printing any vernacular (Scollon and Scollon 2003) resulted in our students being unable to write in Cantonese and having to write in English, a language they spoke imperfectly and unintelligibly.

The program English for Professional Communication was designed to enable students not only to speak and write English that would qualify them to work in English-speaking offices, but to do PowerPoint presentations and video-taping and editing with state of the art equipment. It was an application of the activist sociolinguistics we had pioneered in Alaska, which we came to call Nexus Analysis as we had students engage, navigate and change a nexus of practice in which they found themselves.

Students who lived in crowded tenements now work for NGOs, multinational corporations, courts and schools as professional communicators, their multimodal education paying off with many being paid more than some of their teachers. Before they graduated they had internships requiring them to proficiently manipulate text, images and interaction with mobile phones, videocams and computers. As Hong Kong returned to China in 1997, they were prepared to work not only in Hong Kong but in mainland China, the British Isles or North America. Several projects focused on the transition to Chinese sovereignty as we began theorizing mediated discourse analysis.

Ron's first stab at bridging interactional sociolinguistics and media studies (Scollon 1998) theorized action as the unit of analysis. The individual takes action, or in the case of the syntax and sociology professors who relied on *I.F. Stone's Weekly*, fails to take action, on the basis of mediated discourse. A woman from Beijing traced her relationship to a group practicing taijiquan together with her itinerary from day to day mediated by what she heard on news broadcast from China as the Taiwan Missile Crisis developed. Ron and I, with colleagues and student assistants, collected news in print and broadcast formats for two weeks and worked at seeing what actions were mediated by news discourse in the run-up to Hong Kong's return to Chinese sovereignty.

Discourses, always located in space, were internalized in historical bodies as embodied experience, conscious or unconscious. Action is taken by individuals in social sets we call interaction orders, mediated by discourse in nexus of practice. While Rodney Jones, Sigrid Norris and others developed MDA, Ron and I played with geosemiotics and nexus analysis.

References

Burke, Kenneth. 1950. *A Rhetoric of Motives*. Englewood Cliffs, NJ: Prentice-Hall.
Goffman, Erving. 1983. *Interaction Ritual*. Garden City, NY: Anchor Books.
Scollon, Ron. 1998. *Mediated Discourse as Social Interaction: A Study of News Discourse*. London/New York: Longman.
Scollon, Ron. 2001. *Mediated Discourse: The Nexus of Practice*. London/New York: Routledge.
Scollon, Ron and Suzie Scollon. 2003. *Discourses in Place: Language in the Material World*. London/New York: Routledge.
Scollon, Ron and Suzie Scollon. 2004. *Nexus Analysis: Discourse and the Emerging Internet*. London/New York: Routledge.
Scollon, Suzie and Ingrid de Saint Georges. 2012. Mediated Discourse Analysis. In James Paul Gee & Michael Handford (eds.), *The Routledge Handbook of Discourse Analysis*, 66–78. London/New York: Routledge.
Uspensky, Boris. 1973. *A Poetics of Composition*. Berkeley: University of California Press.

Sigrid Norris
3 Developing multimodal (inter)action analysis: A personal account

Multimodal (inter)action analysis originated from a necessity to find a methodological framework that allowed the analysis of diverse data sets from spoken language to video, music and physical layout to objects in the world, in a comprehensive and integrative manner. Working with Ron Scollon around the millennium as my PhD mentor, the basis of my thinking naturally was in the actions that social actors take in the world. The social in this world comes about because of the things people do, and can thus best be understood through the lens of social action. Everyone acts and meaning is created through action, as Ron had explicated so succinctly with mediated discourse analysis. But what, so remained one of our questions at the time, actually *is* a social action? Is *moving my foot* a social action? Or is my *walking the dog* considered a social action? Is my *flying to Germany to attend a conference and then visit my family* a social action – or are these two or three or many social actions? What we came up with was that all of these were social actions, all of these were mediated in multiple ways, and that they were all of a different level, but had one thing in common: They all had a beginning and an ending point.

Well, this worked. Somewhat – or until I began to study everyday identity production through a participant observation and video ethnography. Both of my participants were stay-at-home mothers. During my study, one of them turned into an artist; and, almost simultaneously, although not necessarily related to the first becoming an artist, the two women decided to start a catering business. Their nationality differed, so that the artist was German and the other woman was German-Italian. The artist expressed much of her identity through her paintings and the German-Italian woman listened to Italian music, watched Italian TV, but only spoke German with her immediate family. The two women were dear friends and they spent much time together, making my data collection quite easy, relatively speaking. I collected the books and magazines the participants read, watched the TV programs that they watched, listened to the music that they listened to, met their immediate and extended families and networks, ate the food they ate, drank the coffee they drank, video and audio recorded large parts of their varied actions – and became utterly confused over what to do with my data once I returned home.

I had collected a huge amount of varied data, had learned much in the field about these two women and their identities, but I had no framework to analyse any of it. Instead, I felt like I had everything to produce a soap opera, and that is what I told Ron during our first meeting after my fieldwork. Without a framework to analyse my data, I could not write a PhD thesis. He looked at me in his calm way, contemplating for a while and then said: 'Well, I guess you have your work cut out for yourself.' As he continued looking at me calmly and confidently, I felt a kind of panic inside. He could not really mean this, for sure. He would have something else to tell me, point me to some readings, give me the suggestion to only look at this or that part of my data, maybe focus on the language and to forget I ever collected the rest? But he said: 'Well, better start thinking about it and we will meet again in two weeks.'

I had too many questions to list, but it became clear that *identity* was the least of my problems. What was needed was a framework to analyse all of the different modes with their different structures and materialities. What this meant for identity would emerge, I thought or at least I hoped.

What was needed was *one* framework that could do it all. My basis, the only one that made sense to me at the time (and the only one that makes sense to me even now, many years later) was social action, the mediated action, to be exact. We had had trouble with delineating a mediated action and always came back to the point that there were many possible levels of action. But how, so was my thinking, do you analyse something with a unit of analysis that has no clear definition? An utterance made sense as a unit of analysis, and I kept returning to it. If only I could find units of this kind in other modes; and so I began looking.

I read everything around each mode that I was investigating. Gesture was the first area that I read about and I found much written on gesture. There, I found that the unit that I was looking for did already exist. A gesture unit. Superb! A gesture, certainly a mediated action, thus became a lower-level action similar to the utterance. I began to feel better and was hopeful to find more units like this. Next, postural shifts and gaze shifts became lower-level actions, and what became obvious was that many units were already established in the literature. However, they were often called various terms by various researchers, and often they were discussed either separately or, sometimes in connection with language, only. Essentially all of these units – now the lower-level actions – were pragmatic meaning units with a beginning and an ending point. That was the easy part.

Meeting with Ron, he would sit there and draw on a piece of paper as he was asking me: 'So we have lower-level actions that are linked like chains you say, through pauses?' 'Yes, pauses. Like an utterance is delineated by in-breaths, a gesture is delineated by pauses before and after – ever so slightly, at times, but there are pauses.' 'But, how,' he would say, 'does it all fit together?' He would draw lines on his paper side by side and crossing each other, each line representing a chain of lower-level actions. 'How do they all make a higher-level action? Like a tapestry?' he'd ask. 'Yes, but no. It's not as ordered as a tapestry.' 'Hm. More like a kaleidoscope?' he pondered, focusing his gaze on his paper in front of him. 'Well, yes. But, no. It's not as clear as a kaleidoscope.' This way, Ron moved me along from figuring out lower-level actions and chains of lower-level actions to thinking about higher-level actions. With his marvellous questions; depicting my thoughts on his piece of paper in playful lines, always ending the session with 'Okay. Let's meet in two weeks and see where you've gotten.'

But how did higher-level actions come about? The answer was that they actually come about through the interweaving of multiple chains of lower-level actions at the same time as they make the interweaving of the chains of lower-level actions possible in the first place. This, of course, opened up more questions and moved me into the direction of attention – or maybe it brought me back to the notion of attention: I had noticed in the field that the women often paid attention to several actions (and these were higher-level actions) at the very same time. It had puzzled me, and really mostly puzzled me that most literature seemed only interested in focused interaction. Even Goffman, who certainly had noticed the same thing as I had, pushed this observation into the background by calling it the disattended channel and placing more weight on that which is focused upon. Now, that lower-and higher-level actions were sorted out, attention levels needed to be dealt with. An email to Ron resulted in his sending me a Theo Van Leeuwen reference on Music and Sound, which proved to be very useful. I was happy to have found some notions that could be applied and expanded, and later met Ron with a happy smile. He nodded gently, sat down, took out a piece of paper and pen and said: 'Well, so, now we have lower-level actions and we have higher-level actions. You speak of the various attention levels, but there are two things that bother me: One is how do you *know* that your participants act on these attention levels; and two what are we going to do with the paintings and other objects?'

Some email exchanges later, Ron sent me the reference for Gunther Kress and Theo Van Leeuwen's new book on multimodality. Heaven sent, I can only say. There it was. Layout! Objects! I was delighted. Ron and I excitedly discussed the book and its new ways of looking at the world of objects and layout. 'Brilliant. All you have to do now is bring it together with your framework. And I'll see you in two weeks.' Those were two hard weeks of thinking. I kept looking at my data. Every object I saw, meant an action to me: When I saw a painting hung on a wall, I saw one of my participants' hanging it there. When I saw several coffee cups, I saw us having had coffee. When I saw dirty children's clothes, I saw that child who had dropped them on the floor. Every object, every layout was made by a social actor, placed by a social actor, and used by a social actor. But was it just me, who saw the world in this way? Was I trying to see the world as acted upon? Was I over-theorizing? I began to talk with friends about objects, not mentioning my position or reason why or even that as I wanted to find out their views. 'Oh, look, a coffee cup,' I'd say and the answer was 'Yes, Vic left it there this morning.' 'Shoes,' I would exclaim, and my friend would say 'Oh, Grason always leaves his shoes in the middle of the hallway.' 'Nice painting,' I told a co-worker and she said 'yes, my boyfriend put it up for me over the weekend.' Actions, all actions. I was pleased and began calling these *frozen actions*, or actions that are embedded in the objects. Ron was also pleased with this notion, but immediately brought me back to the most pressing question: 'How do you know that your participants perform several higher-level actions on different attention levels?' 'You can just tell,' I said and showed him a clip. 'It's obvious.' 'Yes,' he said 'but why is it obvious? How do you *know*?'

Two weeks later, I had no answer. I was stuck. How did I *know*? I just did. So did everyone else I asked – and I asked many people during those two weeks. Everyone could see it. But nobody had an answer to why or how. When I saw Ron next, I brought more clips, tested them out on him and found that he could see it just like everyone else could. 'Sure,' he said, 'I can see it. Everyone can see it. But can *you* explain it? That is the real question.' And the answer was 'no.' I could not explain it and now realised that this was likely the reason why no one else had broached the subject.

Weeks of thinking. Weeks of being stuck. I baked. I walked. I baked more. I walked more. I baked more than I ever had. I always bake when I get stuck in my thinking, which makes family, friends, and neighbours, happy. As I was walking and baking and giving cakes, pastries and breads to lots of people, I felt like I couldn't get un-stuck unless I started from scratch. So, I went back to the beginning. This time, however, I began to think about actions from a different point of view. This time, I looked at action from the little science background that I had acquired some long time ago. If actions, I hypothesised, could be viewed similar to atoms or molecules, then actions could produce different types of density. I took out a graph for water-density and stared at it for a long time. Density changes with temperature. I drew an x-axis for which I already had found the answer that it was decreasing attention from left to right. Then, I drew the y-axis, which I had never even thought of drawing before. Staring at the water-density graph again, I thought 'What if action density changes with level of attention?' and I wrote density above the y-axis. If action-density is what we can perceive when we see that a social actor pays more or less attention to one or the other higher-level action, then each of the higher-level actions has to be made up of either more or less dense chains of lower-level actions. Each chain of lower-level action links to only one mode (although I thought the term itself always as problematical) and thus, I called it *modal density*. But what modal density actually is, is action density. Action density can come about in interaction through verbal, nonverbal modes and objects in the environment or it can come about through frozen actions that are frozen on a computer screen, in a building or in a city.

Ron smiled when we met the next time. He was pleased and said 'Well, so now, what about identity? How are you going to explain your participants' identity with this framework? And have you given multimodal transcription some thought?' and that's how it all started ...

Theo Van Leeuwen
4 About images and multimodality: A personal account

I grew up in a culture of the word. My father was a Protestant minister, later a professor of theology. He approved of the poems I wrote in my late teens and early twenties but did not think that films were capable of depth of meaning and thought that my first film, a portrait of my friend Louk Vreeswijk (which went on to win two prizes) was a bit 'superficial'.

I thought he was wrong and felt that, by the 1960s, film had matured as a fantastic medium of artistic and intellectual expression and that film studies had become as serious an academic pursuit as theology. In 1968 I started studying at the Netherlands Film Academy in Amsterdam and became very interested in the French idea of the *caméra stylo*, the camera as 'pen', as a very personal medium, not only for storytelling, but also for reflective 'essays'. I admired Jean Rouch and Chris Marker, and also discovered Roland Barthes and Christian Metz who used linguistic ideas and methods to study photography and film, thereby elevating it to the status of language. With friends at the Film Academy I started *Skrien*, a film magazine, to write about all this. The only picture in my father's study was a photograph of the Swiss theologian Karl Barth, with whom he had studied for a year, just before the war. I now had my own Barthes! But again my father was not very interested, even though structuralism had by then also begun to influence theology. As you can see, I was trying to break with the past, yet also wanted to please my father.

At a film festival in Amsterdam I met my future wife, Clemency Browne, an Australian artist and filmmaker who had been invited to the festival to screen *Tobias Icarus Age Four*, a diary film about her 4-year-old son Toby. Three years later Clem, Toby and I moved to Australia. I continued to make films and also taught film production at the then new Australian Film and Television School and at Macquarie University in Sydney, where, after a few years, I started studying linguistics in the evenings. My 'film and language' dream had not been forgotten. I thought that if I learnt more about linguistics I might be able to make an original contribution to the semiotics of film and would not just echo the work of the French structuralist semioticians, as I felt some British writers did at the time. In 1980 took my family to Paris and studied for a semester with Christian Metz, but he had given up on linguistics by then and turned to psychoanalysis for inspiration.

The breakthrough came, not in Paris, but in Australia, where I encountered the work of Michael Halliday who had become the Professor of Linguistics at Sydney University. Metz had tried to compare the *forms* of language and film, and found, predictably, that there are no such things comparable to nouns and verbs in film. Halliday made it possible to compare modes of communication in terms of their communicative functions. Perhaps language and film could fulfil *similar* communicative functions *in different ways*. Language, for instance, has modal auxiliaries to express degrees of truth (it *may* be, it *will* be, it *must* be). Clearly film does not have anything like that. But, I thought, film *can* express different degrees of truth in different ways, for instance through the difference between documentary black and white and the fantasy world of Technicolor, as famously in *The Wizard of Oz*, or through the difference between the realism of photography and the less than real world of animated cartoons. I would have to use an interdisciplinary approach, drawing ideas about form from literature about the visual, about film and the visual arts, and ideas about meaning and communicative function from the linguistics of Halliday.

At this point I had the good fortune of meeting Gunther Kress, who had been an examiner of my master's thesis on the intonation of radio announcers. We decided to start some work together and met in his house in Newtown, the inner city suburb of Sydney where I also lived. But what would we do? Gunther said he had already written that it was no longer possible to write about media texts without paying attention to the images, but not yet done anything about it. I said that it had always been my dream to write about 'visual language', but that I had not done anything about that either, even though I had now studied linguistics. Gunther got up and went upstairs, to the bedroom of his then 2-year old son Michael, and came back with two children's books, one by the Dutch illustrator Dick Bruna and almost entirely without words, the other a Ladybird book in which words explained every single picture ('Every night I have a bath before I go to bed' on the left page; picture of a bath with rubber duck on the right page). We talked and made notes about these two books for several mornings, and they eventually became a crucial example in the first chapter of our joint book *Reading Images*.

We always worked with examples on the table, writing down the gist of our ongoing dialogue. We always tried to pay close and focused attention to detail, to specific visual features of the examples, such as whether people in an image are shown in close up or not, or look at the viewer or not, and then we would reason our way into what we hoped would be plausible accounts of the meaning potential of these features, and of its meaning in specific instances. When we had exhausted the children's books, we moved to other material – women's magazines, school textbooks, newspaper photography, cartoons and graphics, art works, always asking how the same features are used in different kinds of images, and always looking for common ground between these different uses. We saw, for instance, that many images created a kind of contrast between what is placed on the left and what on the right, and discussed at length what this might mean. One of our examples was a slimming ad, with an overweight woman on the left and her slimmed down version on the right. What is the meaning of left and right? Time? With the past on the left and the future on the right? Often, but by no means always, as we realized when we looked at other examples. Good versus bad? With the bad on the left and the good on the right? Sometimes yes, sometimes no. We had to find something more general to capture the difference. Then we thought, maybe it is like Halliday's 'Given' and 'New' where the Given comes first and represent the 'point of departure' of the message, something which, in the context, can be taken for granted, and the New comes last and represents the crux of the message, to which the listener must pay attention. In cultures which write from left to right, we reasoned, the left comes first and the right last. Images might be read that way too, all else being equal. And we soon found out that in cultures that write from right to left, the order is indeed reversed – there, slimming ads do have the overweight person on the right and the slimmed down person on the left, for instance.

We continued to work in this way, often starting the day with a swim in Sydney's Nielsen Park and having breakfast before starting our session. Once enough notes had accrued we were ready to draft an article or a chapter. We took turns in doing the first draft and the other would then rewrite, sometimes drastically, then we would swap again, until the result satisfied both of us. We tried out our drafts with our friends from the Newtown Semiotics Circle, which met once a month, always in the evenings, and always in someone's house: we were by no means the only ones who sought to expand Halliday's work beyond language, and the input of key members of the Circle, Jim Martin, Terry Threadgold, Paul Thibault, Anne Cranny-Francis, Radan Martinec and others was crucial.

Though the kind of films I had fallen in love with continued to be made (some of them by the Amsterdam Film School colleagues with whom I had started *Skrien*, such as Annette Apon and Digna Sinke) and though many young filmmakers today continue to be inspired by the ideas and filmmaking practices of the 60s and 70s, mainstream Western film had become obsessed with special effects and remakes, and most French films were not quite what they once were either. In the 80s, after one of my films had ended in financial disaster, I decided to focus more fully on my academic work. Meanwhile a new medium had come on the scene, a medium which, much more fully than the expensive medium of film, realized the ideal of the *caméra stylo*, a medium with which anyone could write 'multimodally', and, with a single tool, the computer, combine image, music and text.

Gunther and I now moved away from writing only about images, and began to focus on what we called 'multimodality', a term which had previously only been used in a more limited sense by psychologists of perception to indicate that different sense perceptions influence each other, and which we now used to signify the integration of different modes which had already been common in the mass media and which now had come within reach of every computer user. In an unpublished early paper we introduced a term which we later dropped and spoke of layout as an 'integration code', a code which can integrate different modes of communication into a multimodal whole. And we increasingly realized that many of the things we had studied as image features applied across different modes of communication. We had begun to study framing, for instance, when we noticed how magazine pages 'frame' different parts of an article visually – through space, through text boxes etc. But we soon discovered that the principle of framing applies to all modes of communication. In language pauses frame parts of the utterance, in buildings activities are framed by empty in-between space, partitions, walls etc. Later we began to pay attention also to the differences between modes, for instance to the different affordances of time-based and space-based modes.

The study of multimodality is very new, and it is a very creative endeavour. Many emerging modes of communication have barely been studied. In our approach to studying them it is essential to begin by making a collection of relevant examples and by focusing on a particular aspect of these examples, describing its forms and seeking a plausible account of its meaning potential in general and the use of that potential in specific examples. A study of apps, for instance, could begin with a small collection of children's stories, say ten, and focus on the different ways in which you can touch the screen. These would first of all be named, described and inventorized (pokes, strokes, wipes, etc.) and then their uses would be systematically investigated. Some uses might be narrative – in a story about a lazy lizard, for instance, a poke wakes up the lizard. Others are not narrative. In an app adaptation of a Dr Seuss story, poking represented objects produces words, so that the story may be interrupted by a game of matching words and pictures. But touching the screen is always interactive, always connects the reader with represented people, places or things. Much has been written about interactivity, but studying apps in this way can make a contribution by detailing and trying to explain in what ways children are made to interact with representations in general, and in specific instances, and why. Can they only interact visually, for instance, or is speech and music also used? Is the interaction integrated with the narrative or not? Studying apps in this way can therefore also show what interactions are *not* possible but might be possible elsewhere, for instance in live puppet or theatre shows.

Studies of this kind are not only interesting, but also important. Software designers now create the semiotic resources we use, the shape of the modes we use to communicate. I recently read about a program for kinetic typography which automatically breaks down the text you type into lines and then lets you choose what 'mood' to give that line, for instance 'assertive' or 'hesitant'. But the software designer has decided what moods will exist and how they will be expressed. The software designer has created the language with which you are to express your 'mood'. This applies not only to software for presentation slides, documents or web pages, it also applies to the systems we use to interact with each other, whether at work, or with our friends and nearest and dearest, as in the case of Facebook. The question has to be asked: What can you do to, or for, or with your friends on Facebook and what can you *not* do? To which degree and how does Facebook structure how we interact? And how does that compare with alternatives? Such studies can and should be critical but in a positive and constructive way, as they uncover new possibilities which have not or not yet been tried.

In the past, new developments in communication have always been preceded and accompanied by new theories, new ideas, and new art forms. Studying the great era of renewal in art and design in the early 20th century brings that out very clearly and can still be a source of inspiration. The changes we experience today are as great or greater than those of the 1920s. Let multimodal theory and analysis be as challenging and exciting today as the groundbreaking ideas of Van Doesburg, Kandinsky, Eisenstein and others in those days.

John Bateman
5 Developing a GeM (genre and multimodality) model

My involvement with multimodality as a resource for communicative expression began with a general development that took place at the beginning of the 1990s. At that time, several research groups that had been involved in automatic natural language text generation had begun expanding the kinds of 'texts' they were concerned with generating. Originally, natural language text generation was the area of computational linguistics concerned with developing computer systems capable of taking some abstract, non-linguistic representation – such as that that might be found in a data base or knowledge base – and turning such representations into natural language texts automatically. To begin with, such texts were sequences of printed characters in a single natural language; but by the end of the 1980s this was being extended to include both multiple languages, in multilingual natural language generation, and spoken language as well (cf. Matthiessen and Bateman 1991: Chapter 3 for a review of that time).

Natural language generation as a field had always had an orientation to the 'goals' of communication and the specific contextual constraints that needed to be considered when attempting the most appropriate satisfaction of those goals. Generated texts could not be seen as occurring in a vacuum and the entire motivation of the enterprise was, and continues to be, to produce natural language texts that are appropriate for their intended readers/hearers and for their contexts of use. In this sense, in the words of one of the founders of the field, natural language generation is necessarily "a process of decision-making under constraints" (McDonald 1983). This meant that once many of the issues of the 'bare bones' of natural language generation, such as producing morphologically, grammatically and semantically appropriate sequences of sentences was reasonably under control, it was natural to begin paying attention to other kinds of 'decisions' that are commonly made when producing and using texts – decisions which, at that time, overlapped with several kinds of 'paraverbal' information as considered within linguistics, such as intonational phrasing for spoken language and punctuation and typography for written language.

The styles of language representations adopted within natural language generation were particularly well suited to extensions of this kind. Typically, a language generation system would produce a syntactic tree on the basis of the decisions it had made to meet some set of communicative goals. This syntactic tree had then to be 'expressed' by reading off a linear sequence of, most typically, words. There was then nothing standing in the way of making further motivated decisions during this process of reading off a linear sequence to respect additional information and sources of constraint. For example, the generation system with which I was working at that time, William Mann's Penman system (Mann 1985; Matthiessen and Bateman 1991), would select punctuation appropriately on the basis of semantically-motivated grammatical features selected during generation: a clause with the grammatical feature 'imperative' would accordingly select a terminating exclamation mark during linearisation of its syntactic structure, whereas a clause with the feature 'interrogative' would select a question mark. There were then two levels of representation involved: the syntactic structure as motivated by the system's grammar and a *presentational* structure including further information. The reader/hearer of a generated text would normally only encounter the presentational form produced.

Structured markup was also beginning to be used for annotating or enriching textual data at that time. Markup, now familiar to everyone in the form of HTML for signalling information such as the presence of headers, paragraphs, bold or italic fonts, etc. in webpages, was originally developed in the publishing industry for specifying formatting and other structurally-relevant information for documents represented electronically (cf. the Standard Generalised Markup Language, SGML: Goldfarb 1990). Non-professional electronic document production was also employing a variety of more light weight annotations – the most successful of which was, and still is, the widely used LAT$_E$X system. A further natural extension to the automatic generation process was thus to start including more of these markup elements in the presentation form produced during linearisation (cf. Hovy and Arens 1991) – thus text generation could begin to include the generation of typographically formatted text: rather than directly 'printing' the presentation form, that form would itself instead be sent first through an appropriate piece of rendering software. This already included at that time the possibility of 'active' presentational forms such as links leading to actions similar to today's hyperlinks (Moore and Swartout 1990). These capabilities are all now basic functionalities provided by our current, much extended version of that earlier generation system, the KPML automatic text generation environment (Bateman 1997).

Automatic text generation was, however, not only concerned with the production of sentences but of entire texts. And so generation systems, including the Penman system, were also including from the mid-1980s onwards notions of text organisation and text structure. The most widespread of these text organisations is still that provided by Rhetorical Structure Theory (RST: Mann and Thompson 1988; Bateman and Delin 2006), which came to be used in a number of automatic generation systems. Generation using RST produces a larger scale structure within which the structure of individual sentences appears at the leaves. It was then natural to again divide such larger scale structures into two forms: a rhetorical text organisation and a presentational form: the latter could then include further typographical considerations beyond the scope of single sentences, such as headings of various kinds, indentations, enumeration and so on. This subsequently formed the basis of several automatic text generation systems producing typographically more sophisticated text (cf. Kruijff et al. 2000; Bouayad-Agha et al. 2000; Power et al. 2003).

One final component setting the scene relevant here was the largely parallel increase in interest at the beginning of the 1990s in multimedia presentations. Starting from work in human-computer interface design and multimedia, several research groups were addressing issues of presenting information to users in different modalities in an orchestrated fashion, whereby different modalities could each contribute to the overall message delivery and interaction experience (Maybury 1993). This had several points of contact with natural language generation research. On the one hand, many of the problems faced in such systems overlapped with issues that had also arisen in automatic natural language text generation: basic questions of what information to include and how it should be presented were common to the two concerns; on the other hand, the consideration of natural language texts as just one type of component in more extensive multimedia presentations was also a natural further development beyond the basic production of written or spoken texts in isolation. As a consequence, several multimedia presentation systems were constructed in which the multimedia presentation was created using an extended notion of rhetorical structure theory. For this, the model was extended so that rather than simply having sentences at the leaves of the rhetorical structure, one might also have information expressed in other modalities, such as visual diagrams or pictures (cf. Feiner and McKeown 1990; André and Rist 1993; Wahlster et al. 1993; Arens 1992). One of the additional 'decisions' added to the generation process was consequently that of determining the modality to be selected for the information to be expressed – rather than forcing this to be an expression in linguistic terms as would traditionally be the case, multimodal presentation systems supported a motivated choice of output modality on the basis of the information to be expressed and the system's communicative goals (Arens and Hovy 1990).

With these components and development in place, we started in the mid-1990s a cooperation between two departments of the German state-funded research institute for integrated publication and information systems (IPSI) in Darmstadt: one department (called KOMET: 'Knowledge-oriented production of multimodal documents'), of which I was in charge, was concerned with automatic multilingual language generation building on the earlier experiences of the Penman project; the other department (called PAVE: 'Publication and advanced visualization environments'), headed by Christoph Hüser, was developing hypermedia techniques involving automatic visualisation and diagram generation for publications and information systems. In order to produce *mutually coherent and supportive* diagrams and texts automatically, it was evident that certain decisions concerning the presentation forms to be selected had to be made prior to handing on control to either natural language generation or diagram generation. Some of these decisions were very similar to the problem of *aggregation* explored within natural language generation, i.e., the question of which information is to be grouped with what other information and on what basis (Dalianis and Hovy 1996).

An example of our early diagram generation is shown in Figure 1, taken from the detailed discussion in Bateman et al. (1998, 2001). Here we see two renditions of information concerning artists, their areas of specialisation (architect, urban planner, designer), their affiliations and time intervals. Depending on which information is grouped together and which not, differing visualisations are produced. This was then completely analogous to decisions possible in the linguistic form, for example, a grouping around specialisations would produce sentences such as "Breuer, Gropius and Hilbersheimer were architects", where a grouping around affiliations would produce sentences such as "Breuer and Gropius were affiliated with Harvard". In both cases our generation was driven by a common approach to fact representation and grouping described in detail in Bateman (1999).

As soon as we were producing blocks of text and visualisations, however, the issue arose of how these elements could be co-presented to readers in a manner that supported their interpretation and expressed their inter-relationships. This led to a consideration of the *layout* of automatically generated presentations. To pursue this in a more principled fashion, we undertook an investigation of a range of 'naturally occurring' examples of layouted documents, including illustrated magazines, scientific texts and the like. Whereas it was common for documents of the kind prepared electronically using markup schemes of the kind mentioned above to include visual materials, this did not appear to go very far towards covering the sheer range of variation observed in many professionally produced publications. A general heuristic of the form 'place the visual material somewhere near the corresponding or rhetorically-related textual material' was clearly severely under-constraining. In fact, the kind of organisation inherent in a heuristic of this form is that underlying just one particular 'semiotic mode' later defined within the Genre and Multimodality framework: the mode of *text-flow*, as Hiippala (this volume) sets out. Linearising a rhetorical structure or other form of document structure model – as commonly

Developing a GeM (genre and multimodality) model — 29

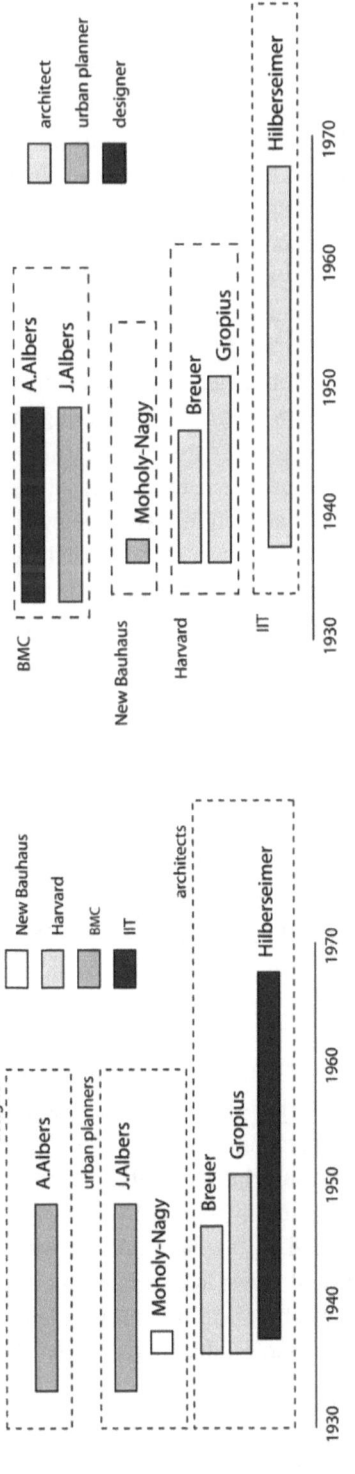

Figure 1: Example generated diagrams contrasting according to differing aggregations

found in the context of the World-Wide Web, for example – often takes this strategy. As we found in our informal analyses of more diverse published materials, however, there was evidently far more being made of the two-dimensional 'real estate' of the page than the text-flow model sensibly describes.

Even when 'rhetorically dysfunctional' layouts had been removed so that information was being presented in a manner in which the visual and spatial distribution on the page was more or less compatible with the rhetorical relationships established or presumed, there was still immense variation. Such variation resulted from widely divergent design decisions and represented a source of constraint that was outside of the mechanisms and information that we had so far considered. To begin describing this area of variation more systematically, we introduced in Reichenberger et al. (1995) the notion of a *layout structure*, a representation particularly targeting the two-dimensional distribution of information on a page, be that a physical page or that of a screen-based medium. This structure captured the notion of hierarchical containment relations of regions on a page as well as dependency constraints between elements, representations of content-types (e.g., textual, diagrammatic, etc.) and targeted 'importance' or 'salience' of elements with respect to each other. The idea of this layout structure was that it could, on the one hand, be used as an input for automatic layouting algorithms that would finally commit to spatial regions within a page and, on the other hand, stand as the output of a transformation process from a rhetorical structure to a committed deployment of graphical, typographic and spatial resources consistent with the rhetorical weights, similarities and differences given by the rhetorical organisation. Since it was already evident that many layout structures could be constructed that were broadly 'compatible' with any rhetorical structure, we deliberately left open at that time the precise nature of the transformation between them, although a sketch of an algorithm was presented in Bateman et al. (2001) and further refined in Henschel et al. (2002) and Bateman and Henschel (2007). Figure 2 shows one of our first examples, a page redesigned according to our principles from material in the German health magazine *Fit for Fun* from 1995. On the left-hand side of the figure we can see the layout structure, in the middle a spatially realised version of that structure satisfying its specified constraints, and on the right a final rendered version with filled content.

This gave us much of the descriptive capabilities we needed to explore alternative designs but we still had no way of systematically enforcing coherent design strategies. We also had no explanation for why particular documents would take on particular visual styles rather than others since this could not be motivated on the basis of the rhetorical organisation alone. This challenge was then the principal impetus for the establishment of the *Genre and Multimodality*

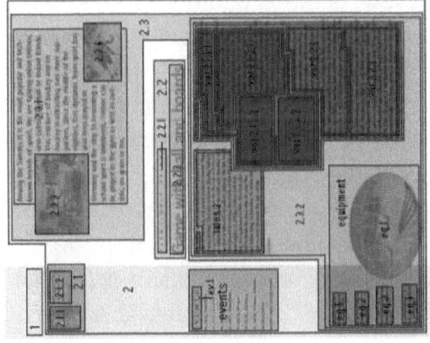

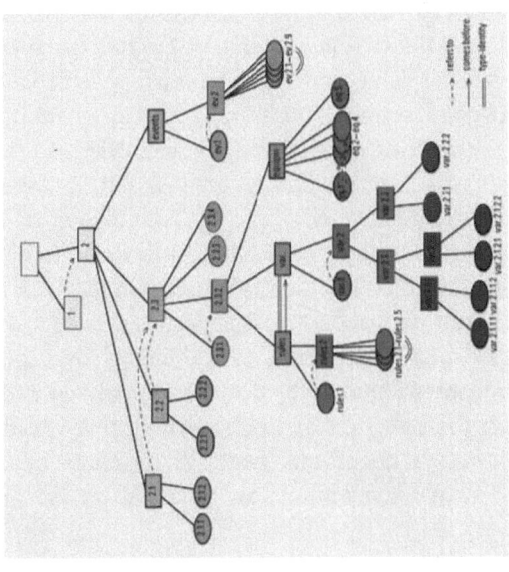

Figure 2: Three stages of page description: layout structure, spatial region allocation and final rendered page

(GeM) research project at the University of Stirling in Scotland in 1999 by Judy Delin, Patrick Allen and myself. The project was funded by the British Economic and Social Research Council (ESRC) and ran until mid-2002, also employing Stewart Pleace and Renate Henschel at various times over its duration and taking in changes in the affiliations of all the project's participants: Renate Henschel and myself moving to Bremen, Patrick Allen to Electronic Imaging and Media Communications in Bradford, Judy Delin taking up positions in Nottingham and Leeds as well as becoming head of research at Enterprise IDU, a company specialising in document design, and Stewart Pleace returning to industry.

The goal of the GeM project was to develop a framework that would let us account for consistencies in visual style (including layout and typographical decisions) in terms of an extended notion of *multimodal genre* – the essential idea here being that, just as genre is traditionally seen as bringing constraints to bear on selections made within the linguistic system in terms of lexicogrammatical, semantic and rhetorical patterns (cf. Swales 1990), then a multimodal account of genre might similarly exercise constraints on selections within layout structures, on their typographical and spatial realisation, and on the transformation processes between layout structure and rhetorical organisations. This approach therefore built on views of genre from literary studies and linguistics, and extended this to include documents that are not single-mode linguistic products. The general framework employed was a combination of the approach of Martin (1992), in which genre is considered to be realized in register configurations which are themselves realized in linguistic (semantic, lexicogrammatical, etc.) configurations, and the idea of a *genre space* proposed by Lemke (1999). Genre was thus considered to be best captured in terms of a description of a space of genre possibilities – movements within this space would then pull the accompanying register configurations in various, systematically specifiable, directions. These register configurations, now conceived multimodally, were taken as a means for capturing consistency in visual style.

The GeM project was designed to be corpus-based. Building on our own previous experiences in linguistic work and on the range of materials that we had explored at IPSI in Darmstadt, we decided to focus on four broad areas of documents in order to characterise their differences in terms of a genre model – bird field-guides, print and online newspapers, and technical manuals. The project was also particularly concerned with avoiding 'over-interpretation' of the import of the properties found in the documents analysed and so took pains to discuss them with the designers and publishers involved in the documents' production; details of the documents analysed, example analyses and the designers consulted within the project can be found on the project website, maintained at http://purl.org/net/gem. Analysis within the project then took the form of a multiple level annotation of the documents considered; these levels are introduced by Hiippala (this volume) and set out at greater length in, for example, Henschel (2002), Bateman et al. (2002) and Bateman (2008).

The GeM experience has suggested that the construction of datasets employing the GeM annotation scheme, or some extension of it, can play a significant role in achieving a sharper and more firmly empirically grounded understanding of the meaning-making practices of multimodal documents. The project taught us a considerable amount about how page-based documents can be characterized and offered new insights concerning the kinds of semiotic modes deployed within such documents. This has now been taken further in work such as Thomas (2007, 2009) and Hiippala (2011), where results with respect to a broader range of multimodal genres have been realized, in Bateman (2011), where the concept of 'semiotic mode' is defined more precisely, and in Bateman (2014), where there is a further consideration of the notion of 'multimodal genre'. Nevertheless, the goal of achieving a general description of the multimodal genre space of page-based documents remains a wide open and long-term enterprise. There is much to be done before well-founded empirical results over a sufficiently broad range of document types are available and the opportunities for further research topics are considerable. A critical step here will be to arrive at generalizations that *explain and motivate* the diversity of realizations taken up in particular multimodal documents – that is, we will need to use the detailed annotations of the GeM scheme as rungs on a ladder of analytic abstraction capable of making visible general mechanisms of multimodal meaning-making. For this, the annotation scheme must be made to function as a tool for isolating significant patterns against the mass of detail that multimodal documents naturally present. Only then will we realistically be able to bring these extremely complex semiotic artefacts under some degree of analytic control.

References

André, Elisabeth and Thomas Rist. 1993. The design of illustrated documents as a planning task. In Mark T. Maybury (ed.), *Intelligent Multimedia Interfaces*, 94–116. Menlo Park (CA), Cambridge (MA), London (England): AAAI Press/The MIT Press.

Arens, Yigal. 1992. Multimedia presentation planning as an extension of text planning. In Robert Dale, Eduard H. Hovy, Dietmar Rösner and Oliviero Stock (eds.), *Aspects of utomated natural language generation*, 278–280. Berlin: Springer.

Arens, Yigal and Eduard H. Hovy. 1990. How to describe what? Towards a theory of modality utilization. In *The Twelfth Annual Conference of the Cognitive Science Society*, 487–494. Hillsdale, New Jersey: Lawrence Erlbaum Associates.

Bateman, John A. 1997. Enabling technology for multilingual natural language generation: the KPML development environment. *Natural Language Engineering* 3(1): 15–55.

Bateman, John A. 1999. Using aggregation for selecting content when generating referring expressions. In *Proceedings of the 37th. Annual Meeting of the American Association for Computational Linguistics (ACL'99)*, 127–134. University of Maryland: American Association for Computational Linguistics.

Bateman, John A. 2008. *Multimodality and Genre: A Foundation for the Systematic Analysis of Multimodal Documents*. London: Palgrave Macmillan.

Bateman, John A. 2011. The decomposability of semiotic modes. In Kay L. O'Halloran and Bradley A. Smith (eds.), *Multimodal Studies: Multiple Approaches and Domains*, 17–38 (Routledge Studies in Multimodality) London: Routledge.

Bateman, John A. 2014. Genre in the age of multimodality: some conceptual refinements for practical analysis. In Paola Evangelisti, Vijay Bhatia and John Bateman (eds.), *Evolution in Genre: Emergence, Variation, Multimodality*. (Linguistic Insights) Frankfurt am Main: Peter Lang.

Bateman, John A. and Judy L. Delin. 2006. Rhetorical structure theory. In Keith Brown (ed.), *The Encyclopedia of Language and Linguistics* 10: 588–596. Amsterdam: Elsevier.

Bateman, John A., Judy L. Delin and Renate Henschel. 2002. A brief introduction to the GEM annotation schema for complex document layout. In Graham Wilcock, Nancy Ide and Laurent Romary (eds.), *Proceedings of the 2nd Workshop on NLP and XML (NLPXML-2002) – Post-Conference Workshop of the 19th International Conference on Computational Linguistics (COLING-2002)*, 13–20. Academica Sinica, Taipei, Taiwan: Association of Computational Linguistics and Chinese Language Processing. http://www.aclweb.org/anthology-new/W/W02/W02-1703.pdf.

Bateman, John A. and Renate Henschel. 2007. Generating text, layout and diagrams appropriately for genre. In Elka van der Sluis, Mariët Theune, Ehud Reiter and Emiel Krahmer (eds.), *Proceedings of the Workshop on Multimodal Output Generation MOG 2007*, 29–40. Centre for Telematics and Information Technology (CTIT), University of Twente.

Bateman, John A., Thomas Kamps, Jörg Kleinz and Klaus Reichenberger. 1998. Communicative Goal-Driven NL Generation and Data-driven Graphics Generation: an architectural synthesis for multimedia page generation. In *Proceedings of the 1998 International Workshop on Natural Language Generation*, 8–17. Niagara-on-the-Lake, Canada.

Bateman, John A., Thomas Kamps, Jörg Kleinz and Klaus Reichenberger. 2001. Constructive text, diagram and layout generation for information presentation: the DArtbio system. *Computational Linguistics* 27(3): 409–449.

Bouayad-Agha, Nadjet, Donia Scott and Richard Power. 2000. Integrating content and style in documents: a case study of patient information leaflets. *Information Design Journal* 9(2): 161–176. http://www.itri.bton.ac.uk/projects/iconoclast/Papers/ITRI.pdf.

Dalianis, Hercules and Eduard H. Hovy. 1996. Aggregation in natural language generation. In Giovanni Adorni and Michael Zock (eds.), *Trends in natural language generation: an artificial intelligence perspective* (Lecture Notes in Artificial Intelligence 1036), 88–105. Springer Verlag.

Feiner, Steven K. and Kathleen R. McKeown. 1990. Coordinating Text and Graphics in Explanation Generation. In *AAAI-90: Proceedings of the 8th National Conference on Artificial Intelligence* Volume I: 442–449. AAAI Press / The MIT Press.

Goldfarb, Charles F. (ed.). 1990. *The SGML Handbook*. Oxford: Clarendon Press.

Henschel, Renate. 2002. *GeM Annotation Manual. GeM Project Report*, University of Bremen and University of Stirling. http://purl.org/net/gem.

Henschel, Renate, John A. Bateman and Judy L. Delin. 2002. Automatic genre-driven layout generation. In *Proceedings of the 6. Konferenz zur Verarbeitung natürlicher Sprache (KONVENS 2002)*, 51–58. University of the Saarland, Saarbrücken.

Hiippala, Tuomo. 2011. The localisation of advertising print media as a multimodal process. In Wendy L. Bowcher (ed.), *Multimodal Texts from Around the World: Linguistic and Cultural Insights*, Basingstoke: Palgrave Macmillan.

Hovy, Eduard H. and Yigal Arens. 1991. Automatic generation of formatted text. In *Proceedings of the 8th. Conference of the American Association for Artifical Intelligence*, 92–96. Anaheim, California.

Kruijff, Geert-Jan, Elke Teich, John A. Bateman, Ivana Kruijff-Korbayová, Hana Skoumalová, Serge Sharoff, Lena Sokolova, Tony Hartley, Kamy Staykova and Jiří Hana. 2000. A multilingual system for text generation in three Slavic languages. In *Proceedings of the 18th. International Conference on Computational Linguistics (COLING'2000)*, 474–480. Saarbrücken, Germany.

Lemke, Jay L. 1999. *Typology, Topology, Topography: Genre Semantics*. MS University of Michigan. http://www-personal.umich.edu/~jaylemke/papers/Genre-topology-revised.htm.

Mann, William C. 1985. An introduction to the Nigel text generation grammar. In James D. Benson and William S. Greaves (eds.), *Systemic Perspectives on Discourse: Selected Theoretical Papers from the 9th. International Systemic Workshop*, 84–95. Norwood, NJ: Ablex Pub. Corp.

Mann, William C. and Sandra A. Thompson. 1988. Rhetorical structure theory: toward a functional theory of text organization. *Text* 8(3). 243–281.

Martin, James R. 1992. *English text: systems and structure*. Amsterdam: Benjamins.

Matthiessen, Christian M. I. M. and John A. Bateman. 1991. *Text Generation and Systemic-Functional Linguistics: Experiences from English and Japanese*. London and New York: Frances Pinter Publishers and St. Martin's Press.

Maybury, Mark T. 1993. *Intelligent Multimedia Interfaces*. Cambridge, Massachusetts: AAAI Press and MIT Press.

McDonald, David D. 1983. Description directed control: its implications for natural language generation. *Computers and Mathematics* 9(1): 111–129. Reprinted in Barbara J. Grosz et al. (eds.). 1986. *Readings in Natural Language* Processing, 519–538. Morgan Kaufman Publishers, California.

Moore, Johanna D. and William R. Swartout. 1990. Pointing: a way toward explanation dialogue. In *AAAI-90: Proc. 8th Nat. Conf. on Artificial Intelligence*, Volume I: 457–464. Menlo Park: AAAI Press / The MIT Press.

Power, Richard, Donia Scott and Nadjet Bouayad-Agha. 2003. Document Structure. *Computational Linguistics* 29(2): 211–260.

Reichenberger, Klaus, Klaas Jan Rondhuis, Jörg Kleinz and John A. Bateman. 1995. *Effective Presentation of Information through Page Layout: A Linguistically-Based Approach*. Tech. Rep. Arbeitspapiere der GMD 970 Institut für Integrierte Publikations-und Informationssysteme (IPSI), GMD Darmstadt. http://www.cs.uic.edu/~ifc/mmwsproc/reichen/page-layout.html. (Paper presented at the workshop *Effective Abstractions in Multimedia, Layout and Interaction*, held in conjunction with *ACM Multimedia '95*, San Francisco, California.).

Swales, John M. 1990. *Genre Analysis: English in Academic and Research Settings*. Cambridge: Cambridge University Press.

Thomas, Martin. 2007. Querying Multimodal Annotation: A Concordancer for GeM. In *Proceedings of the Linguistic Annotation Workshop*, 57–60. Prague, Czech Republic: Association for Computational Linguistics. http://www.aclweb.org/anthology/W/W07/W07-1510.

Thomas, Martin. 2009. Developing multimodal texture. In Eija Ventola and Arsenio Jesús Moya Guijarro (eds.), *The World Told and the World Shown: Multisemiotic Issues*, Basingstoke: Palgrave Macmillan.

Wahlster, Wolfgang, Elisabeth André, Wolfgang Finkler, Hans-Jürgen Profitlich and Thomas Rist. 1993. Plan-based integration of natural language and graphics generation. *Artificial Intelligence* 63(1–2): 387–427.

II Multimodal theory and methodology: What are their facets?

Rodney H. Jones
6 Mediated discourse analysis[1]

Introduction

The world is full of meaning. Written texts surround us in the form of books, newspapers, street signs, tee shirts, labels on products, and words on the screens of computers and smartphones. We hear tens of thousands of words a day, some directed specifically at us, but most broadcast or overheard. And meaning comes not just from language. Colors, shapes, gestures, sounds, smells and tastes fill our environment, communicating everything from traffic regulations to the innermost feelings of our loved ones. Given the cascade of discourse that confronts us in our daily lives, perhaps the most important question a discourse analyst can ask is: 'Where do I begin?' 'How do I know which discourse is relevant and which is not?'

Mediated discourse analysis, an approach to discourse developed by Ron and Suzanne Scollon beginning in the late 1990's (Scollon, 1998; 2001; Scollon & Scollon, 2004), attempts to answer this question by shifting our focus *away* from discourse, and on to the *actions* people use discourse to take. The only way to determine which discourse is worth analyzing, MDA argues, is to first understand what people are *doing*, and then to attempt to determine what role discourse plays in these actions.

The way of approaching discourse through action has enormous practical value not just for discourse analysts, but for all of us as we make our ways through our discursively complex worlds, trying to 'get things done'. The modern supermarket is a good example of this complexity. As soon as we enter a supermarket, multiple forms of discourse vie for our attention. Rows and rows of products in colorful packages covered with pictures and written text surround us. Signs advertise items on sale. Verbal announcements emanate from the PA system over the sound of violin versions of old Beatles songs. Kids scream to their parents, who squint at their scribbled shopping lists. Teenagers stocking shelves wear badges with their names on them. Cash registers beep and flash numbers. Currency, credit cards, and receipts change hands. Customers are told to 'have a nice day'.

---

[1] Research for this chapter was made possible by the General Research Fund Grant 'The Discourse of Food Labeling in Hong Kong: Public Policy and Discursive Practice' (#CityU144110) from the Hong Kong Research Grants Council.

This discursive environment presents challenges to customers trying to complete their shopping, to store managers, trying to decide where to place items on the shelves, to food manufactures and distributors, trying to design packages that will catch the eyes of customers, and to legislators trying to determine how best to regulate what kind to discourse should appear on such packages to prevent food manufacturers from misleading the public. In this chapter I will illustrate how the main analytical tools of mediated discourse analysis can help us to make sense of this kind of discursive complexity through a focus on social actions.

Key terms: discourse itinerary, mediated action, mediational means/cultural tool, site of engagement, social practice

Mediated action

The unit of analysis for the mediated discourse analyst is not the word, nor the sentence, nor the text. Nor is it the image, the gesture or the sound. It is the *action* which makes use of the word, sentence, image, gesture or sound to get done. Words, sentences, texts, images, gestures and sounds are not of much relevance unless they are in some way involved in actions. At the same time, actions cannot be accomplished without the use of things like words, sentences, texts, images, gestures and sounds, as well as other *cultural tools* such as supermarket shelves, cash registers, barcode scanners, and cardboard boxes. In other words, all actions are *mediated* through some kind of cultural tools. Therefore, the real unit of analysis for mediated discourse analysts is not just the *action*, but the *mediated action*.

The roots of this approach come from the work of the Soviet psychologist Lev Vygotsky (1981), who sees all action in the world as mediated by 'cultural tools' which have the effect of either amplifying or constraining those actions. The notion of mediation was important for Vygotsky insofar as it provided a link between social and cultural processes and individual mental processes. Because mental functioning is carried out by mediational means provided by the society, all thought is essentially social. At the same time, individuals appropriate and adapt mediational means for particular concrete purposes. Therefore, the relationship between individual consciousness and the mediational means provided by society is always dialectical, mediational means acting to both afford and limit actions, and individuals constantly adapting mediational means to fit the contingencies of particular circumstances and goals

(Wertsch, 1994). What mediated discourse analysts are interested in is the interplay between social actors and cultural tools (including discourse) as it is expressed in action.

Of course, this attention to 'action' is not entirely foreign to discourse analysis. Many schools of discourse analysis from pragmatics to conversation analysis have been concerned with how people 'do things with words'. In fact, it can be argued that a preoccupation with action – 'language in use' – is at the root of most approaches to discourse. Where mediated action differs is that it is less concerned with 'discourse as action' – how words and texts themselves can constitute actions – as with 'discourse *in* action' – how discourse, along with any number of other cultural tools, contributes to how people are able to perform certain actions in different circumstances. The former approach privileges 'discourse' (texts and spoken language), and generally ignores other things like supermarket shelves, cash registers, barcode scanners, and cardboard boxes. The latter approach privileges action and attempts to account for all the cultural tools that might be implicated in it.

Sites of engagement

When we speak of mediated actions we do not do so in an abstract, decontextualized sense. We do not, for example, speak of the action of choosing a product from a supermarket shelf, for this action is very different depending on what the product is, who is doing the choosing, the particular supermarket in which the choosing takes place, and a host of other conditions. Every action is unique and 'unreproducible', taking place at a single point in history at which particular people, particular cultural tools, particular motivations and particular causes and conditions meet. We call this point the 'site of engagement' for an action.

Many discourse analysts speak of the importance of 'context' – the conditions that surround a text or utterance, but the 'site of engagement' for an action is not the same as the 'context' of a text. It does not merely 'affect' how the action might be carried out or interpreted. It is what makes the action possible in the first place. Scollon defines a 'site of engagement' as a 'window that is opened up through the intersection of social practices and mediational means (cultural tools) that make that action the focal point of attention of the relevant participants' (2001:4). There are several key concepts in this definition, the most important being the 'attention of the relevant participants'. 'Sites of engagement' are created not just through the physical presence of tools, actions and people at a particular place at a particular time, but rather through the 'attention' or 'engagement' of the people involved. The same configurations of tools at the same moments in time and the same points in space may for some people function as sites of engagement for particular actions, whereas for others they may not.

What determines how people focus their attention is a complex question. Attention is partially determined by cultural tools themselves (including what the Scollons in their 2004 book call 'discourses in place'). As scholars of multimodality (Norris, 2004; Kress and van Leeuwan, 1996) have pointed out, configurations of modes and media have a lot to do with this: the placement of objects in images, the use of color and fonts, the posture and gaze of social actors all contribute to the way attention is channeled. Attention is also a product of what the Scollons (after Goffman, 1983) call the 'interaction order', the relationship among participants that is created as they negotiate the ongoing process of giving and getting attention that constitutes social encounters. The final thing that determines how people 'engage' with particular cultural tools to perform mediated actions has to do with the people themselves, the degree of familiarity they have with the cultural tools at hand and the kinds of actions they are accustomed to performing – what the Scollons refer to as the 'historical bodies' (Nishida, 1959) of the social actors.

Social practices and historical bodies

Although the focus of mediated discourse analysis is on situated, 'real-time' mediated actions, it is difficult to understand these actions without taking into account how they fit into the fabric of people's experience and the cultures in which they live. Most of the actions that we perform in the course of a day, actions like choosing products from supermarket shelves, queuing at check-out counters, swiping credit cards, and all of the other actions that are part of grocery shopping, are things that we do on a regular basis. In fact, we are sometimes so accustomed to doing these actions that they have become more or less automatic: they have become 'practices'.

What mediated discourse analysts mean by 'practices' is actions or 'chains of action' that have become 'practiced', that have become submerged into the 'historical bodies' of social actors. The notion of 'practice' links the individual action to a whole history of learning and doing within the mind and body of the individual. It also links the individual action to other actions, since practiced actions rarely occur alone, but usually form part of larger social practices. The action of shaking someone's hand is part of the social practice of greeting. The action of swiping your credit card is part of the social practice of paying. Finally, the notion of practice links individual actions to the groups of people, societies and cultures who practice these actions and who recognize one another as members by the actions they perform. So, although every time we choose a product from a supermarket shelf, we are performing a unique, irreducible and unrepeatable action, we feel like we are doing something that we have done before, and people observing us can recognize and perhaps label what we are doing. They might even be able to tell from how we are doing it whether or not we are a 'seasoned shopper' or a member of the family who usually does not do the shopping but has been called upon to pick up a forgotten item on the way home from work.

Itineraries and resemiotization

As I said above, the way mediated discourse analysts go about deciding what discourse to analyze is by determining the relevant *actions* and determining which discourse plays a role in the accomplishment of those actions. It should be clear from the discussion above, however, that the task of determining the relevant actions at a particular site of engagement is neither simple nor straightforward. For one thing, any given site of engagement may involve multiple social actors using the same cultural tools to perform very different actions. As a customer chooses a product from a supermarket shelf, a store clerk might be stocking products on the same shelf. Second, even a particular social actor my be engaging in multiple activities at once: at the same time he is choosing a product, for example, the customer may be talking on his mobile phone to his wife. The thing that makes this relationship between actions and mediational means most complicated, however, is the fact that every action is part of a long history of actions involving multiple social actors and multiple mediational means. The moment the customer chooses a product from the supermarket shelves is not just part of a longer scale action of a shopping trip, but part of a lifetime of shopping and cooking and consuming food in which all sorts of other people including family members, doctors, advertisers, may all be implicated. And the moment of the store clerk placing the product on the shelf is also part of a long chain of actions involving people like farmers, factory workers, and business executives.

Every social action takes place at the intersection of multiple *itineraries* of discourse and action (Scollon, 2008). Along these itineraries social actors appropriate various mediational means to take actions which in turn give rise to new mediational means which allow them to take future actions, and through this process selves ('historical bodies') are created, social identities are claimed and imputed, and societies and cultures are produced and reproduced. Iedema uses the term 'resemiotization' to describe this process. What he means by resemiotization is that, as we take action, the mediational means that we use to take those actions change: Conversations between a husband and wife, for example, are transformed into shopping lists which are later transformed into products purchased at the supermarket, which in turn are transformed into meals, which (if you want to get technical) are transformed into glucose which fuels the bodies of these social actors to have further conversations, make further lists, and take further journeys to the supermarket.

But mediational means are not the only things that change. Actions and social actors also change as actions along these itineraries are submerged into the 'historical bodies' of participants, becoming 'practices'. The first time I choose a particular item from the supermarket shelves is not the same as the second time or the third time. Many of the mediational means that were very important the first time I bought it – things like its price tag and list of ingredients – are no longer relevant to the accomplishment of the action. That is not to say that the price and ingredients are not important, but the action of determining this information has become part of my 'historical body' and fused with the practice of buying the item to the extent that they do not demand conscious attention to any text, unless, of course, the price or ingredients change for some reason, in which case I might find this practice somehow interrupted.

It is often at these moments when we find our practices 'interrupted' that their real complexity becomes most obvious to us. The multiple chains of action that were so tightly bound into a social practice suddenly unravel, revealing themselves to us. This insight is at the heart of the 'breaching experiments' of the ethnomethodologist Harold Garfinkle (1991), who believed that the best way to understand how people 'do being normal' was to try to poke holes in the fabric of everyday life and observe how people worked together to tie the loose threads back together. It is, however, really not necessary to stage such occurrences. They happen all the time as social actors adjust their actions to the constantly changing convergences of people, tools and social practices that confront them.

Popcorn, movie stars and regulatory discourse

An example of this can be seen in my own act of choosing a box of Newman's Own Oldstyle Picture Show Microwave Popcorn from a shelf in a supermarket in

Figure 1: Newman's Own Popcorn Box (used with permission)

Hong Kong where I live (see figure 1). This purchase is inextricably tied up with my own particular set of practices around shopping, popcorn eating and movie watching. My partner and I have become accustomed to spending our Friday evenings watching a movie on our big screen television, and making a bowl of popcorn has become an expected part of that practice. The practice of eating popcorn while watching movies is of course not unique to us, but has a long history going back to the Great Depression when cinema owners, watching their profits from ticket sales decline, started to sell candy and other snacks in their theaters, and to World War II, when sugar rations resulted in popcorn replacing candy at theater concessions stands. The migration of this practice into people's homes, including my own, can be traced back to other chains of technological development including the invention of 'home theaters' and microwave ovens.

Why I choose this particular brand is slightly harder to unravel. Part of it has to do with the kind of inertia that often accompanies purchasing behavior – I buy this brand because, for as long as I can remember, I have bought it. Part of it has to do with my own 'historical body', the fact that I grew up watching Paul Newman movies, that I'm a Democrat and Paul Newman has always supported liberal causes, the fact that I prefer savory snacks to sweet ones, and a host of other practices and preferences that have become deeply sedimented in my 'historical body'. Also relevant here is the itinerary of discourse and action that led to Paul Newman himself to find his face on a box of microwave popcorn, an itinerary that began with his birth in Shaker Heights, Ohio in 1925, extends through a successful acting career to 1982 when he stared the Newman's Own line of food products, chiefly as a way of earning money for charities for seriously ill children. Finally, this box of popcorn would not be available for me to choose were it not for the itineraries that led up to it being placed on this particular shelf, itineraries that stretch back to cornfields in Iowa, company board rooms in Westport, Connecticut, and factories in China. Finally, this package of popocorn, its presence in this supermarket, and my act of reaching for it are all bound up with the itineraries of large-scale systems of economic exchange, of wealth and poverty, production and environmental degradation over which neither me nor Paul Newman seem to have much control, but which would not function if not for me and people like me taking the tiny action of reaching for a product in a supermarket (Scollon, 2005).

The point is that there are multiple itineraries of discourse and action on many levels from the cultural to the corporate to the personal that conspire to drive the action of me reaching for this package and dropping it into my shopping basket, itineraries that I am not fully conscious of but nevertheless are inseparable from that momentary action and how it gets done. Although most of the chains of action that converge at this moment are deeply submerged in my historical body and in the practices and architecture of the supermarket, the corporate structure of the company that manufacturers the product, and the culture of popcorn eating of movie watchers everywhere, if pressed, I and most other shoppers could unravel these chains, could, for example, explain why we are buying this particular brand or venture a guess as to why Paul Newman is selling it. The reason for this is that we are not separate 'historical bodies' choosing a box of popcorn, but rather members of broader 'communities of practice' (Lave and Wenger, 1991), communities that are bound together by thousands of banal practices like movie going and popcorn eating and supermarket shopping.

Most discourse analysts confronted with this package of popcorn would focus on the strategic use of language and other modes: They might for example point out the interdiscursivity on the front of the package which shows an old style movie marquee in which the name of the product appears like the name of a movie. They might point out the intimacy created by the headshot of Paul Newman gazing directly out at the viewer and smiling. They might point out the grammatical construction of phrases like 'No Trans Fats' and 'All Profits to

Charity', especially how processes are elided. They might point out how the words on the package like 'oldstyle', 'natural' and 'charity' (as in 'All Profits to Charity') go together to reproduce a certain ideology that resonates with customers like me who grew up in the 60s in the US. They might also turn their attention to issues like font and color, pointing out that the word 'Natural' is printed in bold white font against a purple background, as opposed to the word 'flavoring' to the right of it, printed in a harder to see small, dark font.

The problem with such an analysis is that it would totally ignore all of those itineraries mentioned above. Gone would be the movie theater concession stands, the microwave ovens, and the Iowa farmers without which this package would not have been possible. And, most important, gone would be all of the actions in my life that led up to me choosing this product, an itinerary of discourse and action in which the grammar and font of the words on the package are rather peripheral.

In fact, much of the communicative work of the *discourse* on this package play no role at all in the action of me plucking it from the supermarket shelf. The only really relevant thing about the colors, fonts, words and smiling face of Paul Newman for me at this moment is that they make it *recognizable* as the same product that I have bought before. In fact there are large parts of this text that I have never read. I've never read the ingredients or the nutritional information on the side of the box (maybe because somewhere deep down I trust Paul Newman), and I've never, until recently, read the additional promotional paragraph printed on the bottom of the box, which reads:

> Top-of-The-Crop
> Taste. No
> Trans Fats. No
> Hydrogenated Oils!
>
> It's our great,
> crispy, fresh tasting
> popcorn without
> the trans fats and
> hydrogenated oils.
> It's deliciously
> all natural and
> pops to perfection
> in two to five minutes.

A diligent discourse analyst would no doubt have included this passage in her analysis, and there is plenty to analyze here, including more literary uses of language like rhyme and alliteration (Carter, 2004). But as a shopper, this text was completely invisible to me until the last time I went searching for the product and found it altered, portions of it redacted with black magic marker.

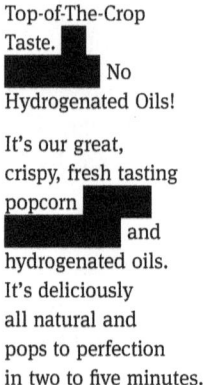

Top-of-The-Crop Taste. ■ ■ No Hydrogenated Oils!

It's our great, crispy, fresh tasting popcorn ■ ■ and hydrogenated oils. It's deliciously all natural and pops to perfection in two to five minutes.

Of course, there is a lot about this new text that is problematic from the point of view of discourse, not least of which is the fact that now it 'means' something totally different than it did before. Before I was buying 'fresh tasting popcorn without … hydrogenated oils', and now I am buying 'fresh tasting popcorn … and hydrogenated oils'. This in itself, however, (since I have very little knowledge of hydrogenated oils) is not nearly as important as the *physical* presence of black marks on the package, the *physical* fact that the product package has been altered by somebody other than Paul Newman or his employees.

Suddenly a piece of discourse that I could safely keep in the background when purchasing this product has been pushed into the foreground, demanding that I take some kind of action with it. But, not understanding the hidden chain of actions that led to these words being hidden, I do not know what action to take. What is important here, what has suddenly disrupted my popcorn purchase, is not *discourse* per se, but *action*, the action of somebody somewhere taking a black magic marker and defacing this package. This 'frozen action' (Norris, 2004) embodied in these black marks on the package is enough to interrupt my purchase, to make me consider buying something else instead.

There is, in fact, nothing sinister going on here. The black marks on this package are the result of an itinerary of discourse and action that can be traced back to the passage of a new Food and Drug Composition and Labeling Regulation by the Hong Kong Legislative Council in May 2008, which imposes strict new rules about what can and cannot appear on food labels. Among these is the rule that in order to make the claim 'zero trans fat', a product must fulfill three conditions: 1) it must contain no more than .03 grams of trans fats per

100 grams; 2) the sum of trans fats and saturated fats must not exceed 1.5 grams per 100 grams; 3) the sum of trans fats and saturated fats must not contribute to more than 10% of the energy. The fact is, Newman's Own Microwave Popcorn, while actually containing 0 trans fats, contains 6.6 grams of saturated fat per 100 grams, and therefore is not legally permitted to bear the claim 'zero trans fats' (despite the fact that the amount of trans fats in the product equals zero).

The fact that this regulation is rather confusing, however, is not the main problem here. The problem comes in the actions that must be taken to comply with the regulation. Since Hong Kong is such a small market, few major food manufactures are willing to change their packages to comply with these unique rules. Therefore, shopkeepers and supermarket employees are forced to alter packages before they put them on the shelves to avoid falling foul of the law. Once the package finds its way onto the shelves ready for me to reach for it, all of those actions of legislation, regulation, and compliance have become invisible. All that is left are the black marks. The problem is not that I don't know what the words *mean*, but that I don't even know what the words are.

The goal of the government was to help me make healthy choices about my diet. However, the result is the opposite. Not knowing what is behind those black marks, I immediately become suspicious of Paul Newman and decide to choose another snack item, one with no unsightly black marks because the manufacturer of this particular item, chock full of trans fats, has chosen not to make any claims to the contrary. And so I trade in a healthy item for a less healthy one, perhaps beginning a new itinerary leading up to possible heart disease in my later years.

The point I'm trying to make here is that the real problem with this text is not so much that I can't figure out what it means as it is that I can't figure out what it *does*. What interrupts my practice of popcorn buying, steering it in a new and dangerous direction, is not discourse *per se*, but the convergence of multiple itineraries of discourse and action, many of which, like the blacked out words, are invisible to me. Not only would analyzing this discourse divorced from the actions it is used to take not help me much in understanding this text, but it is this focus on discourse (meaning) at the expense of considering how it is used to take action that is, in fact, the problem here. In its effort to protect me from the non-existent trans fats in this product, the Hong Kong government has focused only on the words and their 'technical' meanings without considering the complex chains of actions in which these words (and their disappearance) are implicated.

Conclusion

Mediated discourse analysis is designed to help people understand practical problems in the real world, problems as trivial as which box of popcorn to buy and as significant as how to address world hunger. Often the best way to address such problems is not to focus on discourse, but to consider the chains of actions that discourse is a part of. Sometimes, in our efforts to solve problems by altering discourse alone, we end up creating bigger problems. There is no denying that food manufacturers sometimes try to deceive us, and governments must do their best to help prevent that. But simply changing the discourse on food labels is not enough to interrupt the complex and sometimes insidious itineraries of discourse and action that result in the products we find on our supermarket shelves. A better way to address social problems might be to find ways of making these itineraries more visible, and so making the social actors involved in them more accountable. Such an agenda would also involve helping people to make their own itineraries of shopping and eating more visible to themselves and others, and to become more conscious of how even tiny, banal actions of choosing particular products are part of larger social practices, some of which promote health and social justice, and some of which do not. Social change comes not from changing our discourse – it comes from changing our actions.

Further readings

Jones, R. H. 2009. Dancing, skating and sex: Action and text in the digital age. *Journal of Applied Linguistics*, 6(3), 283–302.

Norris, S., & Jones, R. H. (Eds.). 2005. *Discourse in action: Introducing mediated discourse analysis*. Abingdon: Routledge.

Scollon, R. 2001. Action and text: Towards an integrated understanding of the place of text in social (inter)action, mediated discourse analysis and the problem of social action. In R. Wodak & M. Meyer (Eds.), *Methods of critical discourse analysis* (pp. 139–183). London: Sage.

Wertsch, J. V. 1993. *Voices of the mind: A sociocultural approach to mediated action*. Cambridge, MA: Harvard University Press.

Project idea

Choose a practice that you engage in on a regular basis such as shopping at a particular shop, riding on public transportation, or eating in a particular restaurant. Over the course of several weeks make a list of all of the different instances of discourse you encounter when you engage in this practice. Then attempt to account for the role each of these instances of discourse play in your performance of the practice. How does discourse make some actions easier and others more difficult?

Then consider how much of this discourse is 'regulatory discourse', discourse imposed by some authority in order to ensure that people do things 'better'. Using the concepts outlined in this chapter, analyze if and how this discourse has a positive impact on people's actions. Finally, make recommendations regarding how the aims of the regulatory discourse might be better met by focusing more on the itineraries of actions people follow as they move through these sites of engagement.

References

Carter, R. 2004. *Language and creativity: The art of common talk*. New York: Routledge.
Garfinkel, H. 1991. *Studies in ethnomethodology*. Oxford: Polity Press.
Goffman, E. 1983. The interaction order: American Sociological Association, 1982 presidential address. *American Sociological Review, 48*(1), 1–17.
Kress, G. R., & van Leeuwen, T. 1996. *Reading images: The grammar of visual design*. London: Routledge.
Nishida, K. 1959. *Intelligibility and the Philosophy of Nothingness*, Tokyo, Maruzen Co. Ltd.
Norris, S. 2004. *Analyzing multimodal interaction: A methodological framework*. London: Routledge.
Scollon, R. 1998. *Mediated discourse as social interaction: A study of news discourse*: Longman.
Scollon, R. 2001. *Mediated discourse: The nexus of practice*. Oxford: Routledge.
Scollon, R. 2005. The discourses of food in the world system: Toward a nexus analysis of a world problem. *Journal of Language and Politics, 4*(3), 465–488.
Scollon, R. 2008. Discourse itineraries: Nine processes of resemiotization. In V. K. Bhatia, J. Flowerdew & R. H. Jones (Eds.), *Advances in discourse studies* (pp. 233–244). London: Routledge.
Scollon, R., & Scollon, S. 2003. *Discourses in place : language in the material world*: Routledge.
Scollon, R., & Scollon, S. W. 2004. *Nexus analysis: Discourse and the emerging internet*. London: Routledge.
Vygotsky, L. S. 1981. The instrumental method in psychology. In J. V. Wertsch. (ed.) *The concept of activity in Soviet psychology*. Armonk, NY: M. E. Sharpe, pp. 134–143.
Wertsch, J. V. 1994. The primacy of mediated action in sociocultural studies. *Mind, Culture and Activity 1* (4): 202–208.

Yuling Pan
7 Nexus analysis

Introduction

Nexus Analysis (Scollon and Scollon 2004) is an analytical framework that organically grew out of the Mediated Discourse Theory (Scollon 2001). While the Mediated Discourse Theory argues for a discursive approach to analyzing human action, Nexus Analysis focuses on the methodology of how to investigate a social action through the lens of the MDT. Nexus Analysis employs and links multiple analytical perspectives, including interactional sociolinguistics, conversation analysis, anthropological linguistics or the ethnography of communication, and critical discourse analysis.

Methodologically, a nexus analysis is an ethnographic study, involving participant-observation and discourse analysis. Central to Nexus Analysis is social action, which is the unit of analysis and focal point of the study. The social action is mediated by the historical body, discourses in place, and the interaction order. The relationship of all these components is represented in Figure 1 (Scollon and Scollon 2004: 20).

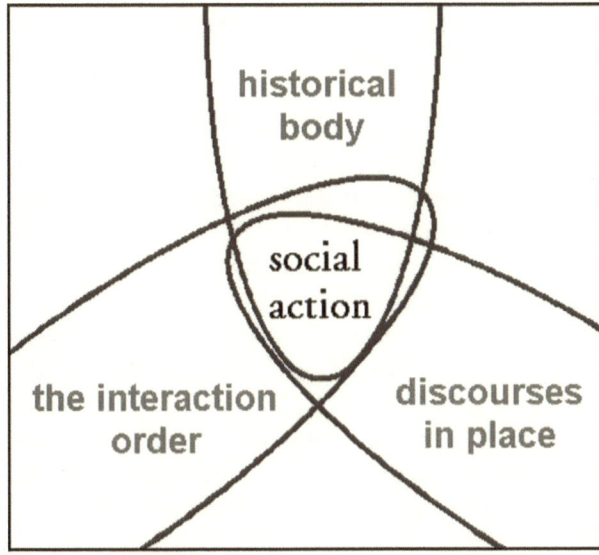

Figure 1: Nexus Analysis

Key terms: Circumferencing, cycles of discourses, discourses in place, historical body, interaction order, social action, zone of identification.

Key concepts

At the center of the diagram is the *social action*. This is any action taken by an individual with reference to a social network. The social action is mediated by three elements: life experiences of the individual social actors (historical body), written or spoken discourses that mark the social setting for the action (discourses in place), and social arrangement by which people come together in social groups (the interaction order). All three elements should be taken into consideration when analyzing the social action.

Historical body is the history of personal experiences inscribed in the individual body of a social actor. It is an abstraction of the aggregation of social practices or repeated experiences of the social actor that others recognize as a repeatable action, such as greeting by speaking, or by putting the palms together in front of the chest, or by raising the eyebrows. It is memories in the form of practices embodied in the historical body of the actor.

Discourses in place are instances of language use, either written or spoken, that mark the environment in which the social action takes place. These discourses can be conceptualized as the following: (1) discourses that circulate on slow time cycles such as environmental markings that bear signs or images for a social action; for example, to study the social action of eating out among friends, the restaurant signage, furniture, and decorative objects all constitute discourses that contribute to the action under examination; (2) discourses that circulate more rapidly such as conversational topics among friends eating together at the restaurant; (3) discourses that are distant and of little direct relevance to the particular social action occurring in that place, such as the design specifications of the tables; (4) discourses that are directly relevant such as the menu from which a meal selection is made.

The *interaction order* refers to the many possible social arrangements through which people form relationships in social interactions. It also includes the roles people take up in social interactions. People as social actors behave differently depending in part on the roles they are in and the people who are there. For example, whether the social actor is alone or with others, how the social actor interacts with people who are there as conversational pairs, or as customer or server.

Analytical tasks/activities

Nexus Analysis uses discourse analysis as its analytical tool. However it is strategically different from traditional discourse analysis as characterized by Scollon and Scollon (2004). They contend that there are generally two levels of discourse analysis. One is the "micro-analysis of unfolding moments of social interaction" (2004: 8), such as analyzing conversation among friends with a focus on how alignment among participants is achieved or how participants take up their position in the conversation. The other level of discourse analysis is "a much broader socio-political-cultural analysis of the relationships among social groups and power interests in the society" (2004: 8), such as "legal discourse" or "medical discourse." Nexus Analysis is a way to strategically unify these two different levels of analysis through the three tasks of *engaging, navigating, and changing the nexus of practice*.

Each of these three tasks consists of a series of activities that aims to recognize and identify the nexus of practice that surrounds the social action under investigation. In order to illustrate how to carry out these specific activities, a case study is presented here to show the steps involved in a nexus analysis.

Case study: Observing census enumeration of non-English-speaking households in the United States

In 2010, the United States Census Bureau conducted its nation-wide census. In order to understand the process of enumerating non-English-speaking populations in the U.S., a research project employing the framework of Nexus Analysis was conceived (see Pan and Lubkemann 2013). A multilingual research team with 28 ethnographers observed live census interviews[1] conducted with respondents who were speakers of seven non-English languages (Arabic, Chinese, Korean,

---

1 The U.S. Census is an address-based operation that consists of two phases. In Phase I, a census form is mailed out to every housing unit with a valid mailing address throughout the nation. Residents of housing units are expected to fill out the census forms and mail them back. When no census form is returned from an address, the Census attempts to collect this missing data through its Phase II operation: in-person interviews. During this second phase, a census taker visits households that failed to return their census forms, and seeks to collect their data through a personal interview.

Portuguese, Russian, Spanish, and Vietnamese). The research team also conducted debriefing interviews with respondents and census takers to obtain their perspectives on the census process. Under the Nexus Analysis framework, the research sought to study the *mediated action* of the census interview by conducting the following activities:

Engaging the nexus of practice

The first task was to engage the nexus of practice. This task involves the following steps:

(1) To identify the mediated action to be studied: In this case study, the mediated action is the act of enumerating non-English-speaking populations through face-to-face interviews. Since Nexus Analysis emphasizes social action and change of nexus practice, it is important to identify an issue that has some social implications. The social implications for studying this mediated action are multi-fold: The Census Bureau's mission is to count everyone in the country, including all those who immigrated to or stayed temporarily in the U.S. Non-English-speaking populations are likely to be missed in the census counting. This may affect the accuracy and reliability of census data and political representation of minority groups. It is, therefore, very important to include non-English-speaking populations in the census.

(2) The next step is to determine who the crucial social actors are for the mediated action of census taking. In this case, the crucial social actors were non-English-speaking respondents and census takers. The key is to explore their identities, social roles, and their individual histories (their historical bodies), and how they are enabled to take the mediated action of participating in the U.S. census.

(3) The third step is to observe the interaction order among the social actors. In this case, we need to discover what the typical interaction orders are within which the census interview occurs. Are people usually alone or with others during the interview? Does the interview action occur in task groups or teams? Who initiates the interaction and in what order does the interaction proceed?

(4) The fourth step is to determine the most significant cycles of discourse. We want to know what discourses are circulating through the census interview. The census interview is an encounter in which the census taker has some kind of power to define significant outcomes for respondents who must account for themselves. Before such an encounter can begin, however, the

census taker must gain access to a respondent. No questioning can take place if a resident does not recognize the census taker and open the door. Personal appearance is thus a significant consideration for the census taker, who must take care to look professional and somewhat official. The personal front is a visual image, a type of discourse in place.

Some discourses circulate on slow time cycles like the housing units of non-English-speaking respondents, i.e, the type of housing and furniture arrangement. More rapidly circulating discourse might include the conversation of the census taker and respondent as the census taker rings the doorbell. Intermediate circulating discourse might be the dress of these social actors.

All these are significant cycles of discourses for the particular scene of census interview. The goal here is to locate the central and crucial discourses which are intersecting the interaction order and historical bodies of the participants to produce the focal mediated actions of the study (Scollon and Scollon 2004: 155).

(5) The last activity is to establish the zone of identification. That is, by conducting preliminary studies of the scene, participants, events, discourses, and actions, our researchers became full-fledged participants in the activities. They gained a place in the nexus of practice of census enumeration as accepted legitimate participants. In the study design, our researchers came from the language community that they were studying and they spent a considerable time with local census offices to get themselves familiar with the census procedures and requirements. They accompanied census takers on interviews for two weeks during the census operation. This enabled them to analyze the social practices of census enumeration so they could make meaningful recommendations to the U.S. Census Bureau to improve the process of enumerating non-English-speaking populations. By doing so, they were engaged in the changes of the nexus of census enumeration.

Navigating the nexus of practice

While the first task of engaging the nexus of practice is the ethnographic component of the research process, the second task of navigating the nexus of practice is largely discourse analysis of central and crucial cycles of discourses, including talk between the census taker and the respondent; signs, images, graphics, clothing of the participants; texts and materials used during the census interview; place and location of the interview.

The research teams were instructed to note down these cycles of discourses during their field work by taking detailed notes and audio-taping the census interview for analysis. The analysis consists of the following steps:

Mapping

The goal of a nexus analysis here is to map out these cycles of discourse from the moment of a census enumeration interview to large discourse-and-practice complexes that make up the powerful census operation in the U.S. and the socio-cultural complexes that are reflected in the historical bodies of immigrants. In this sense, the analysis here does not limit itself to the discourse of interview interaction between the census taker and the respondent. Nor does it focus solely on the broader discourse of the U.S. census. Rather it seeks to link the census event with immigrants' experiences with census taking in the country of origin and in the U.S. and their perception of the census taking as a social practice. To obtain this level of data, the research team asked non-English-speaking immigrants a series of questions about their experiences after the census interview to see if their perception of the U.S. census matched the social practice of census taking in the U.S.

Through this mapping activity, it was found that many immigrants had little understanding of the purpose and procedures of the U.S. census. The lack of knowledge, and thus lack of motivation, is a big barrier for their participation in the U.S. census.

Circumferencing

This step of analysis is to open up the circumference of our analysis to dissect how the habits of historical bodies are related to discourses surrounding the moment of census interview. For example, to understand why some people might be reluctant to open the door to census takers, we need to understand the experience of immigrants. In their experience, it may simply be that they were never interviewed by a stranger. Or they didn't know what the U.S. census was about and why they needed to participate in it.

Furthermore, to understand why some people failed to answer some census questions, we need to look beyond the census questions themselves to understand what each census question entailed from the perspective of immigrants. It may be that the census questions did not make any sense when translated from English into another language. It may be that a particular question was offensive to ask in a certain culture. Or it may be that a certain concept did not exist in the target culture. Our researchers gained this level of knowledge or data by observing the interview interaction and by identifying the interaction order.

Discourse analysis

According to Scollon and Scollon (2004: 173), a nexus analysis examines at least six forms of discourse:
(1) Speech of the participants in mediated actions
(2) Texts used as mediational means
(3) Images and other semiotic systems used as mediational means
(4) Discourse submerged in the historical body of the participants and in the practices in which they engage
(5) Discourse submerged in the design of the built environment and objects
(6) Speech or writing or images of the analysts in conducting the nexus analysis

Discourses under analysis for this case study include: (1) taped census interviews as speech of the participations; (2) debriefings with census takers and respondents to get to the discourse submerged in the historical body of the participants; (3) researchers' observational notes of the interaction and interview environment to note down the images and semiotic systems; (4) texts (e.g., census questionnaire, language materials) that the census takers used during the interview; and (5) researchers' summaries and field reports recording their own reflections on the observations as these occurred.

To be more specific, the taped census interviews are discourses that bear direct relevance to the social action of census interviews and circulate more rapidly. Discourse analysis of this set of data focused on the interaction between the census taker and the respondent to identify any problems with census questions and on-the-fly translation from English into target languages.

The analysis of debriefings focused on census takers' perspective of challenges with enumerating non-English-speaking populations, and the non-English-speaking respondents' view of the census and government. This brings to light the historical bodies embedded in the respondent and the census taker.

The researchers' observational notes contained detailed records of the environmental markings (type of housing, neighborhood, signs, and images, location of the interview), interactional order between the census taker and the respondent, and the materials (census questionnaires, flashcards, target language materials) that the census taker used to complete the task of enumeration. Analysis of this form of discourse shows how these discourses impacted the interview process. For example, it was found that the location of the interview (outside vs. inside the house) played a significant role in securing the interview. Interviews conducted inside the house were complete and the respondents appeared more willing to provide answers to the census questions.

Finally, researchers' summaries and field reports recording their own reflections on the observations as these occurred. The researchers brought their insight and knowledge of the language community that they observed.

Motive analysis

Nexus Analysis seeks to provide explanations for actions and to understand how participants are positioning themselves in giving explanations for their actions. The motive analysis is based on Burke's *grammar of motives* (1969), which proposes that any action can be talked about from any of five points of view: (1) the scene, (2) the social actor, (3) the mediational means, (4) the mediated action, and (5) the purpose. That is, whether participants are taking on full responsibility, or they are displacing responsibility to society or "people," or perhaps to technology, or they are giving purely goal-driven (purpose) explanations. The key question that governs the motive analysis is "How do participants ascribe and allocate motives for their actions among the elements of a nexus analysis?" (Scollon and Scollon 2004: 176).

Our motive analysis focused on how respondents explained their decision to participate in the U.S. census or not. For example, when asked why they did not fill out the census form, some respondents claimed that the census form was lost by someone in their household. This explanation is from the point of view of the scene: other people, and itself is thus a discursive strategy to shift responsibility onto others. Others stated that they did not read English and therefore, they could not fill out the form. This explanation ascribed to the motive of the mediational means (lack of language proficiency).

Conducting motive analyses of the social action gives us a better understanding of how speakers of non-English languages perceived and accounted for their involvement in the social action of participating in the census.

Changing the nexus of practice

The third task of changing the nexus of practice is the activist position for Nexus Analysis, which means a nexus analysis is conducted not for the sole purpose of doing an analysis, but rather for the purpose of changing a nexus of practice. This position answers the question of "what is the point in doing all of it?"

Changing the nexus of practice began when our study was conceived: this was the first study in the history of the U.S. census to observe live census interviews conducted with non-English-speaking immigrants. Upon completion of the fieldwork and analysis, the seven language teams made extensive recommendations on how to improve this process. Recommended changes include strategies to reach out to this segment of the U.S. population, methods to translate the census questions, and design of language and culture training for census takers. Not all recommended changes would take place given institutional constraints, but this nexus analysis made a new start in the nexus of practice for the census enumeration process. Through the research teams' presentations and reporting of findings, issues with enumerating non-English-speaking immigrants were made known and discussed at various levels of the census operation.

Conclusion

Through this case study, it is clear that Nexus Analysis brings together multiple perspectives and methods in analyzing the social action. Its strength lies in the analytical framework of connecting the micro-level of discourse analysis (e.g., conversation analysis and interactional sociolinguistics) with the macro-level of discourse analysis (e.g., critical discourse analysis and linguistic anthropology). More importantly, focusing on the social action, a nexus analysis can bring about meaningful changes to resolve issues in the real world.

Further readings

Scollon, Ron. 2001. *Mediated Discourse: The Nexus of Practice*. London/New York: Routledge.
Scollon, Ron and Suzie Wong Scollon. 2004. *Nexus Analysis: Discourses and the Emergent Internet*. London/New York: Routledge.

Project idea

With the rapid growth of technology, our ways to stay in contact with friends and families are expanding beyond imagination. Some new communication modes or devices sprung into existence and gained popularity almost instantaneously (e.g., iPhone, Facebook). Pick a social action that is mediated by one of the new communication modes and conduct a Nexus Analysis following the steps outlined in this chapter.

References

Burke, Kenneth. [1935] 1965. *A grammar of motives*. Englewood Cliff, NJ: Prentice-Hall.
Pan, Yuling and Stephen Lubkemann. 2013. *Observing Census Enumeration of Non-English Speaking Households in the 2010 Census. Research and Methodology Directorate, Center for Survey Measurement Study Series (Survey Methodology 2013-02)*. U.S. Census Bureau, Available online at <http://www.census.gov/srcl/papers/pdf/ssm2013-02.pdf>.
Scollon, Ron. 2001. *Mediated Discourse: The Nexus of Practice*. London/New York: Routledge.
Scollon, Ron and Suzie Wong Scollon. 2004. *Nexus Analysis: Discourses and the Emergent Internet*. London/New York: Routledge.

Najma Al Zidjaly
8 Geosemiotics: Discourses in place

Introduction[1]

Geosemiotics is an analytical framework created by Scollon and Scollon (2003) to examine public discourse, such as signs, as situated in the material world and shaped by social and cultural use; hence, geosemiotics refers to *discourses in place*. The essence of geosemiotics is that the meaning of public texts like road signs, notices, and brand logos can only be achieved through physical and social contextualization. Only by elucidating the connections among these three elements (i.e., public discourse, situated use, and physical world) can researchers truly understand public discourse and bring about needed social change. This innovative ethnographic method to researching discourse in the material world links sociocultural theory, semiotic theory, and anthropology to examine 1) how meanings of signs are culturally sensitive, and 2) how power is structured in the social world through the public discourses it inhabits.

Geosemiotics complements and extends Kress and van Leeuwen's (1996) visual semiotics, which analyzes the internal grammar of multimodal texts – regardless of their situated use. It does so by enabling researchers to fully analyze public discourse not only in terms of linguistic content but also ethnographically in their physical, social, and cultural contexts. It has indeed led to a recent burst of dynamic multimodal research (e.g., Jones 2005; Norris 2008; Al Zidjaly 2011) that is described by Norris (2011) as the multimodal mediated approach to visual texts. Additionally, geosemiotics contributed to the development of Nexus Analysis (Scollon and Scollon, 2004), the methodological arm of mediated discourse theory (Scollon 2002), which enables researching social action (chapter three of this volume). Most importantly, it has important implications for intercultural communication.

Key terms: Discourse, Geosemiotics, Indexicality, Interaction Order, Place Semiotics, Social Actor, Visual Semiotics.

---

[1] Research for this chapter was made possible by Internal Grants at Sultan Qaboos University, Oman (IG/ART/ENGL/12/01). The funded project is titled, "New Media Technology and Omani (Arabic) Cultural Identity."

Geosemiotics and indexicality

The main focus of geosemiotics is indexicality, "the property of the context-dependency of signs, especially language" (Scollon and Scollon 2003: 3). This is so because signs and communication in general cannot be comprehended nor studied without situated placement and use. This is true whether of a spoken word, a protest flyer, or a stop sign. As the Scollons (p. ix) elucidate, "Language indexes the world. We speak and listen, write and read not only about the world but in the world, and much of what we understand depends on exactly where we and the language are located in the world." Language, additionally, "indexes who and what we are in the world as we use it." I am writing this chapter in English and you as a reader are thus reading it in English. This indexes us as members of a particular social group with access to academic discourse.

As per signs, as social actors (tourists, passers-by, or researchers), we require certain information to decode the public discourses surrounding us: We need to know who created, for instance, the Arabic sign in Figure 1 (Please Wear Proper Clothes), the sign's intended viewer, its exact placement in the physical world (including the culture or society in which it exists), and the significance of the language chosen. Otherwise, the meaning of the sign is not only lost on us, it can have serious ramifications for intercultural miscommunication. That is why geosemiotics as an approach to public discourse analyzes signs not only as they exist in physical and social contexts but also as how people use them in taking actions or orient themselves towards them in everyday actions. Hence, there is an action element to this dynamic framework.

The sign consists of one language: Arabic. On the top right, it requests "Please Wear [female inflection] Proper Attire." In the lower middle, it politely states "Thank you for your Cooperation." In the bottom right, the logo of Muscat City Center is featured, indexing source and authority: Muscat City Center Management. Muscat is the capital city of Oman. The linguistic part of the sign is complemented with an iconic part to the left boxed in a red circle akin to a no smoking sign, but offering two attire options: A long black dress or a T-shirt and long pants. Looking at just the internal grammar of the sign, with limited access to its location, is insufficient to decode, comprehend, and respond to its meaning. Thus, to be able to read the sign in Figure 1 – and, most importantly, to understand it and avoid cultural offence, it must be contextualized by examining the physical and cultural details surrounding it.

The sign's power to address clothing behavior stems only from its location on the entrance doors of Muscat City Center, the major shopping mall in Oman,

Figure 1: Please Wear Proper Clothes

an Islamic Arabian country located in the Arabian Gulf. Muslim Omanis discourage immodest behavior and improper clothing; this has led the management of Muscat City Center to receive numerous complaints about the inappropriate attire some non-Muslim female foreigners have worn in the mall. In 2011, the management decided to put up a sign on all its major entrance doors requesting foreign females to wear proper garments when entering the mall. It is implicit that the intended viewers are foreign women because all female Omanis wear proper apparel when outside. The choice to use Arabic only – though most signs in Oman are written in both Arabic and English, and especially given the addressee, indexes larger sets of discourses that must be considered to accurately decode the sign: the discourses of Arabic Islamic culture and all the modesty it entails. It is thus a reminder to foreigners that this is an Arabic Islamic culture. However, knowing that most foreigners do not speak Arabic, the management complemented the linguistic part of the sign with an iconic part that provides two options: Either adapting to the local culture by donning a long black dress similar to Omani female attire (indexing Islamic local culture), or sticking to Western attire by wearing T-shirts but with long pants only (indexing [and acknowledging] foreign culture).

There is also indexicality of the social actors involved: The foreign females to whom the sign is indirectly addressed, for instance, are positioned in time and space; an "us" (Omani females and those who don't wear proper attire) and "them" (foreign females and those who wear improper attire) dynamic is created. In addition, by the time the intended viewer (foreign female shoppers) see the sign, it is usually too late (for they have arrived at the mall already). As a result, a quick decision is in order: whether to go back home and change, or to enter the mall and disregard the sign. This restricts and limits the reactions of the viewers, which may lead to hasty reactions that have personal and cultural consequences: By going back, one is changing their individual plans, and by stepping in, one is defying not just the sign but the culture it indexes. This indicates that interpreters of signs and watchers too are social actors in real life taking real actions with consequences, and that signs shape those who interact with them.

The example in Figure 1 demonstrates the three main principles of geosemiotics: indexicality, that the meanings of signs are a consequence of their physical and social placement; dialogicality, that signs and public discourses function in accordance with other signs and cultural discourses (the discourses of Western and Arabic attire and behavior as well as other available discourses on site [Muscat City Center is filled with many other types of signs]); and selection, that choice plays a major role in designing and reading signs (e.g., it was a matter of choice by the mall's management to use Arabic only, and the sign can be attended to or ignored). In the case of this sign, the meaning of the sign was actually lost on the foreigners who did not know Arabic. However, the materiality also needs to be considered: The sign was printed on paper, lacking permanency, which may also have contributed to it not being taken seriously. In fact, the sign was removed by the management in just two weeks.

The main tenets of a geosemiotic analysis

The example above illustrates that a geosemiotic analysis consists of analyzing simultaneously three semiotic systems: The interaction order (Goffman 1959) or social arrangement among the participants engaged in the given social action with a particular sign; the visual semiotics of the sign (Kress and van Leeuwen 1996); and the place semiotics of the sign (its inscription, emplacement, code preference, and discourses in time and space). A geosemiotic analysis consists of analyzing these three systems in conjunction with each other, taking into account that they are all based on indexicality, and that the three elements come together in every social action. Hence, a geosemiotic analysis examines not just the visual semiotics of a sign and its physical placement, but also must consider how social actors orient themselves to signs or use them in real time action.

In what follows I explain these elements – the primary semiotic systems of geosemiotics – using a second example (Figure 2) also from Oman.

The example used to illustrate 'how to do a geosemiotic analysis of a public sign' is taken from a larger project I conducted on Social Media and Arab (Omani) Identity (funded by a grant from Sultan Qaboos University, Oman). The years 2010–2011 witnessed a wave of political protests by the youth across the Middle East, including Oman. This came to be known as the Arab Spring. In Oman, unlike other Arab countries, the protests were mainly peaceful, with protesters declaring their love for their leader, and requesting mainly modest financial reforms. While Oman is located in the Arabian Gulf, a region known for its oil, living standards for most Omanis have been low for years, prompting Omanis to demand their government to increase monthly salaries, which did not rise for over 40 years, despite high inflation. A major protest site was Al Khuwair, the chief ministerial city of Oman. The image of the social scene in Figure 2 was taken at this protest site.

Figure 2: Protest Sign in Oman

All human action takes place at the intersection of three semiotic systems – interaction order, visual semiotics, and place semiotics, and all semiotic systems are systems of social positioning. Geosemiotics takes an action perspective on how meaning is made. The social scene in Figure 2 illustrates these points. It entails the interaction order among the social actors standing in the vicinity of the sign – an encounter between a protestor (the man whose back faces the camera) and visitors to the site (the other three men). The visual semiotics of the sign – the design of signs including the language(s) used (e.g., Classical Arabic in this case) – are important as well. Place semiotics, or the built and natural environment in which the sign is situated (Ministerial City) also play a fundamental role in understanding the sign and the social action. These semiotic systems can be sketched as following (adapted from Scollon and Scollon 2003).

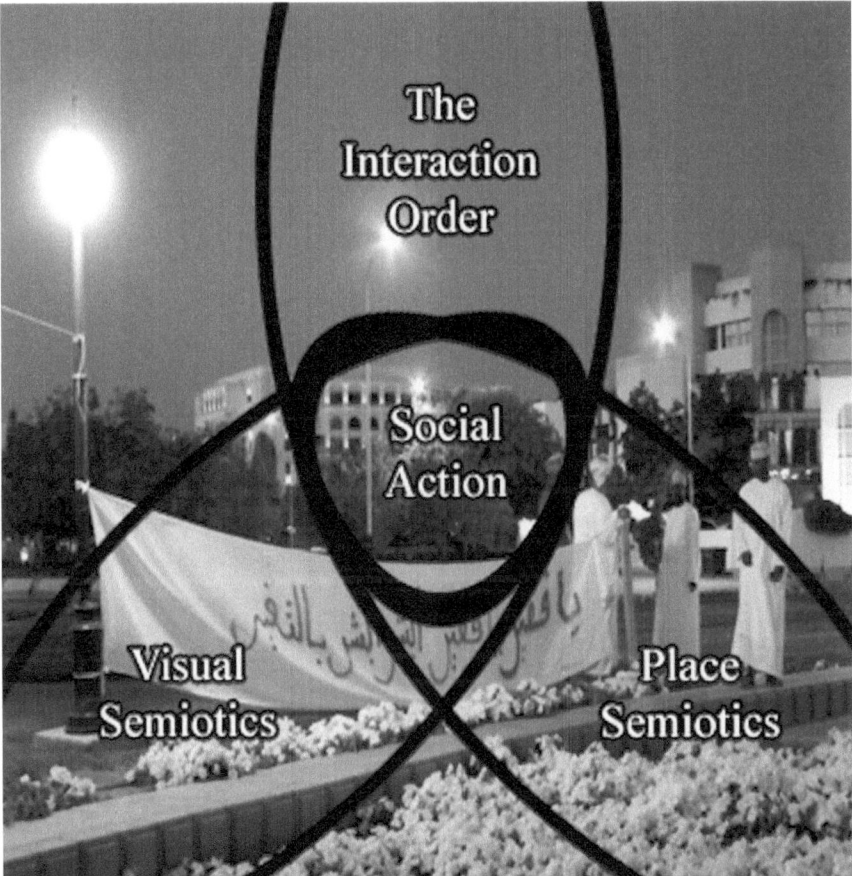

Figure 3: Geosemiotic Systems in Protest Sign in Oman

Place semiotics

Signs, on the surface, can be of three types: Icons (where a sign might resemble an object, such as a smiley icon), symbols (arbitrary representation of an object, such as a green traffic light meaning to continue driving), or an index (a sign meaning something because of where and when it is placed, such as the "Please Wear Proper Clothes" sign. In reality, however, there are two types of signs: icons and symbols because all signs receive their meaning through indexicality. However, rather than focusing on indexicality in language, which has been extensively covered in linguistics, geosemiotics focuses on "the ways in which the sign system of language indexes the other semiotic systems in the world around language;" it is interested in "the *indexical world* than in the systems of Indexicality in language" (Scollon and Scollon 2003: 5).[2] To arrive at the indexical world, a geosemiotic analysis examines four resources: emplacement, code preference, inscription, and discourses in time and space.

Emplacement

This refers to the physical emplacement of a sign in the real world and the affordances and limitations it offers. The ministry park in the city of Al Khuwair was chosen as one of the main camping sites by Omani protesters for two reasons: Al Khuwair is where most Omani government ministries are located (the buildings in the picture's background are official government buildings). So the sign and the camping site in the park in front of the government buildings could not be ignored by the government in Oman. Al Khuwair was chosen also for a second reason: The ministerial park is located right on one of the main highways of Muscat, the capital city of Oman. Thus, the protest sign is placed facing the highway so that drivers can read it. However, to take a good look at the sign, and to show real support to campers, one must park their car on the street from the other side of the park, and come on foot to examine it, and other signs, in depth. In short, this particular choice of emplacement enables the message – the demand of protesters – to reach two targets: the government of Oman and the public.

Code preference

Code refers to the language selected in a particular sign. The preferred code of the sign is Arabic. The sign, which played a major role in hastening the Omani government's response to the request for financial reform, is translated as: *Hear ye, hear ye, o ye poor, tidings of change are at the door.*[3] To the thousands of Omanis who were living below acceptable standards, this is a reassuring, symbolic sign that suggests hope and change (specifically since financial benefit increases were finally on the way, judging by the government's initial response to the protests). Further, other protest signs indicated that the protesters were

---

2 The main indexicals that have been linguistically studied are demonstratives (this, that, these, those), deictic adverbials (here and there), tense and time adverbials (Now and then), and personal pronouns (he, she, they).
3 I am grateful to David Wilmsen for the beautiful translation of the protest sign.

not going to give up until living standards were raised. Choosing only the Arabic code, despite English being the second official language of the country, sends a clear message to the international community that this is an internal matter. Also, while the focus of geosemiotics is not on linguistic indexicality, it still merits examination. In this particular example, there are three kinds of indexicality: indexicality in space (the promised action is taking place in Oman), indexicality of social relationships (the phrase "o ye poor" indexes a social class to which the majority of Omanis belong), and indexicality in time (change is imminent).

Inscription

This semiotic system includes various aspects of the presentation of banners or signs, ranging from font type, size, and color; to material used; to layering (adding comments or other signs on a sign) and changes of state (such as not lighting the protest sign properly resulting in it not being properly visible at night). Any choice within these four elements or resources indexes different meanings. For instance, choosing calligraphy versus handwriting or typing evokes different connotations. The particular protest sign in Figures 2, as most protest signs, is handwritten (though calligraphy is a celebrated art in the Arabic culture). It is simple, yet using the color red indexes urgency, seriousness, and, most possibly, danger if demands are not met. Lack of permanency is indexed by the use of fabric as the sign material and its placement on wooden posts temporarily dug in the park ground. This was necessitated by two facts: Most protest signs are temporary signs, and by law citizens are not allowed to place permanent signs in the government park (only municipal, commercial, or traffic discourses or signs are permitted in the park).

Discourses in time and space

Discourses in time and space refer to "the intersections of multiple discourses and the interaction order in particular places" which form what Scollon and Scollon (2003: 167) call "semiotic aggregates." The main idea is that discourses do not exist in a vacuum but rather interact and integrate with other discourses in and across time and space. Geosemiotics distinguishes between the centrifugal distribution of discourses across time and space, and the centripetal distribution of discourse in time and space. For example, as aforementioned, the protest site hosts an aggregate of various public discourses – including municipal regulatory discourse, commercial discourse, traffic organizing discourse, as well as discourses provided by drivers and passers-by, which protest discourse has to interact with to create meaning. This is an example of interdiscursive dialogicality that features prominently in geosemiotics. According to geosemiotics, the semiotic aggregate in this example is the result of the centripetal forces of aggregation. An example of the centrifugal forces of aggregation in this case is that the protest sign in Al Khuwair can be tracked to other protest signs in other camps in Oman. We can also track the protest sign to the office of protesters where the sign was made. Additionally, this same sign or discourse was debated and quoted in newspapers and was discussed in government reform meetings. It, moreover, ended up being used in Omani law enforcement system. All these connections need to be taken into account to fully understand how signs shape our social world, and how they are shaped by our actions as social actors.

Interaction order

Interaction order is defined by Goffman (1959) as the way social arrangements within societies are produced. It thus "consists of the current ongoing ratified but also contested and denied set of social relationships we take up and try to maintain with the other people who are in our presence" (Scollon and Scollon 2003: 16). A geosemiotic analysis is interested in how the various social structures of social encounters in various cultures are used by people to produce discourses in place. This is so because all semiotic systems (including interaction orders) are "part of the sign equipment we can and do use to produce our actions in the world" (Scollon and Scollon 2003: 17). For instance, where do Omanis feel comfortable chatting and with whom? Do they feel comfortable talking with protesters or not? Do they avoid protesters they see on the streets? Goffman identified 11 types of interaction orders that range from a single person alone in social space, to "withs" (two or more people perceived to be together), to platform events such as academic conferences. These various ways of coming together are socially agreed upon in in-groups and thus vary culturally. This fact is important in a geosemiotic analysis, since, as previously indicated, geosemiotics is interested in how social actors orient to signs or use them in accomplishing social action.

Resources of interaction order

According to Edward T. Hall (1959), interaction orders have four elements: the sense of time, perceptual spaces, interpersonal distances, and personal fronts.

These too are negotiated differently in different cultures because any social action is positioned within the interaction orders appropriate for the particular society. A geosemiotic analysis of discourse in place asks, how do people orient to each other and other people in the social world in which they inhabit in relation to time, space, distance, and personal fronts? How do they index them verbally and non-verbally? For instance, in Arabic cultures, including Oman, time is not of the essence; people have a slow sense of time that is indexed in both their body (how they move) and (inter)actions with insiders and outsiders (they usually take a long time to get things done). As for perceptual space and interpersonal distance, these are minimized, for Arabic cultures are "high involvement" cultures (Tannen 2005). This too is indexed in both body and action (Omanis do not realize the sense of personal and group space, so they tend to stand close and ask very private questions). All these may lead to intercultural miscommunication if not interpreted through the right cultural lens.

Personal fronts

Our discourses in place are not only tied to the material world they inhabit but also are positioned in relationship to others with whom we interact. Hence, the Goffmanian (1959) distinction between frontstage and backstage, meaning that people have different demeanors in public and in private. Distinguishing the line between these two (i.e., public and private) is important because a major concept in how individuals come together in social spaces is personal front. Personal fronts refer to how people present themselves consciously and unconsciously to the world, including what they wear, how they move, what they carry, and so on. Because some aspects of personal fronts are controlled (such as wearing perfume) while others are not (blushing or sweating), Goffman distinguishes further between the expressions a person *gives* and the expressions a person *gives off*. That is, people usually, through their personal fronts, communicate much more than they intend to. This is so because most of our actions are habitual and unconscious; social actors in the framework of geosemiotics are thus "bundles of histories of language, of discourses, and experiences, of social and political performances, as juggling multiple social roles and performance, largely unconsciously" (Scollon and Scollon 2003: 15).

In the protest scene (Figure 2), there are four main social actors: A protester staged next to the protest sign to engage visitors of the camp site (he is wearing a yellow head cover with his hand resting on one of the sign posts), and three protest site visitors. Two are clearly engaged in a conversational encounter with the protestor, though one is keeping unusual distance (uncharacteristic of Omanis engaged in a *with*) while involved in the discussion. The man on the far left is trying to overhear part of the discussion without fully engaging in the encounter; his physical body is clearly indexing he is not a *with* with the other three men (he is there not to discuss but only to check the sign for himself). These various social engagements or interaction orders index that while much action is unconscious, in this social action, both groups (the protester and the three visitors) are acting by choice. The protester by active and conscious choice is engaged in an action that goes against the government, and the visitors by choice have decided to acknowledge (albeit to a different degree) the protests. The way the third visitor's body is positioned gives off that he is not there to actively engage in a political debate. Overall, however, simply in being present in the scene and learning more, all three visitors are distancing themselves from the government and creating public closeness with the protesters.

Visual semiotics

Because the visual semiotics of a sign is an inherent/integral part of its meaning, geosemiotics draws on Kress and van Leeuwen's (1996) social semiotic approach to the internal grammar of multimodal texts, extending this framework to decode the contents of public discourse. The main focus of geosemiotics, unlike Kress and van Leeuwen's approach, is not on the internal grammar of signs per se, but rather on how the interaction order/the real social world/and actions are represented and indexed visually. How, for instance, the sense of time, perceptual space, interpersonal distance, and personal fronts are represented visually to communicate or index certain social and cultural meanings. Thus, a geosemiotic analysis is interested "in how images represent the real social world, in how images mean what they mean because of where we see them, and in how we use images to do other things in the world" (Scollon and Scollon 2003: 84). The purpose thus is on the depiction of action and the invitation of action found in signs such as the invitation for reform found in the protest sign in Figure 2.

To arrive at these outcomes, geosemiotics draws on four elements from Kress and van Leeuwen's (1996) framework that represent how the interaction order can be visually indexed or constructed.

Four visual semiotic elements

The first element in Kress and van Leeuwen's semiotic framework is *represented participants*, which can be indexed conceptually or abstractly as an image (such as the clothing icon in Figure 1 used to represent females and their attire), or narratively (as an unfolding action or a process of change). The second is *modality*, the truth value of a representation, or how well a represented image is similar to the real thing or action. For instance, the iconic image of clothing used in Figure 1 is low modality because high modality or credibility of a representation, while culturally variable, must be a true reflection of an action or image. Third, *composition* has to do with the representation of information on a sign (centralized or polarized layout, each indexing different meanings). For example, in Figure 1, the symbol representing the shopping mall management appears at the bottom of the sign, as if signing off on it. Finally, *interactive participants* refers to the representation of the relationship between the producer of an image and the people/action represented, the relationship among the participants who are represented, and between the participants and the viewer (are the depicted participants looking directly or indirectly at the viewer and what does that entail).

To arrive at how public discourse is used to create actions in real life, geosemiotics complements this visual semiotic analysis with a second framework, nexus analysis (Scollon and Scollon 2004), which is introduced in chapter three of this volume. Nexus analysis allows researchers to examine how images can be used to create social action.

Conclusions

Social change cannot be achieved without systematically examining the inherent linkages between semiotics and the "context" in which they are situated. Only then, as argued in Al Zidjaly (2011), can we begin to realize the full potential of images and how visual materials can perform actions that either create, contest, negotiate, or affirm identities, whether personal or national.

Further readings

Norris, Sigrid. 2011. *Multimodality in Practice: Investigating Theory-in-Practice-through-Methodology*. (Routledge Studies in Multimodality). London: Routledge.

Scollon, Ron. 2009. *Analyzing Public Discourse: Discourse Analysis in the Making of Public Policy*. London: Rutledge.

Project idea

Choose a social issue you feel passionate about and that you would like to investigate; it is highly recommended that you invest in a social cause that would contribute to the general society. Examples of social causes could be disability, anti-government protests, immigration, minority identity and so on.

Once you have selected a social concern you would like to be socially active about, you can do one of two things: i) collect images about the issue, and/or ii) photograph images of the problem under scrutiny. For example, you can collect disability or protest images or take up your camera and visit sites of protests or disability conventions. Once you have a good number of photographs or images, select a few key ones, and apply the analysis provided in this chapter to them.

Keep in mind that a geosemiotic analysis consists of analyzing simultaneously three semiotic systems: interaction order, visual semiotics, and place semiotics of the selected signs. Geosemiotics is an approach to public discourse that analyzes signs not only as they exist in physical and social contexts but also as how people use them in taking actions or orient themselves towards them in everyday actions. So always keep a field notebook with you when doing a geosemiotic analysis.

References

Al Zidjaly, Najma. 2011. Multimodal texts as mediated actions: Voice, synchronization and layered simultaneity in images of disability. In Sigrid Norris (ed.), *Multimodality in Practice: Investigating Theory-in-Practice-through-Methodology*, 190–205. London: Routledge.
Goffman, Erving. 1959. *The Presentation of Self in Everyday Life*. New York: Doubleday.
Hall, T. Edward. 1959. *The Silent Language*. Garden City, New York: Doubleday.
Jones, Rodney. 2005. 'You show me yours, I'll show me mine': Negotiation of shifts from textual to visual modes in computer-mediated interactions among gay men. *Visual Communication* 1 (41): 69–92.
Kress, Gunther and Theo van Leeuwen. 1996. *Reading Images: The Grammar of Visual Design*. London: Routledge.
Norris, Sigrid. 2011. *Multimodality in Practice: Investigating Theory-in-Practice-through-Methodology* (Routledge Studies in Multimodality). London: Routledge.
Norris, Sigrid. 2008. Personal identity construction: A multimodal perspective. In Vijay Bhatia, John Flowerdew and Rodney H. Jones (eds.), *New Directions in Discourse*, 132–149. London: Routledge.
Scollon, Ron and Suzie Scollon. 2004. *Nexus Analysis: Discourse and the Emerging Internet*. London: Routledge.
Scollon, Ron and Suzie Scollon. 2003. *Discourses in Place: Language in the Material World*. London: Rutledge.
Scollon, Ron. 2002. *Mediated Discourse Analysis: Nexus of Practice*. London: Routledge.
Tannen, Deborah. 2005. *Conversational Style: Analyzing Talk among Friends*. Oxford: Oxford University Press.

Jesse Pirini
9 Introduction to multimodal (inter)action analysis

Introduction

This chapter introduces the primary notions of multimodal (inter)action analysis and demonstrates the approach with an example. Multimodal (inter)action analysis was developed by Norris (Norris 2004, 2011) as a way to help her understand identity production during research with participants in Germany. Since then, multimodal (inter)action analysis has been useful in studies that involve social action ranging from marketing, to kite surfing, to vegetarianism. Researchers continually develop the methodology through use, and it has proven especially practical for studies seeking to describe human action that go beyond the mode of spoken language to include all the modes involved in social action.

Multimodal (inter)action analysis draws upon the theoretical notions explicated by Scollon in mediated discourse analysis (Scollon 1998, 2001). As with mediated discourse analysis, the notion of mediated action forms the central unit of analysis, and multimodal (inter)action analysis adds further methodological tools to apply the theoretical principles of mediated discourse analysis to the analysis of social action. These developments include delineating social action into higher and lower levels, and introducing the concept of the frozen action. Norris (2004) also developed the concept of modal density to describe more clearly where higher-level actions are positioned on a foreground-background continuum of attention. These methodological tools are introduced below using an example from research into business coaching.

Key terms: Foreground-background continuum, frozen action, higher-level action, horizontal identity production, lower-level action, mode, modal complexity, modal density, modal intensity, semantic/pragmatic means, vertical identity production.

Units of analysis

A central principle of multimodal (inter)action analysis is that of *mediated action*, which refers to the mediated nature of social action. All actions are mediated by psychological tools and material objects (Scollon 1998, 2001; Wertsch 1998). Multimodal (inter)action analysis delineates actions into higher-level actions, formed by chains of lower-level actions. Also, frozen actions refer to lower- and higher-level actions entailed in objects in the world (Norris 2004). Each of these delineations is described below, with an example.

Mediated action

During an analysis we can delineate actions into higher and lower levels (Norris 2004; Norris and Jones 2005).

Lower-level action

A lower-level action is the smallest unit of an action, with a beginning and an end. In talk, an utterance is a lower-level action. In gesture, a complete gesture from beginning to end is a lower-level action. Lower-level actions can be analyzed from video data, which begins with selecting portions of the data that are of interest. Selection may be influenced by the researcher's experience during data collection, field notes, and repeated watching of video data.

Having selected some data of interest, lower-level actions are carefully transcribed for each relevant mode. For example, the researcher might transcribe the mode of gesture, the mode of head movement, the mode of spoken language and the mode of posture. A separate transcript can be made for each mode. These are then combined to form a final transcript that incorporates all the modes and lower-level actions in a useful way.

By separately transcribing the lower-level actions of each relevant mode the researcher can begin to describe how social actors construct higher-level actions from chains of lower-level actions. This approach does not give one mode primacy over others, providing an equalizing influence and opening the researcher up to detect the importance of all aspects of an interaction.

Figure 1 presents five seconds of data from a business coaching session. The coach's lower-level actions in the mode of gesture have been transcribed. The movements made by the coach have been carefully captured to show each gesture. Beginning and ending points are shown, as well as the peak of the movement.

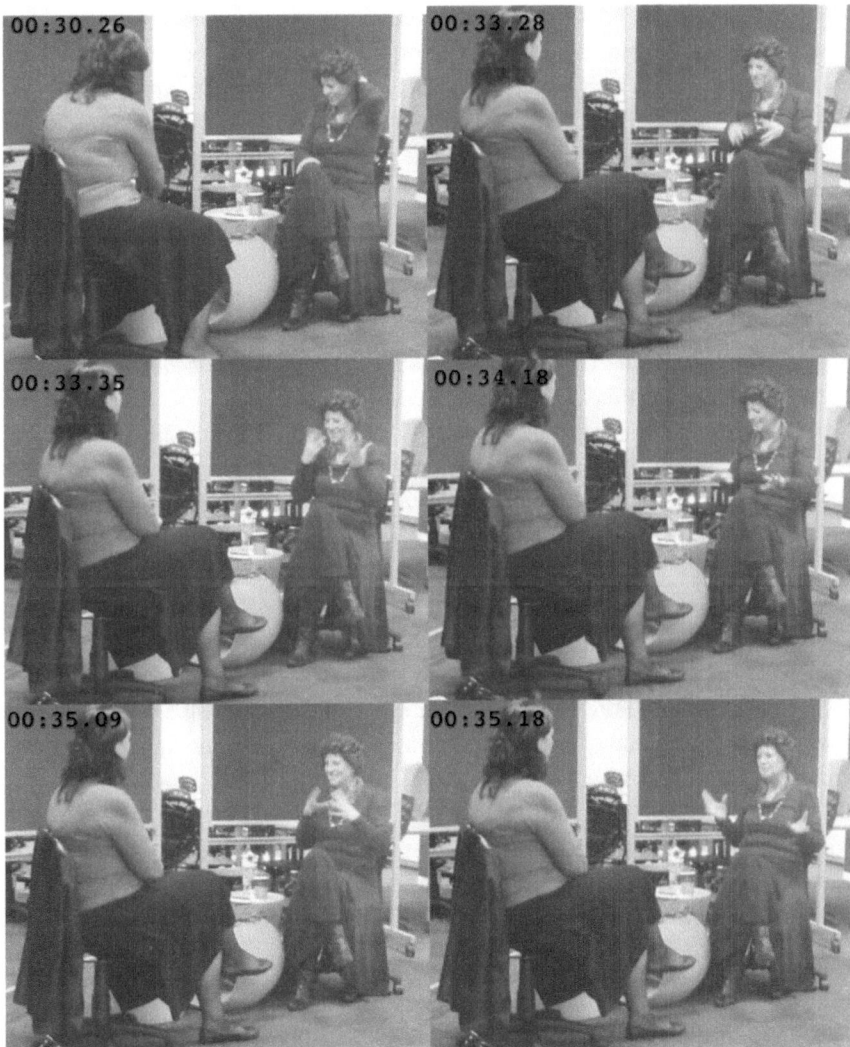

Figure 1: A transcription of the mode of gesture from video data

Higher-level action

A collection of chains of lower-level actions constitutes a higher-level action (Norris 2004), and several higher-level actions can be nested within one another. In the example of a business coaching session, the coaching conversation is a higher-level action, within which are nested several other higher-level actions, all made up of chains of lower-level actions. Note however that lower-level actions are not considered logically prior to the higher-level action, but both constitute each other in interaction. However, when analysing, our focus in transcribing are the chains of lower-level actions.

In the transcript below (figure 2), the coach Linley makes the higher-level action of a request to take a few notes as the session progresses. The action starts with the raising of the coach's finger, after which she states 'So I'm just gonna scope out'. She does not complete this utterance, but reaches for a pad and pen to her right, which she places on her lap. She then says 'Can I- I might just take a few notes' (row 1, 05:11.12). Notably she rephrases her utterance from a direct question to a conditional suggestion with the use of might. The client Carolyn agrees that this is fine. Linley repeats herself adding more information 'I might write the odd word but I'm not intending to write anything really big'. During this utterance Carolyn overlaps with 'yeah'. The coach then goes on to present the issues that the client had previously brought up for discussion.

The transcript shows some of the multiple lower-level actions that were involved in the higher-level action the coach constructed as she began to take a few notes. Through the process of breaking this higher-level action down into lower level actions the researcher was able to show that the coach reaches for the pad and paper prior to verbally requesting that she can take notes. Using the mode of spoken language, the coach starts off formulating a statement that she is 'gonna scope out', and then reformulates it into a direct question 'can I', and then a conditional suggestion 'I might just'.

This section of data formed part of a larger set that examined how a business coaching conversation is constructed. Multimodal (inter)action analysis has been used to show how grasping the notepad and the utterances are coordinated to achieve the goals of a coaching conversation. The coach checks that taking notes is ok with the client, while already reaching for the notepad. The notepad then forms a useful tool for the coach to help the client structure their thoughts, and generate their own solutions. It also gives the coach authority over the structure of the coaching session (Wertsch and Rupert 1993).

The approach taken here shows the higher-level action as a chain of lower-level actions, and illustrates that focusing multimodally provides a detailed analysis of the construction of a coaching conversation.

Frozen action

Frozen actions refer to the chains of lower-level actions that are entailed in material objects within the site of engagement (Norris 2004). In the coaching

Introduction to multimodal (inter)action analysis — 81

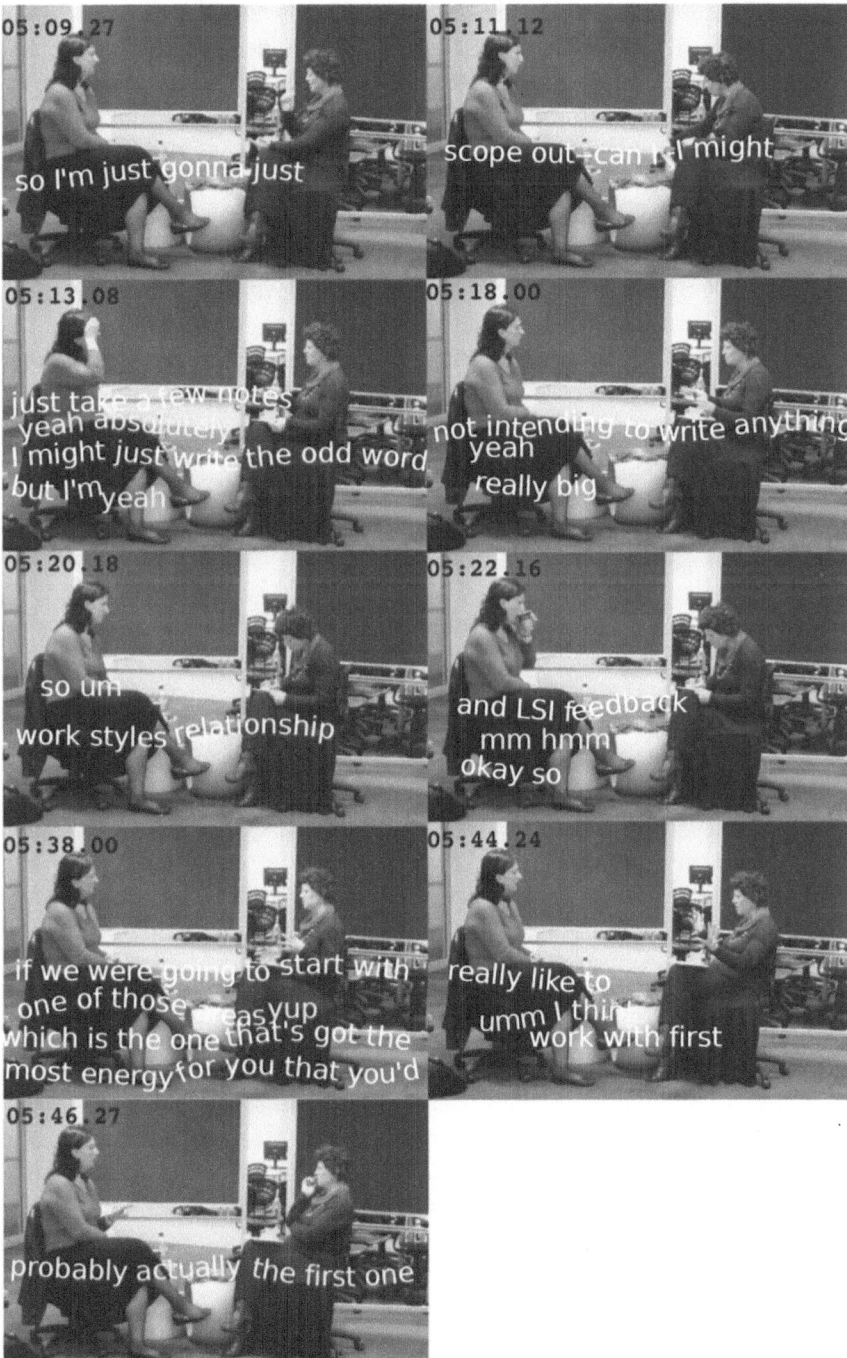

Figure 2: Example of final multimodal transcription of a higher-level action

session the cups of water sitting on the tables between the participants are frozen actions. The researcher carried out a chain of lower-level actions in preparing the space, including placing the cups on the table. When considering the presence of the cups, these actions, and many others, are observable. Material objects in the interaction of interest can be analyzed for the frozen actions they entail, and usually it is the most recent actions that are most relevant to social actors (Norris 2004).

In the coaching interaction the researcher had prepared the space, and placed mobile privacy screens in the arrangement shown below (Note the coach leaning forward to peer between the privacy screens in figure 3 below). The coaching client had requested that if the researcher was to be present, they remain out of sight. It is clear to the participants that the researcher placed the screens, or put another way, the higher-level action of placing the screens is visible to the participants. Frozen actions provide a useful methodological tool for the analysis of material objects by re-making relevant the social actions that led to their presence in an interaction. This reflects also the centrality of social action in multimodal (inter)action analysis.

Multimodal transcription

As noted, the central principle of multimodal (inter)action analysis is the mediated action, and transcripts represent relevant higher-level actions, made up of chains of lower-level actions. Consequently the images that are captured in the transcription are selected based on when actions are carried out, rather than sampling based on a standard of time (e.g. every 0.5s). The transcript therefore expresses the researcher's analysis of mediated actions, and transcribing is part of the analytic process. In the top right corner of each frame is a time stamp that shows the time between frames, which ranges from 1 second to over 13 seconds.

I use transcription conventions that present the data through image and text (Norris 2002, 2004, 2011). Including images in transcriptions allows the reader to gain a rich sense of the actions mediated by social actors. Figure 2 is a final transcription and the images come from single mode transcriptions, which were selected to best demonstrate my analytic points, and provide a clear representation of the actions in play. Sometimes actions such as gaze shifts and gestures will coincide, and other times they will not. Coordination of modes can be analytically useful, and recognizing how actions interrelate arises from careful transcribing of individual modes.

The participants' use of the mode of spoken language is layered over the relevant images, and it is structured to indicate the prosody of the talk it represents. While every gesture, or gaze shift is not present in the final transcription, generally the entirety of the mode of spoken language is. It is important to keep single mode transcriptions, and to note down any insights that arise throughout the transcription process. Through the process of transcription, researchers begin to investigate their data, and can then use the transcripts to present their findings to others.

Modal density

Modes have been defined as semiotic systems with rules and regularities attached to them (Kress and Van Leeuwen 2001) as they are being used (Norris 2009). Norris's addition to this definition emphasises that modes exist as people use them, rather than as resources that exist externally and are drawn upon by social actors.

There are always multiple modes in use during interaction, and these interrelate in complex ways. Modal density is a useful methodological tool to analyze the importance of particular modes to an interaction, and how they interrelate. Modal density is made up of both modal intensity, and modal complexity. Both are used with reference to an action. For example an action can be said to have high or low modal complexity or intensity.

Modal complexity refers to the interrelationship of modes in a particular action. Some actions have a higher modal complexity than others. A face-to-face conversation may have a high modal complexity, as the interlocutors utilize the mode of spoken language, the mode of gesture, the mode of posture and the mode of gaze. A conversation on the telephone may have low modal complexity, because the interlocutors are directly reacting to spoken discourse and other modes have less impact (see Norris 2004: 84 for a discussion regarding the indirect impact of other modes on telephone discourse).

Researchers can also refer to how strongly one particular mode is engaged in during an interaction, or its relative intensity. In the phone conversation for example the mode of spoken language takes on high intensity. When watching a movie the mode of gaze is likely to take on high intensity, and dimming the cinema lights facilitates this. Note that the mode of sound also plays a large part in the movie experience, as does the mode of posture. This illustrates the multimodal nature of actions, and it is important to consider the range of modes present in an action, when considering the intensity of modes.

In the higher-level action of the coaching conversation the various modes utilized support a highly focused one-to-one interaction. The mode of layout contributes to this by positioning the coach and client, and separating them from the researcher with privacy screens. The modes of gaze, posture, gesture, proxemics and spoken language are made highly relevant in the interaction. This is facilitated by the mode of layout providing clear lines of sight and sound, and flexibility regarding proxemics. As the interaction progresses we can use the methodological tool of modal complexity to examine the relative density and intensity of modes as they are in use. This becomes especially relevant when we consider the notion of attention, and the foreground-background continuum.

Foreground-background continuum

Social actors are able to, and usually do, engage in multiple higher-level actions at any one time. Since some of these higher-level actions receive more focus than others, they can be represented at different levels of attention/awareness. An attention/awareness continuum helps the analyst to direct their analytical focus, and present their findings to others (Norris 2004).

The analyst can determine where particular simultaneous higher-level actions rest along a continuum of attention/awareness through examining their relative modal density. Actions can achieve high levels of attention/awareness through high modal complexity, high modal intensity, or both. The higher-level action of the coaching conversation has high modal complexity. Many modes come together, and are directed towards the coaching conversation. Contrast this with an action that has high modal *intensity*, such as reading. The mode of gaze is very intense here. One way to think about this is to consider what would happen if you removed a mode. In the case of reading, it is not possible without gaze. In contrast, coaching sessions can happen on the phone, or over the Internet. In both reading and coaching, certain higher-level actions are at a high level of attention/awareness and this can be analyzed through modal density (either complexity or intensity).

As social actors often engage in simultaneous higher-level actions, the notion of modal density can be used to show which actions are in the foreground of attention/awareness, and which actions are in the mid-ground and background of attention/awareness.

The transcript below is taken from the very end of the coaching session, as the coach leans forward and looks behind the screen (figure 3) to indicate that the session is over to the researcher. The researcher is never mentioned by the

Introduction to multimodal (inter)action analysis — 85

Figure 3: Coach leans forward and looks between privacy screens to signal end of session through gaze

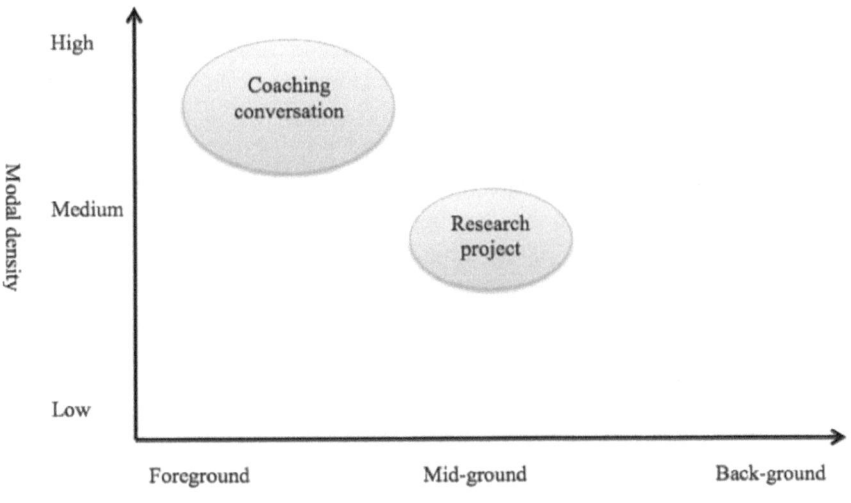

Figure 4: Graph of attention/awareness showing where the higher-level actions of coaching conversation and research project are placed for coach and client

participants, and they specifically asked for him to be behind a screen. This allows them to give a high level of attention and awareness to the coaching conversation. The privacy screens decrease the modal complexity and intensity of the higher-level action of being part of a research project, by interrupting the mode of gaze between the participants and the researcher.

If we consider the foreground/background continuum we can place the two higher-level actions on different levels (figure 4). This is important because it means that as a researcher we can discuss the coaching session, and point out that there is some impact from the researcher, but that this has been purposefully minimized by lowering the modal density of this higher-level action.

Semantic/pragmatic means

Changes from more to less modal density can indicate that a higher-level action is shifting from the foreground of one or more of the participants' attention and awareness, to the mid-ground or background (or vice versa) (Norris 2004). As modal density changes, this signals a change in the participants' orientations to the higher-level actions they are involved in, which in turn reflects their focus on relevant actions.

A shift in focus from one higher level action to another is often accompanied by some form of gesture, postural shift or facial expression that can both help the performer of the action to structure their own interaction, and signal to others that a shift is about to, or has just occurred. These pronounced lower-level actions have been referred to as semantic/pragmatic means because of how they function. As Norris (2004) states:

1. A *means* functions semantically by marking the end of a foregrounded higher-level action (or the beginning of a new higher-level action), facilitating the organization of higher-level actions in the performer's own mind.
2. A *means* functions pragmatically by communicating the upcoming occurrence of a shift in foregrounded higher-level action to the other participants.

(Norris 2004: 88, italics in original)

Throughout interaction, observing instances of semantic/pragmatic means helps explicate how participants structure the interaction, and what higher-level actions they are focusing on.

The example below (figure 5) shows the coach raising their finger. This pronounced lower-level action comes as the coach introduces the higher-level action of taking notes about the session. The coach carefully negotiates this

Figure 5: Transcription of coach performing a semantic/pragmatic means

higher-level action, taking care to ensure that the client still feels in control of the session, and is aware of why the coach is taking notes. The semantic/pragmatic means in this case indicates to the researcher that the coach is shifting her focus to a different higher-level action, communicates that pragmatically to the client, and helps the coach structure the addition of this higher-level action to the coaching conversation.

Identity

Norris initially developed multimodal (inter)action analysis to describe the identity production of two participants that she spent a year with. She was noticing that identities are produced on many different levels simultaneously, and current methodologies did not provide for simultaneous higher-level actions at different levels of attention. These simultaneous actions give off identity elements, which can stand alone as complete units, and also come together as part of a whole. Multimodal (inter)action analysis thus emerged as a way to describe social action while maintaining its complexity.

Norris (2011) refers to two types of identity production. The first is horizontal, and refers to simultaneous higher-level actions carried out at different levels of attention and awareness. The second is vertical, and refers to the various layers of discourse that people operate within, each impacting upon identity elements they produce.

Horizontal production

As noted, social actors produce identity elements through their actions. Social actors produce multiple identity elements as they carry out multiple simultaneous higher-level actions. These are produced at different levels of attention/awareness, and can therefore be plotted in a graph of attention/awareness. We can visualize identity elements spread horizontally across a graph, in the foreground, mid-ground and background of attention/awareness. Thus this is referred to as the horizontal production of identity.

Researchers can use this to show how identity elements are coordinated between social actors, and often not matched in interaction. We can also consider the notions of appropriation and mastery of identity elements. Social actors can master identity elements, without appropriating them. In this case the associated higher-level action that produces the identity element will rest at the foreground of attention/awareness. When a person appropriates an identity element, often it will move to the mid or background of attention/awareness, as they often are able to carry out the action without focused awareness or attention.

Vertical production

Just as identity is produced through actions, it is also produced through discourses. Discourses can be referred to as mediational means, with affordances and constraints. Norris (2011) delineates discourses into three layers, but points out that while these layers help to make discourses analyzable, there are ever more layers that could be teased out. The three layers are the outer layers, the intermediary layers and the inner layers. These layers exert forces on social actors, and produce different types of identity elements.

The outer layer of discourse is formed by the larger society, and is enforced by extended networks and institutions. This outer layer produces general identity elements, and is largely invisible when social actors comply and produce the general identity elements enforced by societal forces. These forces become apparent when social actors do not comply. Norris (2011) uses the example of a woman who is going through a divorce, and as she is in court either side argues over how she can be interpreted in the marriage: as caring mother, or selfish woman seeking to hurt her husband? The institution imposes these general identity elements and it is very difficult not to comply with them to some extent.

The intermediary layer of discourse is formed by the social actor coordinating with, and through, their immediate and extended networks. This layer impacts upon longer-term actions carried out with these networks, and produces continuous identity elements. The example Norris (2011) uses is again from a woman going through a divorce. Her friends produce her as a divorcee, and she struggles to move away from this production, eventually deciding to move cities and provide some distance between herself and this network. This enabled her to also move away from the continuous identity element of divorcee that was being produced for her, and which she no longer felt comfortable with.

The central layer of discourse refers to immediate higher-level actions that the social actor produces, and forces upon others. At this level the social actor is viewed as mostly agentive, even if they are acting in compliance with the higher levels of discourse. At this level the affordances and constraints of the mediational means impact upon what a social actor can do.

Multimodal (inter)action analysis starts with these three layers of discourse, however we can take each layer as multiple also. These layers provide a framework for examining the impact of discourses upon the social actor, how their actions are interpreted, and how this influences the identity elements that are produced. This model can also be used to consider agency in identity, and action (see Norris 2011 for further discussion of agency and the layers of discourse model).

Conclusion

Multimodal (inter)action analysis provides methodological tools and theoretical concepts for the analysis of social action in its complexity. This framework takes social action as the unit of analysis, produced by social actors with tools, with the environment, and with each other. These actions can be delineated into higher- and lower-level actions, and frozen actions. Social action is complex; modal density and the foreground/background continuum provide tools to investigate how social actors construct various higher-level actions, sequentially and simultaneously.

This focus on actions means the analyst can examine the complexity of interaction, providing for a holistic analysis that does not bias the research towards specific actions such as speech or writing. Consequently multimodal (inter)action analysis has proven useful in a wide range of fields. Norris has applied multimodal (inter)action analysis extensively to the study of identity, and developed the notion of vertical and horizontal identity production to describe simultaneous identity elements, and the influence of layers of discourse upon action, and identity.

Multimodal (inter)action analysis can be used anywhere that researchers want to investigate social action. Kite surfing, vegetarianism and marketing are three recent areas of application. Geenen (forthcoming) examines the sport of kite surfing, both through participating in the sport and by carrying out an ethnography. White (2011, 2012) uses multimodal (inter)action analysis to examine how people engage with marketing messages in action, challenging prevailing views of consumer engagement. Makboon's current research examines identity production in Thai Vegetarians and the links to Buddhist practice. Due to its well-developed methodological tools, multimodal (inter)action analysis has proven particularly useful to describe and analyze a wide range of social phenomena, and will continue to develop further with the field of multimodality.

Further readings

Norris, Sigrid. 2004. *Analyzing multimodal interaction: a methodological framework.* London: Routledge.

Norris, Sigrid. 2011. *Identity in Interaction: Introducing Multimodal Interaction Analysis* (Vol. 4). Berlin, New York: Mouton De Gruyter.

Project idea

Choose an activity that interests you. Either find a video on YouTube related to that activity or find a public spot where you can observe people. Take time to focus on individual modes, spending a few minutes on each. What impressions do you get about how people are structuring their actions?

References

Kress, Gunther and Van Leeuwen, Theo. 2001. *Multimodal Discourse: The modes and media of contemporary communication.* London: Edward Arnold.

Norris, Sigrid. 2009. Modal density and modal configurations: multimodal actions. In C. Jewitt (Ed.), *The Routledge Handbook for Multimodal Analysis*. London: Routledge.

Norris, Sigrid. 2011. *Identity in Interaction: Introducing Multimodal Interaction Analysis* (Vol. 4). Berlin, New York: Mouton De Gruyter.

Norris, Sigrid. 2004. *Analyzing multimodal interaction: a methodological framework*. London: Routledge.

Norris, Sigrid. 2002. The implication of visual research for discourse analysis: transcription beyond language. In B Dicks (Ed.), *Digital Qualitative Research Methods*. London, New Delhi: Sage.

Norris, Sigrid and Jones, Rodney. H. 2005. *Discourse in action: Introducing mediated discourse analysis*. New York: Routledge.

Scollon, Ron. 1998. *Mediated Discourse as Social Interaction*. Addison Wesley Publishing Company.

Scollon, Ron. 2001. *Mediated discourse: the nexus of practice*. London; New York: Routledge.

Wertsch, James V. 1998. *Mind as action*. New York: Oxford University Press.

Wertsch, James V. and Rupert, L. J. 1993. The Authority of Cultural Tools in a Sociocultural Approach to Mediated Agency. *Cognition and Instruction*, 11(3 & 4), 227–239.

White, Paul. 2011. Reception as social action: The case of marketing. *Multimodality and practice: Investigating theory-in-practice-through-methodology*. New York, NY: Routledge.

White, Paul. 2012. Multimodality's challenge to marketing theory: a discussion. *Multimodal Communication*, 1(3), 305–323.

Carmen Daniela Maier
10 Multimodal analysis of new corporate genres

Introduction

Contemporary corporate communication is characterized by a constant diversification of its persuasive strategies across several genres and media. Cornelissen foregrounds that as consumer groups are "more fragmented and less homogenous than before", corporations "have to use more channels and different media to reach them" (Cornelissen 2008: 24). For example, in order to meet the expectations of existing and prospective (younger) consumers, major companies have a video channel now on YouTube where these consumers can watch videos and comment upon them. Furthermore, corporate communicative strategies have to keep pace with these consumers' genre preferences and up-to-date expertise. Therefore, the videos that can be viewed on corporate video channels reflect a development and spreading of genres across specific business domains as these channels include a more and more diversified range of genres. This range incorporates, apart from classic commercials, several other genres which structure new knowledge about the respective companies and new perspectives on their products and services.

Key terms: Corporate video, "the making of" video.

Corporate videos between documentary sobriety and marketing persuasion

Among the newest phenomena is the proliferation of genres that have been borrowed from film business context; for example, the teasers and "behind the scenes" videos that accompany the commercials before and after their release. Borrowed from film business context, the "behind the scenes" videos – usually called "The Making of" – present the creation of a commercial which advertises a certain product. In film business context, together with teasers and film trailers, "The Making of" videos belong to the genre network of promotional videos that accompany the release of a new film. It is usually considered a documentary and sometimes it can even have the length of a feature film. It consists of shots selected from the advertised feature film which are accompanied by shots filmed on the film's location while the shooting process took place, and by shots of interviews with film crew members.

In other business contexts, in which "The Making of" video shows how a commercial and not a feature film is made, such a video elevates the status of that commercial because, just like a blockbuster, when a commercial "deserves" to be followed by "The Making of" video, then it is obvious that the respective commercial is considered to be or become a successful piece of work. Implicitly, both the commercial and the advertised product become more worthy of public attention. Certainly, "The Making of" video increases the number of viewings, maximizing the number of prospective customers that might buy the product advertised in the respective commercial.

In order to clarify the new dimensions of these videos when colonizing other business contexts than film industry, I have chosen to explore multimodally several "The Making of" videos uploaded by car companies on their YouTube channels. Usually, car companies upload the following videos on their YouTube video channel: commercials, "The Making of" videos about how those commercials have been created, videos about company's values and activities, videos about how the cars have been manufactured, and videos created by fans as responses to any of the above mentioned company's videos. It should be mentioned that all these videos are accompanied by the on-going comments of various users, and that some of these videos are uploaded again by other users of YouTube on their own channels.

Usually, "The Making of" videos tell the story of how and why a commercial has been created through voice over commentaries and interviews of film crew members, actors and company representatives. The shots that construct the video are shots filmed on location and in the lab, and selected shots from the respective commercial. In some cases, the whole commercial is also embedded at the end of "The Making of" video and, consequently, some of the commercial's shots can appear twice in "The Making of" video. However, due to their placement in the structure of the video, they have different communicative purposes.

By identifying and explaining the meaning-making resources of "The Making of" videos of car companies, this chapter intends to show how visual and textual modes are seamlessly employed in a complex interplay that incorporates elements belonging to two different genres: documentary and commercial. The present exploration is also meant to suggest a possible model of multimodal discourse analysis from a social semiotic perspective of the "The Making of" videos regardless of the business context in which they appear.

Theoretical background

Looking at the complex structure of "The Making of" videos, it is clear that an interdisciplinary perspective is of importance in any analytical endeavour, and therefore I combine several approaches from film theory to social semiotics and discourse analysis in order to clarify the kinds and effects of the meaning-making resources that characterize this genre.

As already mentioned, the proliferation of such genres can be linked with the on-going social changes that have taken place in the last decade in terms of not only enhanced expertise and expectations of consumers, and enhanced mediated interaction opportunities, but also in terms of enhanced reflexivity. Inspired by Giddens (1991), when explaining how discourses work within social practices, Fairclough highlights that today "reflexivity is an inherent property of all social practices – any social practice includes the constructions of that practice produced by its practitioners as part of that practice "(Fairclough 2010: 548). The way in which the social practice of shooting a commercial is mediated in "The Making of" videos is just one of the symptoms through which this phenomenon of enhanced reflexivity manifests itself in corporate communication context. The fact that reflexivity is a characteristic that marks prominently the genre of documentary film is relevant for the present analysis because "The Making of" video is a genre that combines generic elements of the documentary with those of a commercial.

The tension between the pretense of an 'objective' recount of the sobriety discourse of a documentary (Nichols 1991: 3) and the persuasive strategies in the promotional discourse of a commercial is in fact a distinctive feature of this genre. "The Making of" video shares several traits with the documentary genre: the organizing logic, "the evidentiary editing" (Nichols 2001: 30), and a prominent role of speech directed at the viewer. The organizing logic is a common trait because "The Making of" video also displays a wide range of shots and scenes that are brought together by "a controlling perspective": "places and things may appear and disappear as they are brought forward in support of the film's point of view and perspective" (Nichols 2010: 23). From Nichols' perspective, evidentiary editing "may sacrifice spatial and temporal continuity to rope in images from far-flung spaces if they help advance the argument" (Nichols 2001: 107). The prominent role of speech directed at the viewer also characterizes a "The Making of" video as it will be explained below. However, "The Making of" video departs from the documentary genre which is supposed "to produce a suitably authenticated account of a real-life event" (Kilborn and Izod 1997:

19), because this video promotes explicitly both the commercial and the advertised product. Furthermore not only parts of the commercial but even the whole commercial can be actually embedded in it.

In order to understand this generic complexity and its meaning-making potential, it is important to address genre from a social-semiotic point of view. Kress points out that "genre mediates between the social and the semiotic: it points to social organization and provides semiotic arrangements which realize these" (Kress 2010: 116). In order to be able to provide sufficient explanations of how meanings are recurrently shaped, the discourses that emerge from the above mentioned generic combination also have to be addressed from this perspective. Kress suggests that the questions to be asked when employing a social-semiotic approach are: *Whose interest* and *agency* is at work here in the making of meaning? *What meaning* is being made here? *How* is meaning being made? With *what resources*, in *what social environment*?" (Kress 2010: 57). These questions are relevant from a social semiotic perspective upon discourse because, according to social semioticians, discourses are "socially specific ways of knowing social practices" (Van Leeuwen 2008: 6). But discourses do not only represent what happens in the context of a social practice; when social practices are recontextualized in discourses, the recontextualization is marked by various processes of transformations among which evaluations occupy a prominent role. For this specific investigation, the analysis of evaluations is relevant because "which kinds of evaluation will occur in a particular recontextualizing social practice will, again, depend on the concerns and values of that practice" (Van Leeuwen 2008: 21).

Therefore, one of the main questions that arise when trying to explore this complex genre is: how does it disguise what it presents the viewers as something obvious and objective?

Data and method

In this chapter, I illustrate the social semiotic approach to the multimodal discourse analysis of "The Making of" videos by employing examples from five videos uploaded by Dodge, Nissan, Renault, Toyota and Volkswagen companies on their YouTube channels. These videos are longer than the commercials and they are quite popular in terms of number of views.

Table 1: Car commercials and the accompanying "The Making of" videos

Company, name & year	Commercial		"The Making of" ...	
	Time	Views	Time	Views
Dodge (*Challenger Freedom* 2011)	1:01	1,606,387	3:53	79,627
Nissan (*Polar Bear* 2011)	1:02	1,668,697	3:38	56,078
Renault (*Ballet* 2007)	1:34	1,049,983	4:39	146,123
Toyota (*Harmony* 2010)	0:30	735,843	4:44	175,094
Volkswagen (*The Dog Strikes Back* 2012)	1:16	14,450,878	6:41	1,080,239

Each of these videos deconstructs the commercial and combines fragments of it with new footage filmed behind the scenes. Obviously, there are several social practices that are thus recontextualized, namely both those related to "The Making of" video and those represented in the respective commercial. I have chosen three main aspects of the recontextualized social practices to present in this chapter: the social actors in terms of multiplicity of voices and roles; the social actions in terms of multi-layered environments; and the multimodal strategies of evaluations through which these are (re)contextualized. Following Van Leeuwen, I analyze these aspects highlighting how "some discourses provide discursive resources for other discourses" (Van Leeuwen 2009: 152). My choice is primarily motivated by the double articulation of "The Making of" video as a documentary and as a commercial.

Table 2: The social practice elements

Genre elements			
Social practice elements	Social actors	Social actions	Evaluations
Documentary	Actors (as testifiers) Film crew members Company representatives	Location-related Lab-related	Commercial and filming process Advertised car Actors
Commercial	Actors (as actors)	Commercial-related	Advertised car

The analytical work has been conducted in detail at the level of shot, and is based on multimodal transcriptions captured in *Microsoft Word* tables. The multimodal strategy of transcription has been chosen because "multimodal transcriptions are ultimately based on the assumption that a transcription will help us understand the relationship between a specific instance of a genre, for example a text, and the genre's typical features" (Baldry and Thibault 2006: 30). The movie-making software program *Adobe Premiere* has been used for segmenting each video at one frame intervals and thus acquiring the representative frames

Table 3: A sample of the transcription strategies employed to record specific aspects of Renault's *Ballet*

Time Frame	Frame attributes Text	Generic element	Social actors	Social actions	Evaluations
01:20	Medium close up Eye contact with viewers Superimposed name & function	Documentary	Individualized crew member	Lab-related: retrospective interview	Verbal: on screen: verbal evaluation of the filming process' difficulty: *We only had ten cars …*
01:45	Long shot Camera crew member on car filming		Non-individualized crew member	Location-related: live dynamic shooting sessions voice over commentary	off screen: *and three days to shoot.*
01:48	Extreme long shot Cars running in the desert	Commercial	Renault cars	Commercial-related Location-related: voice over commentary	off screen: verbal evaluation of the filming process' difficulty: *That was the challenge and one hell of a ride.*

of each shot. These stills have been introduced in the tables together with information concerning the frame's visual and textual attributes, and the shot's length. Each shot has been annotated in terms of its belonging to the documentary or commercial generic element, and in terms of the selected elements of the social practice.

Researchers in multimodality have reached "a general agreement concerning the existence of several semiotic modes that interrelate in meaning-making systems in most contemporary texts" (Maier et al. 2007: 460), and this agreement is translated in detailed analyses that incorporate several semiotic modes from (still and moving) images, to written text, speech, sound, music, gesture, etc. The need to explore "The Making of" videos multimodally, namely to address their complex "modal configuration", is obvious. Although the main focus of this exploration is related especially to the roles of images in the construction of this genre, it is not possible to ignore the role of on- and off-screen texts in connection with this analytical purpose. Therefore, aspects related to text and image-text interplay are also taken into consideration. Kress stresses the different meaning-making potentials of these two semiotic modes: "image *shows* what takes too long to read, and writing *names* what would be difficult to *show*" (Kress 2010: 1). The focus on the combination of images with the superimposed written text is also motivated by the fact that the visual appearance of the textual information affects both the meanings of the respective words and of the whole video (Van Leeuwen 2011).

In what follows, the analytical findings related to the social actors and the social actions and their evaluative recontextualizations are explained in detail in order to reveal the communicative balancing act of these persuasive videos between evidence and argument.

Analytical findings

Social actors

The social actors included in these videos are film crew members, company representatives and actors. The film crew members are presented while working on location and/or in the lab, or while being interviewed, and they surface in the video in various ways and for various purposes. First of all, they are individualized in medium & close-up shots while being interviewed, and they are collectivized in long shots when the shooting takes place in various locations. When individualized, both their names and functions are revealed in superimposed captions. The company representatives are also individualized in medium and close-up shots while being interviewed, and their names and functions are also revealed in superimposed captions. When recontextualized in "The Making of" video, the commercial's actors are reallocated other roles. The actors playing in the commercial – be they human or animals – are represented both as actors in the recontextualized shots of the commercial, and as testifiers when they are "actors" in "The Making of" video. When recontextualized, the actors of the commercial are represented either by means of visual "passivation" (Van Leeuwen 2008: 32) while being prepared on location for the shooting session, and/or by means of verbal "activation" (Van Leeuwen 2008: 32) when they talk about their work in the interviews. Visually, the viewers experience how the actors leave behind their personalities as they are given the necessary costumes and are prepared by makeup artists and hair stylists.

Simultaneously, the viewers hear their confessions regarding their work as actors in the respective commercial. Evidently, the viewers are allowed to immerse themselves in the practice of filmmaking by witnessing multimodally what happens before a shooting session and hearing the actors' explanations. In *The Dog strikes Back*, even the dog, Bolt, that is the main actor of the commercial is given a voice. His barking answers are translated into English and superimposed on the images in captions. For example, when the voice over

Figure 1: Screen shot from *Polar Bear* with the actor wearing the bear costume

Figure 2: Screen shot from *The Dog strikes back* with the Bolt, the dog actor

interviewer asks him "How did you feel when you got the part?" (*The Dog strikes back*[1] 2012), the words "excited" and then "happy" have been superimposed on the long shot of Bolt when he is barking the answer.

The wide range of social actors and locations that surface in "The Making of" videos is brought together by logic of implication "which bridges these leaps from one person or place to another" (Nichols 2010: 23) that is specific to documentaries. The appearance of each category of social actors and locations support seamlessly and in specific ways the story of how the commercial has been made and its persuasive argumentation. The fact that, when interviewed, all these categories of social actors maintain eye contact with the viewer minimizes the distance between these viewers and what is going on the screen, enhancing the feeling of being a part of the fascinating world of film making.

Social actions

Apart from the social actions appearing in the commercials, the social actions visualized in "The Making of" videos are related to two social practices and environments: location-related and lab-related actions. The location-related actions are represented by three types of shots: shots of shooting sessions, of prospective discussions among film crew members, and either prospective or retrospective individual interviews with crew members and/or company representatives. The live dynamic shooting sessions are usually preceded or followed by shots from the commercial facilitating an understanding of the working process. The long shots with off screen explanations are preferred to represent the shooting sessions because in this way both aspects of the commercial and of the filming process can be incorporated in the same shot contributing in this way to the seamless combination of documentary and commercial features. The viewers can experience in these long shots both what has been filmed and how it has been filmed.

The prospective discussions among crew members allow the viewer to witness at close hand the process of finding solutions to complex shooting problems. In *Ballet*, the off screen words of the safety officer/chief rigger, "we have two cars flying through the air and hitting in mid-air" (*Ballet* 2007), can be heard off screen while, in a long shot, the viewers can see a group of crew members looking at the director who is drawing something. The words are also superimposed on the screen.

---

[1] In order to ease the reading process, the names of the commercials are used whenever quotations are given from their respective "The Making of" videos.

Figure 3: Screen shot from *Ballet* with the film crew members

The usage of the personal pronoun "we" and the present tense "have" facilitate the inclusion of the viewers in the film's universe, helping them to become a part of that group who has to solve the respective shooting problem. The retrospective interviews are meant both to reveal the level of difficulty related to filming certain shots and scenes, and to clarify the purposes of certain choices. For example, in *Harmony*, the creative director admits that "we wanted to put the Prius in a world that is exclusively made out of people" (*Harmony* 2010).

The lab-related actions presented in the videos are visually "agentialized" (Van Leeuwen 2008: 67) through medium or long shots of crew members working together in the lab. The "deagentialized" (Van Leeuwen 2008: 67) lab-related actions are visualized through close up shots of computer screens showing the details of specific technical solutions. The verbal track that accompanies such types of close up shots oscillates between the intimate explanatory comments of a voice over or the almost coded dialogue of the working experts.

Evaluations

In terms of the evaluations that are added to the elements of social practices when these are recontextualized in "The Making of" videos, I have found several types depending on the object/subject of evaluation.

Figure 4: Screen shot from *Challenger Freedom* with the cars and the American flag

First, the product's values are verbally evaluated both by film crew members, company representatives and actors. For example, in *Challenger Freedom*, a close up shot of the car is accompanied by the following voice over commentary of one of the crew members: "The engine sounds actually really nice ... You don't see that in cars anymore" (*Challenger Freedom* 2011). Visually, the product's evaluations are usually represented by close up shots. When investigating film trailers, Maier explains that "the combination of a character's comments and a close-up can enhance the evaluative effects of both" (Maier 2009: 169). This multimodal evaluation strategy is recurrently used in "The Making of" videos. The close up shots of the car can be both new shots filmed for "The Making of" video, or can be recontextualized shots from the commercial. When evaluating the promoted products, these are also commented in terms of general values. For example, in *Challenger Freedom*, the car represents more than just another Dodge car: "He's these 3 things: Dodge, freedom and America" (*Challenger Freedom* 2011). These words are accompanied by shots in which the car and the American flag are represented together.

If this statement hints at perennial national values, in *Polar Bear*, the evaluative statement invokes the future: "The Nissan Leaf is the 1st step towards a brighter future" (*Polar Bear* 2011). By inserting such statements, "The Making of" video hints to certain value systems that are supposed to be similar to that of

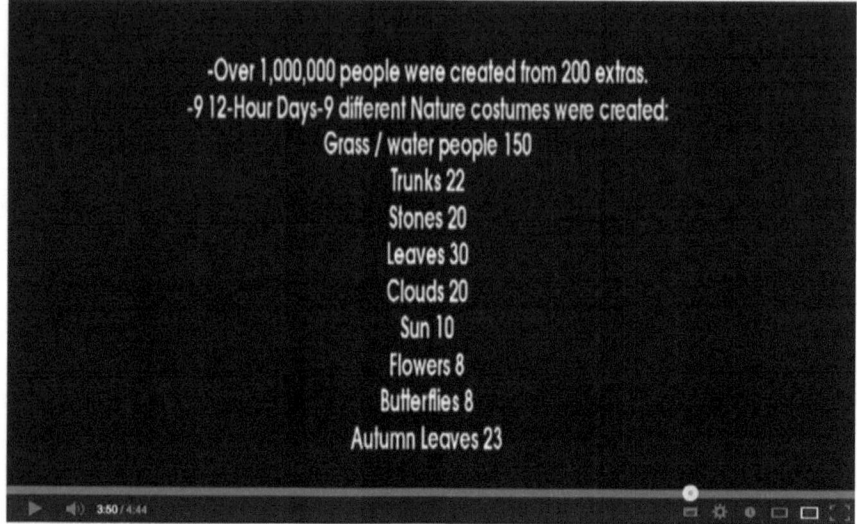

Figure 5: Screen shot from *Harmony* with evaluative information about the cast

the prospective customer. Apart from advertising the specific product, these types of evaluative assumptions are also meant to build or strengthen the relation with the prospective customers that are viewing the video. The company's values are especially evaluated in interviews by the companies' representatives. In *Ballet*, The Renault's Director of Road Safety Policy claims that "Group Renault executes its global strategy for active and passive safety with an interdisciplinary approach combining both: medical and technical competence" (*Ballet* 2007). The words are uttered in a convincing tone while he keeps eye contact with the viewers.

Second, the verbal evaluations marking the location- or lab-related social actions are clustered around the practical problems of the shooting process and the creative qualities of the commercial. For example, in *Ballet*, the director explains that they "only had ten cars and three days to shoot", and he confesses: "that was the challenge and one hell of a ride" (*Ballet* 2007). In *The Dog Strikes Back*, not only the words, but also the intonation, the voice's volume and rhythm contribute to the evaluative effect: "All of this stuff here it was done in two weeks ... uh ... it was ... a lot of long hours" (*The Dog Strikes Back* 2011). In *Harmony*, the director of photography confesses in the very first shot of the video that he has "never seen a storyboard or an animatic for an idea like this before", while the 1st assistant director explains that "the concept is very high art" (*Harmony* 2010). The verbal evaluation takes also visual forms when the following white coloured words appear superimposed on a completely black screen: "Over 1,000,000 people were created out of 200 extras" (*Harmony* 2010).

The visual evaluations are to be found either in interplay with the textual ones or independent of them. In *Ballet*, the shots visualizing from different angles the shooting of the real crashes in South Africa are accompanied either just by the music track or by voice over commentaries. The visual evaluations are realized through specific types of shots. For example, long shots are employed to show the difficulty or complexity involved in shooting certain scenes while close ups are employed to reveal the innovation of other scenes. The commercial shots are also selected as evaluative evidence of the products' qualities (close-up shots of various parts of the product), of the actors' performance (close-up shots and slow motions), and of the film crew's expertise (by preceding or following explanatory interviews). Maier finds that "the evaluative stance in the visual mode is created through an intensifying or repetitive use of close-up shots, camera movements, captions and various special effects" (Maier 2009: 167). In *Harmony*, one of the special effects that are employed in order to evaluate the huge amount of work done by the crew members and actors is time lapse filming. This special effect allows the viewers to see in a couple of seconds the tedious process of creating natural elements like trees out of many actors.

The multimodal evaluations are the most often employed evaluations in all the analysed videos. For example, at the end of *Ballet*, the words "eight models awarded five stars in the Europe NCAP Crash Test" and five yellow stars are superimposed on the long shot of eight Renault cars.

Finally, what should be also highlighted here is the fact that in "The Making of" video, the voice over commentaries evaluate the commercial implicitly when addressing the viewers as *connoisseurs* who may already have seen the commercial and who "may follow what is occurring due to their *background knowledge* concerning the types of events, entities, properties and their interrelationships that are being depicted" (Bateman and Schmidt 2012: 152).

The following table displays the main representation strategies of the social actors and social actions appearing in "The Making of" video. The representation strategies employed for the evaluations that surface when these two categories of the social practices are recontextualized in such a video are also included in the table:

Table 4: Main representation strategies of the social actors and social actions appearing in "The Making of" video

Social practice elements		Representation strategies
Social actors	Actors (as testifiers)	Multimodal individualization (close up), nominalization (name)
		Visual passivation and verbal activation (before shooting) and multimodal activation (while shooting)
	Film crew members	Multimodal individualization (close up), nominalization (name) and functionalization (profession)
		Visual collectivization
	Company representatives	Multimodal individualization (close up), nominalization (name) and functionalization (position)
Social actions	Location-related	Live dynamic shooting sessions
		Prospective discussions (group of crew members)
		Prospective & retrospective interviews (individual crew members)
	Lab-related	Visually agentialized
		Visually deagentialized
Evaluations	Commercial and filming process	Multimodal evaluation of innovation, difficulty and complexity
	Actors	Multimodal evaluation of their performance
	Advertised car	Multimodal evaluation of product and its values
		Multimodal evaluation of product and general values
		Verbal evaluation of companies' values

Conclusions

In this chapter, I have attempted to show how a social semiotic approach to multimodal discourse analysis can be employed in order to explain how visual and textual modes are seamlessly combined at the intersection of two different genres: documentary and commercial.

My main question that I have posed in the beginning of this chapter, namely how does "The Making of" genre disguise what it says as something objective and obvious, could be given an answer now, because the tension between the pretense of an 'objective' recount of the sobriety discourse (Nichols 1991: 3) and the persuasive strategies of the promotional discourse seems to be negotiated primarily through an evaluative expert discourse.

Layers of this evaluative expert discourse dominate multimodally the recontextualization of the two social practices which are brought together in this genre: the filming of a commercial and the advertising of a specific product. By employing this all-embracing discourse, the generic complexity of "The Making of" videos becomes viable, and both the generic elements of the documentary and of the commercials seem to accomplish their functions, even reinforcing each other in this process.

Through this discursive strategy, "The Making of" video accomplishes its communicative purposes. The viewers' awareness of the amount and quality of work put into such creative processes is definitely heightened especially by getting the feeling of being "involved" in what happens on the screen. The video also implies that it discloses "insider" information through objective investigation and observation due to the intimate or authoritative tone of the commentaries accompanying shots in which the crew members are followed while working. These shots are marked by "authenticity" in terms of live shooting sessions and rough filming style.

This discursive strategy also contributes both explicitly and implicitly to the enhancement of the credibility of commercial's claims regarding the product's qualities when it selectively recontextualizes some of the commercial's shots accompanied by the highly professional commentaries of experts. It also reinforces explicitly and implicitly the commercial's overall persuasive aims through evaluative coherence and enhancement when interweaving multimodal types of evaluations.

This multimodal analysis can definitely be expanded by also taking into consideration other semiotic modes, and by examining "The Making of" videos made for commercials advertising other kinds of products in order to assess differences and similarities in terms of discursive strategies.

Further readings

Bateman, John A. and Karl-Heinrich Schmidt. 2012. *Multimodal Film Analysis. How Film Mean*. New York: Routledge.

Project idea

Analyze some videos incorporated in a corporate YouTube channel by companies that produce similar products (cars, cosmetics, food items, etc.) in order to reveal how they employ the persuasive interplay of several semiotic modes in different ways.

References

Bauldry, Anthony and Paul J. Thibault. 2006. *Multimodal Transcription and Text Analysis*. London: Equinox.
Bateman, John A. and Karl-Heinrich Schmidt. 2012. *Multimodal Film Analysis. How Film Mean*. New York: Routledge.
Cornelissen, Joep. 2008. *Corporate Communication. A Guide to Theory and Practice*. London: Sage.
Giddens, Anthony. 1991. *Modernity and Self- Identity*. Cambridge: Polity Press.
Kilborn, Richard and John Izod. 1997. *An Introduction to Television Documentary. Confronting Reality*. Manchester: Manchester University Press.
Kress, Gress. 2010. *Multimodality. A Social Semiotic Approach to Contemporary Communication*. London: Routledge.
Maier, Carmen D., Constance Kampf and Peter Kastberg. 2007. Multimodal analysis – an integrative approach for specialized visualizing on the web. *Journal of Technical Writing and Communication* 37: 453–478.
Maier, Carmen D. 2009. Visual evaluation in film trailers. *Visual Communication* 8(2): 159–180.
Maier, Carmen D. 2011. Knowledge communication in green corporate marketing: A Multimodal analysis of an Ecomagination video. In Kay L. O' Halloran and Bradley A. Smith (eds.), *Multimodal Studies: Exploring Issues and Domains*, 153–169. New York: Routledge.
O'Halloran, Kay L. 2004. Visual semiosis in film. In Kay L. O' Halloran (ed.), *Multimodal Discourse Analysis*, 220–246. London: Continuum.
Nichols, Bill. 1991. *Representing Reality. Issues and Concepts in documentary*. Bloomington: Indiana University Press.
Nichols, Bill. 2001. *Introduction to Documentary*. Bloomington: Indiana University Press.
Nichols, Bill. 2010. *Introduction to Documentary*. 2nd edition. Bloomington: Indiana University Press.
Norris, Sigrid. 2009. Modal density and modal configurations: multimodal actions. In Carey Jewitt (ed), *The Routledge Handbook of Multimodality*, 78–91. London: Routledge.
The Making of "Ballet". 2007. Online video accessed on *YouTube*, 5 January 2012.
The Making of "Challenger Freedom". 2011. Online video accessed on *YouTube*, 5 January 2012.
The Making of "Harmony". 2010. Online video accessed on *YouTube*, 30 July 2012.
The Making of "Polar Bear". 2011. Online video accessed on *YouTube*, 5 January 2012.
The Making of "The Dog Strikes Back". 2012. Online video accessed on *YouTube*, 30 July 2012.

Van Leeuwen, Theo. 2008. *Discourse and Practice. New Tools for Critical Discourse Analysis*. Oxford: Oxford University Press.
Van Leeuwen, Theo. 2009. Discourse as the recontextualization of social practice: a guide. In Ruth Wodak and Michael Meyer (eds.). *Methods of Critical Discourse Analysis*, 144–161. London: Sage Publications.
Van Leeuwen, Theo. 2011. *The Language of Colour. An Introduction*. London: Routledge.

Tuomo Hiippala
11 Multimodal genre analysis

Introduction

The concept of genre is frequently invoked in multimodal analysis for a variety of reasons. In most cases, genre is used to describe multimodal phenomena and their properties. From a methodological perspective, it may be argued that genre is often used to circumscribe the analysed phenomenon. For instance, Held (2005: 193) describes magazine covers as a 'contact-and-advertisement' genre, whose function is to showcase the magazine's contents and to attract the reader's attention – a task which the proposed genre fulfils by using multiple semiotic resources. Tan (2010: 93), in turn, uses genre to characterize the multimodal features and the semiotic potential of websites as a form of digital media:

> Newly emergent media such as internet web-pages – an innately hybridic genre that generates a multitude of intertextual possibilities by assembling texts from various modes and discourses (e.g. verbiage, image, sound, activity) that are then represented in multiple relations to one another...

As the work of Held (2005) and Tan (2010) shows, genre is used to cover a wide range of multimodal phenomena, extending from specific page types within an artefact – a magazine cover – to particular forms of digital media, that is, websites. The question that immediately arises is whether genre can be theoretically useful, if the concept can be freely applied to such diverse examples without constraints and criteria.

Indeed, there are growing concerns that genre has not received the theoretical consideration it warrants. Although the previous work includes both theoretical explorations (Lemke 2001, 2005; van Leeuwen 2005) and methodological proposals (Baldry and Thibault 2005; Bateman 2008), in many cases the concept of multimodal genre lacks a solid theoretical foundation due to the scarcity of empirical research and analytical scrutiny. The lack of a definition with firm boundaries is of concern, because the concept is often tasked with abstract description of complex multimodal phenomena – that is, the entire artefact or situation – without the required theoretical foundation. The purpose of this chapter is to outline the current research on multimodal genre, beginning with the initial linguistic models of genre and then moving towards the state-of-the-art in multimodal research. I emphasize the position of genre in multimodal analysis, because a well-formulated theory requires establishing the relations of genre to other central theoretical concepts such as *medium* and *mode*. In this chapter, the discussion of genre is limited to static multimodal artefacts in print media: I will begin by tracing some of the functions that have been traditionally assigned to genre.

Key terms: Discourse semantics, image-flow, material substrate, page-flow, semiotic mode, text-flow.

The underlying theories in genre research

As several influential multimodal theories draw on both social semiotic and systemic functional theories of language (cf. Halliday 1978; Halliday and Matthiessen 2004), it is necessary to consider how genre has been described in these theories. Firstly, the motivation for deploying genre needs to be established. Bateman (forthcoming: 2) identifies three broad purposes:
1. comparing texts and events, and describing their properties,
2. describing the expectations that genre creates for the reader,
3. describing the social functions of genre.

The above points have been extensively investigated in linguistic studies of genre (see e.g. Miller 1984; Ventola 1987; Swales 1990; Bhatia 1993; Hasan 1996; Christie and Martin 1997; Lemke 1999; Martin and Rose 2008). The detailed description of each point is not feasible here due to limitations of space; I simply wish to underline that all of the above points are still relevant for multimodal genre. However, novel approaches are required if we wish to extend genre analysis from linguistics to multimodality.

This brings us to the second point of consideration, that is, the structure of linguistic genre. Traditionally, the structure of genre has been considered *linear* and *staged*. In both spoken and written discourse, genre is seen to unfold through multiple stages, which work towards accomplishing the intended social function. However, the principle of linearity becomes problematic when the analysis is extended from a purely linguistic environment to a multimodal one. It appears that the linear principle applies mainly when linearity is essential for interpreting multimodal discourse, such as in serial graphics (Holsanova et al. 2009: 1223).

There have been propositions to reinstate the principle of linearity by moving away from the artefact structure and towards the observer (Bateman forthcoming: 4). For instance, van Leeuwen (2005) proposes that multimodal artefacts act as an environment for the genre. In this environment, the notion of a reading path could be used to trace the hypothetical, linear path taken by the observer to accomplish the social function performed by the genre. However, there is considerable evidence that visual perception is largely task-driven and unlikely to follow a strictly predefined pattern, which contests the notions of linear, observer-based approaches to the study of multimodal genre (cf. Hiippala 2012b).

To conclude, it appears that the principle of linearity cannot be used to establish reliable criteria for genre analysis, which would support sequential staging in multimodal artefacts. While the attempts to define the social functions of genre remain largely valid, the absence of linearity or any other principle leaves us with few analytical tools to identify genre structures. Consequentially, genre currently appears as a grey area between the social function of a multimodal artefact and its structure. At the same time, the concept of genre can be useful only when it is defined clearly with sufficient analytical constraints and when its relations to other theoretical concepts are clearly stated.

In order to work towards a definition of genre, the first step is to identify where to look for genre structures. Bateman (forthcoming: 3) suggests that genre is a 'multi-stratal' phenomenon, which means that the 'semiotic work' required for deploying a genre involves making choices on several strata. Martin (1999: 38–39) has proposed a similar principle for language, which he calls *meta-redundancy*. According to Martin (1999: 38), "genre is a pattern of register patterns just as register patterns represents patterns of language patterns", that is, linguistic genre metaredounds with register, and register metaredounds with language.

In monomodal contexts, describing the contribution of different strata to genre is by no means a simple task due to various approaches to language (and genre), which have their own theoretical frameworks and concepts, and their interrelations (cf. Martin 1997; Biber and Conrad 2009; Dorgeloh and Wanner 2010). With the move to multimodality, the same principles of theory-building should apply to the definition of theoretical concepts, their interrelations and strata. For this reason, I will now move to describe the concepts relevant to multimodal genre.

Towards multimodal genre analysis

If multimodal genre is viewed as a stratified phenomenon, then we need analytical tools that could allow us to identify the semiotic choices that contribute to genre structures on multiple strata. Moreover, we need to be able to do more than state that the artefacts deploy language and image simultaneously. We also need to say what language and image do in different contexts and how they do it. For this purpose, we need the concept of a semiotic mode to describe the structure and functionality of language, image, or combinations thereof in a given context. Only then does it become possible to proceed towards more abstract levels of description in genre analysis. It should be noted, however, that the concepts of a semiotic mode and that of a semiotic resource are still being developed (see e.g. Kress 2009; Elleström 2010). Due to restricted space and methodological focus, the current discussion focuses on the model proposed in Bateman (2011).

Rhetorical strategies

Before discussing the semiotic modes, the related concept of *rhetorical strategy* needs to be outlined. According to Bateman (forthcoming, p. 8), a broad definition of rhetorical strategy consists of the 'communicative goal' of an artefact and the contribution of the semiotic modes towards the realization of this goal. In other words, rhetorical strategies are established means of doing particular kinds of communicative work by deploying and making selections in the available semiotic modes.

Previously, Lemke (1999) has suggested that artefacts with similar social functions may also be structurally similar: the aforementioned notion of semiotic mode allows us to capture and compare these multimodal structures. The structural properties of multimodal artefacts can then be described using a *topology* – a genre space – that describes the range of choices in the semiotic modes which realize a particular rhetorical strategy. Thus, the rhetorical strategies establish a space, which is populated by the genres that do similar communicative work (Bateman 2008: 223–225).

However, before we may proceed to discuss the abstract semiotic levels of genre or rhetorical strategy, we need a solid analytical tool to account for the deployed semiotic resources. Therefore, I will now turn to the notion of a semiotic mode.

Semiotic modes and media

Bateman (2011) proposes that a full-blown semiotic mode needs three strata: (1) a *material substrate*, which carries (2) the *semiotic resources*, whose interpretation is guided by (3) their *discourse semantics*. Firstly, the underlying stratum of a material substrate will be discussed shortly in connection with the notion of medium. Secondly, the semiotic resources are modeled as "paradigmatic systems of choice together with a syntagmatic organization for re-expressing paradigmatic choices in structural configurations" (Bateman 2011: 20). This means that the semiotic resources allow a range of choices, and the results of these choices may then be combined into structures. Thirdly, the stratum of discourse semantics guides the contextual interpretation of the semiotic resources: it directs the reader towards the correct interpretation in a given context (Bateman 2011: 21). I will now highlight aspects of both semiotic resources and discourse semantics using Figure 1.

The location description in a tourist brochure, shown in Figure 1, is realized using both language and image, and therefore involves choices in both semiotic resources. Previous multimodal research on tourism discourse (see e.g. Hiippala 2007; Kvåle 2010; Francesconi 2011) has described aspects of the choices in lexicogrammar and their relation to the accompanying images. However, what needs to be understood in this context is that the visual-verbal description is a result of choices in both semiotic resources. Consider, for instance, the choice of MOOD in the linguistic structure, where declarative is preferred over alternative choices, such as imperative (Halliday and Matthiessen 2004: 23). Similarly, choices in photography, such as camera angle and settings (aperture, exposure, focal length) contribute to the appearance of the photograph (for choices in image and typography, see also Lim 2004; O'Halloran 2008).

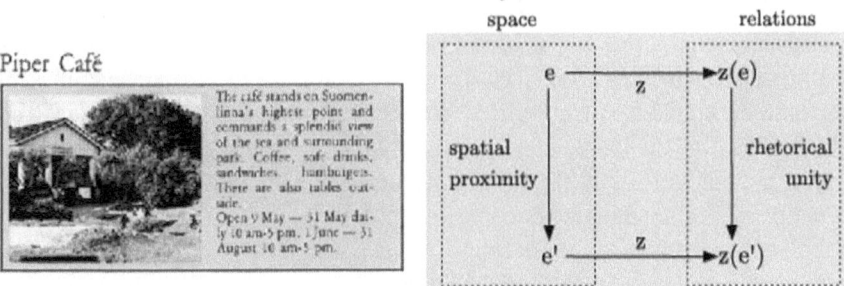

Figure 1: An extract from *Suomenlinna Seafortress in Helsinki* (1988)

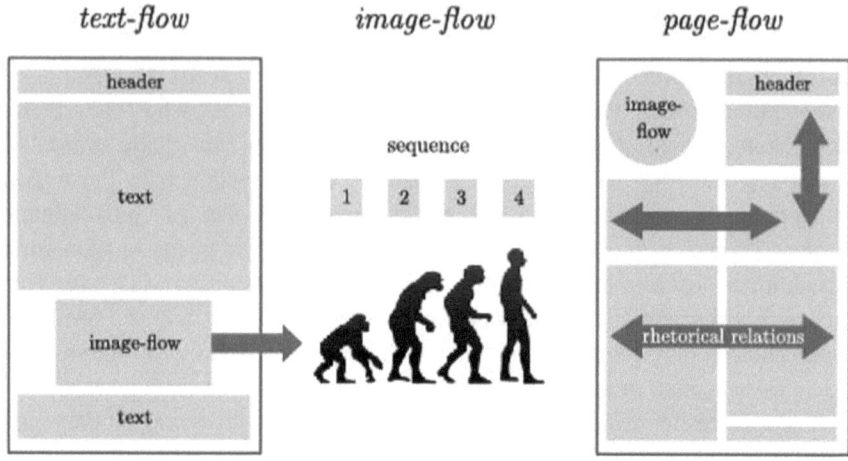

Figure 2: Three semiotic modes: text-flow, image-flow and page-flow

The following question is how the instances resulting from these choices are to be interpreted together? In the "back-and-forth" diagram (see Bateman 2011: 28–29) in Figure 1, the left-side domain of layout space is mapped with the domain of rhetorical relations on the right-hand side. The mapping relation z indicates a relationship between the spatially proximate entities e and e' in the layout domain and their counterparts $z(e)$ and $z(e')$ in the rhetorical domain. In plain words, the spatial proximity of the photograph (e) and the verbal description (e') indicates that they are to be interpreted together. According to Bateman (2009: 61), the use of the layout space to communicate additional meanings is characteristic of a particular semiotic mode, which he refers to as *page-flow*.

In addition to page-flow, Bateman (2009) identifies two other semiotic modes in print media, which are termed *text-flow* and *static image-flow*. Text-flow is characterized by linear-interrupted text, much like this chapter: diagrams, images, tables and such may occasionally interrupt text-flow, but the two-dimensional space is not used to communicate additional meanings. This distinguishes text-flow from page-flow. Therefore, the discourse semantics of text-flow resemble a much reduced version of those outlined for language in Martin (1992). Static image-flow, in turn, organizes graphic elements into meaningful sequences (cf. e.g. Figure 2 above and Hiippala 2012b: 323). These three semiotic modes are illustrated in Figure 2.

Finally, we arrive at the concept of a *medium* and its relation to the semiotic modes. It was established above that full-fledged semiotic mode requires a material substrate to carry the semiotic resources. Furthermore, the material substrate needs to be sufficiently controllable so that a group of users may put the material to 'semiotic' work. At the same time, it has to be noted that semiotic modes do not appear suddenly, but instead they emerge when a suitable substrate comes available and develop over time (cf. O'Halloran 2009). Consider, for instance, the emergence of screen-based displays as a material substrate alongside page-based print media, whose predecessors have included parchment, papyrus and clay tablets. As Bateman (forthcoming: 12) writes:

> [A] medium is seen as a historically stabilized site for the deployment of some selection of semiotic modes for the achievement of varied communicative purposes [...] it is possible for an unrestricted range of genres to be carried within [a] medium.

To exemplify, Bateman (forthcoming: 12) suggests that books constitute a medium in which several semiotic modes may be deployed. Another proposed medium is the newspaper, which has similar affordances in terms of semiotic modes (cf. Gibson 1979), but significantly different practices of consumption and distribution. Bateman (forthcoming: 12) also insists on a clear demarcation between (1) features that arise from the medium, such as page numbering, margins, etc. and (2) selections in the semiotic modes that contribute towards the genre structures in a multimodal artefact, which will be made explicit later in this chapter. This concludes the theoretical discussion of genre and related concepts. In the following section, I will show how the *Genre and Multimodality* model (hereafter GeM; see Bateman 2008) may be used to identify and capture aspects of genre structure in multimodal artefacts.

Identifying genre structures

The GeM model is a model of multimodal document structure which attends to several aspects of multimodal artefacts: the semiotic resources and their typographic and graphic features, the layout and its hierarchical organization, rhetorical structure, and navigation. The model also comes with an XML-based annotation scheme for the creation of multimodal corpora. As the name of the GeM model suggests, genre is a foundational notion within the model, whose aim is to provide a consistent analytical method for describing and comparing multimodal artefacts. Because genre is considered a multi-stratal phenomenon, the GeM model provides multiple analytical layers that are cross-referenced in the annotation. A full discussion of each analytical layer is not possible here; the distinct layers and their contribution to the GeM model are listed in Table 1.

The model provides a list of *Recognized Base Units* (RBUs), which can be picked up in subsequent analytical layers (Bateman 2008: 111). According to

Table 1: The layers of the GeM model

Layer name	Descriptive function	Analytical unit and examples
Base layer	Provides a list of base units that may be analysed as a part of other layers.	*Base units*: sentences, headings, drawings, figures, photos, captions, list items, etc.
Layout layer	Groups the base units together based on similar properties in the three domains below.	*Layout units*: paragraphs, headings, drawings, figures, photos, captions, list items, etc.
Structure	The hierarchical structure between layout units.	
Area model	The placement of layout units in a layout.	
Realisation	Typographical or visual features of layout units.	
Rhetorical layer	Describes the rhetorical relations holding between the identified rhetorical segments.	*Rhetorical segments*: base units with rhetorical functions
Navigational layer	Describes the navigational structure by defining pointers, entries and indices.	*Pointers, entries and indices*: base units and layout units with navigation functions

Source: Hiippala (2012a: 108)

the list of RBUs, sentences, headings, page numbers, list items, photographs, diagrams, etc. are identified as base units. The layout layer describes the hierarchical structure of the identified RBUs, their positioning in the layout, and their typographic or graphic features. The relationships between base units are described using an extension of *Rhetorical Structure Theory* (hereafter RST; see Mann and Thompson 1988; Taboada and Mann 2006). Finally, the navigation structure describes the structures provided to facilitate the use of the artefact.

I will now illustrate how the GeM model may be used to identify multimodal genre structures, using the example shown in Figure 3. The data in Figure 3 were retrieved from a GeM-annotated corpus and visualized automatically using scripts developed for this purpose (Hiippala 2013). The upper part of Figure 3 shows the hierarchical layout structure of a double-page in a tourist brochure. The double-page is represented by the parent node in the center of the diagram. From here, the hierarchical structure extends all the way to the child nodes on the outer circle, which consist of layout units such as headings, paragraphs, photographs, maps and so on (see Table 1). The layout units annotated as graphics are marked using color. The lower part of Figure 3, which I shall explain shortly below, shows a part of the brochure's rhetorical structure.

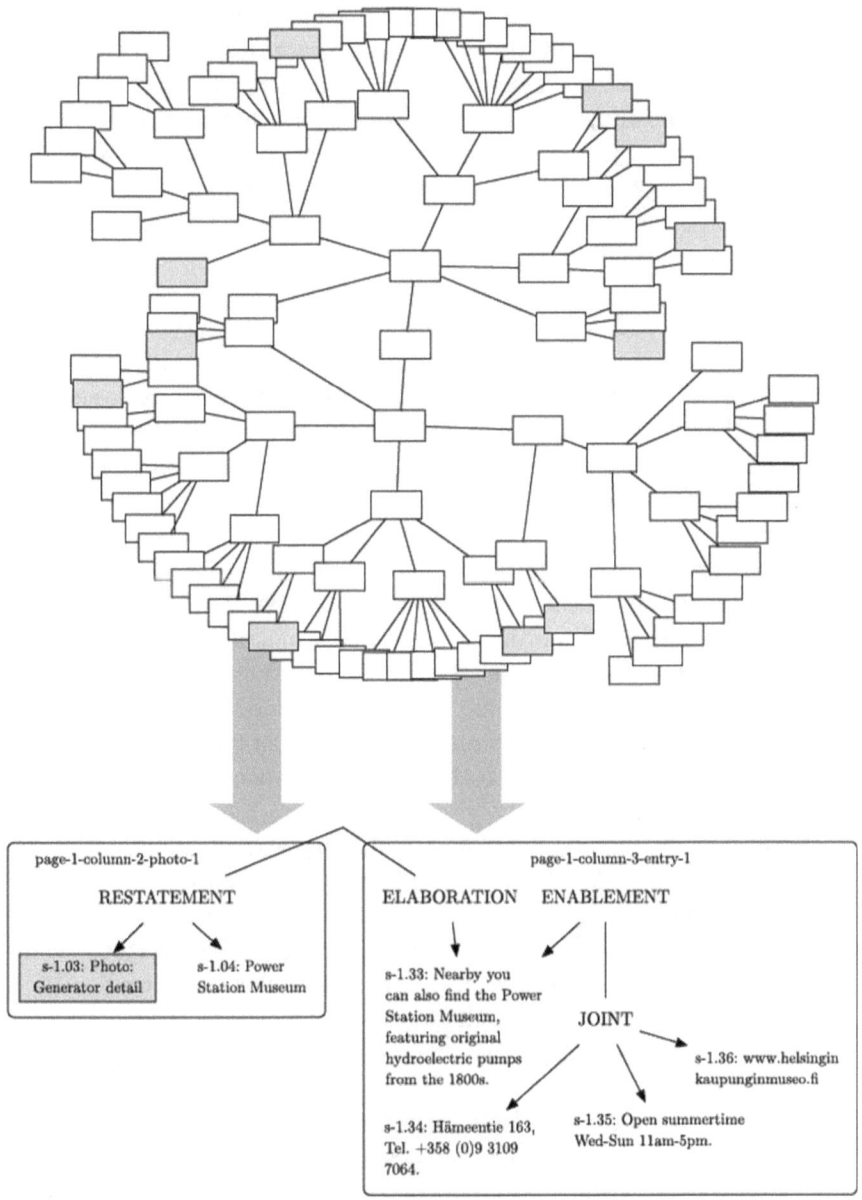

Figure 3: The layout and rhetorical structures in *Helsinki Visitors Guide* (2008) (Hiippala 2013: 220)

As Figure 3 shows, the layout structure of the tourist brochure is fragmented and has a deep hierarchy. In the most extreme case, reaching the outermost child nodes requires a total of five steps from the center node. Now, considering the layout structure and its functions – organizing the content into larger structures and establishing part-whole relationships (Bateman and Schmidt 2012: 53) – we may ask what enables the reader to make sense of the complex layout structure in Figure 3? One possible answer may be found in the interaction between the layout structure and the rhetorical structure.

The layout structure is not arbitrary, but functionally motivated. The communicative function of a multimodal artefact defines its structure, which may be captured using the rhetorical layer of the GeM model. This can be seen in the lower part of Figure 3, which shows parts of the rhetorical structure and their relation to the layout structure. In this case, the bounding boxes around the RST structures indicate that the rhetorical segments belong under the same parent node in the layout structure.

On the left-hand side, we have a photograph and an accompanying caption, which participate in a RESTATEMENT relation. Structurally, this configuration of layout and rhetorical structures is close to the example shown in Figure 1, as their structure and spatial proximity in the layout indicate that they are to be interpreted together. Moreover, the photograph and caption elaborate a verbal description located elsewhere in the layout, as indicated by the RST structure on the right-hand side. This RST structure comprises an introductory sentence, which is complemented by travel and contact information using the relation of ENABLEMENT.

What is worth acknowledging here is that these kinds of rhetorical configurations may also be found elsewhere. For instance, the upper part of Figure 3 contains several layout 'chunks' with two child nodes, in which one of the child nodes is a graphic element. In most cases, these image-text combinations in the layout structure possess a similar rhetorical configuration: the same applies to the verbal descriptions which fulfill similar communicative tasks. It may be argued that this kind of patterning allows the reader to negotiate the complex layout structure.

The tourist brochures may prefer certain multimodal structures, while artefacts with different communicative purposes may rely on different types of structure (see e.g. procedural texts in André and Rist 1995; Martinec 2003). These patterned structures have evolved over time to perform certain communicative tasks, and they also respond to the reader's expectations towards the multimodal structure of artefacts (see also Waller 2012). Together, the configuration of these patterns may also signal how the entire artefact is to be interpreted. In the case of Figure 3, the fragmented configuration may encourage an interpretation using the discourse semantics of page-flow, which prefers a selective reading strategy, as opposed to a linear interpretation based on the semiotic mode of text-flow.

Finally, it is also important to note that not all tourist brochures are structured this way in terms of the layout and rhetorical structure. What we have accomplished here is simply a brief description of one possible configuration among many alternatives. To account for these alternative structures, we need more data, preferably in the form of annotated corpora. For this reason, future work on multimodality and genre is likely to benefit from optical character recognition to speed up the creation of corpora and the development of concordancers for their exploration (see e.g. Thomas 2007, 2009; Parodi 2010).

Further readings

Bateman, John A. 2008. *Multimodality and Genre: A Foundation for the Systematic Analysis of Multimodal Documents*. London: Palgrave Macmillan.

Bateman, John A. 2011. The decomposability of semiotic modes. In Kay L. O'Halloran & B. A. Smith (eds) *Multimodal Studies: Multiple Approaches and Domains*. London: Routledge.

Bateman, John A. forthcoming. Genre in the age of multimodality: some conceptual refinements for practical analysis. In Paola Evangelisti-Allori, Vijay K. Bhatia and John A. Bateman (eds) *Evolution in Genres: Emergence, Variation, Multimodality*. Frankfurt am Main: Peter Lang.

Project idea

Compare two multimodal artefacts with different communicative purposes, for example, an information brochure and an instruction manual. How is the verbal and visual content organized? How are the relationships between the content signaled?

References

André, Elisabeth and Thomas Rist. 1995. Generating coherent presentations employing textual and visual material. *Artificial Intelligence Review* 9: 147–165.

Baldry, Anthony P. and Thibault, Paul J. 2005. *Multimodal transcription and text analysis*. London: Equinox.

Bateman, John A. 2008. *Multimodality and Genre: A Foundation for the Systematic Analysis of Multimodal Documents*. London: Palgrave Macmillan.

Bateman, John A. 2009. Discourse across semiotic modes. In Jan Renkema (ed.), *Discourse, of course: An overview of research in discourse studies*, 55–66. Amsterdam/Philadelphia: Benjamins.

Bateman, John A. 2011. The decomposability of semiotic modes. In Kay L. O'Halloran and Bradley A. Smith (eds) *Multimodal Studies: Multiple Approaches and* Domains, 17–38. London: Routledge.

Bateman, John A. forthcoming. Genre in the age of multimodality: some conceptual refinements for practical analysis. In Paola Evangelisti-Allori, Vijay K. Bhatia and John A. Bateman (eds) *Evolution in Genres: Emergence, Variation, Multimodality*. Linguistic Insights, Frankfurt am Main: Peter Lang.

Bateman, John A. and Karl-Heinrich Schmidt. 2012. *Multimodal Film Analysis: How Films Mean*. London: Routledge.

Bhatia, Vijay K. 1993. *Analysing Genre: Language Use in Professional Settings*. London: Longman.

Biber, Douglas and Susan Conrad. 2009. *Register, Genre, and Style*. Cambridge: Cambridge University Press.

Christie, Frances and James R. Martin (eds). 1997. *Genre and Institutions: Social Processes in the Workplace and School*. Continuum: London.

Dorgeloh, Heidrun and Anja Wanner (eds). 2010. *Syntactic Variation and Genre*. Berlin/New York: Mouton de Gruyter.

Elleström, Lars. 2010. The modalities of media: A model for understanding intermedial relations. In Lars Elleström (ed), *Media Borders, Multimodality and Intermediality*, 11–48. London: Palgrave.

Francesconi, Sabrina. 2011. Images and writing in tourist brochures. *Journal of Tourism and Cultural Change* 9(4): 341–356.

Gibson, James J. 1979. *The Ecological Approach to Visual Perception*, Boston: Houghton Miffin.

Halliday, Michael A. K. 1978. *Language as a Social Semiotic: The Social Interpretation of Language and Meaning*. London: Arnold.

Halliday, A. K. Michael and Christian M. I. M. Matthiessen. 2004. *An Introduction to Functional Grammar*. London: Arnold.

Hasan, Ruqaiya. 1996. *Ways of Saying: Ways of Meaning: Selected Papers of Ruqaiya Hasan*. Edited by Carmel Cloran, David Butt and Geoffrey Williams. London: Cassell.

Held, Gudrun. 2005. Magazine covers – a multimodal pretext-genre. *Folia Linguistica* XXXIX(1–2): 173–196.

Hiippala, Tuomo. 2007. Helsinki: A multisemiotic analysis of tourist brochures. Master's thesis, University of Helsinki.

Hiippala, Tuomo. 2012a. The localisation of advertising print media as a multimodal process. In Wendy L. Bowcher (ed.), *Multimodal Texts from Around the World: Linguistic and Cultural Insights*, 97–122. London: Palgrave.

Hiippala, Tuomo. 2012b. Reading paths and visual perception in multimodal research, psychology and brain sciences. *Journal of Pragmatics* 44(3): 315–327.

Hiippala, Tuomo. 2013. Modelling the structure of a multimodal artefact, PhD thesis, Department of Modern Languages, University of Helsinki. http://hdl.handle.net/10138/41736

Holsanova, Jana, Nils Holmberg, and Kenneth Holmqvist. 2009. Reading information graphics: the role of spatial contiguity and dual attentional guidance. *Applied Cognitive Psychology* 23: 1215–1226.

Kress, Gunther. 2009. What is mode? In Carey Jewitt (ed.), *The Routledge Handbook of Multimodal Analysis*, 54–67. London: Routledge.

Kvåle, Gunhild. 2010. Invitasjon til destinasjon: Multimodal retorikk i turistkommunikasjon. In Martin Engebretsen (ed.), *Skrift/bilde/lyd: Analyse av sammensatte tekster*, 39–55. Kristiansand: Hoyskoleforlaget.

Lemke, Jay L. 1999. *Typology, topology, topography: genre semantics*. MS University of Michigan.

Lemke, Jay L. 2001. Discursive technologies and the social organization of meaning. *Folia Linguistica* XXXV(1–2): 79–96.

Lemke, Jay L. 2005. Multimedia genres and traversals *Folia Linguistica* XXXIX(1–2): 45–56.

Lim, Victor F. 2004. Developing an integrative multi-semiotic model. In Kay L. O'Halloran (ed.), *Multimodal Discourse Analysis: Systemic Functional Perspectives*, 220–246. London: Continuum.
Mann, William C. and Sandra A. Thompson. 1988. Rhetorical Structure Theory: Toward a functional theory of text organization. *Text* 8(3): 243–281.
Martin, James R. 1992. *English Text: System and Structure*. Amsterdam: Benjamins.
Martin, James R. 1997. Analysing genre: functional parameters. In Frances Christie and James R. Martin (eds), *Genre and Institutions: Social Processes in the Workplace and School*, 3–39. London: Continuum.
Martin, James R. 1999. Modelling context: A crooked path of progress in contextual linguistics. In Mohsen Ghadessy (ed.), *Text and Context in Functional Linguistics*, 25–61. Vol. 169 of Amsterdam Studies in the Theory and History of Linguistic Science: Series IV – Current Issues In Linguistic Theory, Amsterdam: Benjamins.
Martin, James R. and David Rose. 2008. *Genre Relations: Mapping Culture*, London: Equinox.
Martinec, Radan. 2003. The social semiotics of text and image in Japanese and English software manuals and other procedures. *Social Semiotics* 13(1): 43–69.
Miller, Carolyn R. (1984). Genre as social action, *Quarterly Journal of Speech* 70: 151–167.
O'Halloran, Kay L. (2009). Historical changes in the semiotic landscape: from calculation to computation. In Carey Jewitt (ed.), *The Routledge Handbook of Multimodal Analysis*, 98–113. London: Routledge.
Parodi, Giovanni. 2010. Research challenges for corpus cross-linguistics and multimodal texts. *Information Design Journal* 18(1): 69–73.
Swales, M. John. 1990. *Genre analysis: English in Academic and Research Settings*. Cambridge: Cambridge University Press.
Taboada, Maite and William C. Mann. 2006. Rhetorical structure theory: looking back and moving ahead. *Discourse Studies* 8(3): 423–459.
Tan, Sabine. 2010. Modelling engagement in a web-based advertising campaign, *Visual Communication* 9(1): 91–115.
Thomas, Martin. 2007. Querying multimodal annotation: A concordancer for GeM. In *Proceedings of the Linguistic Annotation Workshop*, Association for Computational Linguistics, Prague, Czech Republic, 57–60. URL: http://www.aclweb.org/anthology/W/W07/W07-1510
Thomas, Martin. 2009. Localizing pack messages: A framework for corpus-based cross-cultural multimodal analysis, PhD thesis, University of Leeds.
van Leeuwen, Theo. 2005. Multimodality, genre and design, in Sigrid Norris and Rodney H. Jones (eds), *Discourse in Action: Introducing Mediated Discourse Analysis*, 73-94. London: Routledge.
Ventola, Eija. 1987. *The Structure of Social Interaction: A Systemic Approach to the Semiotics of Service Encounters*. London: Pinter.
Waller, Robert, Judy Delin and Martin Thomas. 2012. Towards a pattern language approach to document description. *Discours* 10. DOI: 10.4000/discours.8673.15

Acknowledgements

I would like to thank John Bateman and Ivan Berazhny for their insightful comments on earlier drafts of this chapter.

III Conducting multimodal research

Carey Jewitt
12 Multimodal approaches

Introduction

Multimodality is used to refer to a theory, a perspective, a methodological application or a field of enquiry. It attends to the full repertoire of resources that people use to communicate and represent phenomena and experiences including speech, sound, gesture, gaze, body posture and movement, writing, image and so on. Thus language/talk is not the given starting point or anchor for meaning. The use of these resources is understood as shaped by the social norms operating at the moment of making meaning, and influenced by the motivations and interests of people in a specific social context.

Multimodality has been taken up within four main disciplines: Conversation Analysis, Systemic Functional Linguistics, Anthropology, and Social Semiotics, and combinations of these. Theoretical and methodological connections distinguish the focus of these disciplines from other takes on communication and meaning making. Notably, the fine grained analysis and the need to understand the details of texts and interactions, the focus on meaning making as social and semiotic/material, the interest in the place of language within a communicational ensemble and the need to broaden conceptions of communication beyond language in order to understand social practices. The origins, key concepts, and focus of these disciplinary approaches to multimodality are outlined in this chapter.

Key terms: Anthropology, conversation analysis, social semiotics, systemic functional linguistics.

Conversation analysis and multimodality

Conversation analysis (CA) is a discipline that was developed by sociologists in the USA in the 1960s to investigate the social and situated use of language in the organization of action in situ. 'Action' is a central unit of analysis, with actions seen as being connected over time to constitute sequenced or chained. Originally CA focused exclusively on spoken interaction and it is known for its detailed, moment-by-moment transcription and analyses of speech (including voice, rhythm). Classic studies include analysis of talk-in-interaction such as phone calls or face-to-face meetings, and describe what its participants orient to and how they jointly accomplish the tasks at hand, for instance the role of turn taking as an organizing structure in talk (e.g. Sacks, Schegloff, and Jefferson, 1974).

Although much of CA analysis remains focused on speech, there is considerable acknowledgment that people always mobilize facial expression, gesture, and space in face-to-face situations – including when on the telephone (Mondada 2008). Video recordings are increasingly used in CA studies to conduct close observations of people's speech, gesture, physical interaction with artefacts and use of space, notably within workplace studies, interaction in auction houses, health consultation rooms and transport control rooms (Heath, Hindmarsh and Luff 2010), and work of archaeologists and air controllers (Goodwin 2000).

This work applies (and redefines) key concepts in CA to the study of multimodal communication, such as the opening and closing of interactional units, turn taking, and indexicality. It makes use of fine-grained transcription and analysis of short (e.g. 10 second) fragments of video recordings to explore how multimodal interaction unfolds moment-by-moment. It is this micro-analytic scale and the rigorous systematic attention to sequential interaction that distinguishes CA from most other approaches to multimodality that focus on texts and discourse on a larger scale (Streeck, Goodwin, LeBaron 2011). These studies demonstrate how people coordinate their actions and anticipate the actions of others in collaborative work; how people negotiate roles and position themselves in relation to others; and how participants use all parts of their body alongside or in the absence of speech to achieve this. Goodwin connects the CA shift toward multimodality with changes in how talk and interaction have been reconfigured or adapted by technology-remediated environments that re-orientate face-to-face communication (e.g. video conferencing) and provide new multimodal communicational challenges to be examined.

Conversation analysts define their work in terms of interaction and action rather than communication or multimodality: CA is firmly focused on the simultaneous structured exchange with an insistence 'that embodied interaction in *the material world*, which includes material objects and environments in the process of meaning making and action formation, is primary' (Streeck, Goodwin, LeBaron, 2011: 9). This contrasts with the analytical focus of some semiotic-orientated multimodal research, and with multimodal approaches focused on discreet modes. CA has its origins in talk-as-interaction, and much of its analytical tools are rooted in talk. It remains the case that for some CA analysts who draw on multimodal perspectives language is the most important form of interaction, and thus speech is regarded as the best analytical 'starting point' even when it is not the starting point within the interaction to be analyzed (Streeck, Goodwin, LeBaron, 2011: 12). For instance, it is routine for a CA analyst using video to start with what is said and to use the visual data to add to the understanding of the verbal. Nonetheless, the term multimodality is beginning to gain currency with CA and this disciplinary formation of action sequences has much to offer multimodality.

Systemic functional linguistics

Linguist Michael Halliday developed Systemic Functional Linguistics (SFL) in the early 1960's (Halliday 1985). It is a theory of language that is primarily concerned with what language does, and how it does it, with a focus on the linguistic choices present in a communicative utterance. This focus on meaning as choice provides the central theoretical framework for Systemic Functional approaches to multimodality to analyse the function and meaning of language use alongside other semiotic resources (Halloran 2004). Semiotic resources are theorised as realising three different meaning functions (known as meta-functions in SFL terms). This meta-functional system is used to interpret how a person's choice of a semiotic resource simultaneously indicates something about 'the world' (Ideational meaning), positions the interpreter in relation to someone or something (Interpersonal meaning) and produces a structured text (Textual meaning). SFL approaches to multimodality develop a theoretical framework for describing the meta-functional based systems for each semiotic resource and the intersemiotic mechanisms through which semiotic choices combine in multimodal discourse. The purpose of this theoretical framework is to analyse multimodal phenomena.

This disciplinary approach to multimodality involves a focus on describing the networks of choice available in a semiotic system and the choice of semiotic resources realises meaning – that is, the system in use. (This contrasts with CA and Anthropology that focus on linguistic and multimodal practices – resources in use.) SFL concepts and categories (e.g. the concepts of rank, clause, phase, stratification, register, and genre) are applied beyond language to support the development of systems for semiotic resources. The analytical focus is on accounting for and describing the semiotic instantiation of these – how a system achieves this focus, how the meta-functions are realized through the systems of meaning which constitute the meaning potential of semiotic resources, and how system choices integrate in multimodal phenomena to create meaning in the context of the situation and the context of culture.

The systemic functional linguistic emphasis is clear in Michael O'Toole's analysis of the Sydney opera house, for example, 'Like a clause in language, a building incorporates Types of Process and their Participants; its specific functions are modified in terms of material, size, colour and texture; and its component elements are organized taxonomically like lexical items in the vocabulary of our language'. (O'Toole, 2004: 15). This approach foregrounds choice of syntax – level rank-scale (a hierarchical organization of elements) as one of its starting points differentiating between the options available at lower ranks in relation to those available at higher ranks. This interest in rank choice is seen in the work of Anthony Baldry who argues for the 'need to show how meaning is built up as a series of functional units – typically sub-phases, phases' (Baldry, 2004: 84). His analysis of a car advert focuses on its phasal and meta-functional organization in order to show the values that are associated with the advert and to provide a systematic description of these. A SFL approach has been extended by Kay O'Halloran (2005) to examine the integration of mathematical symbolism, images and mathematical symbolism in mathematics texts, and semiosis in film (2004).

SFL development of multimodality aims to produce a meta-theory capable of theorizing semiotic resources, their functionality and meaning potential, and their integration in multimodal phenomena that are interpreted in the context of situation and culture. The emphasis is placed on understanding and describing semiotic resources and principles of their systems of choice in order to understand how people use these resources in social contexts for specific purposes. In summary a SFL approach to multimodality is primarily concerned with the multimodal system – understanding and examining semiotic resources as systems of meaning, rather than the sign maker or process of meaning making.

Anthropology and multimodality

Anthropology is a discipline that has evolved from its early origins in the late 1800's into a diverse interdisciplinary field combining cultural studies, linguistics and sociology. It studies the relationship between means of communication and cultural practices and culture, viewing language, gesture and other communicative means as cultural resources. Within Anthropology, notably linguistic anthropology, the methodological privileging of language is reflected in the number of studies based on the assumption that speech or writing is always dominant and carrying the 'essence' of meanings and through notions like 'non-verbal', 'paralinguistic' or 'context' to describe space, gesture, gaze etc.

Ethnography, and participant observation (video recording and interviews) are used to gather detailed documentation of what speakers say and do as they engage in daily social activities. The analytical focus is on how communicative practices come to have meaning, often in unexpected ways, in social and cultural contexts and how the use of communicative resources both presuppose and create social relations in cultural contexts (Duranti 1997). Some classic studies within this discipline have used ethnographic methods to document and analyze multimodal communication in ways that have informed a range of approaches (although they do not commonly use the term multimodality).

Edward Hall's work on proxemics, for example, *Silent Language* (1959) and *The Hidden Dimension* (1966), analyzed the many ways that people unconsciously structure micro-spaces through the distance they establish between themselves and others in everyday transactions, the organization of space in houses and buildings, as well as the layout of cities. Through detailed observation he provided insights into how people communicate without talking, with a focus on temporal and spatial dimensions, such as the physical distances people maintain, and how these practices are molded and patterned by cultural contexts. In their book *Discourses in Place* (2003) Scollon and Wong-Scollon combined the work of Hall, discourse studies and multimodal semiotics to explore how the physical, spatial and material characteristics of language as it is situated in the world give meaning to people's actions. Kress and van Leeuwen have also built on the work of Hall to theorize the semiotic potentials of visual distance and spatial arrangements.

Some anthropologists foreground the significance of particular modes and transcribe them in conjunction with speech or writing. In the study of the practices of musical traditions of Jazz and classical spaces, for example, Havilland (2011) examines the semiotic resources that musicians use to communicate with both in performance and in practice attending to talk, sounds musical and otherwise, bodies, physical objects, and space. He shows how the spaces in which musicians play are put to work for communicating: 'the layout of the playing area, its physical characteristics and those of the instruments, and the bodies of the musicians themselves – structure and are structured by musical and para-musical interaction, including what might be called social structure' (Haviland, 2011: 300). Through his micro-ethnographic observation he demonstrates 'how different problems of musical coordination arise, with solutions shaped by the spatial arrangements of musicians and their instruments, and as a result of constraints imposed by the musical traditions and the musical forms themselves' (ibid). With a focus on classroom interaction, McDermott et al. (1978) show that people are expected to respond to such shifts and notes the wide range of different modes and their mutually modifying effect, emphasizing the different potentials and constraints of different modes: they 'not only organize themselves posturally in relation to what they are doing together, but they take on the postures characteristic to what they are doing together at exactly the same moment' (McDermott et al., 1978: 257).

Social semiotics and multimodality

Social semiotics is a term introduced by Halliday in his book *Language as a social semiotic* (1978) and developed further by Robert Hodge and Gunther Kress in their book *Social Semiotics* (1988). Social semiotics argues against the traditional semiotic separation between language as a formal system and its use in the context of social relations and processes including power and ideology. This work informed the development of Critical Discourse Analysis (CDA) which also views language as a form of social practice and which focuses primarily on the ways social and political domination are reproduced in text and talk (Chouliaraki and Fairclough, 1999). Kress and van Leeuwen (2001, 2006) extended and adapted social semiotic concepts in combination with a range of other social theories that go beyond linguistics to theorize social meaning making across a number of semiotic modes; including Hall as noted in the previous section, interactional sociology particularly the work of Goffman, as well as film theorist Metz, art history and Iconography notably the work of Panofsky, and musicology.

In their book *Reading Images* (2006) Kress and van Leeuwen set out a social semiotic account of how meaning is realized visually, through concepts such as composition, modality and framing. Together they set out to describe available choices and visual semiotic resources as having meaning potentials and to show how choices of visual semiotic resources are used to communicate ideologies and discourses. This laid the groundwork for extending and adapting social semiotics across a range of other semiotic modes to describe their semiotic resources, material affordances, grammar-like organizing principles, and cultural references. This evolving inventory of semiotic modal resources includes Van Leeuwen's (1999) work on the materiality of the resources of sound, speech and music (e.g. pitch, volume, breathing, rhythm and so on). The work of Kress et al. (2001, 2005) analyses how these modes interact and interplay in the classroom.

A social semiotic approach to multimodality has a growing emphasis on how the context of communication and the sign maker shaped signs and meaning.

Social semiotic approaches to multimodality use a flexible notion of grammar, with a focus on people's situated use of resources rather than emphasizing the system of available resources. A primary focus of social semiotic multimodal analysis is on mapping how modal resources are used by people in a given community or social context. This foregrounds the question about what choices people make (from the resources available to them) and what motivates these choices. There is therefore a strong emphasis on the notion of context within social semiotic multimodal analysis. The context shapes the resources available for meaning making and how these are selected and designed. Signs, modes, and meaning making are treated as relatively fluid, dynamic and open systems intimately connected to the social context of use. There is less focus on the development of general modal networks and systems. Research within this approach is concerned with the resources of modes, gesture or image for example, but this concern centers on mapping resources through detailed observational accounts of these mode as they are realized in a given social context.

Combined approaches to multimodality

Leading scholars in the field of multimodality have developed approaches that combine elements from the disciplines outlined in the previous section with a range of theories and methods. Here three notable examples are foregrounded.

Multimodal Interactional Analysis (Norris 2004; Norris and Jones 2005) draws on theories of mediated discourse, gesture studies, sociolinguistics, social semiotic approaches to multimodality, and the ethnographic study of the everyday identity construction. Norris's focus is on social interaction and the variety of modes and inter-semiotic relationships brought into and constitutive of social interaction, identities and relations, with a particular interest in habitus and embodiment (Norris 2009). An important consequence of this focus on multimodal interaction is that the modal system is no longer a primary concern. Modes are understood as made and constituted through interaction and action, and thus there is no notion of a modal system outside of interaction – mode, social actor, and context are too intimately connected to tear apart (Norris 2009).

Multimodality has been brought together with concepts and practices of corpus linguistics in interesting ways, notably in the work of John Bateman and colleagues on multimodal genre (2008). This work combines practices of corpus linguistics with multimodal concepts developed from social semiotics

(Kress and van Leeuwen), genre theory (Jay Lemke) and film theory. Through his empirical studies Bateman has examined how the notion of genre is realized across different modes and texts and developed methods for the corpus analysis of multimodal documents.

Scholars working within literacy have combined Multimodality with New literacy Studies (NLS) to explore the physical semiotic features of a text as signifiers of contextual meanings as well as where, how, and by whom a text is made (Street, Pahl and Rowsell, 2009). New Literacy Studies is used to provide a lens through which to theorize literacy as a set of situated social practices, while multimodality provides conceptual tools to get at the material qualities of texts and how ideologies become materialized in texts.

In short, multimodal approaches to meaning making can be combined with different social science theories in innovative and productive ways that extend multimodal research, and understanding of representation and communication.

Conclusions

This chapter has provided a brief introduction to the complex contemporary landscape of multimodality, its origins and current forms, connections and divergences. Each of these disciplinary takes on multimodality described in this section is valid and useful, however, each offers a particular starting point and pathway into multimodal research. The question of which perspective is 'best' is dependent on the interests of a researcher and what it is that they want to investigate.

Further readings

Jewitt, Carey (ed.). 2013. *The Routledge Handbook of Multimodal Analysis*, Second Edition. London: Routledge.

Project idea

Discuss the similarities and differences between the various approaches to multimodality as explicated in this chapter.

References

Baldry, Anthony. 2004. Phase and transition, type and instance: patterns in media texts as seen through a multimodal concordance. In Kay O'Halloran (ed.), *Multimodal Discourse Analysis: Systemic Functional Perspectives*, 83–108. London/New York: Continuum.

Bateman, John. 2008. *Multimodality and Genre: A Foundation for the Systematic Analysis of multimodal documents*. London: Palgrave Macmillan

Goodwin, Charles, Jürgen Streeck and Curtis LeBaron (eds.). 2011. *Research on Human Behavior, Action, and Communication*. Cambridge/New York: Cambridge University Press.

Chouliaraki, Lilie and Norman Fairclough. 1999. *Discourse in Late Modernity: Rethinking Critical Discourse Analysis*. Edinburgh: Edinburgh University Press

Duranti, Alessandro. 2001. Linguistic anthropology. In *International Encyclopedia of the Social and Behavioral Sciences*. Elsevier Science.

Goodwin, Charles. 2000. Action and embodiment within situated human interaction. *Journal of Pragmatics*, 32: 1489–522.

Hall, Edward T. 1959. *The Silent Language*. Garden City, New York: Doubleday.

Hall, Edward T. 1966. *The Hidden Dimension*. Garden City, New York: Doubleday.

Halliday, Michael A. K. 1978. *Language as Social Semiotic: The Social Interpretation of Language and Meaning*. London: Edward Arnold.

Halliday, Michael A. K. 1985. *An Introduction to Functional Grammar*. London: Edward Arnold.

Havilland, John, B. 2011. Musical spaces. In Goodwin, Charles, Jürgen Streeck and Curtis LeBaron (eds.), *Research on Human Behavior, Action, and Communication*: 289–304. Cambridge/New York: Cambridge University Press.

Heath, Christian, Jon Hindmarsh, Paul Luff. 2010. *Qualitative Video Analysis*. London: Routledge.

Hodge, Robert and Gunther Kress. 1988. *Social Semiotics*. Cambridge: Polity.

Kress, Gunther and Theo van Leeuwen. 2001. *Multimodal Discourse: The Modes and Media of Contemporary Communication*. London: Arnold.

Kress, Gunther and Theo van Leeuwen. 2006. *Reading Images: The Grammar of Visual Design*. London: Routledge.

Kress, Gunther, Carey Jewitt, Jill Bourne, Anton Franks, John Hardcastle, Ken Jones, and Euan Reid. 2004. *Urban Classrooms, Subject English: Multimodal Perspectives on Teaching and Learning*. London: Routledge Falmer.

Kress, Gunther, Carey Jewitt, Jon Ogborn, and Charalampos Tsatsarelis. 2001. *Multimodal Teaching and Learning: The Rhetorics of the Science Classroom*. London: Continuum.

McDermott, Ray, Kenneth Gospodinoff and Jeffrey Aron. 1978. Criteria for an ethnographically adequate description of concerted activities and their contexts. *Semiotica* 24(3–4): 245–276.

Mondada, Lorenza. 2008. Using Video for a Sequential and Multimodal Analysis of Social Interaction: Videotaping Institutional Telephone Calls. Forum Qualitative Social Research / Forum: Qualitative Social Research. Available at: <http://www.qualitativeresearch.net/index.php/fqs/article/view/1161/2566>. Date accessed: 18 Jun. 2012.

Norris, Sigrid. 2009. Modal density and modal configurations: multimodal actions. In Carey Jewitt (ed.), *The Routledge Handbook of Multimodal Analysis*, 78–90. London: Routledge.

Norris, Sigrid. 2004. *Analyzing Multimodal Interaction: A Methodological Framework*. London: Routledge.

Norris, Sigrid and Rodney Jones (eds.). 2005. *Discourse in Action: Introducing Mediated Discourse Analysis*. London/New York: Routledge.

O'Halloran, Kay L. 2005. *Mathematical Discourse: Language, Symbolism and Visual Images*. London/New York: Continuum.

O'Halloran, Kay L. (ed.) 2004. *Multimodal Discourse Analysis*. London: Continuum.

O'Toole, Michael. 1994. *The Language of Displayed Art*. London: Leicester University Press.

Sacks, Harvey, Emanuel A. Schegloff and Gail Jefferson. 1974. A Simplest Systematics for the Organisation of Turn-taking for Conversation. *Language* 50(4/1): 696–735.

Scollon, Ron and Suzie Scollon. 2003. *Discourses in Place: Language in the Material World*. New York: Routledge.

Street, Brian, Kate Pahl and Jennifer Rowsell. 2009. Multimodality and New Literacy studies. In Carey Jewitt (ed.) *The Routledge Handbook of Multimodal Analysis*, 191–201. London: Routledge.

Van Leeuwen, Theo. 1999. *Speech, Music, Sound*. London: Macmillan Press.

Van Leeuwen, Theo. 2005. *Introducing Social Semiotics*. London: Routlegde.

Kay L. O'Halloran and Victor Lim Fei
13 Systemic functional multimodal discourse analysis

Introduction

Systemic Functional Multimodal Discourse Analysis (SF-MDA) is an extension of Michael Halliday's Systemic Functional Theory (SFT) which informs Systemic Functional Linguistics (SFL). Halliday originally developed SFL for teaching Mandarin in his seminal paper Grammatical Categories in Modern Chinese (Halliday 1956/1976) (see Fawcett 2000) before extending the approach to the English language (e.g. Halliday 1994; Halliday and Matthiessen 2004). Halliday (1985: 4) explains that linguistics is a "kind of semiotics" because language is viewed as "one among a number of systems of meaning that, taken all together, constitute human culture". Therefore, SFT is a theory of meaning, which was first applied to language through SFL, and more recently through SF-MDA to other semiotic resources (e.g. O'Halloran 2008, see Knox 2009).

Key terms: Multimodal analytics and state-transition diagrams.

Systemic functional multimodal discourse analysis

Halliday (1978) uses the term 'social semiotics' to describe "the way people use semiotic 'resources' both to produce communicative artefacts and events and to interpret them ..." (van Leeuwen 2005: xi). SF-MDA is the sub-field of social semiotics that focuses on the 'grammatics' of semiotic resources with a view to understanding the contributions of different resources and the meanings which arise as semiotic choices combine in multimodal phenomena over space and time. The SF-MDA approach is based on Halliday's premise that the organization of semiotic resources reflects the social functions which the resources are required to play. The key concepts of SF-MDA are described below and a sample analysis of a video text is provided. Following this, we discuss the advantages of the SF-MDA approach which include the development of 'multimodal analytics' (O'Halloran, E and Tan 2013) for the systematic study of semantic patterns in multimodal texts.

Systemic

The use of the term 'systemic' in SF-MDA follows Halliday's (1985: 4) view of social systems and "modes of cultural behaviour" as inter-related systems of meaning which construe social interactions and practices, and indeed society itself. Halliday (1978: 12) sees semiotic resources and society as a "unified conception" which needs to "be investigated as a whole". The same understanding is extended to the inextricable relationship between multimodal semiotic resources and society in SF-MDA. In this case, the principle that "[c]ontext determines systems in language; but it is also construed by them" (Matthiessen 1995: 33) is extended to multimodal resources.

The term 'systemic' also describes the underlying organization of semiotic resources which enable the resources to be used for different purposes. The systems of meaning are typically modeled as inter-related 'system networks' (e.g. Halliday and Matthiessen 2004; Martin 1992; Martin and Rose 2007; Kress and van Leeuwen 2006 [1996]) to describe the meaning potentials of semiotic resources. The options in the systems represent the paradigmatic choices from which selections are made in multimodal texts. In addition, parametric systems are used to model simultaneous systems for certain 'modes' of meaning (e.g. sound quality, colour and typography) (e.g. van Leeuwen 1999, 2009, 2010; see also Kress and van Leeuwen 2001). Parametric system choices are described as graduations on a scale between two opposite poles (e.g. sound quality: tense/lax, loud/soft, high/low, rough/smooth and so forth) (van Leeuwen 1999), rather than discrete options in the system networks.

The paradigmatic options modeled through system networks and/or parametric systems foreground the importance of choice in SFT. Halliday (1994: xiv) explains that "systemic theory is a theory of meaning as choice, by which language, or any other semiotic system, is interpreted as networks of interlocking options". As Halliday (1994: xiv–xxvi) further explains, the choice is "not a conscious decision made in real time but a set of possible alternatives" from which choices are made in actual texts. These choices usually "result from a convention followed unthinkingly, a habit acquired unreflectively, or an unconscious impulse" (van Leeuwen 1999: 29). Such choices are always, however, motivated according to the interests of the meaning-maker (e.g. Kress 1993, 2010).

Other key principles in SFT are stratification and constituency, where the semiotic resources are conceptualized according to strata and ranks. In terms of stratification, it is understood that language has an expression stratum (i.e. the actual words and sounds) and a content stratum (i.e. meaning and context) (Halliday 1994/1985, Halliday and Matthiessen 2004). In terms of constituency, the different levels in the content stratum are constituents of higher ones (e.g. language is organized according to the ranks of word, phrase, clause and clause complex). While the degree of fidelity to these principles differs in the various approaches to multimodality, the SF-MDA approach generally adheres to these principles and applies them to the other semiotic resources where appropriate. For instance, O'Toole (2011 [1994]) extends the principle of constituency to images in his seminal work *Language of Displayed Art* where he organizes images according to the ranks of Member, Figure, Episode and Work. Likewise, O'Toole (2004) applies the same principles and approach for the analysis of the Sydney Opera House. Baldry (2004: 84), in his analysis of television advertisements, also argues "for the need to show how meaning is built up as a series of functional units – typically sub-phases, phases, but also potentially macrophases, minigenres and genres".

One of the advantages of foregrounding the notions of meaning potential and choice in inter-locking systems along the principles of constituency and stratification in the SF-MDA approach is, as Machin (2009: 182) observes in O'Toole's (2011 [1994]) approach to displayed art, "to replace terms such as 'evoke' and 'suggest' that we often use to discuss works of art with systematic and stable terms that allowed us to talk in concrete terms about how such a composition communicates". This is enabled through the meta-language which SFT offers and the theoretical perspective which SF-MDA presents.

Functional

SFT is concerned with the functional meanings of semiotic resources in society. Halliday (1994: xiii) explains that the use of the term 'functional' in SFT is critical "because the conceptual framework on which it [the approach] is based is a functional one rather than a formal one". As Halliday states, "[e]very text ... unfolds in some context of use". As such, SFT aims to conceptualize, analyze and interpret meanings in different social contexts.

For Halliday (1978: 2), language as a social semiotic means "interpreting language within a sociocultural context, in which the culture itself is interpreted in semiotic terms as an information system". Hence, a major tenet in SFT is that meaning is made and can only be interpreted in context. Halliday and Hasan (1985) conceptualize the context of situation, that is, the immediate environment in which a particular instance of language is actually occurring, namely the field (what is happening), tenor (who is taking part) and mode (role assigned to language) of discourse. In addition to the context of situation (register) stratum,

Martin (1992) develops the context of culture (genre) as a higher stratum. Martin (1992) models language and context through the concept of semogenesis; that is, the unfolding of meanings along different time scales (e.g. the text, the individual and culture). The notion of context is also important in critical discourse analysis, as observed by Machin (2009: 189): "it is notable that two of the best-known critical discourse analysts, van Dijk (1993) and Fairclough (1995), both stress the need for contextual knowledge". In keeping with this, the SF-MDA approach interprets meanings made by the semiotic resources within its specific contexts of situation and culture.

Halliday's (1978) social semiotic theory models the functions of language (i.e. the meaning potential) in terms of four metafunctions: 1) interpersonal meaning: to enact social relations; 2) experiential meaning: to express our experience of the world; 3) logical meaning: to make logical connections in that world; and 4) textual meaning: to organize the message. Similarly, the meaning potential of the various semiotic resources is also described metafunctionally in SF-MDA. The metafunctional organization of meanings is particularly useful because it provides a common set of fundamental principles to compare semiotic resources and the meanings which arise when semiotic choices integrate in multimodal texts. That is, the organization of metafunctional meanings offers a unifying platform for studying semiotic resources and their inter-semiotic relations.

Multimodal

Within SFT, there has always been recognition that language is but one of the many semiotic resources used in meaning making. For instance, Halliday and Hasan (1985: 4) articulate:

> There are many other modes of meaning, in any culture, which are outside the realm of language. These will include both art forms such as painting, sculpture, music, the dance, and so forth, and other modes of cultural behaviour that are not classified under the heading of forms of art, such as modes of exchange, modes of dress, structures of the family, and so forth. These are all bearers of meaning in the culture. Indeed we can define a culture as a set of semiotic systems, as a set of systems of meaning, all of which interrelate.
> (Halliday and Hasan 1985: 4)

The term 'multimodal' describes both the nature of discourse and the type of approach undertaken in SF-MDA. Adding the modifier 'multimodal' to describe the nature of any discourse is probably unnecessary, given that all discourses are arguably multimodal. However, given that most discourse analysis approaches have tended to focus on language or a specific semiotic resource, the inclusion of the modifier 'multimodal' serves to differentiate the SF-MDA approach and theoretical orientation from other approaches to multimodal texts.

Discourse

Gee (1990/2008) specifies the distinction between the terms 'Discourse' and 'discourse'. "A Discourse is a socially accepted association among ways of using language, of thinking, feeling, believing, valuing, and of acting that can be used to identify oneself as a member of a socially meaningful group or 'social network', or to signal (that one is playing) a socially meaningful 'role'" (Gee 1990: 143). However, discourse (i.e. not capitalized) is simply "connected stretches of language that make sense, like conversations, stories, reports, arguments, essays; 'discourse' is part of 'Discourse' – 'Discourse' with a big 'D' is always more than just language" (Gee 1990: 142). SF-MDA aligns with Gee's (1990/2008) use of 'Discourse' and follows Kress and van Leeuwen's (2001: 4) general definition of it as "socially constructed knowledge of (some aspect of) reality".

Jewitt (2009: 31) observes that "O'Halloran's multimodal discourse analysis approaches 'discourse' at the micro-textual level". While detailed fine-grained analysis is a distinctiveness of the SF-MDA approach, the discourse is also related to the macro-social context and vice versa, following the underlying principles of SFT. O'Halloran (2011: 135), for example, emphasizes that "[c]ontext is an essential part of any analysis, not just the immediate context of situation (the ... event and subsequent resemiotizations of that event), but the context of culture in general". In explaining that SF-MDA "reveals how instances of multimodal semiotic choices function inter-semiotically in ways which ultimately create and answer to larger patterns of social context and culture", O'Halloran (2011), in a sense, draws the conection from discourse to Discourse.

Analysis

One of the distinctive features of SF-MDA is the bottom-up orientation where theories and ideologies are extrapolated from the intensive analysis of actual texts. A rigorous analysis in SF-MDA usually involves detailed transcription and annotation of the multimodal corpus. Working with multimodal texts is demanding because of many and often complex parameters and dimensions involved, particularly for videos, hypertext and other dynamic media. For example, the

SF-MDA approach takes into account the semiotic resources, metafunctions, systems (at different levels), system choices and the inter-semiotic relations which unfold across space and/or time in multimodal texts.

Existing analytical approaches in multimodal studies include repeated viewing of data at variable speeds, and zooming into marked or particularly unusual occurrences. As Flewitt (2006: 28) explains, the video sequence can be reviewed "several times, with sound, without sound, in real time, slow motion and fast forward". While repeated viewings of multimodal sequences are essential in many cases, the resulting interpretation may be more discursive than empirical if comprehensive transcriptions and annotations are not undertaken. That is, fine-grained multimodal analysis presents empirical evidence to support the claims made about the text and context. O'Halloran (2009: 101) explains that SF-MDA "transcends the boundaries of a discursive description through the analysis of the actual choices which are made against the backdrop of other possible choices which could have been made".

Sample SF-MDA Analysis

The SF-MDA approach is demonstrated through an analysis of the 'Dreams' television advertisement commissioned by the Republic of Singapore Air Force (RSAF)[1] (O'Halloran, Tan and E 2013). The advertisement is part of an ongoing integrated campaign in Singapore involving television, online, outdoor and print platforms to advertise careers with the RSAF. The career advertisements target a broad spectrum of viewers (e.g. children, young people and parents) with view to promoting a promising career with the RSAF. In this case, the 'Dreams' advertisement works on the basis that all children (and their parents) have dreams and aspirations about the future that can be fulfilled through a RSAF career.

O'Halloran, Tan and E (2013) investigate the connotative ideas, values and myths (Barthes [1957], 1987) in the 'Dreams' advertisement, which are interpreted in relation to the role of the military in Singapore. The analysis is undertaken using prototype software developed in the Multimodal Analysis Lab at the National University of Singapore. The advertisement was found to focus on positive personal qualities and cultural values such as dreams, freedom, ambition and hope, where scenes of children engaging in childhood activities like flying kites, cycling and playing with paper planes are contrasted to air force activities, capabilities and infrastructure. As O'Halloran, Tan and E (2013)

Systemic functional multimodal discourse analysis — 143

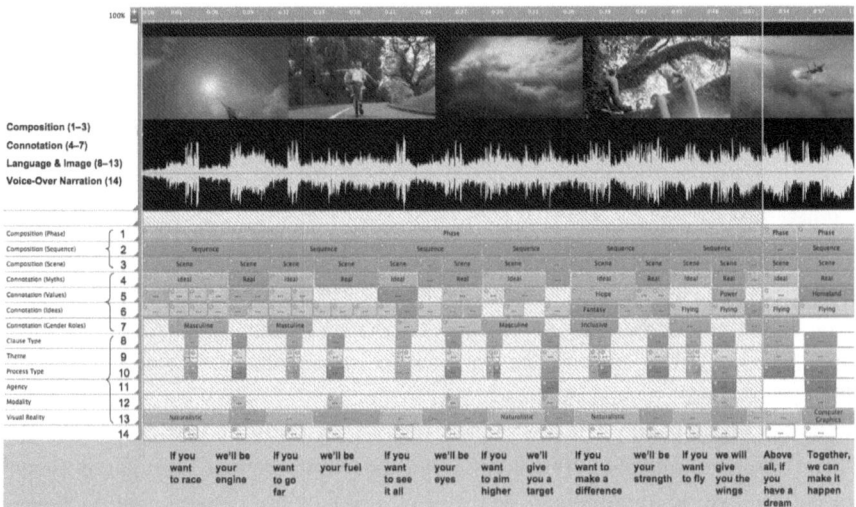

Figure 1: SF-MDA Analysis of 'Dreams' Advertisement

explain, "[t]hese contrasting scenes move towards a climax which reinforces the primary message that the RSAF is the ideal employer if one aims to achieve the various manifestations of success referred to in the advertisement". The 'Dreams' advertisement is a career advertisement that promotes RSAF as a technologically advanced military force that plays a prominent role in Singapore society.

To enrich this higher-level connotative analysis, a SF-MDA approach is adopted to analyze the specific semiotic selections from language, images and music which orchestrate the climax of the advertisement where certain values, attitudes, and beliefs are reinforced. As we shall see, the SF-MDA approach encompasses both orders of analysis; that is, the higher-order analysis undertaken by O'Halloran, Tan and E (2013) and the fine-grained analysis presented here. In fact, O'Halloran, Tan and E (2013) discuss the semiotic choices which construct the connotative meanings of the 'Dreams' advertisement, but do not present a systemic analysis of these choices as they combine over time. In this case, we present the connotative analysis in relation to SF-MDA semiotic analysis using *Multimodal Analysis Video* software[2] (see Figure 1) which permits time-stamped annotations for the different systems to be coded and stored in database for later retrieval and analysis.

O'Halloran, Tan and E (2013) analyze the composite structure of the 'Dreams' advertisement in terms of scenes (camera remains in one time-space), sequences (camera moves with specific characters/sub-topics) and phases (patterns of inter-semiotic choices), following Baldry and Thibault (2006). There are 3 phases (i.e. Phases 1–3), 8 sequences and 16 scenes in the 'Dreams' advertisement, as displayed in rows 1–3 in Figure 1, where Phase 1 has been highlighted using the selection tool (which permits repeated viewings of video segments) in *Multimodal Analysis Video* software. O'Halloran, Tan and E (2013) analyze the connotative myths of the 'Ideal' world of childhood dreams and the 'Real' world of the RSAF in Phases 1–3 terms of values (i.e. happiness, freedom, power, homeland, intelligence, achievement, hope, safety and security and ambition) and ideas (i.e. flying, technology, fantasy, nature, help, wonder and curiosity) which, in some cases, have gender roles attached to them (masculine, feminine and inclusive). The connotative analysis for the myths, values and ideas for Phases 1–3 are displayed in rows 4–7 in Figure 1.

The climax of the 'Dreams' advertisement occurs in Phases 2–3, where the 'Ideal' world of ambition and flying (with masculine gender role) is contrasted to the 'real' world of homeland security and RSAF fighter planes (with no gender role attached). In what follows, the semiotic choices which construct the climax (see rows 8–13 in Figure 1) are analysed to investigate how the main message of the 'Dreams' advertisement is communicated and emphasised through the orchestration of specific linguistic and visual choices which both reinforce and contrast the choices made in Phase 1. The textual organization (in terms of the clause relations and topic of the clause), experiential meaning (in terms of process type and agency) and interpersonal meaning (in terms of modality or truth value) of the linguistic selections and the visual reality of the scenes are examined. In addition, the music in the soundtrack is also considered. As O'Halloran, Tan and E (2013) claim, the climax is effective for reasons which are further explored below.

Language

The linguistic choices in the male voice-over narration in the 'Dreams' advertisement form a pattern of clause complexes (see transcription in Figure 1), where a causal-conditional dependent clause (e.g. "If you want to race") is logically connected to the independent clause (e.g. [then] "we'll be your engine") (see 'Clause Type' in row 8 in Figure 1). The textual organization is marked (i.e. atypical) in the sense that the point of departure is the dependent clause. The length of the clause complex in Phases 2–3 is considerably longer (given the pauses in the voice-over narration) for added effect, even though these phases are considerably shorter than Phase 1 (see Figure 1).

The marked organization of clause complexes is consistent throughout the entire 'Dreams' advertisement. However, in the final clause complex "Above all, if you have a dream, together we can make it happen" in Phases 2–3, the marked textual organization extends to the two clauses in the clause complex, where the topics "above all" and "together" form the points of departure for the dependent and independent clauses respectively (see 'Theme' in row 9 in Figure 1). The marked organization of the clauses provides a contrast to earlier selections and increases the intensity of the message which is delivered in the climax.

Experientially, the viewer is positioned as having aspirations ("if you want") for certain actions ("to race", "to go far", "to aim higher" and "to fly"), perceptions ("to see it all") and positive attributes ("to make a difference" and "to have a dream") (see 'Process Type' in row 10 in Figure 1). In Phases 2–3, there are two attributive relational processes selected, which forms a contrast with previous process selections. The marked textual organization of the first clause ("above all, if you have a dream") reinforces the main premise of the advertisement while playing on the notion that RSAF is "above all", both literally (i.e. in the sky) and metaphorically (i.e. in terms of capability, infrastructure etc). In "together we can make it happen" in Phase 3, the viewer and the RSAF are bought "together", suggesting a collective responsibility where both the viewer (i.e. the potential candidate and his family) and the RSAF must collaborate to "make it happen". In a sense, Phase 3 can be likened to a call for action, which is a common generic feature in advertisements.

The only participant granted agency in the 'Dreams' advertisement is RSAF (i.e. "we will give you a target" and "we will give you the wings") until the final clause where the viewer joins forces with the RSAF ("we can make it happen") (see 'Agency' in Strip 11 in Figure 1), adding emphasis in the climax where the connotative vale of homeland security and ideas about flying are synchronized.

In terms of interpersonal meaning, the statements provide information for viewers. The modality (or truth value) is consistent through the choice of "will" until the last clause when the modality changes to "can", which suggests both the ability and commitment of the RSAF to "make it happen" (see 'Modality' in row 12 in Figure 1).

The linguistic choices in Phases 2–3 in the 'Dream' advertisement form patterns of textual, logical, experiential and interpersonal choices, where certain meanings are reinforced (e.g. logical meanings in the dependent–independent clause complexes) and others are contrasted (e.g. the marked topics "above all' and "together", relational attributive processes, agency for RSAF and "we", and the change in modality to "can") in the climax of the advertisement. As we shall see, the visual and music resources also unfold in recognizable patterns to co-contextualize and reinforce the message which reinforces ambition, flying and homeland security.

Image

As O'Halloran, Tan and E (2013) explain, the visual sequences in the 'Dream' advertisement are presented in an 'Ideal–Real' format (see row 4 in Figure 1) where childhood activities are contrasted with the real activities of the RSAF. The idealized world of childhood is presented in naturalistic colours, with added sepia effects for nostalgic purposes (see row 13 in Figure 1), while the real world of the RSAF takes the form of computer-generated images which construct a 'hyperreal' world where simulations stand for reality (e.g. Eco 1987; Baudrillard 1994). In effect, the 'real' world of the RSAF moves beyond dreams and reality itself.

The parallelism is broken for strategic effect in Phases 2–3 where the ideal world of the dream (a boy in a bomber jacket and goggles) merges with the world of the RSAF (a squadron of fighter planes) in the same visual frame. The personification of this merger is the boy in a bomber jacket and goggles who bears a look of determination on his face. Hence, the climax of the 'Dreams' advertisement is achieved when the dream-like sequences of Phase 1 are replaced with the boy who embodies the potential talent which the RSAF is seeking to recruit. The final scenes in Phase 3 are images of the sky with the slogans of "Above all" and "dream", where the squadron of RSAF planes emerges from clouds to fly over the modern Singapore landscape. The planes fly towards the viewer while forming a frame around the words 'Republic of Singapore, The Air Force, Above All'. The planes disappear and the final frame contains the written text, the website for RSAF careers and associated logos which reinforce the 'call to action' which is effected linguistically.

Music

The music in the soundtrack in the 'Dreams' advertisement adds to the dramatic effect. As O'Halloran, Tan and E (2013) explain, a 'bell-like riff' is layered and repeated throughout the entire advertisement without a change in texture or rhythm. Instrumental and percussion sounds are added to create a fuller effect as the advertisement unfolds with an increased tempo. The effect is heightened in the climax with the extended voice-over narration (see sound wave in Figure

1). In this way, the music functions to achieve the desired effect in Phases 3, accompanied by the loud sound effects for the RSAF planes in the final scene.

Language, image and sound

The orchestration of the linguistic, visual and music selections function to foreground certain logical, experiential and interpersonal meanings which co-contextualize each other to powerfully communicate the meaning of the 'Dreams' advertisement where 'the emphatic climax that creates the desired impact' (O'Halloran, Tan and E 2013). As we have seen, the semiotic choices in Phases 2–3 form repeated and contrasting patterns to Phase 1, where the connotative ideas (i.e. ambition, flying and homeland security) reinforce established ideologies in Singapore in juxtaposition with symbols of Singapore's success (i.e. the Singapore landscape with Marina Bay and the Central Business District) in a hyperreal world which is both appealing and emphatic. As O'Halloran, Tan and E (2013) claim, "[it] is by no means a coincidence that the final scene features these two iconic symbols which the targeted viewer can have a part in protecting Singapore as a member of the RSAF".

The SF-MDA approach to the 'Dreams' advertisement demonstrates how "naturalized" knowledge presents a platform for investigating ideologies, in this case where the important role of the armed forces is integrated into the consciousness of Singapore society. The military has also recognized the need to brand their institutions in order to attract the best talent in Singapore, as illustrated in this advertisement. While the multimodal analysis provided here is not exhaustive, it serves to indicate how the lens afforded by the SF-MDA approach helps to comprehend the meanings of multimodal texts and the semiotic strategies which realize those meanings. In what follows, we explore the benefits of the SF-MDA approach.

SF-MDA and multimodal analytics

The SF-MDA approach provides several distinct advantages with regard to the analysis and interpretation of multimodal texts. Firstly, SF-MDA offers a comprehensive theoretical framework for modeling semiotic resources based on the metafunctional principle where the internal organization of semiotic resources is seen to reflect their respective functions. This permits the semantic contributions of semiotic choices and the meaning arising from the inter-semiotic relations between semiotic choices at different levels of analysis to be investigated. In this way, the SF-MDA approach attempts to bridge the semantic gap between the low-level features (i.e. the actual words, images and sound track) and their associated strands of meaning to be interpreted in relation to the situational and cultural context of the multimodal text.

Secondly, the actual analysis of the multimodal text provides feedback into the SF-MDA theoretical framework and systems, leading to a 'bottom-up' and 'top-down' recursive process which tests the productivity of the proposed SF-MDA frameworks. This iterative process informs the system and serves to advance the theoretical understanding of multimodal semiosis based on empirical analysis (e.g. see Lim 2011). In the iterative process between 'theory guiding practice' and 'practice informing theory' (e.g. see Norris 2012), the analytical interpretation of the multimodal text is enriched and the theoretical apparatus is refined. As O'Halloran and Smith (2013) note, "both the empiricism of detailed, exhaustive text analysis (coping with the challenges this raises) and the ongoing problematisation and exploration of theoretical generalization and abstraction are needed for the development of resources and the practice of multimodal text analysis". As the SF-MDA approach relates the close multimodal analysis to larger social systems and processes, the approach may be used to investigate the 'resemiotization' of social practices (Iedema 2001, 2003) over space and time.

Thirdly, as demonstrated in this paper, the SF-MDA approach lends itself to the development and use of specialist multimodal analysis software to alleviate the complexity and time-consuming nature of multimodal analysis (e.g. O'Halloran, Podlasov, Chua and E 2012; Smith, Tan, Podlasov and O'Halloran 2011). Software applications such as *Multimodal Analysis Video* provide facilities and functionalities for entering system networks and transcriptions and performing time-stamped and/or spatial annotations which are stored in an integrated database for later retrieval and analysis. From the beginning, systemic functional theory lent itself to computational approaches (e.g. Halliday 2005; O'Donnell and Bateman 2005).

Fourthly, the SF-MDA approach leads to 'multimodal analytics' where the complex multidimensional data structures arising from close multimodal analysis are interpreted using mathematical techniques and scientific visualizations to detect multimodal semantic patterns which otherwise would not be discernible. For example, the mathematical techniques that have been applied to multimodal data include singular value decomposition and recurrence diagrams (E et al., 2012), temporal interval logic (O'Halloran, E, Podlasov and Tan 2013) and k-means clustering (O'Halloran, Tan and E, in press-b). In this way, the complexity of the multimodal data is reduced in order to capture patterns and trends which can be visualized and related to higher orders of analysis.

In addition, state-transition diagrams have been used to display configurations of systemic choices in dynamic media such as videos (e.g. Podlasov, Tan

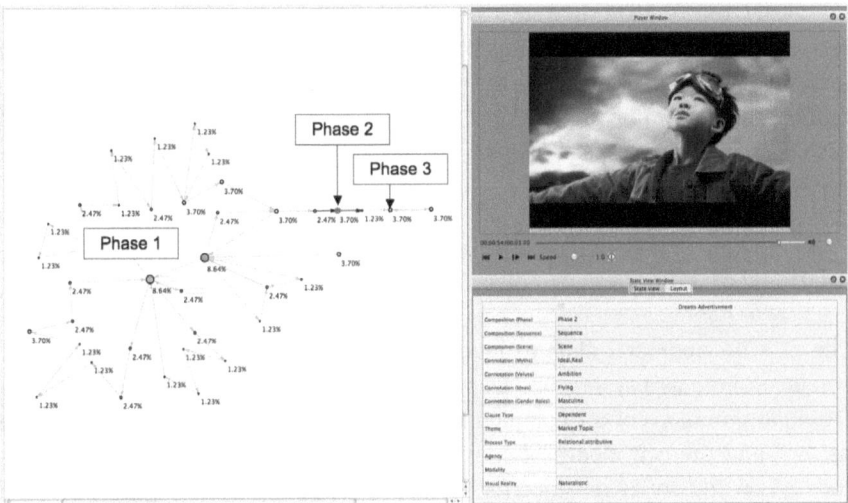

Figure 2: State-Transition Diagram

and O'Halloran 2012; Lim, O'Halloran and Podlasov 2012). For example, the state-transition diagram for the 'Dreams' advertisement in Figure 2 was generated using functionalities in *Multimodal Analysis Video* software which converts the time-stamped multimodal data into a visualization where the different 'states' or combinations of systemic selections are displayed. In this case, the 'nodes' in the visualization display the compositional, connotative, linguistic and visual choices made in the different phases, sequences and scenes in 'Dreams' advertisement and 'transitions' indicate the movement between those different states. The state transition visualization is dynamic so that the nodes and transitions are highlighted as the video is played. In this way, the overall patterns of systemic choices in the video and the time allocated to those combinations of choices are discerned and related to higher levels of analysis in the video. For example, the state-transition diagram in Figure 2 shows that the multiple states in Phase 1 connect to two main states (i.e. 'Real' and 'Flying'; and 'Ideal', 'Happiness-Innocence', 'Flying' and 'Masculine'), each of which occupy 8.65% of the total time in the 'Dreams' advertisement. Phase 2 commences in the scene where the 'Real' merges the 'Ideal' in the form of the boy with the bomber jacket and goggles (as displayed in Figure 2). From here, Phase 3 unfolds as the climax of the advertisement with new combinations of multimodal choices which connect flying and the RSAF with values of homeland security in modern-day Singapore. As we can see from Figure 2, the combinations of systemic choices in Phases 2 and 3 are different from those found in Phase 1.

Lastly, the SF-MDA approach permits the semantic patterns in multimodal text types and genres to be compared and contrasted. In this way, SF-MDA and multimodal analytics embrace the goals of digital humanities, which aim to harness the power of computational and visualization techniques to understand socio-cultural patterns and trends, in this case informed by social semiotic theory.

Conclusion

The SF-MDA approach aims to investigate the 'complementarities' of semiotic resources, both as a system and as multimodal phenomena, following Halliday's (2008) formulations of the complementarities of 'language as system', 'language as text' and the two modes of spoken and written forms. Halliday has always focused on "theory as resource for solving problems" (Halliday 2008: i), and in this case, the problems of multimodal analysis are immense, given the complexity and multidimensionality of multimodal semiosis. For this reason, the SF-MDA approach has led to multimodal analytics, where systemic analyses relate low-level features of the multimodal texts to different strands of meaning using specialist multimodal analysis software to produce multimodal databases which can be mathematically modeled and visualized in order to detect semantic patterns, which in turn can be compared and related to higher order social systems of meaning, and vice versa. In this way, SF-MDA is an inclusive (rather than an exclusive) approach which can be productively employed in collaboration with other social theories and disciplines to investigate and understand the increasingly complex semiotic world of today.

Further reading

O'Halloran, Kay, Lynette. 2011. Multimodal discourse analysis. In Ken Hyland and Brian Paltridge (eds), Companion to Discourse Analysis. London: Continuum, 120–137.

O'Halloran, Kay Lynette, Marissa E Kwan Lin and Sabine Tan. 2013. Multimodal analytics: Software and visualization techniques for analyzing and interpreting multimodal data. In Carey Jewitt (ed.), Handbook of Multimodal Analysis (2nd edition), 384–394, London: Routledge.

O'Halloran, Kay, Lynette, Sabine Tan and Marissa E Kwan Line. 2013. 'Above all': The myth of 'dreams' as advertising tool. In Pennock-Speck, Barry and del Saz-Rubio, Maria Milagros (eds.) The Multimodal Analysis of Television Commercials, 113–135. University of Valencia: University of Valencia Press.

O'Halloran, Kay, Lynette, Alexey Podlasov, Alvin Chua and Marissa K. L. E. 2012. Interactive software for multimodal analysis. In Jana Holsanova (ed.), Special Issue: Methodologies for Multimodal Research, Visual Communication, 11(3): 352–370.

Project idea

Select a short film advertisement and apply the SF-MDA approach to critically analyse the text. Then discuss the meanings made in the advertisement with close reference to the textual evidence from the multimodal analysis, relating the meanings made to the prevailing ideologies in the societal context within which the advertisement is situated.

References

Baldry, Anthony P. 2004. Phase and transition, type and instance: patterns in media texts as seen through a multimodal concordancer. In Kay Lynette O'Halloran (ed.), *Multimodal Discourse Analysis: Systemic-Functional Perspectives*. London/New York: Continuum, 83–108.
Baldry, Anthony P. and Paul J. Thibault. 2006. *Multimodal Transcription and Text Analysis*. Oakville, CT: Equinox Publishing.
Barthes, Roland. [1957] 1987. *Mythologies*. New York: Hill & Wang.
Baudrillard, Jean. 1994. *Simulacra and Simulation*. Translated by Sheila Faria Glaser. Ann Arbor: University of Michigan.
E. Marissa K. L., Kay L. O'Halloran, and Kevin Judd. 2012. Combining computational tools with systemic functional theory for discourse analysis. In Sigrid Norris (ed.). *Multimodality in Practice: Investigating Theory-in-Practice through Methodology*, 153–173. Routledge Studies in Multimodality Book Series. London: Routledge.
Eco, Umberto. 1987. *Travels in Hyperreality*. Translated by William Weaver. London: Picador in association with Secker & Warburg.
Fairclough, Norman. 1995. *Critical Discourse Analysis*. London: Longman.
Fawcett, Robin. 2000. *A Theory of Syntax for Systemic Functional Linguistics*. Amsterdam/Philadelphia: John Benjamins
Flewitt, Rosie. 2006. Using video to investigate preschool classroom interaction: Education research assumptions and methodological practices. *Visual Communication*, 5: 25–50.
Gee, James Paul. 1990/2008. *Social Linguistics and Literacies: Ideology in Discourses, Critical Perspectives on Literacy and Education* (3rd edition). USA/Canada: Routledge.
Halliday, Michael. A. K. 1956/1976. Grammatical categories in modern Chinese. *Transactions of the Philological Society* 1956: 180–202.
Halliday, Michael. A. K. 1978. *Language as Social Semiotic: The Social Interpretation of Language and Meaning*. London: Edward Arnold.
Halliday, Michael, A. K. 1985. Part A. In Michael A.K. Halliday and Ruqaiya Hasan (eds.), *Language, Context, and Text: Aspects of Language in a Social-Semiotic Perspective*, 1–49. Geelong, Victoria: Deakin University Press.
Halliday, Michael A. K. 1994/1985. *An Introduction to Functional Grammar* (2nd edition). London: Arnold.
Halliday, Michael A. K. 2008. *Complementarities in Language*. Beijing: The Commercial Press.
Halliday, Michael A. K. and Christian M. I. M. Matthiessen. 2004. *An Introduction to Functional Grammar* (3nd edition, revised by C. Matthiessen). London: Arnold (1st edition 1985).

Halliday, Michael A.K. and Ruqiya Hasan. 1985. *Language, Context, and Text: Aspects of Language in a Social-Semiotic Perspective*. Geelong, Victoria: Deakin University Press.
Iedema, Rick. 2001. Resemioticization. *Semiotica*, 137 – 1/4: 23–39.
Iedema, Rick. 2003. Multimodality, resemioticization: Extending the analysis of discourse as a multisemiotic practice. *Visual Communication*, 2(1): 29–57.
Jewitt, Carey. 2009. Different approaches to multimodality. In Carey Jewitt (ed.), *The Routledge Handbook of Multimodal Analysis*, 28–39. London/ New York: Routledge.
Knox, John S. 2009. *Multimodal discourse on online newspaper home pages: A social-semiotic perspective*. Unpublished Ph.D. Thesis, University of Sydney, Sydney.
Kress, Gunther. 1993. Against arbitrariness: The social production of the sign as a foundational issue in critical discourse analysis. *Discourse and Society*, 4(2): 169–191.
Kress, Gunther. 2010. *Multimodality: A Social Semiotic Approach to Contemporary Communication*. London/New York: Routledge.
Kress, Gunther and Theo van Leeuwen. 2001. *Multimodal Discourse: The Modes and Media of Contemporary Communication*. London: Arnold.
Kress, Gunther and Theo van Leeuwen. 2006 [1996]. *Reading Images: The Grammar of Visual Design* (2nd Edition). London: Routledge.
Kress, Gunther, Carey Jewitt, Jon Ogborn and Charalampos Tsatsarelis. 2001. *Multimodal Teaching and Learning: the Rhetorics of the Science Classroom*. London/New York: Continuum.
Lim, Fei Victor. 2011. *A Systemic Functional Multimodal Discourse Analysis Approach to Pedagogic Discourse*. Doctoral thesis. National University of Singapore. Retrieved from http://scholarbank.nus.edu.sg/bitstream/handle/10635/29928/Victor%20Lim%20Fei%20%28VLF%29%20PhD.pdf?sequence=1
Lim, Fei Victor, Kay L. O'Halloran and Alexey Podlasov. 2012. Spatial pedagogy: mapping meanings in the use of classroom space. *Cambridge Journal of Education* 42(4): 235–251.
Machin, David. 2009. Multimodality and theories of the visual. In Carey Jewitt (ed.), *The Routledge Handbook of Multimodal Analysis*, 181–190. London/New York: Routledge.
Martin, James R. 1992. *English Text: System and Structure*. Amsterdam/Philadelphia: John Benjamins Publishing Company.
Martin, James R. and David Rose. 2007. *Working with Discourse: Meaning beyond the Clause*. London/New York: Continuum.
Matthiessen, Christian. M.I.M. 1995. *Lexicogrammatical Cartography: English Systems*. Tokyo: International Language Sciences Publishers.
Norris, Sigrid (ed.). 2012. *Multimodality in Practice: Investigating Theory-in-Practice through Methodology*. Routledge Studies in Multimodality Book Series. London: Routledge.
O'Donnell, Mick and John Bateman. 2005. SFL in computational contexts: A contemporary history. In Ruqiya Hasan, Christian M. I. M. Matthiessen and Jonathon Webster (eds.), *Continuing Discourse on Language*: Volume 1, 343–382. London: Equinox.
O'Halloran, Kay L. 2008. Systemic Functional-Multimodal Discourse Analysis (SF-MDA): Constructing ideational meaning using language and visual imagery. *Visual Communication*, 7(4): 443–475.
O'Halloran, Kay L. 2009. Historical changes in the semiotic landscape: From calculation to computation. In Carey Jewitt (ed.), *The Routledge Handbook of Multimodal Analysis*, 98–113. London/New York: Routledge.
O'Halloran, Kay L. 2011. Multimodal discourse analysis. In Ken Hyland and Brian Paltridge (eds.), *Companion to Discourse*, 120–137. London/New York: Continuum.

O'Halloran, Kay L., Alexey Podlasov, Alvin Chua and Marissa E Kwan Lin. 2012. Interactive software for multimodal analysis. In Jana Holsanova (ed.), Special Issue: Methodologies for Multimodal Research, *Visual Communication*, 11(3): 352–370.

O'Halloran, Kay L. and Bradley A. Smith. 2013. Multimodal text analysis. In Carol A. Chapelle (ed.), *Encyclopaedia of Applied Linguistics*. New Jersey: Wiley-Blackwell.

O'Halloran, Kay L., Marissa E Kwan Lin and Sabine Tan. 2013. Multimodal analytics: Software and visualization techniques for analyzing and interpreting multimodal data. In Carey Jewitt (ed.), *Handbook of Multimodal Analysis* (2nd edition). London: Routledge.

O'Halloran, Kay L., Sabine Tan and Marissa E Kwan Lin. 2013. 'Above all': The myth of 'dreams' as advertising tool. In Barry Pennock-Speck and Maria Milagros del Saz-Rubio, (eds.) *The Multimodal Analysis of Television Commercials*, 113–135. University of Valencia: University of Valencia Press.

O'Halloran, Kay L., Marissa E Kwan Lin, Alexey Podlasov and Sabine Tan. 2013. Multimodal digital semiotics: The interaction of language with other resources. In G. Thompson (ed.), *Text and Talk: Special Issue for Michael Halliday*. 33(4–5): 665–690.

O'Toole, Michael. 2011 [1994]. *The Language of Displayed Art* (2nd edition). London/New York: Routledge.

O'Toole, Michael. 2004. Opera Ludentes: The Sydney Opera House at work and play. In Kay Lynette O'Halloran, ed. (2004) *Multimodal Discourse Analysis: Systemic Functional Perspectives*, 11–27. London/New York: Continuum.

Podlasov, Alexey, Sabine Tan and Kay Lynette O'Halloran. 2012. Interactive state-transition diagrams for visualization of multimodal annotations. *Intelligent Data Analysis: An International Journal* 16(4): 683–702.

Smith, Bradley, Alexander, Sabine Tan, Alexey Podlasov and Kay Lynette O'Halloran. 2011. Analyzing multimodality in an interactive digital environment: Software as metasemiotic tool. *Social Semiotics*. 21(3): 359–380.

van Dijk, Teun, A. 1993. Principles of Critical Discourse Analysis. *Discourse & Society* 4(2): 249–283.

van Leeuwen, Theo. 1999. *Speech, Music, Sound*. London: Macmillan.

van Leeuwen, Theo. 2005. *Introducing Social Semiotics*. New York: Routledge.

van Leeuwen, Theo. 2009. Parametric systems: The case of voice quality. In Carey Jewitt (ed.), *The Routledge Handbook of Multimodal Analysis*, 68–77 (1st edition). New York: Routledge.

van Leeuwen, Theo. 2011. *The Language of Colour: An Introduction*. New York: Routledge.

Website

1. http://www.mindef.gov.sg/rsaf/careers/media/tvc.html
2. http://multimodal-analysis.com/products/multimodal-analysis-video/

Jeff Bezemer
14 Multimodal transcription: A case study

Introduction

A recurring challenge in my work and that of many others who are interested in multimodal interaction is transcription. Whenever I analyse a video recording of an interaction the question I am having to address is: how can I represent gesture, for instance, or gaze, or speech, and the alignment between all these different means of communication in writing and perhaps in video stills or drawings? There are at least two reasons why so many researchers take on that challenge. First, making a transcript is an invaluable analytical exercise: by forcing yourself to attend to the details of a strip of interaction you gain a wealth of insights into the situated construction of social reality, including insights in the collaborative achievements of people, their formation of identities and power relations, and the socially and culturally shaped categories through which they see the world. That is the epistemological function of transcription. Second, transcripts can be included in academic publications, which by and large are still paper-based. That way the transcript becomes verifiable 'evidence' of the argument that is developed in the publication. That is the rhetorical function of transcripts.

There are many different approaches to multimodal transcription. In previous, collaborative work we tried to make sense of some of the differences and similarities. By comparing a number of different published transcripts we reconstructed some of the epistemological and rhetorical choices that the transcribers made (see Bezemer and Mavers 2011). Note that in acknowledgement of the significance of all these choices and its analytical potential, multimodal transcription is usually done by the researchers themselves, and not 'outsourced' to external transcribers (who commonly transcribe interviews, for instance). Indeed, like any text, transcripts reveal as much about what is represented as they do about the text maker and the context in which they were produced. For instance, transcribers make choices about which clips to transcribe, which of the modes captured in the clip to transcribe, and how to represent these. All of these choices reflect the interests of the transcribers, their professional vision; And they have epistemological implications: the *re*-making of video-recorded interaction as a multimodal transcript leads to fresh insights.

In this chapter I provide a reflexive account of how I made a detailed multimodal transcript for one particular study. The study was on communication in the operating theatres of an inner-city hospital in London (Bezemer et al. 2011). The question that the transcript was designed to help me answer was: how do the members of a surgical team communicate to accomplish an operation? The transcript is a representation of an exchange between two surgeons and a scrub nurse. It was selected from a set of ten video-recorded operations. Instead of using wide-angle video cameras to capture what happens around the operating table, we used a camera fitted to a light handle, allowing us to capture the features that the participants in the interaction typically orient to, that is, their hands and those of their colleagues, their instruments, and the parts of the patient's body that they operated on. We used a wireless microphone worn by one of the surgeons to record the audio. In addition to these recordings we took photographs and kept detailed field notes of all the operations that we observed, particularly noting changes in the spatial configuration of participants around the operating table.

The transcript I will discuss might look quite different from many other multimodal transcripts, but I take it that researchers go through a number of similar steps to make them. These steps are outlined in figure 1. In what follows I discuss each of these steps, illustrating them using the research described above as a case study.

> Choose a methodological framework
>   Review multimodal frameworks
>   Consider rhetorical status of the transcript
> Define purpose and focus of transcript
>   Select episode and features to transcribe
>   Define questions to address
> Design the transcript
>   Create a template
>   Define transcription conventions
>   Fill in the template
> Read the transcript
>   Annotate the transcript
>   Recount the transcript
> Draw conclusions
>   Address questions
>   Make connections with other studies and theoretical constructs

Figure 1: How to transcribe multimodal interaction?

Key terms: Multimodal transcription, transcription conventions.

Choosing a methodological framework

Making a multimodal transcript starts with choosing a methodological framework that is apt for doing multimodal analysis. These frameworks have distinctly different takes on multimodality and work with different notions of validity and that is reflected in the multimodal transcripts. The transcript that I am discussing here was made for a paper (Bezemer et al. 2011) in which my co-authors and I adopted a conversation analytic approach. Originally focused on the study of talk, a growing body of work in Conversation Analysis (CA) now deals with a range of modes of communication. Much of this work is focused on medical work. Some of these studies are focused on surgical activity (Mondada 2003; Koschmann 2011; Svensson et al. 2009). Adopting the methodology underlying this body of work had a number of important implications for transcription.

First, it meant that I would select a small timescale, say, snippets of no more than a minute or so, so that the selected video clip can be reviewed frame-by-frame (there are 30 frames in one second). It is probably fair to say that the more detailed the multimodal transcript, the smaller the timescale that the researcher can afford to select. Had I adopted a different approach then I might have chosen to analyze clips second-by-second, or minute-by-minute, allowing me to cover more material. That might then have enabled me to made different claims, for instance, about the frequency of occurrence of a certain analytical category.

Second, adopting the methodology underlying the 'multimodal' studies in conversation analysis on medical work meant that I was going to make the transcript not just for myself but also for an audience, i.e. for the readers of our paper. Not just that, it was going to feature as 'evidence' for the arguments I was going to develop in the paper, giving the transcript a particular status within the manuscript. In CA, transcripts are not presented as illustration of a main body of text, they are presented as the object of analysis, as the main text that its surrounding text comments on, 'contextualizes'; a bit like the semiotic relation between a painting in a museum and its caption. All claims made in the surrounding text need to be grounded in the transcript (and not so much in, say, an interview with one of the people featuring in the transcript or in ethnographic insights of the researcher). CA transcripts tend to follow transcription conventions originally defined by Gail Jefferson, one of the 'founders' of

CA. However she only suggested conventions for the transcription of speech. A variety of forms are now used to transcribe communication in other modes in a way that is 'acceptable' and convincing to conversation analysts. That means, for instance, that it has to represent in detail the temporal unfolding of the interaction in all modes included for transcription.

Third, it meant that I was going to use some of the categories and concepts that are consistent with the approach I adopted. In the penultimate section of the chapter I will connect the insights I gained from making the transcript with the observations of other researchers who studied multimodal interaction. For instance, I draw on Kendon (1990) and Norris (2004) to explore how people participate in more than one activity at the same time; and I draw on Goffman (1971), Hindmarsh and Pilnick (2007), and Scollon and Scollon (2004) to understand how people read the bodies of others. Paradoxically, in this study, while clearly 'multimodal' in its outlook, I didn't use the notion of 'mode' to separate out different *sets* of socially and culturally organised meaning making resources (Kress 2009). Instead I separated out the different parts of the body that were available to and used by the participants as resources for making meaning (and visible on the recording) alongside the use of speech: head, upper body and arms and hands. The reason for not identifying modes, at least not *a priori*, was my being a complete outsider of the professional community of operating theatre staff. Hence I did not know how its means of communication were organized.

Define purpose and focus

Researchers select episodes for transcription for any number of reasons. In previous research I was often drawn to occasions where the interaction order is disturbed, making visible some of the ideologies operating in that context. For instance, I transcribed an excerpt from a video recording of a secondary school classroom in which a student threw a pack of chewing gum to his classmate while the teacher, who noticed this, was giving instruction to the class (Bezemer 2008). The transcript allowed me to investigate the regulation of displaying orientation through the body. The episode described in this chapter was selected for a different reason. Now my attention was drawn to the apparent seamlessness of the interaction between a junior surgeon on the one hand, and a consultant surgeon and a scrub nurse on the other hand.

Having replayed the clip a number of times I noticed that two activities occurred at the same time, involving different sets of participants. The consultant is tying knots, which is facilitated by the first assistant, a senior surgeon, who provides the necessary traction by holding a retractor in place. The consultant and the first assistant are talking about the management of beds. The SHO, a junior surgeon or 'senior house officer' (SHO), is within earshot of this conversation but is not a 'ratified participant' (Goffman 1981) in it. The episode starts at the point where the SHO makes a request for and subsequently receives scissors from the scrub nurse. It ends after the SHO has applied the scissors to cut a suture that the consultant has just finished tying. All this happens in less than 15 seconds. I noticed that the SHO was ready to apply the scissors exactly at the point where the consultant needed someone to cut the suture he had just tied. That raised questions such as, How did the SHO know that she was expected to cut the suture at that point in time and at that point of the suture without having received any spoken instructions from the consultant or first assistant? And where did these scissors come from? It took me (and all others I showed this clip to) several rounds of playing the episode in slow-motion to discover how the consultant used his body to signal to the SHO where and when to cut the suture; and to discover how the SHO had used her body (and speech) to make a request to the scrub nurse for scissors.

Having roughly defined what the boundaries were of the episode I then had to choose exactly what the beginning and the end points of my transcript were going to be. As starting point I chose what I came to see as the onset of the SHO's request, that is, the point that she begins to turn her body away from the operative field and towards the scrub nurse. As end point I chose the point immediately after the SHO had cut the suture. I also had to consider what features I wanted to transcribe. That was shaped, in part, by the partiality of the frame of the video recording. Since this camera was inside one of the operating lights, it moved along as the surgeons adjusted the positioning of the light. In the clip selected for transcription the SHO can be seen from her back and from a high angle. Her face is invisible, and so are her left arm and hand and her legs. What I could transcribe were the movements she makes with her head (suggesting the direction of her gaze), her trunk/upper body, and her right arm and hand, and her use of speech. So that's what I chose to transcribe. More specifically, I identified three dimensions of the use of head, trunk and arm and hand that I wanted to detail: their temporal and their spatial organization (up/down, left/right). I excluded the talk between the consultant and the first assistant as it plays no role in the interactions that the SHO is engaged in. I also excluded the body movements of the first assistant (whose task is to hold a big retractor) and I only selectively transcribed the movements of the consultant.

As I was selecting the episode and the interactional features I was formulating questions at the same time. I went back and forth between defining and redefining questions and honing in on a particular episode. Being both 'commissioner' and 'designer' of the transcript, I had to brief myself before doing any transcription at all. I was particularly interested in two questions. First, how does the SHO communicate with the scrub nurse and with the consultant, respectively. For instance, how does she signal to the scrub nurse that she requires scissors? And how does the consultant signal to the SHO when and where to cut the suture he's holding? Second, how does the SHO manage to remain involved in two activities at the same time, namely the requesting and passing of an instrument, and the knot tying and cutting? Drawing on the CA studies cited above and other multimodal research I assumed that the SHO and the other participants would use their bodies to achieve all this. So I had to find a way to represent how the various movements of body parts map onto each other. More specifically, the transcript had to show a) how the body movements of one person are (dis)aligned, for instance to make a request; b) how the body movements of different people are (dis)aligned, for instance, when a request is acknowledged.

Design the transcript

Having established the focal episode and the purpose of the multimodal transcript I then had to design it, by creating a template and defining the conventions for transcribing the features I had included. I considered a number of different designs. Multimodal transcripts are not only 'multimodal' in that they represent multimodal interaction, they are also multimodal in that multiple modes operate in the transcript, usually a combination of writing, typography, image, and/or layout. Each of these reshape the focal interaction in particular ways. Since I had chosen to represent the selected episode frame-by-frame the use of photographic stills seemed inapt – it would take 300 stills to represent one second. However by drawing lines of various kinds on grid paper I felt I could represent the timing and direction of the movements that the SHO made with the body parts I was focusing on. This approach was inspired by the work of Christian Heath and colleagues (2010).

As I was interested in the temporal unfolding and the synchrony between body movements I designed a template in which temporality is arranged horizontally, with the different body parts to be detailed separated out on the vertical axis. I drew a horizontal time line on a piece of grid paper and worked out how many frames or seconds each millimetre would stand for. For instance, you could take 1mm per frame, that's 30 mm per second. That means that in landscape orientation you could fit 9 seconds across the full width of the sheet. If you took 1cm per second, that's 1 mm per 10 msecs, you could fit 27 seconds on one line. I had just under 15 secs to transcribe, so I did 1mm per 3 frames. I could now draw lines below the time line, each line representating a different body (part).

I then defined what I wanted to transcribe on each line. The first line was going to represent the consultant's actions; they were broadly described in terms of 'tying knots' and "holding thread tight." The following four lines were to represent the SHO; one line for her use of upper body, one for her use of right arm, one for her use of head, and one for use of speech. I also defined conventions for expressing movement and fixation of these body parts. I used a dotted line for movement, and a continuous line for fixation. Discontinuations of lines indicate 'invisibility' of a feature on the video record, for instance, when the SHO's head temporarily blocks the view of the consultant's hand movements. I described these movements as 'up/down' and 'left/right'. Speech is used at only one point in this episode and was transcribed using conventional orthography and placed on a separate line. The time lapse of speech is detailed as a dotted line.

With the template designed, I started to fill it in using a media player that allowed me to forward frame-by-frame and to vary the playing speed. I focused on one body part at the time as that is the easiest way to keep track of the minute movements I was interested in. As I replayed the clip I decided where a movement started and where it ended, and in what direction it went, and translated that into pen strokes and annotations on my template. That way I filled in the empty fields on the template. Some time later, as I was preparing the manuscript in which the transcript was to appear, I 'digitized' the transcript by remaking it in Windows Paint. That's the version of the transcript that is reprinted here as figure 2.

162 — Jeff Bezemer

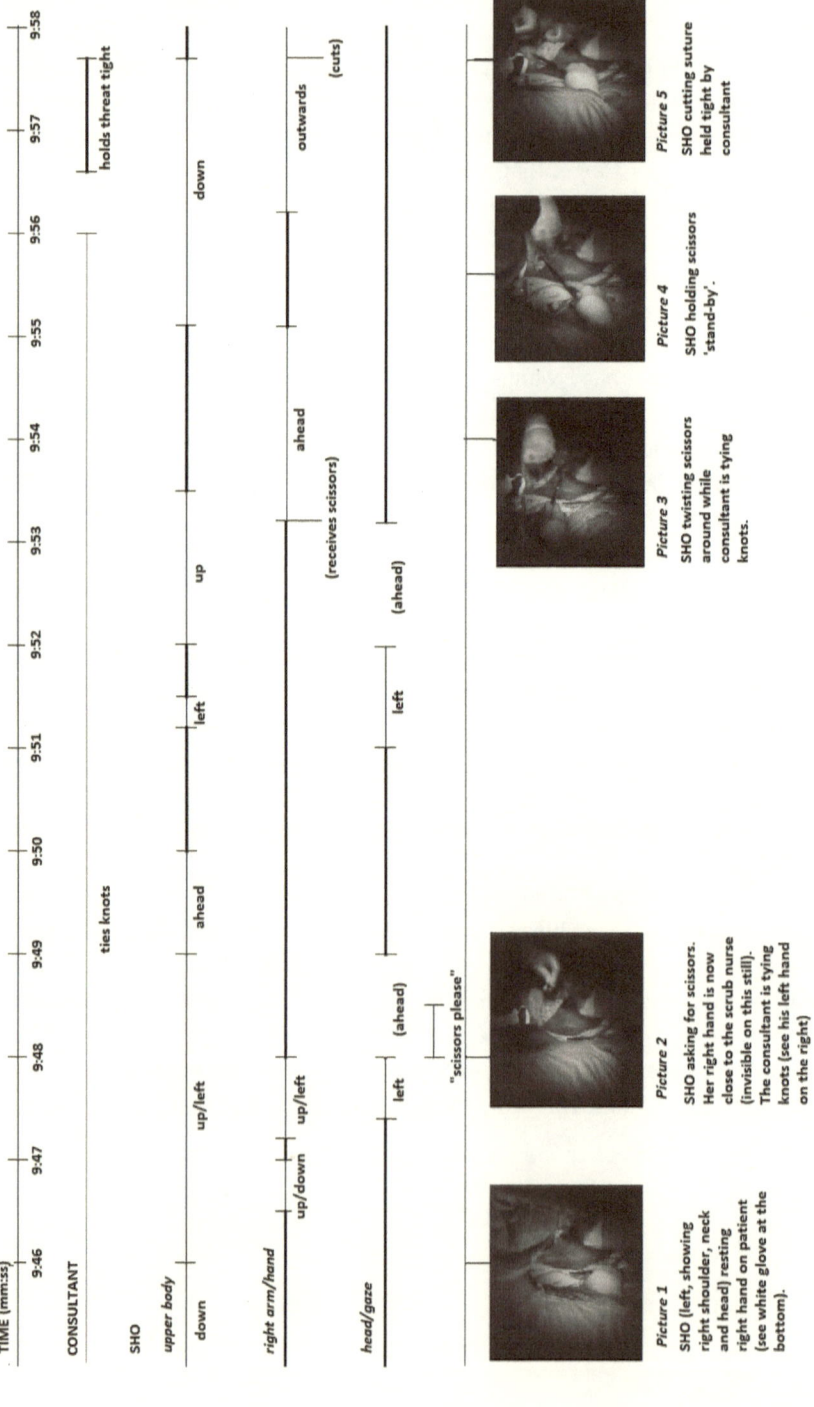

Figure 2

Read the transcript

Transcripts don't speak for themselves. You need to read them, mark points of interest, annotate them, and refine them. For instance, I found it useful to draw vertical lines across what seemed 'critical moments' to see if the reconfiguration of bodies does indeed mark a shift of some kind (I subsequently deleted these lines again from the transcript). I also added stills to depict bodily configurations at certain points in the episode. A good way to then organize your thoughts is to begin writing your interpretation of the transcript. As author you are expected to take readers through your transcript. Now the challenge is not to translate a video clip into a multimodal transcript, but to translate the multimodal transcript into a (written) 'recount'. As in the transcription stage you make selections and highlight interactional features for your audience, and you gain new insights by systematically describing what you see in the visual representation you made. Figure 3 shows what I wrote about my transcript.

Upper body

The SHO stands between the patient's legs, which are bent and which rest on frames (see Figure 2). The scrub nurse and the consultant are on her left, and the registrar is on her right. The SHO has little room to maneuver, yet she can and does move her *upper body* sideways and upward and downward to get the view and make the hand movements that she needs. Moving her trunk downward and upward allows her to respectively get physically closer to and to move away from the operative field. Moving slightly to the left allows her to get physically closer to the scrub nurse. Thus the movements of her upper body are suggestive of her orientation toward the various actions of others unfolding around her. Tilting toward the operative field suggests an increased engagement with the consultant's manual actions. Erecting her upper body and bending slightly to the left but without actually pivoting her trunk suggests a decreased engagement with the consultant's manual actions, but without a complete withdrawal, while suggesting the onset of a temporary engagement with the scrub nurse. Thus she can display her engagement with the actions of two people who at that point are themselves not oriented toward each other.

The SHO begins to tilt toward the operative field as the consultant begins to tie knots. At 9:46:00 she begins to move back up and tilts slightly to the left, suggesting engagement with the scrub nurse, without entirely withdrawing from the consultant's manual actions. Three seconds later she moves back to the middle of the space between the patient's legs, where her trunk remains in a more or less stable position for just over a second. Thus she has disengaged with the actions of the scrub nurse and displays an increased orientation to the operative field. She then turns slightly to the left again, stays in that position for half a second and then moves farther upward for a second and a half. In this way she displays engagement with the scrub nurse again while sustaining the consultant's actions. She maintains that position for just over one and a half seconds and then begins to tilt toward the operative field again, until 9:57:21. She has disengaged with the scrub nurse again and is now displaying orientation to the operative field only. She maintains that position for the rest of the clip. So in this fifteen-second clip the SHO engages momentarily with the scrub nurse twice, without ever completely moving away from the operative field and the consultant's manual actions.

Arms and hands

The SHO's *left arm* is invisible in the clip, but it looks like she is resting that arm on the patient. Her *right arm* and *hand* play a crucial function in her coordination. At the start of the clip, when the consultant is tying knots, her right hand is still resting on the patient. At 9:46:15 she moves her hand up, only to let it rest again. Moments later she moves her hand up again while stretching her arm and moving it to the left. This happens as she is moving her upper body up and tilts slightly to the left. This accentuates her engagement with the scrub nurse. Her right hand is now in front of her trunk, and while she soon starts shifting away from the scrub nurse, again she maintains that position of arm and hand until she has received the scissors from the scrub nurse at 9:53:08. That way she continues to display orientation to the scrub nurse, signaling to the scrub nurse that she is available for receiving the scissors she requested while moving closer to the operative field again. The scrub nurse is likely to have anticipated the request. Only moments ago she has passed a stitch to the consultant, and she is well aware that the attached thread will have to be cut when he has completed the knot tying.

When the SHO has received the scissors she moves her arm back to the right, accentuating her withdrawal from the scrub nurse's actions. As she moves her arm closer to her trunk she twists and grasps the scissors, moving her fingers into its rings (see Figure 2, Picture 3). From 9:55:03 she holds the scissors in a fairly fixed position, apparently ready to apply them (see Figure 2, Picture 4). At 9:56:18 the consultant stops moving his *hands and fingers*, holding the thread in a fixed position using both hands, in such a way that it can be cut (only) by someone else (see Figure 2, Picture 5). His hand positioning "broadcasts" to the SHO the request that the thread needs to be cut. The SHO then moves closer to the thread, and at 9:57:21, just over a second after the consultant started holding the thread fixed and tight between his fingers, she cuts it (see Figure 2, Picture 5). She then moves her arm and hand back to her trunk while rotating the scissors on her fingers and grasping it such that it points upward.

Head gaze

The SHO's shifting head position and gaze direction is a further indication of her orientation toward the actions of others around her. Moving her trunk without also moving her head allows her to display dual orientation toward the operative field and the scrub nurse, and to gradually engage more with the one and less with the other. When she first turns her head to the left, at 9:47:12, she has already begun to move her trunk up and to tilt it slightly to the left; she also has already begun to move her arm and hand toward the scrub nurse. Thus the turn of her head, which allows her to direct her gaze to the scrub nurse, is the

> third indicator of her increased engagement with the scrub nurse, alerting her to an upcoming request. Then, at 9:48:00, she verbalizes the request: "scissors please" (see Figure 2, Picture 2). Now that the request has been completed, she turns her head back to the right, allowing her to look into the operative field again. She knows that soon the scrub nurse will offer her the scissors, and she still holds her open hand within the scrub nurse's reach. At 9:51:00 she turns her head to the scrub nurse again. The positioning of her head and direction of her gaze is not visible on the video record until she receives the scissors just over two seconds later and turns her head back to the operative field.

Figure 3: A recount of the multimodal transcript (Source: Bezemer et al. 2011: 406–408. Time is indicated in minutes:seconds:frames)

Drawing conclusions from the transcript

As I had completed the recount I returned to the questions I had asked myself when I selected a strip of interaction and began to connect the insights I had gained to account for similar actions. My question was, first, how does the SHO manage to remain involved in two activities at the same time, namely the requesting and passing of an instrument, and the knot tying and cutting? Second, how does the SHO communicate with the scrub nurse and with the consultant to achieve those two activities?

Engaging in simultaneously unfolding activities

The SHO managed to help sustain and complete one activity (knot tying) through the timely initiation and completion of another (instrument exchange), each with its own set of participants. The SHO managed to simultaneously engage in those two activities by using her body in particular ways. This observation relates to findings on multimodal interaction in other settings. For instance, Norris (2004) transcribed a video recording of a school crossing guard helping children cross a street. She shows that

> "while the crossing guard shifts her focal attention from directing the cars to directing the children and back again, she simultaneously engages in two-higher level actions on different levels of attention/awareness. In other words, when the traffic guard is directing traffic, she is engaged in focused interaction with the drivers, while she is simulatenously engaged in interaction with the children at the corner: making sure that they are safe. Her engagement in the interaction with the children at this time is not as focused as her interaction with the drivers, but is clearly ongoing." (p. x).

Like the crossing guard, the SHO is juggling between two activities, each of which require her attention: she needs to keep her eyes on the consultant, so as to know when and where to cut. She also needs to keep an eye on the scrub nurse, first to make a request for scissors and then to receive the scissors. The transcript shows how the SHO uses her body to manage this multiple engagement, namely through what Kendon (1990) calls the 'f-formation.' Looking at 'informal' gatherings, he shows how participants standing in a social circle with two others can temporarily turn their head away from the center point of this 'f-formation' while sustaining their involvement in the talk. They keep their lower body in line with the center of the f-formation to express engagement with the talk and use the upper body to engage, temporarily, with someone situated outside the formation. The multimodal transcript suggests that the SHO positions herself in a similar way, with her lower body still aligned with the operative field and the consultant, and her head turned away momentarily at various points to engage with the scrub nurse.

If I had to summarize this in one sentence, I might say, the body is a vital resource for managing one's participation in simultaneously unfolding activities.

Reading bodies

By mapping the bodily movements of the SHO I made visible what Goffman (1971) calls a 'body gloss', i.e., a gloss to broadcast one's interactional positioning. The SHO made a *body gloss* designed to signal, first, to the scrub nurse that she is about to ask her to pass some instrument and, second, to the consultant, that she is ready to apply the scissors whenever he is ready. She can see that the consultant is tying knots, she knows that soon the thread will need to be cut, and she knows that the consultant will be expecting her to do that. She has to calculate the time it will take her to request and receive the scissors, and she has to consider the availability of the scrub nurse for receiving the request, as she may be occupied by, for instance, talking to one of the circulating nurses. We also saw the consultant displaying a body gloss designed to signal to the SHO where and when she was expected to cut: in this case, a discontinuation of knot tying and stretching of the thread.

In other words, the transcript makes visible how the participants in the interaction "gloss" with and "read" bodies, and how that enabled them to "seamlessly coordinate emerging activities" (Hindmarsh and Pilnick 2007: 1413). Similar observations have been made in studies of interaction in classrooms. For instance, Scollon and Scollon (2004) describe the actions involved in a teacher handing a paper to a student. They note that before the handing can occur two conditions have to be met: 'First, the two participants in this action have to come to agreement that it is going to occur, then, secondly, they must position themselves appropriately.' (Scollon and Scollon 2004: 64). In their example, the first condition is met by the teacher calling the student's name and the teacher and student establishing eye contact; the second condition is met by the teacher and student positioning themselves at the right distance (e.g. the teacher walks to the student, the student reaches out his arm). The actual handing is achieved through 'micro-movements that are adjusted to the weight of the object and the timing of the movements of their hands toward each other'. To some extent, these actions correspond with the actions involved in the request for and passing of the scissors. For instance, I noted the SHO's body movements that signal 'what is going to occur' and enable her to establish eye contact and ultimately receive the scissors from the scrub nurse. The name calling is not required at the operating table; by default, all requests for instruments are directed to the scrub nurse. By making comparisons like these we can begin to recognize, at a micro level, how recurring actions (such as handing objects) are differently and similarly achieved across different social (institutional) contexts.

Conclusion

As with any multimodal transcript, the one discussed here is only a partial representation of the interaction it is based on. This partiality is the result of both spatial and temporal limitations. The temporal partiality is rather significant (although perhaps backgrounded in the transcript and its recount): I transcribed less than 15secs from an operation that lasted more than 3 hrs. An example of the spatial limitation is that what was framed by the camera excludes a great number of other, simultaneously unfolding activities. For instance, at the patient's head end an anaesthetic team was engaged in activities which had a direct effect on the work of the surgeons. It is useful to reflect on these limitations, to check that the transcript does indeed match your original questions, your interpretation and your conclusions, and, last but not least, to anticipate what effect the transcript might have on its readers. As I pointed out at the beginning of this chapter, different research traditions have different ways of transcribing multimodal interaction, so it's important to pitch your transcript to the right audience. What may seem an entirely 'valid' transcript in one (academic) context may seem to be lacking in validity in others.

The multimodal transcript discussed in this chapter was made without any transcription software package, of which there are now quite a few available. When choosing transcription software it is important to still consider all the choices discussed in this chapter. A lot of them are being made for you by the software developers, and it's worth checking that they match yours. For the purposes of the transcript discussed here ELAN, a free package developed by the Max Plank Institute of Psycholinguistics, would have been a good option. In ELAN (Wittenburg et al. 2006) you can create the type of template I made on grid paper, with a horizontal time line as a base, and 'tiers' below it, each of which describe a particular interactional dimension (in my case, 'upper body', 'right arm' and 'head gaze'.) ELAN is particularly helpful if you aim to analyze small strips of interaction second-by-second or in even greater detail.

I like to conclude this chapter by going back to the comparison between the passing of the scissors in my multimodal transcript and the passing of the paper in the account of Scollon & Scollon. The Scollons use the notion of the 'historical body' to highlight the embodied resources that people develop through practical experience. The teacher and student, and the SHO and the scrub nurse had been involved in 'handing' certain objects in their respective settings many time before, which allowed them to perform these actions relatively effortlessly in the instances described. It is unlikely that the student or SHO were ever 'taught' how to hand these objects, or that they found instructions on this in the textbooks or syllabi they studied. The notion of the 'historical body' connects with a range of theories about knowledge, learning and the body, in philosophy, anthropology, sociology and psychology (think about terms like, 'tacit knowledge', 'practical knowledge', 'procedural knowledge', 'habitus', et cetera). While these theories acknowledge the significance of the body in social interaction they are rarely accompanied by multimodal transcripts that visually represent that significance. That is an important function of multimodal transcripts: to show aspects of social interaction which often remain unarticulated in the narratives provided by researchers and the people they study. It is these 'hidden' dimensions that can provide inroads into understanding substantive issues (in my case, the safety and quality of surgical care).

Further readings

Flewitt, Rosie, Mirjam Hauck, Regina Hampel and Lesley Lancaster. 2009. What are multimodal data and transcription? In Carey Jewittt (ed) *The Routledge Handbook of Multimodal Analysis*, 40–54. London: Routledge.

Heath, Christian, Jon Hindmarsh, and Paul Luff. 2010. *Video in Qualitative Research: Analysing Social Interaction in Everyday Life*. Los Angeles: Sage.

Norris, Sigrid. 2004. *Analyzing Multimodal Interaction*. London: Routledge.

Project idea

Choose a focus for a small study on multimodal interaction. Use a video on Youtube that speaks to that question and discuss how you would go about making a multimodal transcript of that video using the steps outlined in this chapter.

References

Bezemer, Jeff and Diana Mavers. 2011. Multimodal Transcription as Academic Practice: A Social Semiotic Perspective. *International Journal of Social Research Methodology*. Special Issue on Video based Social Research: Theory and Practice. 14(3): 191–207.

Bezemer, Jeff, Ged Murtagh, Alexandra Cope, Gunther Kress and Roger Kneebone. 2011. "Scissors, please" The practical accomplishment of surgical work in the operating theatre. *Symbolic Interaction* 34(3): 398–414.

Goffman, Erving. 1971. *Relations in Public: Micro Studies of Public Order*. New York: Basic Books.

Goffman, Erving. 1981. *Forms of Talk*. Philadelphia: University of Pennsylvania Press.

Heath, Christian, Jon Hindmarsh and Paul Luff. 2010. *Video in Qualitative Research: Analysing Social Interaction in Everyday Life*. Los Angeles: Sage.

Hindmarsh, Jon and Alison Pilnick. 2007. Knowing bodies at work: embodiment and ephemeral teamwork in anaesthesia." *Organization Studies* 28: 1395–416.

Kendon, Adam. 1990. *Conducting Interaction: Patterns of Behavior in Focused Encounters*. Cambridge: Cambridge University Press.

Kress, Gunther. 2009. What is mode? In Carey Jewitt (ed.) *The Routledge Handbook of Multimodal Analysis*. London: Routledge.

Koschmann, Timothy, Curtis LeBaron, Charles Goodwin and Paul Feltovich. 2011. 'Can you see the cystic artery yet?': A simple matter of trust. *Journal of Pragmatics* 43: 521–41.

Mondada, Lorenza. 2003. Working with video: How surgeons produce video records of their actions. *Visual Studies* 18: 58–73.

Svensson, Marcus, Christian Heath and Paul Luff. 2007. Instrumental action: The timely exchange of implements during surgical operations. In Liam Bannon, Ina Wagner, Carl Gutwin, Richard Harper, and Kjeld Schmidt (eds.) *Proceedings of European Conference on Computer-Supported Cooperative Work* 2007, 41–60. Limerick: Springer.

Wittenburg, Peter, Hennie Brugman, Albert Russel, Alex Klassmann, Han Sloetjes. 2006. ELAN: a professional framework for multimodality research. In *Proceedings of LREC 2006, Fifth International Conference on Language Resources and Evaluation*, 1556–1559.

Emilia Djonov and John S. Knox
15 How-to-analyze webpages

Introduction: Why do multimodal discourse analysts need to study Web communication?

Since its emergence in the early 1990s, the world wide web has become widely accessible and proven to be, alongside the internet, one of the most important social transformations since at least the 15th century and Gutenberg's printing press. It has powered a rapid expansion in new meaning-making practices (e.g. emailing, blogging, micro-blogging, online reading) that have become a significant part of the everyday life of private citizens and public institutions. This expansion has motivated educators and discourse analysts to explore how these practices have developed and how 'old' practices are done anew as existing institutions (e.g. governments, mass media institutions, museums) have adopted the web and adapted it to their communication purposes.

Webpages pose a number of unique challenges for discourse analysis. Every webpage is related to all other pages within the same website, and each website is related to all other websites comprising the web. Many webpages feature dynamic content that runs automatically or may be 'altered' or 'set in motion' by the reader (e.g. video, animation, 'rotating' zones on pages, selectable tabs and rollovers). Their content may also be frequently updated (e.g. in news websites several times a day) and the website they belong to may undergo periodic re-design or even restructuring, which can change the information appearing on webpages, how it is presented, the significance assigned to some pages over others, the interaction between individual pages and the website as a whole, and the relationship between website authors and readers.

Webpages are multi-semiotic (employing a range of semiotic resources such as written language, speech, image, colour, layout, music, and movement) and typically also multi-channel documents (employing visual, aural and increasingly also tactile communication). In complex multimodal documents of this kind, visual design is key to organising meanings on and beyond the page, and provides analysts with a coherent 'way in' to the data. It is for this reason that in this chapter we approach webpages as visual units.

In this chapter we first discuss issues in the collection of webpage data. Then, we outline an approach for analysing webpages, using the homepage of the Parliament of Australia website (Commonwealth of Australia, n.d.-a) at www.aph.gov.au (hereafter APH for Australian Parliament House) as an illustration.

Key terms: Hyperlink, hypermedia, hypermodality, hypertext anchor, hypertext mark-up language (html).

Data collection

One way to collect webpages is to save them as html files using a web browser. Such saves, however, tend not to preserve the way advertisements, images, animations, and page layout were rendered at the time the webpage was saved. For this reason, it is good practice to take an image (i.e. screen capture) of any webpage being analysed. There are readily accessible browser plug-ins or other software tools (some free) that can capture single screens and scrolling screens (or full windows). Yet, a saved html file or a static image of a scrolling webpage can not accurately represent dynamic content on webpages such as zones that scroll sideways, videos, tabs, and roll-overs.

Additionally, webpages are 'instantly impermanent' (Perlmutter 2003). If the analyst misses a webpage, it is sometimes possible to locate it in an archive (either on the host website, or on another archive such as the 'wayback machine' at www.archive.org), but archived pages, like browser-saved html files, often render differently to 'live' pages, and the archived version may be from a different date or time to the version being analysed. A solution to some of these problems is to use a tool like *ScrapBook*, which downloads pages so that they appear the same as on the web and have live hyperlinks (see Zhang 2012). Such tools vary in their stability and functionality. In short, there is no single 'best way' to collect webpages for data analysis, and the approaches taken depend on the purposes and methods of analysis.

Tools for webpage analysis

Anyone undertaking serious webpage or website analysis should develop a familiarity with the field represented by the text under analysis (e.g. for an online newspaper website, news reporting and specific news institutions), and with the multidisciplinary field of web design (see Garrett 2011[2003]). This chapter presents a social semiotic framework for webpage analysis that takes both into account.

Technically, a website is a group of hypertext mark-up language (HTML) documents, or webpages, housed within the same WWW domain and must have one of these designated as its homepage. The homepage is a file typically called 'index', 'default', or 'home' that can be opened when only the domain address of a website is specified in the Universal Resource Locator (URL) bar of a web browser. The URL http://www.aph.gov.au/ will open the homepage of the Parliament of Australia website.

Webpages are documents stored on web servers, opened with a web browser, and displayed within a single browser tab on various devices. They are the building blocks (or 'hypertext nodes') of websites and provide 'departure' and 'destination' ports for hyperlinks (cf. Landow 1987). Hyperlinks are the connections that define the web as the world's largest and most complex hypermedia environment. They are activated through clickable visible webpage areas ('hypertext anchors'). But webpage design is the interface through which users navigate through the web, usually exploring a webpage at a time and relying on the interaction of various semiotic resources to make navigation choices, orient themselves, and make sense of the information presented within and across webpages and websites.

The webpage is thus a unit of analysis that reflects the role of technology in web communication (i.e. it is technologically as well as semiotically motivated) and allows researchers to take into consideration the perspectives of website designers and users alike. The social semiotic framework for analysing webpages presented in this chapter combines elements of two earlier frameworks specifically designed for analysing web texts. The first (e.g. Knox, 2010) was developed through the analysis of online newspapers and provides tools for considering how meanings are made within and across different 'levels' on the webpage. The second offers tools developed through the analysis of the interaction between children's website design and use, primarily for the purpose of identifying how website design affects users' orientation, engagement, and learning on the web (Djonov, 2007, 2008; Stenglin and Djonov 2010).

The framework adopts a broad notion of text as an "exchange of meanings" (Halliday 1985: 11) "with socially ascribed unity" (Hodge and Kress 1988:6), and adapts to web communication Halliday's metafunctional framework for analysing language, according to which every text simultaneously makes three broad kinds of meaning (known as 'metafunctions'):

- ideational: the representation of patterns of experience and the logico-semantic relations that connect these patterns
- interpersonal: the ways in which social relationships and values are construed
- textual: the interweaving of ideational and interpersonal choices into cohesive and coherent units of meaning, that is, texts.

The framework presented here also builds on Kress and Van Leeuwen's (2006 [1996]) influential grammar of visual design, which extends Halliday's metafunctional framework beyond language, and responds to Lemke's (2002) call for developing social semiotic tools for studying 'hypermodality' – the meanings created as hyperlinks interact with language, visual design and other modes.

Analysis of the Australian Parliament House homepage

The framework introduced in this chapter is presented as a series of questions which are addressed by taking the APH homepage as a starting point and then, where necessary, considering its relationship to other webpages within the same website (see Figure 1).

The decision to analyse a homepage is based on the dominance of analyses and discussions of homepages in research on web communication, which reflects the important technical as well as semantic status of the homepage. Semantically, every homepage serves three important functions (Krug 2006 [2000]; Lynch and Horton 2008 [1999, 2001]; Nielsen and Tahir 2002):

(i)   to show visitors the website's main parts together with any popular or timely information, regardless of where in the website this information may be (which maps on to the ideational metafunction)
(ii) to establish the identity and mission of the website and the institution/s it represents (which maps on to the interpersonal metafunction)
(iii) to reveal how the site is structured and what options for navigation it offers (which maps on to the textual metafunction).

Page and purpose

What is the purpose of the website and webpage under analysis?

Websites have different functions, depending on the institution, organisation, or individual they belong to. For example, online news sites provide information to readers, enable advertisers to reach an audience, and promote the ideologies of the institution (Knox 2007; Zhang and O'Halloran 2014). The structure of online newspapers is determined in part by the organisational structure of the news room, and how the news institution 'divides up' the 'world of news' for its readership (Knox 2007, forthcoming). (See Suen 2009; Zhang and O'Halloran 2012;

> **Page and purpose**
> - *What is the purpose of the website and webpage under analysis?*
>
> **Ideational meanings**
> - *What content is included on or excluded from the page? How is content on the page classified?*
> - *What logico-semantic relations (e.g. exemplification, temporal sequence, contrast) reveal the organisation of content of the website as a whole?*
>
> **Interpersonal meanings**
> - *How is the content presented to the reader (e.g. as rational, factual, or sensational)? What kind of relationship is construed visually between the reader, the content, and the author?*
> - *How does the webpage align users attitudinally towards the website and its content?*
>
> **Textual meanings**
> - *How is the page composed to make each screen, and the entire page a meaningful 'whole'?*
> - *To what extent does the homepage reveal the organisation of the website as a whole? What navigation choices does it offer and privilege? Does it support user orientation?*
>
> **Social context and interpretation**
> - *In what ways are the multimodal and hypermodal structures of the webpage and their meanings related to social context? How can you explain these relations?*

Figure 1: Summary of framework for analysing webpages introduced in this chapter

Carreon, Watson Todd, and Knox forthcoming on the functions and structure of respectively hotel, university and private hospital homepages.)

The APH website (see Figure 2) functions simultaneously:
- to represent and enact Australian democracy, both by informing readers how the parliament and its institutions work, and by providing access to those institutions and their processes (which itself is an important aspect of democracy)

- to promote and preserve the particular approach to government used in Australia by presenting the parliament in a positive manner, construing its structure and work as natural rather than controversial or subject to possible change at the will of the people
- to advertise the Australian Parliament House as a tourist destination.

These functions are clearly reflected on the homepage by: the prominent links to the houses of parliament, the House of Representatives and the Senate; dominant images of Australian Parliament House; and other content and links promoting it as a destination (e.g. 'News & Events', 'Visit Parliament', an item on anniversary celebrations, a calendar of events).

In addition to considering the purpose of the entire website, when analysing a webpage, it is important to understand the place and function of the page in relation to the website to which it belongs. In what section is the page located, and what role does it serve (e.g. presenting content vs. providing information about the website)? Homepages typically reflect the purposes and organisation of the entire website, as discussed above. Given these important functions, it is not surprising that the homepage is the most highly valued page within a website.

Ideational meanings

What content is included on or excluded from the page? How is content on the page classified?

The spatial organisation of the webpage is an important resource for 'packaging' meaning. Different content may be placed in different 'zones' on the page, and a range of visual devices can be used to distribute content on the page, and to classify information.

The first thing to consider is the broad structure of the page. The APH homepage can be seen as a photograph of the front of the Australian Parliament building, with a webpage 'laid over' the pond which takes up most of the image (Figure 2). The effect, when viewed on-screen, is to make the iconic building the header of the page. Coupled with the coat of arms at top left, this presents a strong visual representation of the Parliament, which we call the 'banner' of the webpage (Figure 3).

Moving down the page, the first zone of information after the banner is a horizontal bar, classified by colour and language into House of Representatives and Senate. It offers links to important information related to the two chambers,

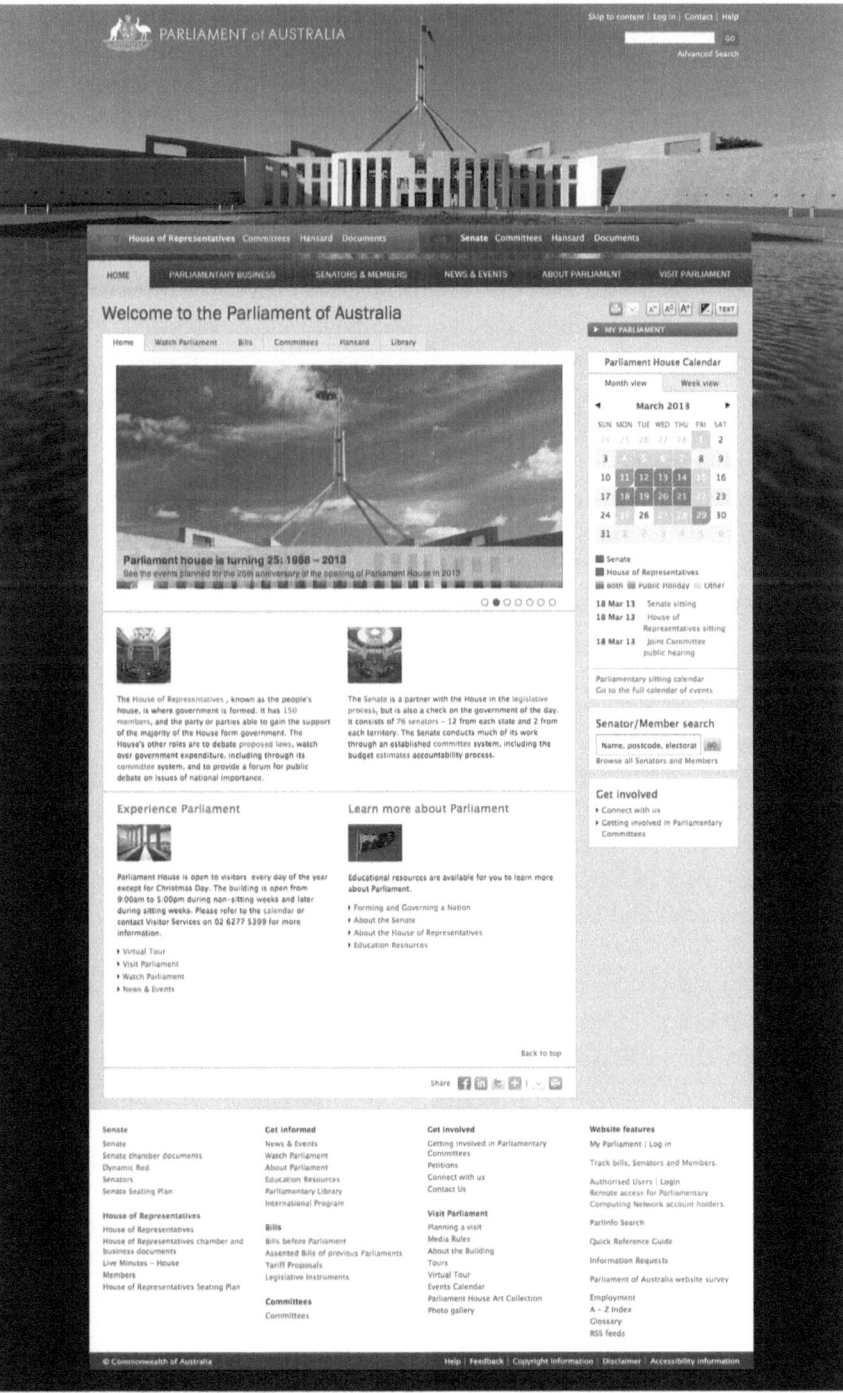

Figure 2: APH homepage

and employs red and green, the colours representing each chamber. This is a 'navigation zone'. Navigation zones typically have a dual purpose of providing navigation links and classifying the content of the website. The more prominent a navigation zone is, the more important the second of these purposes. Navigation zones typically appear on all pages of a website in the same, or a similar, format and location.

Moving further down the page, the second visual block is divided into four areas by background colour. The first of these areas consists of six tabs organised horizontally. They have a dark grey background, and the selected tab (the default selection is the HOME tab) has a light grey background, matching that of the content zone below. These tabs constitute a second horizontal navigation zone.

Further down is the main section of content, a content zone, with a grey background and 'blocks' of content with a white background (these are discussed further below).

Below the content zone are two more zones which also appear on all pages. One has a white background and four columns of links classified with headings: a third navigation zone. The other, across the bottom, has a black background with a copyright mark and a horizontal menu: the 'signature'.

Thus, this page has a banner, three navigation zones, a content zone, and a signature (see Figure 3). These components are found on many homepages, but some webpages have fewer zones and some have zones not discussed here (e.g. advertising zones).

Navigation zones are related to the content on the entire website more than that of a single page, and are as important for interpersonal and textual meanings as they are for ideational meanings. Similarly, the banner and signature present 'content' but serve important interpersonal and textual functions too. The interpersonal and textual functions of all these zones are discussed further below.

Content zones on homepages usually provide some kind of introduction to information that appears elsewhere on a website and is considered important by its authors. They usually classify this information through headings and sub-headings, and/or various visual devices. On the APH homepage, the left column of the content zone has four areas, each with a white background (see Figure 3). The topmost of these is divided horizontally into its own tabs with headings, and the Home tab at this level has a series of seven images that rotate.

Through different webpage design devices, the content zone thus construes a taxonomy of information. A partial taxonomy of content on the APH homepage is shown in Figure 4. Italics show items that are not named on the homepage but by the analysts. Such categories can be considered 'covert', whereas categories named by the website authors can be considered 'overt'.

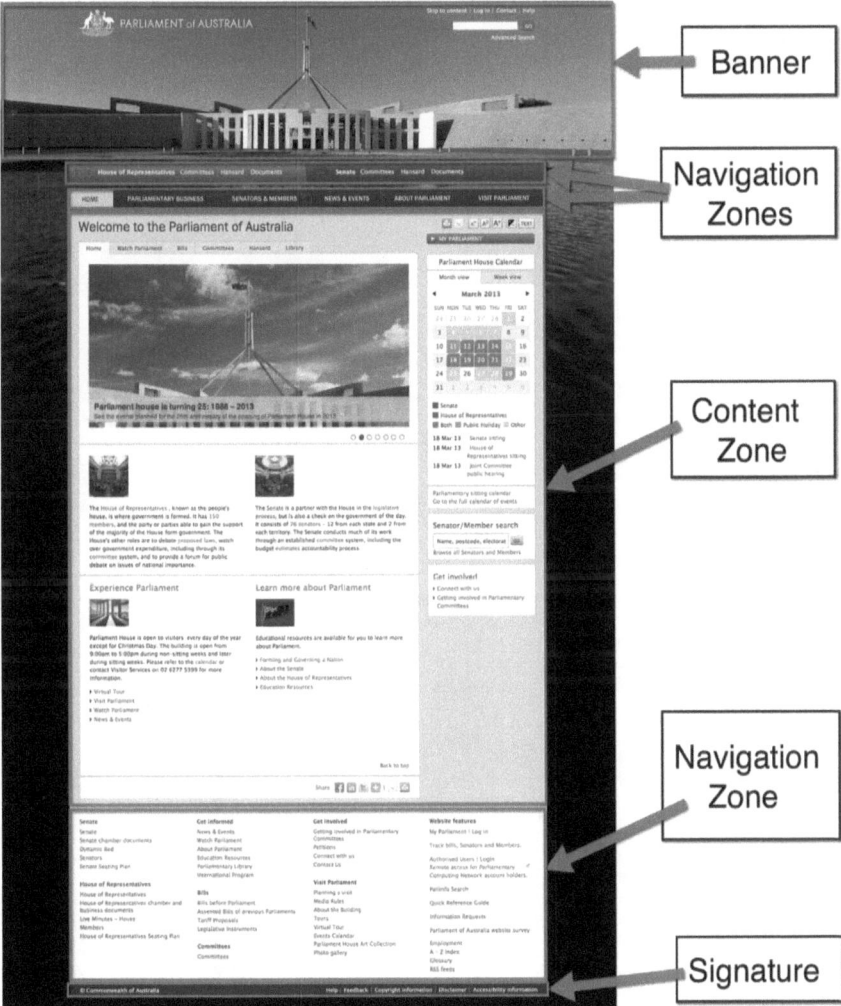

Figure 3: APH homepage with zones indicated

Rendering the taxonomy of content on a webpage (especially a homepage) in this way allows us to question what content is included, what is excluded, and how it is classified. Choices in the classification of information on homepages are sometimes inconsistent, and sometimes apparently illogical. For example, 'social media' might be more logically presented as a 'utility', but its positioning as 'information' reflects the importance of social media to the institution.

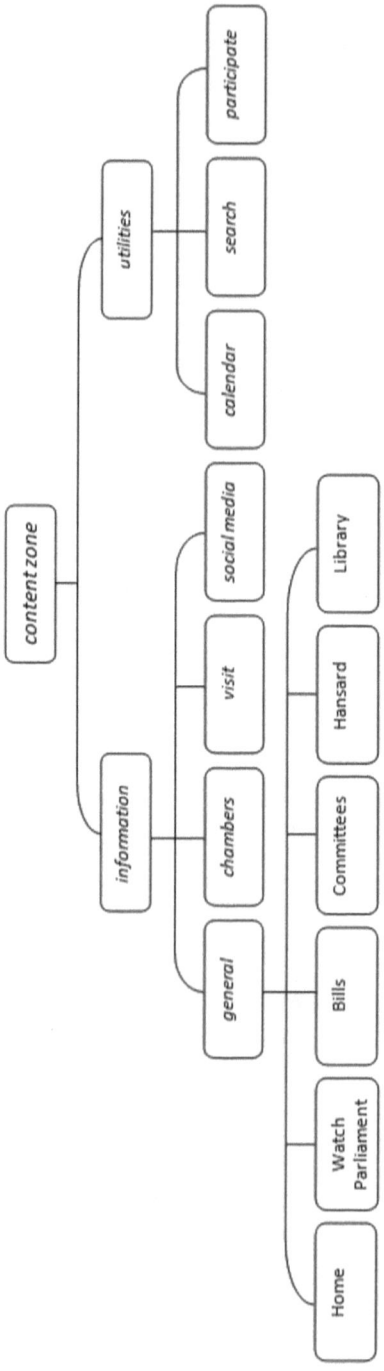

Figure 4: Classification of content in the content zone of the APH homepage

This highlights that classification is not a 'neutral' or 'natural' activity. Classification of content on webpages may reflect the structure of the institution, the values of the authors, and/or the purposes of the website. For example, while the two chambers, the House of Representatives and Senate, are employed to subcategorise and cross-classify information available on the website (e.g. documents, speeches, live updates), and each also appears in the content zone on the homepage, neither the Queen (of England and Australia) nor the Governor-General are 'built into' the structure of the website, nor do they appear in the content on the homepage. Yet: "The Parliament consists of the Queen, represented by the Governor-General, and two Houses – the House of Representatives and the Senate" (Commonwealth of Australia, n.d.-b). Clearly, the undemocratic role of a foreign monarch in governing Australia is omitted from the structure of the APH website and the content of the homepage, raising issues of nationalism, Australian independence, and the very system of government.

What logico-semantic relations (e.g. exemplification, temporal sequence, contrast) reveal the organisation of content of the website as a whole?

Webpage design plays an important role in revealing the logical relations used to organise the website's content and structure, and can therefore affect both learning and orientation within a website. Adapting social semiotic principles for analysing conjunctive relationships in verbal discourse (Halliday, 1994 [1985]; Halliday and Hasan, 1976; Halliday and Matthiessen 2004; Martin 1992), Djonov (2005) proposes several parameters for describing the logico-semantic relations (LSRs) that can be used to organise information in websites. Three of these are especially relevant for webpage analysis.

Scope concerns the size of the related units. A LSR can connect:
- elements occupying the same webpage
- whole webpages, which may or may not be hyperlinked with each other
- whole website sections or sub-sections, which too may or may not be hyperlinked with each other.

Webpages or webpage elements may also function to represent much larger units of discourse. For instance, the website banner, like the homepage, represents the website as a whole. Also, a website section's title and icon, like its main page, represent the section as a whole.

Examples on the APH homepage are the section titles 'Parliamentary Business', 'Senators & Members', 'News & Events', 'About Parliament' and 'Visit

Parliament' (Figure 2). These are designed with the same font and colour background. They are tabs that occupy the same navigation zone and function as anchors to the website's main content sections. This design on the homepage signifies that the website sections represented by these tabs have equal status and similar function.

Type refers to the meaning of LSRs (e.g. clarification, generality, similarity/contrast, causality, etc.). To illustrate, on the APH homepage there is a clarification relationship between the picture of the Senate, and the paragraph below it, which explains the functions and composition of the Senate (the paragraph clarifies the image). In the topmost navigation zone, there is a generality relationship between the headings 'House of Representatives' and 'Senate' on one hand, and the anchors to specific information ('Committees', 'Hansard' and 'Documents') from each house on the other (the headings are more general than the anchors belonging to them).

Two or more units can also be related in terms of degrees of similarity and/or contrast. Similarity/contrast relations are essential for presenting the distinction between the two core types of website sections found on most websites:
- content sections, which provide information on certain topics and related activities
- functional sections, which offer information about the website, its designers, and/or organisation or functional features such as search and email forms.

On the APH homepage, as discussed above under 'Scope', the five main content sections ('Parliamentary Business', 'Senators & Members', 'News & Events', 'About Parliament' and 'Visit Parliament') are shown as similar to each other. At the same time, they are different from the functional sections (e.g. 'Contact', 'Help', 'Feedback', 'Copyright Information'), whose titles/anchors use smaller font and occupy different zones of the homepage.

In webpage design the same units can be simultaneously signalled as related in terms of both similarity and contrast. For example, the navigation menus 'House of Representatives' and 'Senate' occupy the same navigation zone, have the same structure and use the same font, but have different colour backgrounds.

LSRs may also involve one unit qualifying another by reference to location (in space or time) or cause (reason, purpose or means). The headings 'Experience Parliament' and 'Learning more about Parliament', for example, highlight the purpose (or motivation) for selecting the links under each heading.

Explicitness defines the extent to which a LSR is clearly signalled. LSRs in websites may be implicit, and rely for their interpretation on readers' familiarity with the website, its field (e.g. Australian politics) and/or web design conventions. A LSR may also be more or less explicit depending on which and how many semiotic resources (e.g. colour, font type, layout) are co-deployed to signal its presence or both its presence and its meaning.

Interpersonal meanings

How is the content presented to the reader (e.g. as rational, factual, or sensational)? What kind of relationship is construed visually between the reader, the content, and the author?

These questions can be explored through Kress and Van Leeuwen's (2006 [1996]) notion of 'modality', or truth value, in visual design. Knox (2009) identifies three variables that contribute to assigning different status to the information presented on a webpage, and that thereby construe particular relations between its authors, readers and the website. These are stasis, shape and space, and colour.

Stasis concerns degrees of movement (e.g. animation, rollovers, flashing elements) on a page. Less movement helps present a page as less 'playful' and visually adds to its credibility as a source of information by making the page more like print and therefore more 'conservative', and by focussing attention on the content rather than on the hypertext resources (Knox 2009: 256; Kok 2004).

Turning to *shape* and *space*, generally a squared, ordered page with clearly defined and consistently designed spaces for content visually presents information as rational, ordered, and logical (regardless of the actual logic or order of the information itself). A page using oblique angles, varied shapes, and/or a cluttered or 'chaotic' 'jigsaw' design, by contrast, presents information as random and chaotic (see Knox, Patpong and Piriyasilpa 2010).

With regard to *colour*, black (or near-black) text on a white (or near-white) background draws on the tradition of print. The further webpages move away from this, the more they bring attention to their 'impermanency' as web texts. Following established web design conventions (e.g. coloured font for hyperlinks and sparing use of colour for headings) also presents very differently to using a wide range of font colours or coloured backgrounds.

These three factors are 'read' in combination. We can describe pages that are relatively static, squared and ordered, and conservative in colour use as having relatively 'high modality' or high truth value from the perspective of a non-specialist audience, as they present the content in an apparently factual, reliable manner. (See Kress and Van Leeuwen 2006[1996]: 163–166, on the ways modality values may vary with the perspective from which viewers interpret visual representations). Pages that use a lot of movement, less conventional shapes, less neatly ordered space, and more varied colours present content as less reliable, and less likely to be factual. This, of course, has nothing to do with the actual factuality of the content, but is about the way visual design contributes to the relationship between the reader, the content, and the author.

Another factor, not discussed in depth here due to space limitations, is the authority of the website. The APH website is authored by the Parliament of Australia and the Australian coat of arms appears at the top of every page. This gives the content of the website an 'official' and trustworthy status it otherwise would not have.

In terms of modality, the APH home page uses a photographic image as background to the whole page, thus the page (and particularly the first screen) is framed in colour. This is offset by the use of a much more traditional colour scheme in the content zone and the third navigation zone, so much of the written text is black on white. The combination of the use of colour, the squared, compartmentalised, and 'uncluttered' use of shape and space, and the relatively static page (the animated 'rotating' images change slowly, and fade relatively slowly one into another when they do change; the only other animation is drop-down menus from the main tabs) contributes to a relatively high degree of factuality in the visual presentation of information on this web page.

How does the webpage align users attitudinally towards the website and its content?

To fulfil its purposes, the APH homepage should create a sense of comfort and security and align readers positively towards the values it seeks to promote. To understand how it is designed to achieve this, we can employ two tools that Stenglin and Djonov (2010) adapt to hypermedia, which were originally developed by Stenglin (2004) for the analysis of 3D space: Binding and Bonding.

Binding concerns "the way a space closes in on a person or opens up around them" (Stenglin 2004: 115). Spaces invoke security by providing protection and comfort (if Bound) or freedom of movement (if Unbound). Spaces that are Too Bound or Too Unbound typically create a sense of insecurity, of feeling either smothered or exposed and dwarfed (see further Stenglin, 2008). Following Stenglin and Djonov (2010: 196), design that simultaneously supports user orientation and freedom of navigation creates a sense of comfort, while disorientation or entrapment into a single navigation path can both cause frustration (see Figure 5).

The APH homepage provides a balanced sense of orientation and freedom of navigation. To illustrate, both are supported through the dropdown menu

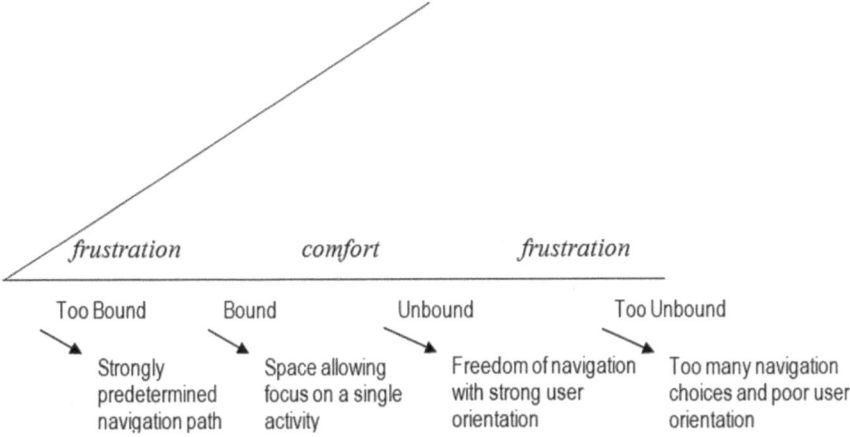

Figure 5: Binding in hypermedia (adapted from Stenglin and Djonov, 2010: 195)

that appears when each of the main section titles is activated as a rollover (i.e. the cursor is moved over it without clicking), offering a preview of what each section has to offer. This is shown for 'Visit Parliament' in Figure 6. Similarly for Binding, the coat of arms/website logo and the HOME tab serve as anchors allowing users to access the homepage directly from anywhere in the website and (re)orient themselves. A sense of comfort is also fostered through the conventional placement of the website logo and anchors to functional sections (e.g. 'Help', 'Disclaimer', 'Copyright Information').

Freedom of navigation is supported through alternative routes for accessing the same information. For instance, the section 'Visit Parliament' can be accessed both through the tab in the navigation zone at the top and from the list of links below the heading 'Experience Parliament' in the bottom navigation zone.

Bonding interacts with Binding to create communities around shared values, and involves aligning a particular field to positive or negative attitudes about it. Aligning people around shared values is facilitated through the use of **Bonding Icons**, "attitudinal alignments that have achieved stability and become social emblems [e.g. buildings, famous people, flags and symbols, iconic works of art and buildings] that people rally around in acceptance or rejection of shared values" (Stenglin and Djonov 2010: 196).

APH's website relies on the established value of Parliament House as an architectural icon designed to integrate with the Australian landscape (e.g. the building is built into the earth), to symbolise democracy (e.g. its lawns go over the whole building, so people can walk across the roof and 'over' Parliament), and to serve a range of functions (e.g. hosting public ceremonies and functions,

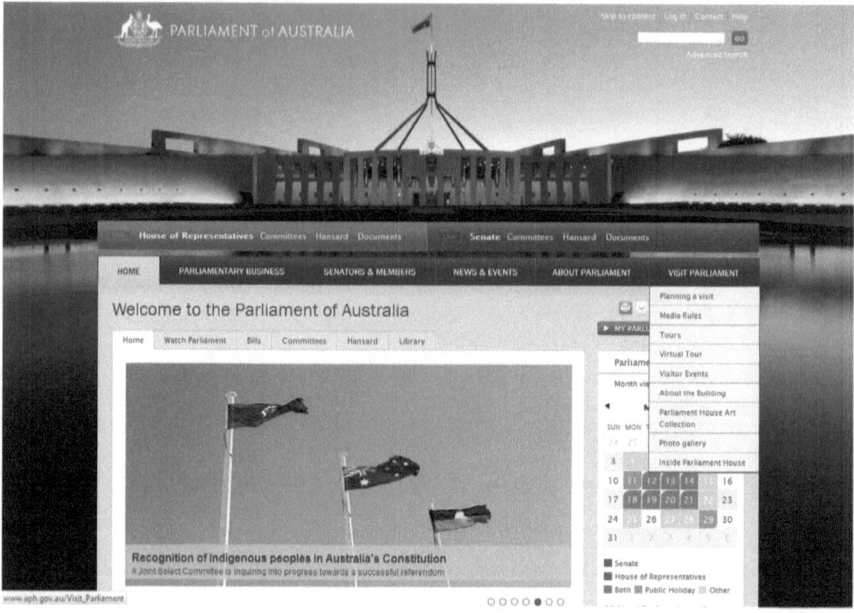

Figure 6: APH homepage's 'Head' with 'Visit Parliament' section's dropdown menu, with background showing Parliament House at night

housing art works, permanent and temporary exhibitions, and the Australian Parliament).

The APH homepage employs the building as a familiar Bonding Icon through the use of different photos of the house from both outside and inside. One is the background photo, which gains in interpersonal appeal for readers who notice that it changes from a day to a night shot of Parliament House as day changes to night in Australia (see Figure 6). This image is a long, eye-level shot that echoes the building's open, 'embrace-shaped' façade and human scale (cf. Kress and Van Leeuwen, 2006 [1996] on power relations in visual communication).

The rotating-image area features other Bonding Icons too. One image shows the Torres Strait Islander, Australian national and Aboriginal flags (Figure 6). Another shows the Magna Carta, a Medieval English document described on the APH website as "a foundation stone of constitutional and parliamentary government"; this Bonding Icon then presents the Australian Parliament, a relatively new and local institution, as a continuation of the 13th century origins of European democracy.

Textual meanings

How is the page composed to make each screen, and the entire page a meaningful 'whole'?

Building again on Kress and Van Leeuwen's (2006 [1996]) work, we can identify three factors that are important for achieving visual cohesion in the composition of webpages: information value, salience, and framing. Framing refers to the visual devices used to connect or separate 'packages' of content on a webpage. Devices such as borders, spacing, background colour, and lines can be used to frame content. Here, we only consider framing as it relates to information value and salience.

Webpages are viewed onscreen, and the most important information typically appears on the first screen of a page. Therefore, in the design of webpages that extend beyond a single screen, there is typically a top-bottom distinction between the first screen and the remainder of the page. Knox (2007) calls this a 'Head-Tail' opposition. The boundary between Head and Tail cannot always be clearly identified because webpage designers cannot specify where a page will be 'broken' on different computer screens. Many webpages also segment the content positioned in the Tail in a way that approximates a 'screen-full' of information. Regardless, the content of a webpage "decreases in impact and immediacy as the reader scrolls down" (Knox 2007: 38).

The Head of the APH homepage ends with the horizontal separation line immediately below the rotating-image area, and therefore includes the banner with the iconic image of Parliament House, the coat of arms, and the top two navigation zones, which classify the website's content (Figure 6).

Salience, or what webpage elements stand out the most, is, of course, not limited to proximity to the top of the page. Factors such as size, movement, and contrast all contribute to salience, and there is no 'formula' for determining their contributions. Commonsense predicts that images will be more salient than written text, but findings from eye tracking research are ambivalent about this, and some suggest that readers' gaze is typically attracted to writing first (Leckner 2012). However, eye movements do not necessarily equate with salience, so arguments about the relative salience of elements on the page need to be based on a combination of factors.

When viewing the entire APH homepage as a visual unit (as viewed in Figure 2), the most visually salient elements are the top image of Parliament House, and the second, large, 'rotating' image, due to their size and placement in the Head area, the animation of the large image, and their contrast with the rest of the page (colour versus grey scale, image versus written text). When viewing only the Head of the page on-screen, however, most of the screen space is taken up by images, and is a mix of colours (see Figure 6). In effect, there is not necessarily a single 'standout' feature on the page in terms of salience, which may encourage viewers' eyes to 'roam the page' rather than settling on a particular element.

To what extent does the homepage reveal the organisation of the website as a whole? What navigation choices does it offer and privilege? Does it support user orientation?

A webpage is expected to provide navigation options and reveal its place in the website to which it belongs. Additionally, a homepage should show both the navigation possibilities of the site as a whole and its structure. For these reasons, Djonov (2007) considers the homepage as serving a function analogous to that of the title of a chapter in a book or the first sentence in a paragraph, that is, as a 'Theme' (Martin 1992; Martin and Rose 2007 [2003]). The homepage can then be defined as the highest-level Theme in a website, the main page of a website section as a Theme below the level of the homepage, and so on. In Djonov's (2007) model of website hierarchy, these relations form a hierarchy of Themes, and each section, subsection, etc. branches into a separate hierarchy of Themes. The homepage is the point that unifies all the hierarchies of Themes within a website.

In this model, hyperlinks are categorised first as website-external, leading to another website or application, or website-internal. The latter are then sub-categorised as either vertical (if they connect different levels within the same hierarchy of Themes, e.g. the main page of a section to another page of that section) or horizontal (if they connect different hierarchies, e.g. from one website section to another). Both horizontal and vertical hyperlinks may obscure a website's structure if they allow a destination webpage to be reached directly, without visiting pages that function as higher-level Themes in the hierarchy of Themes to which the webpage belongs (e.g. returning to the homepage directly from a page presenting a story within a particular website subsection or switching from one website section to another without having to visit the homepage). Although potentially increasing disorientation, these hyperlinks enable freedom of navigation and are indispensable for a website's attractiveness. This is why it is important that such hyperlinks are combined with webpage design that reveals a website's hierarchical organisation (Djonov 2008).

The APH homepage reveals the organisation of the website into functional and content sections through the positioning of their titles/anchors in the banner and signature zones and tab-based navigation zone respectively. The tab-based navigation zone not only provides access to the website's main content sections, but also reveals the organisation of each through a dropdown menu that offers direct access to its subsections. As this zone appears on every webpage of APH's site, it provides considerable freedom of navigation along both the website's vertical (e.g. from a section's main page to another of its pages) and its horizontal dimension (e.g. from one (sub)section to another).

The APH homepage also provides alternative routes to subsections belonging to the main content sections. For example, the subsection 'Virtual Tour' belongs to the section 'Visit Parliament' and can be accessed from the section's dropdown menu in the tab-based navigation zone or from the link below the heading 'Experience Parliament' in the content zone.

Navigation options on the APH homepage vary in the degrees of orientation associated with them. For example, the rotating-image area provides direct access to items deeper within the website but does not reveal the (sub)sections to which each belongs. To find this out, readers must rely on the webpage of each feature. For example, selecting the item titled "Where can you learn more about the House of Representatives?" leads to a webpage with a 'breadcrumb trail' showing its location in the website's hierarchical structure as being four levels below the homepage: "Home » About Parliament » House of Representatives » Powers, practice and procedure » Infosheets".

The homepage appears to offer no access to destinations outside the website. Selecting the items titled "Parliament house is turning 25: 1988–2013" and "Explore Magna Carta online" from the rotating-image area, however, leads to pages with markedly different design. Their distinctive design may be motivated by a desire to attract to them a wider audience, including readers who do not engage in current politics or do not support Australia's parliamentary structure, but who are interested in history or politics in general.

The examples in this analysis of navigation options offered on APH's homepage point to the need to consider any webpage as a hypermedia unit and explore its actual and potential hypertextual links to other webpages within and beyond the website's boundaries.

Conclusion

This chapter has presented a social semiotic framework for analysing webpages as visual units in terms of their purpose, ideational, interpersonal and textual meaning (see Figure 1). As the analysis reveals, the same feature can have repercussions for all three types of meaning. For example, the dropdown menus for each main section classify information, present the website subsections as similar, allow readers to access those subsections directly while supporting their orientation, and reveal the hierarchical organisation of the site. Applying the framework to the homepage of the Parliament of Australia website revealed that the APH homepage serves the purpose of representing, enacting, and educating viewers about Australian democracy as well as promoting Australian Parliament House as a tourist destination.

Ideationally, content on the page is presented in several zones, including three navigation zones that classify the content of the website. The content zone on the page is classified in a covert taxonomy divided into 'information' and 'utilities', but there are inconsistencies in this classification. Further, important content about the Australian Parliament (the role of the Queen and Governor-General) is completely absent from the homepage content and website structure. Logico-semantic relations between elements on the homepage function primarily to represent relations between the website's sections, and are mostly explicitly signalled. They distinguish content from functional sections, and present sections about the Australian Parliament and about visiting Australian Parliament House as being of similar status, in accord with the website's purposes.

Interpersonally, the APH homepage is constructed to appear factual and authoritative; to create a sense of comfort by balancing freedom of navigation with strong support for user orientation; and to align readers around positive, shared values towards Australian history and politics through images of potent iconic objects such as Parliament House, the Australian and Indigenous flags, and the Magna Carta.

Textually, the most important ideational and interpersonal meanings are constructed on the first screen, or the 'Head' of the page, which features most of the images of iconic objects, and two of the three navigation zones. These zones serve to provide access to and classify website content. The homepage supports a high degree of freedom of navigation, by offering alternative as well as direct routes to information – up to four levels deeper within the website's hierarchical structure. It also supports a high degree of user orientation, by allowing readers to predict the destinations of most hyperlinks departing from the homepage.

Finally, taking a social semiotic approach requires that multimodal or hypermodal structures and their meanings be systematically related to social context. To achieve that, analysts need knowledge of the field of the website. Familiarity with Australian politics, for example, reveals a significant hypermodally-constructed 'fiction' on the APH homepage – the absence of a foreign monarch, who in reality sits above the two chambers described as "the people's house"

(House of Representatives) and "a check on the government of the day" (Senate) on the homepage.

Thus, the APH homepage is a coherent, authoritative and positive representation of the Parliament of Australia that enacts certain aspects of democracy, but does so in a way that also reproduces undemocratic aspects of the social order. As this example suggests, then, the social semiotic framework for webpage analysis presented in this chapter holds considerable value for the critical multimodal discourse analysis of web texts.

Further readings

Djonov, Emilia. 2007. Website hierarchy and the interaction between content organization, webpage and navigation design: A systemic functional hypermedia discourse analysis perspective. *Information Design Journal* 15(2): 144–162.
Knox, John S. 2007. Visual-verbal communication on online newspaper home pages. *Visual Communication* 6(1): 19–53.
Lemke, Jay L. 2002. Travels in hypermodality. *Visual Communication* 1(3): 299–325.

Project idea

Choose a website from a field in which you have knowledge or expertise. Find 2–3 different versions of the homepage of that website from different time periods on www.archive.org. Analyse each using the framework introduced in this chapter. Do the results of the analysis reflect changes in the structure and values of the institution and its field? Were there aspects of webpage design that required additional or different analytical tools?

References

Carreon, Jonathan R., Todd R. Watson and John S. Knox. forthcoming. Medical tourism communication of a Thai private hospital website. *Journal of Applied Linguistics and Professional Practice*.
Commonwealth of Australia. (n.d.-a). Parliament of Australia website (Creative Commons Attribution-NonCommercial-NoDerivs 3.0 Australia licence) Retrieved March 31, 2013, from http://www.aph.gov.au/
Commonwealth of Australia. (n.d.-b). Parliament of Australia Infosheet 20: The Australian system of government (Creative Commons Attribution-NonCommercial-NoDerivs 3.0 Australia licence) Retrieved March 31, 2013, from http://www.aph.gov.au/About_Parliament/

House_of_Representatives/Powers_practice_and_procedure/00_-_Infosheets/Infosheet_20_-_The_Australian_system_of_government

Djonov, Emilia. 2005. Analysing the organisation of information in websites: From hypermedia design to systemic functional hypermedia discourse analysis. PhD Thesis. University of New South Wales, Sydney. Retrieved from http://handle.unsw.edu.au/1959.4/23915

Djonov, Emilia. 2007. Website hierarchy and the interaction between content organization, webpage and navigation design: A systemic functional hypermedia discourse analysis perspective. *Information Design Journal* 15(2): 144–162.

Djonov, Emilia. 2008. Children's website structure and navigation. In Len Unsworth (ed.), *Multimodal Semiotics: Functional Analysis in Contexts of Education*, 216–236. London: Continuum.

Garrett, Jesse J. 2011[2003]. *The Elements of User Experience: User-Centred Design for the Web and Beyond* (2nd ed.). Indianapolis, Indiana: New Riders Publishing.

Halliday, Michael A. K. (1985). Part A. In Michael A. K. Halliday and Ruqaiya Hasan (eds.), *Language, Context, and Text: Aspects of Language in a Social-Semiotic Perspective*, 1–49. Geelong, Victoria: Deakin University Press.

Halliday, Michael A. K. 1994 [1985]. *An Introduction to Functional Grammar* (2nd ed.). London: Arnold.

Halliday, Michael A. K. and Ruqaiya Hasan, R. 1976. *Cohesion in English*. London/New York: Longman.

Halliday, Michael A. K. and Christian M. I. M. Matthiessen. 2004. *An Introduction to Functional Grammar* (3rd Edition). London: Arnold.

Hodge, Robert and Gunther Kress. 1988. *Social Semiotics*. Cambridge: Polity Press.

Knox, John S. 2007. Visual-verbal communication on online newspaper home pages. *Visual Communication* 6(1): 19–53.

Knox, John S. 2009. *Multimodal discourse on online newspaper home pages: A social-semiotic perspective*. PhD thesis. University of Sydney, Sydney. Retrieved from http://ses.library.usyd.edu.au/handle/2123/7696

Knox, John S. 2010. Online newspapers: Evolving genres, evolving theory. In Caroline Coffin, Teresa Lillis and Kay L. O'Halloran (eds.), *Applied Linguistics Methods: A Reader*, 33–51. London: Routledge.

Knox, S. John. forthcoming. Online newspapers: Structure and layout. In Carey Jewitt (ed.), *The Routledge Handbook of Multimodal Analysis* (2nd ed.). London: Routledge.

Knox, John S., Patama Patpong, and Yupaporn Piriyasilpa. 2010. ข่าวหน้าหนึ่ง (Khao naa nung): A multimodal analysis of Thai-language newspaper pages. In Monica Bednarek and James R. Martin (eds.), *New discourse on language: Functional perspectives on multimodality, identity, and affiliation*, 80–110. London: Continuum.

Kok, Arthur K. C. 2004. Multisemiotic mediation in hypertext. In Kay L. O'Halloran (ed.), *Multimodal Discourse Analysis:Systemic-Functional Perspectives*, 131–159. London/New York: Continuum.

Kress, Gunther and Theo Van Leeuwen. 2006 [1996]. *Reading Images: The Grammar of Visual Design* (2nd ed.). London: Routledge.

Krug, Steve. 2006 [2000]. *Don't Make me Think!: A Common Sense Approach to Web Usability* (2nd ed.). Berkeley, CA: New Riders.

Landow, George P. 1987. Relationally encoded links and the rhetoric of hypertext. In *Proceedings of the ACM Hypertext '87 Conference*, 331–343.

Leckner, Sara. 2012. Presentation factors affecting reading behaviour in readers of newspaper media: An eye-tracking perspective. *Visual Communication* 11(2): 163–184.
Lemke, Jay L. 2002. Travels in hypermodality. *Visual Communication* 1(3): 299–325.
Lynch, Patrick J., and Sarah Horton. 2008 [1999, 2001]. *Web Style Guide: Basic Design Principles for Creating Web Sites* (3rd ed.). New Haven/London: Yale University Press.
Martin, James R. 1992. *English Text: System and Structure*. Amsterdam/Philadelphia: John Benjamins Publishing Company.
Martin, James R. and David Rose. 2007 [2003]. *Working with Discourse: Meaning Beyond the Clause* (2nd ed.). London: Continuum.
Nielsen, Jakob and Marie Tahir. 2002. *Homepage Usability: 50 Websites Deconstructed*. Indianopolis: New Riders Publishing.
Perlmutter, David D. 2003. The internet: Big pictures and interactors. In L. Gross, Julian S. Katz and Ruby Jay (eds.), *Image Ethics in the Digital Age* (Vol. 1–25). Minneapolis: University of Minnesota Press.
Stenglin, Maree. 2004. Packaging curiosities: Towards a grammar of three-dimensional space. PhD dissertation, Sydney: University of Sydney. Retrieved from http://ses.library.usyd.edu.au/handle/2123/635
Stenglin, Maree. 2008. Binding: a resource for exploring interpersonal meaning in 3D space. *Social Semiotics* 18(4): 425–447.
Stenglin, Maree and Emilia Djonov. 2010. Unpacking narrative in a hypermedia 'artedventure' for children. In Christian R. Hoffmann (ed.), *Narrative revisi4ted. Telling a story in the age of new media*, 185–212. Amsterdam/ Philadelphia: John Benjamins.
Zhang, Yiqiong. 2012. Representing science: A multimodal study of science popularization on institutional and mass media websites. PhD Thesis, National University of Singapore, Singapore. Retrieved from http://scholarbank.nus.edu.sg/handle/10635/36378
Zhang, Yiqiong and Kay L. O'Halloran. 2012. The gate of the gateway: A hypermodal approach to university homepages. *Semiotica* 190: 87–109.
Zhang, Yiqiong and Kay L. O'Halloran. 2014. From popularization to marketization: The hypermodal nucleus in institutional science news. In Emilia Djonov and Sumin Zhao (eds.), *Critical Multimodal Studies of Popular Discourse* 160–177. London/New York: Routledge.

Acknowledgements

The authors would like to thank Dr Maree Stenglin for insightful comments on Binding and Bonding in the Australian Parliament House as an architectural text and on the APH homepage.

Rick Iedema
16 A participatory approach to 'analysing' visual data: Involving practitioners in visual feedback

Introduction

This chapter considers the use of video data feedback to intervene in the quality and safety of clinical processes in health care. Intervening in these processes is important, because health care is extremely complex and its processes are frequently multi-stranded and fast-paced at the same time. Clinicians often do not have or take the time to think and talk about how to organise their processes across units and services. Instead they maintain a narrow focus on the more technical and purely medical aspects of care. Yet they are faced with rising numbers of patients who are chronically ill, and many of whom have multiple problems or 'co-morbidities'. This means that care trajectories involve multiple specialties and services, thereby becoming more intricate and more challenging to organise, and hence more difficult to keep safe.

I personally am not a clinician and do not have clinical experience. I am frequently challenged trying to understand the processes of care that I study. For patients and their family members this is a problem too: they are frequently confused about what is going on and whom they are dealing with. Even clinicians who become patients themselves frequently report confusion about the processes of care that unfold around them (Berwick 2009). For researchers to make sense of what goes on in health care on their own, without the input of practitioners, is therefore hard, and sometimes impossible.

Another confounder may be the methods and analytical schemas that researchers seek to apply to explain health care practice. These may suit researchers' analytical interests and understanding, but they may not satisfy or meet the needs of practitioners and patients. Research methods and analytical schemas may even be experienced as not making sense given the complexity of the 'logic of [clinical] practice' (Bourdieu 1990). For these reasons, researchers' collaborating with clinician-practitioners and patients is an increasingly critical strategy. Collaboration helps the researcher-analyst to work out what issues are important to focus on, what data are collected and how, and what exactly is to be done with that data. Important to note here is that this means that the primacy of analytical methods can neither be posited nor presumed. This is due to the complexity of the practices that are in focus, the multiple stakeholders in these practices, and the different expectations now bearing on the research, its processes, and its outcomes.

I suggest collaboration with those whose practices we are interested in enriches research because it enables negotiation of aspects of clinical processes whose logic and meaning are difficult to discern for non-initiates, like myself. Collaboration also makes for a less predictable and more exciting research process. It opens research up to different views and expectations. Further, collaboration leads to a much more direct impact on practice, particularly when practitioners and the patients learn about care practice by being involved in the overall research process, and are enabled to articulate changes to better suit their contexts and purposes.

Another critical dimension to my research is the use of video. Because clinical processes unfold so quickly and have so many strands, I felt it would be advantageous to *video* health care processes. Video-ing these processes might not just give a richer record of what goes on, but it might also frame practice in a 'visual language' that is more easily accessible to practitioners and patients compared to other ways in which researchers frame and present their data (transcripts, diagrams, formal analyses). Indeed, I regard video-ing practice and showing the results back to those who appear in the video footage and involving those people in making sense of that footage as a deliberate democratic strategy and ethical act.

In what follows I will set out the basis for participatory research in complex organisational settings. I will then expand on the use of video, and particularly video feedback in such settings. Following that I will explain how one of our projects unfolded, how we orchestrated it, and what the outcomes were. In my conclusion, I draw the various strands of the chapter together to advocate for an ethics of research practice. This ethics is not one of critique, and justified on the grounds of analytical dissection. Instead, it is one of participation and collaboration, defined by and enacted through our approach, our methods, our outcomes, and our social and practical impact.

Key terms: Affect, diffraction, participative enquiry, video-reflexive ethnography.

Participatory research in action

In recent years, the practice of involving in the research the people whom researchers want to study has taken on increasing importance. Particularly researchers in the areas of disability research, multi-ethnic research and social justice research have become acutely aware of the need to share research strategies, rationales, learnings and outcomes with what were commonly regarded as 'the subjects of research' – the people who were studied by being observed, interviewed, or subjected to tests (Mertens 1998; Mertens 2009).

If as yet infrequently practised, collaborative enquiry and participatory research are now regarded as valid and credible variations on more established forms of action research (Reason 1999; Reason and Bradbury 2008). The reasons given in favour of these endeavours by researchers working with disadvantaged people tend to centre on their subjects' difficulty of access for themselves to research funding, project investigation decisions, research literatures, and research findings. These reasons are valid and important. In this chapter, I want to add two other reasons to this list, arguing for research subject participation in social research *per se*.

First, participatory research is critical in circumstances where there is a high level of practical complexity and rapidly unfolding and changing processes. Analysing what people do in such circumstances using formal analytical tools and resources risks producing findings and conclusions that may not be relevant to those who have a stake in those practices and processes. Findings may be obtuse to practitioners, and conclusions may be out of date by the time they are articulated due to the speed of change in practice.

Second, involving practitioners in the research short-circuits what questions are asked, how they asked, by whom, and with what effect. That is, researchers' approaches and foci, when open to practitioners' concerns, are likely to benefit from their practical insights as well as from persistent confusions. This is because a participative approach ensures they inform not merely the findings of the research, but also its orientation, its structure, its ability to change direction, and its ultimate practical outcomes, by feeding back into practitioners' awareness of how they carry out their work.

In short, participatory research has particular importance for rendering research more sensitive and more immediately relevant to the way practices are enacted in the here-and-now. It has effect on those involved in the research, because they have been given a stake in it and its outcomes. Such research thereby bypasses the perpetual triumvirate of problems of argumentation, dissemination and implementation.

Involving research subjects in video reflexive ethnography

The use of video to enable health care practitioners to reflect on their practices is by no means new (Hargie and Morrow 1986). Mostly though, video feedback has been restricted in two ways. It has been used predominantly with junior trainees, and it has been deployed in domains where technical-medical skills are at issue or where one-on-one communication skills are practised. Until recently, video feedback has been used only rarely in complex organisations such as hospitals, to focus on real-time *in situ* work processes involving senior clinicians from nursing, medicine, allied health and management, capturing both clinical-technical and relational processes, and including patients as central stakeholders in care provision and in care improvement.

When I began involving practitioners and patients in selecting and scrutinising footage of their own care processes, two things became apparent. On the one hand, people were frequently surprised by what they saw. They might have worked in the setting filmed for years, and yet be taken aback by what they saw unfolding on the screen. On the other hand, people often saw beyond what was displayed on the screen, out across the organisation, back into the past, or forward into the future, linking what was shown to what was known (Iedema, Mesman, and Carroll 2013).

These were critical findings. They indicated that the visual medium, alongside capturing aspects of practice that might be transparent for practitioners and patients, could also reveal practices in ways that were not (or no longer) evident to those inhabiting those practices themselves. Thus, I realised that our video footage was not simply a means to gain clarity about what goes on. Focusing clinicians' (and patients') attention on specific aspects of practice was no guarantor for getting a firm or a single explanation.

Rather, the footage revealed itself to harbour facets of practice of which practitioners and patients themselves were not necessarily aware, or no longer consciously aware. In that way, the footage *re-minded* people. The footage enabled people to view their practices from a different angle. This made evident that reflection was not an adequate descriptor for what transpired during the visual feedback meetings. Showing the footage enabled people to explain *only in part* the context and logic of practice, and enabled me, the analyst, to apply my analytical tools *only in part* to reveal important patterns and unrecognised regularities. What happened most frequently, in these meetings, was that practitioners and patients had to produce new explanations for what went on. In doing so, they tended to formulate questions about what went on. They also appeared to realise, for the first time, the problems inherent in what went on.

Importantly, it was this process that led to another: people started to notice opportunities for *changing* what went on. Hence, viewing footage was no longer about producing explanations and clarifications for my benefit. It was instead about partaking in conversations that were exploratory, experimental and creative. Instead of reflection, or even reflexivity, therefore, the effect of showing people video footage of their own ways of doing, being and saying may be better characterised as one of incurring *diffraction* (Haraway 1998).

Diffraction is explained as follows in Haraway's original text:

> Diffraction does not produce 'the same' displaced, as reflection and refraction do. Diffraction is a mapping of interference, not of replication, reflection, or reproduction. A diffraction pattern does not map where differences appear, but rather maps where the effects of difference appear. (Haraway 1992: 300)

Diffraction is what makes negotiating with people what to video and showing them video footage of their ways of being in the world so productive. It is this that drives much of the participative video work we have done over recent years (Iedema, Merrick, Rajbhandari, Gardo, Stirling, and Herkes 2009a).

The data focused on in this chapter

The data focused on in this chapter is derived from a large clinical handover project which I and a team of researchers conducted for the Australian Commission on Safety and Quality in Health Care between 2007 and 2008. Many similar studies have been done since then (Iedema, Mesman, and Carroll 2013), but this clinical handover project included developing and publishing a comprehensive statement setting out the video-reflexive ethnography approach (Iedema, Merrick, Kerridge, Herkes, Lee, Anscombe, Rajbhandari, Lucey, and White 2009b; Iedema and Merrick 2008).

The clinical handover project involved filming of how clinicians engaged in handing over clinical information to their colleagues as part of shift changes in two large teaching hospitals. Our team collected 16 hours of visual data over a period of ten months, involving four hospitals, 150 clinicians and 5 patients. The visual data produced from the project was used to generate discussions among the clinicians involved in the handovers. The purpose of this was to enable the clinicians to think about how they might be able to systematise their information exchanges and render their practice more predictable and structured. This was an important aim, given that numerous clinical incidents occur as a result of inadequate and ineffective team-to-team and department-to-department handovers leading to misunderstandings, inaccurate reporting, and incomplete information, and ultimately to potentially disastrous errors and failures in care (ACSQHC 2008).

A 'how-to' of participatory video-based research

Participatory video-based research, referred to here as video-reflexive ethnography or 'VRE' (Iedema, Long, Forsyth, and Lee 2006), starts with a collaborative identification of a research problematic or priority. At times, such problematic and priority may be evident from how research funding opportunities are designed and defined by the health industry (i.e. the health bureaucracy). The project described here was designed and funded by a government agency, a federal or national agency overseeing the quality and safety of health care in Australia. This agency had established that clinical handover was a critical process in the overall trajectory of patients' care. The agency had funded a number of projects that would generate resources for practitioners to make their clinical handovers safer.

Instead of proposing to implement a predesigned handover protocol and test clinicians' compliance with the protocol, we sought to involve clinicians in scrutinising their existing handover practices, and develop their own unique protocol. This was to ensure that local practitioners felt ownership over the protocol, knew how to redesign it in case circumstances changed, and knew how to integrate it into their existing practices.

The process we designed to achieve this was as follows (table 1).

Table 1

Step	Description
1. Engaging management	It is critical to obtain management support for the method. While this will not guarantee frontline clinician support, it promotes faith in the positive impact of the method and reassures staff that the risk of capturing potentially subpoenable material is outweighed by management support for the method and their prioritizing of team learning over defensive risk management attitudes.

2. Familiarizing frontline staff with the video method	Frontline staff needs to believe that their involvement will provide a means for them to take action in some way with regard to their own ways of working. To achieve this, facilitator-researchers need to work on developing trust relationships with those clinicians who are willing to participate in the video-ing. Trust is engendered by facilitator-researchers spending time on the wards or in the relevant departments as non-participant observers, before bringing along their video cameras. Also, a series of meetings needs to be arranged with frontline staff, to explore: their understandings of the video method, their responsibilities when signing up, ground rules (about ending one's relationship with the project or questioning the video-ing of specific events), as well as practical issues that they find worthy of being video-ed.
3. Videotaping and 'hot feedback'	Handover events are videotaped over a set period of between a few days and a couple of weeks (depending on resources available). On the day of video-ing and once the video-ing has concluded, sections of the videos can be immediately shown back to individual professionals (one-on-one). This hot-feedback component signals to clinical professionals that the facilitator-researchers value their input, and that they have a role to play in deciding what is valuable footage and what is not. It also enables facilitators to gain initial insight into prominent issues in the footage, relevant foci for improvement, as well as sensitive matters (pertaining to specific individuals or actions visible in the footage and which may be detrimental if shown publicly). Hot feedback also offers the facilitator-researchers the opportunity to ask for permission to show the recordings to others. In doing this, facilitators are enabled to fine-tune their video-ing, building confidence they are video-ing the right thing, that the participating professionals are happy with what is going on, and that they are capturing useful data. The facilitators stop with video-ing when time runs out (and not much footage is needed to have a good reflexive session!), or when saturation is reached (when no new issues are captured). Depending on the level of detail required, and depending on the degree of familiarity on the part of the researcher with the site and the practice, saturation tends to set in anywhere between a week and three weeks, but this is a rough guide only. At the

	end of step 2 many if not most professionals have seen some footage, feel comfortable with the process, and may have ideas for how to intervene in their handover communication practice.
4. Selecting and editing video fragments	Based on the input of the professionals and the facilitators' own expertise, the facilitator-researchers make compilations of video clips that capture the discussion themes and/or specific issues, problems, or successes. Clips used for feedback should not be more than a couple to 4 minutes long. Before being shown in public, clip selections should be tested one-on-one with on-site champions to ensure no sensitive actions or questionable behaviours are shown publicly, potentially damaging relationships. Facilitator-researchers have to have a bank of clips and work out how to structure the discussion; that is, they need to be clear about the questions and issues they would like to see raised, even if the resulting deliberations end up moving in very different directions.
5. Multidisciplinary feedback	The selected clips are presented at feedback sessions. The facilitator-researchers may structure their presentation on the basis of what they have video-ed and heard during previous meetings and during the hot feedback. The feedback meeting may be video-ed to capture the groups' responses and creative thinking. Frequently, the discussion will flow quite freely and touch on a great variety of topics. Here, facilitation comes into its own: the facilitators need to skillfully guide the participants to address matters that matter and that can be feasibly changed. In many instances too, groups will steer the discussion towards important issues and useful outcomes. Ideally, the meeting concludes with an agreement on a change, and identification of a person responsible for overseeing the change and its communication to staff, and a starting date.
6. Recording the change	When the change that was devised during the feedback meeting or meetings (e.g. a new handover format, or a handover form, or a checklist, etc) is put into practice, it is important that this change and the new practices buttressing it are video-recorded. Time needs to be allowed of course for the practice to 'gain traction'. A date is agreed when the teams are ready to be video-ed enacting the change. A further set of feedback meetings or evaluations can be initiated with the purpose of engendering conviction among staff that they are capable of 'continuous improvement'.

In what follows I first present a formal analysis of some of the handover communication that we video-ed. Following that I describe how practitioners themselves saw the footage, what their comments were, and what they decided to do in response to viewing it.

Analysing clinical handover communication

Clinical handovers were filmed in (among other places) the Emergency Department or 'ED'. Before showing footage segments back to ED staff, the research team selected clips and produced transcripts to use for the feedback meetings. The extract below is one such transcript. In the original clip, the night (junior) doctor (here DR1) presents a handover to the senior day doctor about a motor-vehicle-accident patient he cared for during the night. The reason we chose this clip is that the junior doctor seemed unusually vague and confused, those attending the handover did not seem very interested and engaged, and some even started their own conversations while the handover was unfolding. We wanted to explore how these issues were interpreted by the practitioners involved.

Extract 1: Medical night shift to medical morning shift (DR = doctor)

DR1: Well he he when he came in he was writhing around on the floor. He was just in referred pain. So he had indomethacin and about twenty morphine in five milligrams lots. About twenty morphine in five milligram lots too.

DR2: how long ago did he have the morphine

DR1: uh I'm not suite sure when his last one was is- it- he took twenty basically straight away to get him down

DR2: uh what time vaguely

DR1: ah probably about one o'clock would've been

DR2: so he's been pain free for si-

DR1: oh he had fi- he went to sleep then he had five sometime between now and then um

DR2: so he's had repeated doses

DR1: just one

DR2: oh okay

DR1: There's not much else to do in terms of that.

DR2: mm

DR1: Wait for the CT.

DR2: Is the pain completely gone?

DR1: Yeah. Last we checked yeah. He is being seen by the urologist um (who was seeing him) about a month ago (and he knew that there was something bilaterally). But they weren't (inaudible). So we'll see what's going on at the moment.

DR3: Is he having indomethacin for this?

DR1: Yes he has.

DR3: Yeah yeah right and that didn't work much and that's why he had a (whole lot of) morphine.

The transcript shows that the junior doctor (DR1) sounds quite tentative in his responses ("Um I'm not quite sure"). He also is quite unspecific about the drugs he administered: "he had indomethacin and about twenty morphine in five milligrams lots". The senior doctor asks, "so he's had repeated doses", but we are not clear to which drug is being referred. The reply to this question is "just one". In the absence of clarification which drug is at issue, we remain unclear whether this means the indomethacin was administered separately and only once, or whether it contradicts the earlier '5 mg lots' comment. Not much later during the same exchange, related issues are brought up (extract 2).

Extract 2: Medical night shift to medical morning shift (DR = doctor)

DR1: and er left-sided er (inaudible) groin pain came on quite suddenly. Um required indomethacin and morphine when he came in. Um he's also had some (inaudible) since the pain started and um he was had blood in his urine. Afebrile. By the time I saw him he was kind of settled and pain free. (I examined) his abdomen and it was nice and soft. And on his bloods he did have a raised blood cell of fourteen (inaudible) otherwise normal. We were gonna- he was pain free for like five hours or so so we were gonna get- he's got the (specialist) reports so we were going to try and get him home. Gave him a sat dose of (inaudible) in case this was a a UTI[1] [inaudible] kind of picture.

DR2: [inaudible]

DR1: hm?

DR2: [inaudible]

DR1: yeah yeah they were at the time but he'd had quite a bit of morphine and stuff so. But then when I was just about to get him home he (writhed) in pain again. He didn't need morphine, he settled with panadeine forte. It wasn't severe. Anyway he's now booked in for a CT [inaudible]. I've spoken to the radiologist this morning now.

DR2: Renal function normal?

---

1 UTI stands for urinary tract infection.

DR1: Renal functions normal. So I was yeah he's had couple- he's a stat dose of (gen) (and some *Keflax*) as well just or- um just in case. And his MSUs gone off just 'cause his white cells were raised. But he's been afebrile. He's actually been quite settled for the most of the night...

Again, the communication shown here comes across as *ad hoc* and unstructured. Earlier points are repeated, but now with different emphases and details. The junior doctor handing over mentions again that he administered two drugs, without specifying the amounts administered nor the times at which the drugs were administered. The footage shows he had no documentation handy from which he could have obtained these details. No one else present referred to paperwork to clarify the issue. Overall, the handover comes across as 'laboured': people look elsewhere, they appear bored, no one except the senior doctor asks questions, and some people even start up a separate conversation.

Another clinical question arises around the doctor's overall perception that the patient's pain had reduced during the night. He says that less strong painkillers were needed as time progressed, and that the patient was being prepared to go home. Yet a subsequent episode of pain meant the doctor had to ask for a CT scan. Interestingly, this issue of whether the patient was or had been in pain was not pursued during the handover. No one present thinks it important to clarify it.

The tenor and the orientation of the senior doctor's questions suggest that she regards this exchange as being about both information and education. There is a degree of leniency in her questioning ("what time, vaguely"), accommodating the junior night-doctor's obvious fatigue evident from his tentative answers and imprecise diagnosis. However, both as pedagogic event and as patient handover communication, this exchange would appear to suffer from several shortcomings: the junior doctor's lack of factual knowledge about potentially dangerous drug administrations appears to be condoned; no attempt is made on the part of the senior staff member to clarify the drug or the pain details, and there is no pedagogic (in contrast to service-centred) questioning of the junior doctor or any of the others present about the medical and clinical content of the handover.

These are some clinical observations that an outsider-researcher might derive from analysing the footage. Delving more deeply into some of the bodily comportments that are evident in the footage (Knoblauch, Schnettler, Raab, and Soeffner 2006), we could comment on the excessively tired-looking junior doctor, the bodily disengagement of the other junior clinicians, the concurrent conversation between a doctor and a nurse over some unrelated paperwork, and the somewhat exasperated questioning by the senior doctor.

Conveying such analytical claims to practitioners is difficult however. They may bare taken-as-given conducts and be experienced as confronting. The advantage of video of course is that practitioners may be able to view their own conducts and draw their own conclusions. Indeed, enabling them to observe their own behavioural practices and discuss these tends to intensify their engagement with the feedback process, and lead to creative insights into how to change how they communicate about and organise their care.

Video-reflexive ethnography

As noted, the project was designed as a participatory study. Participation occurred at different levels. First, we negotiated with clinicians what and where to film. We also discussed with them what to edit into the feedback materials, liaising with all stakeholders to make sure no inappropriate or undesirable footage was shown. Finally, rather than privileging our own readings and analyses, and instead of promoting our own conclusions, we sought to give prominence to practitioners' interpretations and insights into change.

During the feedback sessions, practitioners' comments revealed that they readily connected the brief sections of footage (1–3 minute clips) to the broader clinical context, as well as to specific treatment activities. This provided reassurance that while the footage might not fully capture all possible handover practices, it was relevant and meaningful to the practitioners reflecting on handover communication as practice[2].

The absence of structure in the handovers was regarded as of interest. However, practitioners homed in on how the footage of their handover communication foregrounded issues pertaining to intra- and inter-professional *relationships*. Thus, they honed in on the junior doctor's exhaustion, and how it conflicted with the professional imperative to impress one's colleagues. Equally, they commented on the lack of engagement between nursing and medical staff, and the consequences of this for information handling. This latter concern was evident from this comment made during one feedback session:

---

[2] The objection that video can only ever show a narrow slice of practice can be countered by pointing to how practitioners see video footage as *hologrammatic*. From their comments, it is evident that they see *through* the video footage: using their intimate knowledge of practice and its context, they see back to past activities, out to concurrent ones, and forward to future ones.

"One thing that sort of struck me is, the nurses come along they do a big handover, work out what's going on, the medical people come along do a handover and get what's going on, but there is no real cross-communication between the two, I mean there is a lot of information that we both need to share, and we are doing two separate handovers. What would be the benefit of combining a medical and nursing handover?" (ED nursing clinician, feedback session, 2008)

Another clinician comments on the problem of professional teams 'working on their own', without communicating with other staff:

"One thing I really noticed is that every team just works on their own, like when you notice, when the seniors come around they do their thing, then the juniors are doing their thing ... everything changes minute to minute, and sometimes you are completely outdated with the information." (ED medical clinician, feedback session, 2008)

These comments suggest that reflexive video viewing may lead people to comment on the bodily and behavioural dimensions of what goes on. This means that video feedback may have in the first instance an *affective* impact on those captured in the footage (Iedema et al. 2009a). Others too have found that video data engage people *affectively*; that is, at the level of how relationships are enacted and experienced, and how they figure in those relationships.

I suggest that the prominence of the relational, produced through witnessing oneself interact with colleagues in the video footage, is what introduces a special energy to the feedback meetings. It is this energy that enables practitioners to *diffract* what is; that is, transform their perspective on what might otherwise appear as taken-as-given, unchangeable, or not in need of change because normalised and naturalised. The visual *affects* people, and thereby it *diffracts*. It makes them see previously taken-as-given things differently.

The relational energy and diffraction produced by video feedback have been explained in different ways. MacDougall, a participatory documentary maker, explains video's impact by suggesting that footage is capable of at once distancing 'the real' (i.e. what people regard as 'the real') and bringing 'the real' closer. It distances by compressing and shrinking 'the real' down to fit onto a flat, 2-dimensional screen. At the same time, it brings 'the real' nearer by re-playing activities and events that we experience as intimately familiar (MacDougall 2006). For those featuring in the footage, this dual pull may engender surprise and wonder.

Another commentator, Massumi, also writes about a dual effect when people engage in video feedback. He refers to the "continuous displacement of the subject, the object and their general relation" (Massumi 2002: 51). This displacement harbours transformative potential, in that the subject (the practitioner) and the object (the clinical unit, handover practice, the patient) are removed from their usual way of relating. Massumi suggests that transformative energy springs from the footage 'de-subjectifying' the viewer and 'de-objectifying' her context and practice. Put differently, viewing video footage creates a diffractive space where "[t]he objectness of the object is attenuated, as the subject, seeing itself as others see it, comes to occupy the object's place as well as its own. Simultaneously occupying its place and the object's, the subject departs from itself" (Massumi 2002: 50).

It was evident during the project that the practitioners who participated experienced something unique. The process motivated them to intervene in their own everyday ways of doing, being and saying. In the sites where this handover study was conducted, and in sites where similar research was done, practitioners designed and almost immediately after initiated new handover communication processes (Carroll, Iedema, and Kerridge 2008; Iedema, Ball, Daly, Young, Green, Middleton, Foster-Curry, Jones, Hoy, and Comerford 2012; Iedema et al. 2009b).

Important to mention is that what was proposed as part of these studies contrasted sharply with the one-size-fits-all protocol-based solutions that are currently being imposed on handover practice by change consultants and safety experts (e.g. Haig, Sutton, and Whittington 2006). Instead of producing simply lists of information items, participating practitioners devised innovative relational solutions. Thus, they generated more cross-professional information exchange opportunities, more suitable contexts for handover communication, more efficient filtering-down processes to include junior staff, and more opportunities for revising the solutions settled on when circumstances were to change in the future.

The following extract is a transcript of a reflexive feedback meeting during which staff express surprise at the inefficiencies that are evident from how they do handover (SN = Senior Nurse).

SN1 – Yeah looking at it ...

All – [inaudible, laughter]

SN1 – when you step back it from it all you notice a lot of inefficiencies and a lot is happening, and there's a lot of places where information can fall through, uh, if you tied the whole thing up

SN2 – the environment is changeable, so changeable, so what are we all doing standing there, things have changed by the time we got back to it

SN3 – yeah that's the thing, from the time we have our handover to the time they have their handover a lot has happened.

SN1 – [there's ...

SN3 – [so ...

SN1 – well I was going to say, there's two processes, there needs to be a clinical information handover with the medical and nursing staff and teams, and there needs to be a logistical handover between the senior NUMS and the staff specialists, so there needs to be two separate types of handover

Others – yeah, yeah

Within a minute of viewing their own handover footage, these senior clinicians worked out what kinds of handover changes were needed in their unit. The changes put in place soon after amounted to a shared nurse-doctor team leader ward round, and better supervision opportunities for junior staff. In the first instance relational rather than procedural solutions, these interventions capitalised on the affective intensity and learning that this reflexive video process generated for the practitioners involved. Their familiarity with what they were witnessing on-screen enabled them immediately to devise a change that was commensurate to and could therefore be integrated in their existing ways of working.

Conclusion

I draw the following conclusions from involving practitioners in video-based research. When shown footage of their own work, practitioners become acutely attuned to the kinds of solutions that are possible. This is all the more remarkable, given their work "is unstable, resists attempts at control and standardisation, and requires rapid integration of expertise from various locations and traditions ..." (Engeström 2008: 230). Instead of conceptualising handover improvement as conditional upon the formulation of a step-by-step procedure, practitioners conceptualise improvement as contingent on opportunities for dialogue – a loosely coupled process. Construing what is needed in terms of a communicative opportunity space rather than 'a communication recipe', they show understanding of the notion that flexible communication offers the best opportunity for 'taming' complexity (Woods, Patterson, and Cook 2007).

Equally, while our multimodal analyses of interaction may identify bodily and behavioural peculiarities, these issues may not be easily communicated to those in the footage. Our findings may confront, precisely because they delve below the level of everyday consciousness, accessing the more embodied, and therefore normalised and naturalised aspects of experience. Indeed, the frameworks for and outcomes from multimodal analysis may objectify practice in ways that neither suit practitioners' priorities, nor match the temporalities of in situ practice, nor are attuned to practitioners' sensibilities. Moreover, such analytical frameworks pre-empt the *diffractive* potential inherent in practitioners scrutinising their own practices.

Of course, disciplinary analytical frameworks draw their legitimacy from time-honoured modes of reasoning and theorising. Within the discipline, research is cast as the practice of refining these procedures and categories for the benefit of theoretical progress. Given the complexity of contemporary social and organisational phenomena, however, research is increasingly faced with having to respond quickly and innovatively. To adequately address complexity, then, research needs to transcend social, knowledge and disciplinary boundaries, and create opportunities for diffraction. The research modality needed under these circumstances makes possible intense dialogue with – as in 'mutual shaping of' – complex socio-organisational phenomena. Only this ensures that research is not only sensitised to the various dimensions and implications of that complexity, but also that it capitalises on its diffractive potential.

In sum, given the ubiquity of complexity and uncertainty in contemporary workplace practice, prevailing disciplinary and analytical approaches cannot but leave a significant and critical remainder. Inevitably, the quest to 'understand' practice will remain constrained by the way we approach it, and the degree to which we objectify it. To some extent, this reduction can be countervailed by converting our research into a process that, besides producing formal conclusions derived from formal analytical procedures, integrates with practitioners' reflexive learning, and nurtures their diffractive capacity for practice expansion. In this context, research enabling practitioners' involvement in sense-making of complex processes provides an important counter-balancing strategy. It may enable researchers to initiate novel forms of engagement, revise their own disciplinary assumptions, articulate significant research outcomes, and gain practical (and policy) traction in their areas of research interest.

Further readings

Iedema, Rick, Jessica Mesman and Katherine Carroll. 2013. Visualising health care practice improvement: Innovation from within. Oxford (UK): Radcliffe Medical Press.

Iedema, Rick and Katherine Carroll. 2011. The clinalyst: Institutionalising reflexivity and flexible systematisation in health care organisations. Journal for Organizational Change Management. 24(2): 175–190.

Iedema, Rick and Katherine Carroll. 2010. Discourse research that intervenes in the quality and safety of care practices. Discourse & Communication. 4(1): 68–86.

Project idea

Video reflexive ethnography can be deployed to investigate the potential for workplace practice change in sites where rising levels of practical complexity create practical challenges for practitioners and learners. A particularly fruitful focus for this method is the introduction of new technologies and their effects on existing practices. For example, the introduction of a new information technology system into a workplace may entrain a host of behavioural responses and changes, many of which workers may not have the time to think about and come to terms with. Video-ing the ways in which the information technology perturbs existing ways of working, and showing the resulting footage back to workers may enable workers to come to terms with and confront challenges more effectively. The research project could focus on two or more groups of workers, but involve only one group in video reflexive ethnography, to test its effects on workers' capacity to accommodate (and perhaps even adjust) the affordances of the new information technology.

References

ACSQHC. 2008. Priority Program 5: Clinical Handover. vol. 2008. Sydney: Australian Commission for Safety and Quality in Health Care.
Berwick, Donald. 2009. What patient-centred should mean: Confessions of an extremist *Health Affairs* 28:555–565.
Bourdieu, Pierre. 1990. *The Logic of Practice.* Cambridge: Polity Press.
Carroll, Katherine, Rick Iedema, and Ross Kerridge. 2008. Reshaping ICU ward round practices using video reflexive ethnography *Qualitative Health Research* 18:380–390.
Engeström, Yrjö. 2008. *From teams to knots: Activity-theoretical studies of collaboration and learning at work.* Cambridge/New York: Cambridge University Press.
Haig, Kathleen M., Staci Sutton, and John Whittington. 2006. SBAR: A shared mental model for improving communication between clinicians. *Journal on Quality and Patient Safety* 32:167–175.
Haraway, Donna. 1998. The Persistence of Vision. In Nicholas Mirzoeff *The Visual Culture Reader*, 191–198. London: Routledge.
Hargie, Owen and Norman C. Morrow. 1986. Using videotape in communication skills training: a critical evaluation of the process of self-viewing. *Medical Teacher* 8:359–365.
Iedema, Rick, Jessica Mesman and Kathleen Carroll. 2013. *Visualising health care improvement: Innovation from within.* Oxford UK: Radcliffe.
Iedema, Rick, Eamon T. Merrick, Dorrilyn Rajbhandari, Alan Gardo, Anne Stirling, and Robert Herkes. 2009a. Viewing the taken-for-granted from under a different aspect: a video-based method in pursuit of patient safety. *International Journal for Multiple Research Approaches* 3:290–301.

Iedema, Rick, Chris Ball, Barbara Daly, Jacinta Young, Timothy Green, Paul Middleton, Catherine Foster-Curry, Marea Jones, Sarah Hoy, and Daniel Comerford. 2012. Design and evaluation of a new ambulance-to-ED handover protocol: 'IMIST-AMBO'. *BMJ Qual Saf* 21:627–633.

Iedema, Rick, Debbi Long, Rowena Forsyth, and Bonne Lee. 2006. Visibilizing clinical work: Video ethnography in the contemporary hospital. *Health Sociology Review* 15:156–168.

Iedema, Rick, Eamon T. Merrick, Ross Kerridge, Robert Herkes, Bonne Lee, Mike Anscombe, Dorrilyn Rajbhandari, Mark Lucey and Les White. 2009b. 'Handover – Enabling Learning in Communication for Safety' (HELiCS): A Report on Achievements at Two Hospital Sites. *Medical Journal of Australia* 190:S133–S136.

Iedema, Rick and Eamon Merrick. 2008. *Handover – Enabling Learning in Communication for Safety (HELiCS) – A DVD/Booklet-based Kit for Handover Improvement*. Australian Commission on Safety and Quality in Health Care & University of Technology Sydney, Sydney.

Knoblauch, Hubert, Bernt Schnettler, Jürgen Raab, and Hans-Georg Soeffner. 2006. *Video Analysis: Methodology and Methods*. Bern: Peter Lang.

MacDougall, David. 2006. *The corporeal image: Film, ethnography and the senses*. Princeton: Princeton University Press.

Massumi, Brian. 2002. *Parables for the virtual: Movement, affect, sensation*. Durham NC: Duke University Press.

Mertens, M. Donna. 1998. *Research Methods in Education and Psychology: Integrating Diversity with Quantitative and Qualitative Approaches*. Thousand Oaks, CA: Sage.

Mertens, M. Donna. 2009. *Transformative research and evaluation*. New York: Guildford Press.

Reason, Peter. 1999. Integrating action and reflection through cooperative enquiry. *Management Learning* 30:207–226.

Reason, Peter and Hilary Bradbury. 2008. *The Sage Handbook of Action Research: Participative Inquiry and Practice*. London: Sage.

Woods, D. David, Emily S. Patterson and Richard I. Cook. 2007. Behind Human Error: Taming Complexity to Improve Patient Safety. In Pascale Carayon (ed.) *Handbook of Human Factors and Ergonomics in Health Care and Patient Safety*, 459–476. Mahwah, NJ: Lawrence Erlbaum Associates.

Sigrid Norris, Jarret Geenen, Thomas Metten and Jesse Pirini
17 Collecting video data: Role of the researcher

Introduction

In this chapter, we discuss three different projects and three different types of researcher roles when collecting video data. The chapter is a discussion of the roles that we have taken up in actual research projects. We describe some how-to notions from camera positioning to interacting with participants and some of the problems that we found. While there is little literature that the reader is pointed towards within the chapter, the reader can find some useful literature in the Further Readings section at the end.

Key terms: Audio-video data, co-researcher, researcher role.

Role of the researcher

The social sciences have seen a marked increase of researchers employing audio-video technology as a data collection tool (Dicks et al. 2011; Pink 2011; Holsanova 2012; Luff and Heath 2012). While there has been quite extensive discussion regarding how to collect and analyse audio-video data collected using contemporary technologies, the employment of cameras unequivocally affects the kinds of positions and/or roles, the researcher may find themselves in while engaged in the field. As a result, the employment of audio-video technology and the collection of video data requires a consideration about the multiple and multifarious roles which manifest in and through the research process itself.

The three different examples of roles for a researcher that we have taken up came about through the different foci of study as well as the different situations that we found ourselves in. We have chosen to focus on these three to offer the reader a glimpse of what one can expect when one collects video data. However, while these three examples are quite different from each other, these are just three of many more possibilities.

In example one, the researcher studied coaching. This was a small student research project with limited scope: the student researcher video recorded two one-hour coaching sessions with the same coach and client team.

Example two was a larger project of an experienced researcher. In this example, the researcher was interested in a participant's own video recording and documentary-making. The experienced researcher was accompanied by a research assistant, who, at the time, was learning hands-on how to conduct participant-engaged research.

In the third example, from a school setting, the researcher engaged in a long-term ethnographic study playing a participant observational role for the first time. Here, we illustrate the video data that was collected in a design classroom, discuss the notion of relationships and what it means to be involved in the field. After the three examples, we discuss some main points and conclude our chapter.

Example 1: Coaching sessions

In this example we describe the role of the researcher in collecting video and audio data as well as observational notes of coaching sessions. The coaching sessions were semi-natural, i.e.: the researcher had selected a place (a classroom) in which the coaching session took place, but coach and client conducted an authentic coaching session. Figure 1 illustrates the setting and camera positioning. Coach and client were sitting across from each other with a small table in between and slightly to the right of them. Their interaction was filmed with three video cameras, positioned on tripods (C1, C2, and C3). Besides the three video cameras, an audio recorder was placed on a soft surface and positioned on the small table between coach and client.

While the three video cameras were used in order to film the interaction from various angles, the audio recorder in close proximity to the participants was used in order to pick up any audio noise that the video cameras might miss.

This project was the first research project that the young researcher conducted. The researcher explains:

As this was my first research project I was nervous, but I was also prepared. I had run training sessions for groups before and I drew on this experience when setting up the room and preparing for the participants to arrive. I made sure that they had water, and that the space was comfortable. I placed the chairs so that the video cameras could pick up a range of views, and also so that the participants would be orientated comfortably. The cameras had a wide enough range of field to allow some flexibility to the participants about where they positioned themselves.

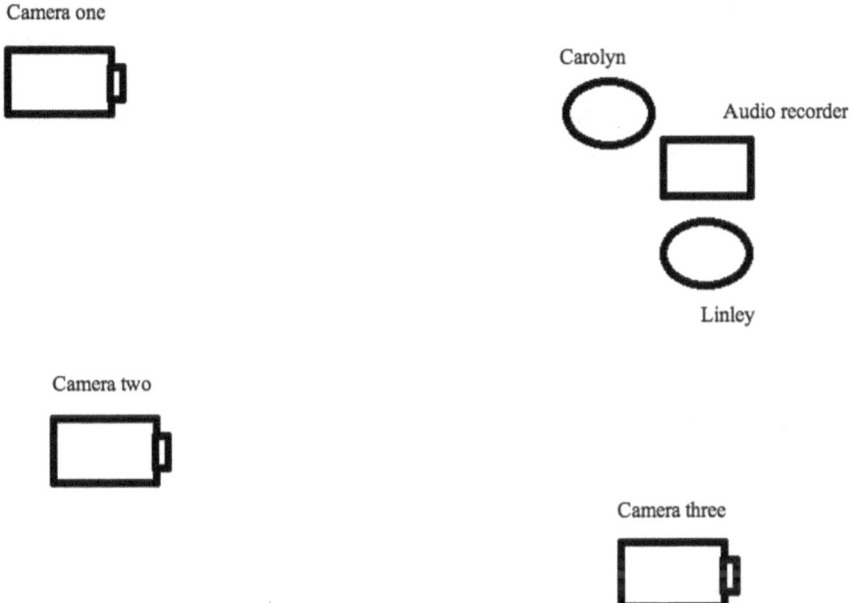

Figure 1: Layout of research space

Initially I did not want to be present in the room during the session, however an experienced researcher advised me that the video cameras and audio recorder would not pick up the whole interaction, and that I should ask to be present to take field notes about how I felt things were going, about what I thought was relevant to my research question, and about elements of the interaction space that the video could not pick up – such as the 'vibe' of the room.

Before the first session was recorded, the researcher thus inquired if coach and client would be happy for the researcher to be present. The researcher says:

The coach was fine with me being present, and the client was also happy to have me there, but she requested that I was not visible to her.

Luckily, the researcher had set up the session in a flexible learning space with mobile privacy screens, which could easily be moved to partition off the area in which the researcher sat.

Beginning the coaching session

Once the cameras had been turned on, the researcher retreated behind the partitions.

The participants orientated to me at the beginning and end of the coaching sessions. As I turned on each of the cameras they carried out small talk unrelated to coaching, or to the upcoming coaching session. Once the cameras were going, I placed a voice recorder between them and told them that I would leave them to it, before retreating behind the privacy screens. In both sessions the coach then initiated the coaching session.

Figure 2 illustrates how the coach moves the interaction from small talk at the beginning when the researcher is in sight to the actual coaching session right after the researcher has retreated behind the screen.

When looking closely at images 2 and 3 in Figure 2, we can see the researcher's legs below the privacy screen (while walking in image 2 and being seated in image 3). Both women are looking to the right and downwards (image 1) as the coach is slowly moving into the coaching session by stating 'so I guess this is it we're ready' before straightening up in image 2 to begin their conversation. Thus, here we see how both coach and client wait for the researcher to disappear behind the screens, before they engage in the interaction that the researcher is actually studying.

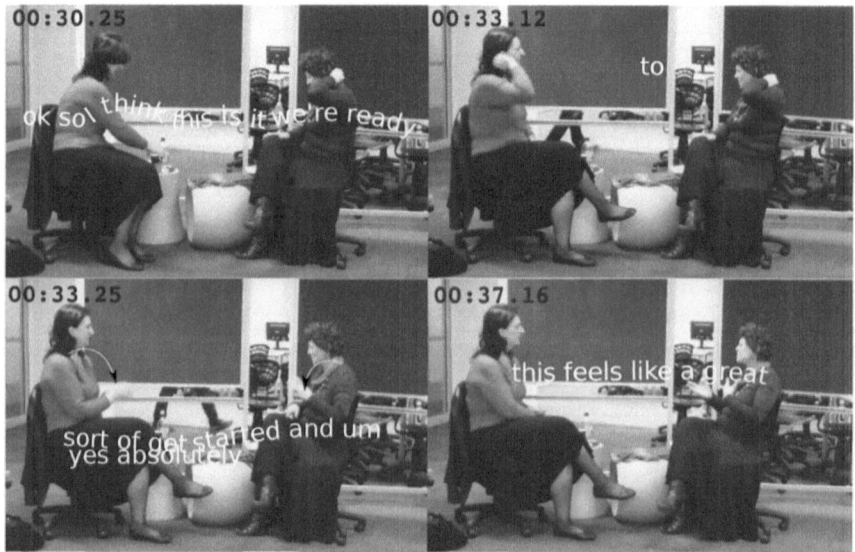

Figure 2: Coach indicating the beginning of the actual coaching session

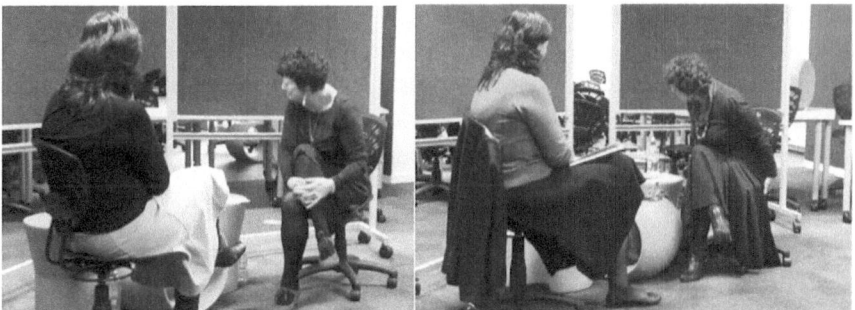

Figure 3: End of the session. The coach looks between screens to where the researcher is seated

Ending the coaching session

Something similar happens at the end of the coaching session. In the researcher's words:

The coach also determined the end of the session, but took care to check with the client as the coach states "So I think we're pretty much ... are you ready to wrap up or ... ?" The client provides an evaluation of the session, saying that it went well, and confirming that she is ready to finish. Both participants never addressed me directly, assuming I was following the conversation and was aware that they were finished. I was cautious not to appear too early, and the coach looked around the screen to further indicate to me that the session was over.

Figure 3 illustrates how the coach looks between the screens to locate the researcher, overtly demonstrating the end of the coaching session.

Problems that emerged

Even a fairly straight forward and easy setting to film can run into glitches. The researcher tells of one of these:

In the second session I had to emerge from behind the screen to remove a chair that I had noticed was in the way of one of the cameras. I tossed up the options for a while, either lose the data from one camera, or interrupt the session. I decided to interrupt the session by knocking on the privacy panel three times and then entering the space to remove the chair. This had very little impact on the coach and client.

Here, the researcher had to weigh the options. Interrupting the coaching session and possibly straining the interaction between coach and client for a moment or leaving the chair where it was and having to disregard one camera angle for the complete session. Seemingly not a very big issue, it is a real toss-up when collecting a limited amount of data.

Researcher presence and taking observational notes

This researcher had received advice from an experienced researcher to be present during data collection. The young researcher contemplates:

It was extremely useful for me to be present in the room, even behind a screen. I could see parts of the coach and client that were not visible to the cameras, and took notes about hand clenching that I could see. I also took notes about how people felt (more relaxed in the second session) and about what I could sense was going on (this included notes on the 'vibe' and whether it was sombre, or more positive). This proved useful when I went over the video footage. The coaching sessions did not seem to be affected by my presence; the sessions were engaging and useful for the client, who at times expressed strong emotions which may indicate she was comfortable with my presence.

For the sessions, the researcher's presence marked the beginning and end of the coaching. As the researcher retreated behind the screens the sessions began, and as the sessions finished the coach motioned the researcher back by looking through the gap in the screens. While the researcher could hear and observe the tone and feel of the situation, the researcher missed seeing the participants' faces, and the researcher states:

For all that I was only a few meters away it seemed to make a difference that I could not see the participants' faces.

But of course, there was more that the researcher could not see while collecting data. Some of the modes such as upper body movements, head movements, and gaze, are very important in interaction (Norris 2004, 2011) and much information is lost without being able to see them. However, the cameras made up for much of this information and in the end, the researcher was able to reconstruct quite a full picture.

Figure 4: Participant, researcher and camera

Example 2: How do you Flip?

In this example we describe the role of two researchers, one experienced and one emergent, in collecting video data as well as researcher involvement in ethnography of user-generated video using Flip cameras and software. Figure 4 illustrates the natural setting of the participant's own home, the participant as well as the Research Assistant and a Flip camera.

The Flip camera was recording keyboard and screen, while the actual image is a still from a large movie camera placed across the room. Camera positioning was heavily influenced by the material configuration of the living space and the natural lighting and was not easy to position in a way that was conductive to the project. The sun was bright and the computer reflected the participants' faces and fingers. Because of these conditions, researchers and participant worked together to achieve the best set-up for recording. Here, we see that researchers and participant built a team from the very beginning and the participant acted as co-researcher and, as discussed in detail below, the young researcher acted as co-participant in some parts of the data collection. In this project, researcher and participant roles were merged, juggled, and negotiated throughout. While the emergent researcher and the participant at times acted as co-participants and at other times enacted co-researcher roles, the experienced researcher operated the cameras and allowed things to unfold in a natural way. The emergent researcher explains:

Coming to this particular situation, was a seasoned researcher in the role of project leader along with a novice researcher (myself) with graduate level research experience. Previous ethnographically oriented and case study based research experience equipped me with basic understandings of etiquette and protocol, however, such explicit involvement with the participant as part of the site of engagement was a novel situation, and one requiring some careful navigation.

Personally I had no previous relationship with the participant. However, the project leader had what seemed to be a reasonably cordial interpersonal relationship with the participant insofar as the previous stages of the research project had given impetus to interaction and familiarization. Some general information about the participant was shared between the project leader and myself as a very surface level character briefing prior to undertaking this stage of data collection.

When we take a closer look at the emergent researcher's contemplations above, we find that there is a strong emphasis on personal relationships. In fact, in this kind of ethnographic data collection, researcher and participant build a quite close relationship. Because of this kind of a relationship, participants move the project – as far as the intended research project allows – in their direction. In other words, the participants want to get something out of the project. Here, in this example, the participant learned how to produce a mini-documentary, or video-postcard about her brother. Through the project, the participant not only learned to use new hardware and software, but also realised that she learned something new about her brother because she was asking questions for the little documentary that she had never asked him before. Thus, she learned to see the world from a different angle.

Of course, since the participant was conducting interviews with and filming her brother for the project, she in reality became a researcher. Her involvement as viewing the world from a researcher's perspective added to the familiarity with and understanding of how important camera angle and lighting was for the project. Thus, when she interacted with the emergent researcher, she indeed was seeing the difficulties with set-up through a researcher's lens. However, the emergent researcher interacted with a slightly different understanding:

The interpersonal dynamic was created through the process of data co-construction. Sociocultural norms of visitation and accessibility influenced the particular area of the house in which editing would occur (areas such as the lounge or kitchen). Similarly, furniture configuration coupled with light saturation and interpersonal proximity requirements resulted in setting up the editing site at the kitchen counter which provided enough space for comfortable computer use and multiple camera positions.

The participant was seated at the counter with her back to the lounge seating area. I was located to the participant's right approximately half a meter away, close enough to see the screen but providing enough distance to denote that the task was basically autonomous. To the left of the participant, on a small flexible tripod, stood a Flip video camera which captured all computer screen activity. To my right, the project leader stood, operating a tripod supported camera, within speaking distance but not in view of the computer screen. The interrelationship of our body positioning supported the associated situational roles: the participant as the key social actor engaged in a semi-autonomous task, supported by a research assistant in close proximity, further supported by the project leader if necessary.

Emergent researcher's actions

Similar to the way in which interpersonal orientation and body positioning was heavily influenced by facets relating to the participants' living environment, my role as a researcher became established in real-time, through the research process itself. Following a task briefing by the project leader, I took up the role of assistant in a comprehensive manner. With software familiarity on the part of the participant unknown, I functioned as a support mechanism in case of usability issues or editing road blocks. As such, initially my actions were given explicit impetus through participant initiation of interaction in the form of questions as seen in the verbal transcript below.

(1)	Kate:	hahahaha,
(2)		she's like a famous person in the video (watching video)
(3)		ok so what can I do with this ...
(4)		(watching video and going through dialogue boxes)
(5)		(attempting to cut or edit)
(6)		hahahahaha,
(7)		ok so do I want to do this?
(8)		do I need to stick them all in here to create a movie?
(9)	Researcher:	well that one's already in there
(10)		so now if you want to add other stuff to it ...
(11)	Kate:	Ok.
(12)	Researcher:	so,
(13)		um this will be ... think of that as your project
(14)	Kate:	ok.

(15) Researcher: So that is your whole project.
(16) Kate: yep.
(17) Researcher: and,
(18)   so if you want you can grab other things ...
(19) Kate: well because I'll,
(20)   surely I'll want heaps in there.
(21) Researcher: yep.
(22) Kate: so can I just,
(23)   is it better to just chuck them all in here right now?
(24) Researcher: perfect,
(25)   ya you can if you'd like

In this instance, Kate appears unsure about the task requirements and the functionality of the editing software. The apprehension is exemplified in the ways in which she positions herself lexically and requests reaffirmation about the editing process. In so doing, the participant concretises my role as an assistant who is not only in support of the process, but an individual who is engaged alongside herself. This is verbally represented in questions like "so do I want to do this?" and "Well because I'll, surely I'll want heaps in there?" Here, Kate establishes the process as one in which I, as the research assistant have some solidified goal in mind. Thus, accomplishment is closely aligned with meeting this conceptual goal. The interrogatives situate me not explicitly as knower of her desires "do I want to do this?" but rather as 'knower of how her actions relate to my goal'.

Thus, throughout the course of the editing process, Kate's explicit requests and positioning of the emergent researcher as engaged in the task alongside her established a situation in which they were working together.

Experienced researcher's actions

The experienced researcher at times re-established the role of the project leader as the individual who could provide operational and goal clarification to the two of them. When the young researchers' actions in the process meandered away from the purpose of the task, the project leader would interject to re-establish a working direction:

(1) RESEARCHER: you might want to just think about
(2)   what you would like to do with these clips ...
(3)   because I mean

(4)		your next
(5)		your next challenge will be
(6)		to take those clips
(7)	Kate:	umhm
(8)	RESEARCHER:	and cut them
(9)		ya,
(10)		and then produce a little bit of a little documentary.
(11)	Kate:	ya
(12)	RESEARCHER:	about your brother,
(13)		that kind of tells us who
(14)		who
(15)		who your brother is
(16)	Kate:	ya I,
(17)	RESEARCHER:	now,
(18)		how do you want to do that?
(19)		what is it you need to know
(20)		before you can do that?
(21)		that's why we're here,
(22)		that's why we're
(23)	Kate:	ya,
(24)		ya,
(25)		so I need to
(26)	RESEARCHER:	do you actually know what you,
(27)		what you want to do,
(28)		that you can do that?

In this instance we see an explicit re-constitution of the goal of the editing session. However, here the experienced researcher not only re-establishes the goal of the session for Kate, but implicitly also for the emergent researcher. This illustrates that it needs a lot of experience to interact naturally, to build co-researcher relationships with participants, without, however, losing sight of the project itself.

Possible problems: A collaborative approach

When running into problems with data collection, these issues are solved collaboratively. As discussed in our example above, our first problem was lighting. The participant as co-researcher was just as interested and involved in solving the problem as were the researchers collecting the data. Or, when participant and research assistant were moving into a direction that was outside of the intended project, the experienced researcher re-adjusted the goal for both, helping them to stay on task.

Example 3: Schools as institutions of cultural memory

In this example we describe the role of a researcher in an ethnographic project in a secondary school. In this project, the researcher was conducting participant observations, taking extensive field notes and collecting audio-video data.

Video recording in a school setting

Collecting video data always brings with it ethical as well as practical questions. Particularly when studying minors in a school setting, ethical questions arise. The researcher in our school project solved the issue in the following way:

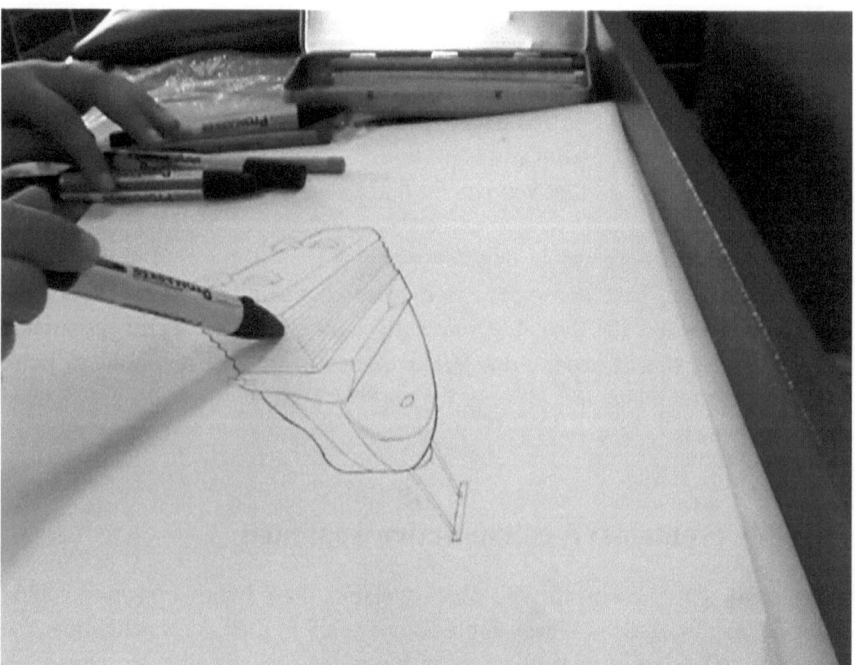

Figure 5: Top of the table, the working hands, and the materials

As far as possible I tried to avoid filming the students' faces and mostly focussed on the design process. Pointing a camera on someone always has its effects: As mostly is said, the people might forget about the camera after a while. However, to me this seems to be only half of the truth: In many situations I noticed that the students kept aware of the camera and from time to time they interacted with it. Above all, this never was a problem. To keep the process most transparent, the students were told that they always can have a look on the camera. Because they knew about my research interests, they also controlled the camera position from time to time and sometimes re-positioned it or used the zoom to get a better perspective on the drawing. Usually the camera here was fixed on the table in front of the students. This was the only possible position to get a good view on the sketching process.

Because the tables in the class were fixed and the rows were narrow it was impossible to use a normal tripod. Thus, the camera was fixed on the front of the table and by this showed the top of the table, the working hands, the materials and the page.

Field notes and other material

The researcher collected video recorded data in a Graphic Design and Visual Communication class to gain a deeper understanding of the drawing process.

As a researcher I was always very welcome in class. The teacher was a young woman and it was her first year in school; but she already was very confident and professional in her teaching. The 25 students in class respected her a lot and she was able to keep the atmosphere friendly and focussed. When I first brought the camera into class, I was already known by the students. A few weeks before, I had given a short talk to the class to introduce myself and my research interests. Some of the students also met me in other classes, and I had a few conversations with some of them about my topic.

They sometimes wondered about the amount I wrote, but besides this, I was fully accepted in class.

While the camera recorded the drawing process, the researcher was taking extensive field notes:

The field notes included everything from the setting, the seating plan in class, the music playing in the background up to the teacher's instructions and notes on students' interactions.

Furthermore, I collected and analysed the materials used in class such as books, information given to the students, images and examples that were pinned on the walls and the guidelines for the design process. As part of the collection of materials I also took photographs of the environment, the walls and the chalk board as well as the setting in class.

Besides video recording, taking field notes and photographs of aspects in the environment, the researcher also became involved in some of the students' work:

While the camera mechanically records the on-going action, videoing is never able to replace emotions, impressions or the experience a researcher has in a situation. However, actually getting involved in a situation means to become experienced. Thus, experience provides the basis for understanding a situation. Without experience one will not be able to decide if today's lesson in school went on as usual or was led by particular events.

Here we see just how important experience is for the researcher.

Relationships

Relationships in an ethnographic project are of great importance. There are many relationships that a researcher engages in and the researcher explains:

While the relation to every single person in the field was special, I generally was involved in three different groups: the students, the teachers and the senior management.

All of these groups in the institution 'school', and each relationship with the individuals within the groups are different:

While the principal and the management of the school are the general gatekeepers that every researcher has to get past, every teacher again is the gatekeeper of his own class.

Once I became involved in the school, the role I played constantly changed depending on the relationships with particular social groups, their status and the time I spend with them.

First, I was walking around in school with other teachers. This went on for a while until the students got to know me; after this I became more and more part of the student body. I entered class with them, left when the students were allowed to leave and had random conversations with my neighbours in class, always taking care that the teacher did not pay attention. If a new teacher recognized me in his class and asked who I was, sometimes the students told him that I am the new student in class.

However, I still had lunch with the teachers. And in many situations it felt like having a double-faced identity, especially when conflicts came up between teachers and students.

Problems

I remember one situation, when a teacher asked me how I thought about a situation and what I would have done, while on the other side, the students involved me in their position. The situation was thus: A young teacher was thinking about giving a student a "not achieved" because the teacher had the impression that the student had copied all of the answers in his exam from another student. In a discussion, the student seriously tried to pretend having done all work by himself. But as soon as the teacher left the class he and his friends were extensively talking about how they copied their answers from each other while I was with them.

What made me really feel bad in this situation was that the teacher seriously trusted me and asked me for advice before the lesson. Thus, the conflict between the teacher and the student became an inner conflict for me, and the most basic ethical question arose: What should I do? For sure, there are ethical questions, that are much more serious than this one, but the example shows how easily the researcher can get caught in the middle.

Involvement

This story of an ethical issue illustrates that a distanced and neutral positioning of a researcher is not possible. But, in our view, it is also not desirable. We genuinely believe that ethnographic researchers ought to get involved. What we mean by involvement is that the researcher develops honest relationships with others; and this is where the above researcher's ethical issue stems from. There, the researcher was torn: Who was the group that the researcher was going to align with? Was it the students or was it the teachers?

But how does one answer such a question? It is not as easy as to go back to the original idea about the research and focusing on what is being studied. Thus, one cannot simply say that, if the researcher studies students, the researcher should align with the students; nor can we assume that, if the researcher studies teachers, the researcher can simply align with the teacher. Rather, the answer will emerge from a deep inquiry of the ethics and the morality that is linked to the problem. Here, the researcher needs to take a perspective that is good for all involved, and part of this will have to do with the consequences of aligning with one individual/group or the other individual/group or mediating between the two.

The involved researcher thus is an ethical and moral researcher, who at times interferes in the field, and always juggles various relationships. When finding incommensurate issues such as the one discussed above, the researcher, who has the overview of the actual problem, has a chance to improve the situation through well-thought-out steps.

While the researcher is embedded in the field and thus is a part of the project, the researcher is also the one who experiences the institution in a more holistic way than any one individual from any of the three groups (students, teachers, administrators). The researcher may be seen by the students as similar to other students; viewed by teachers as similar to other teachers; and seen by administrators as similar to other administrators. Because of this, the researcher's experience is much richer than the experience of actual individuals belonging to any of these groups. Yet, in a participant-ethnography where all individuals involved are aware of the research, the researcher does not belong to any of the groups. Because of this, the researcher's experience will also never be as rich as that of any actual individual in any one of these actual groups.

Thus, there are two contradictory forces that a researcher experiences: belonging too much to all groups and belonging too little to any one group. These forces build a certain amount of tension that the researcher has to continuously manage. This is an issue that researchers, who are new to participant-ethnography, as the researcher in our example, often struggle with. But it is also a tension that allows the researcher to learn as much about themselves as they do about the institution/group/individual that is being studied.

Conclusions

In this chapter, we used three different examples to give a glimpse of the complexity of video recording.

First, we looked at coaching sessions and illustrated that the participants' wishes have to be respected by the researcher. There, one of the participants' requested that the researcher was not in sight. However, rather than leaving the room, the emergent researcher negotiated the situation and was allowed to be present behind some dividers.

The coaching sessions were then begun and ended with the researcher vanishing behind the dividers and being called back into sight. But even here, in a semi controlled environment, a problem arose as the researcher missed rearranging a chair that inhibited one of the cameras from filming the interaction. Such little mishaps can easily happen, especially if a researcher is working with several cameras simultaneously.

Second, we examined the filming of teaching/learning of documentary software. Here, we discussed the emergent researcher's, the participant's (or co-researcher's) and the experienced researcher's actions. However, the most important point in this section was the collaborative nature of the project.

The emergent researcher, the participant (or co-researcher), and the experienced researcher first collaboratively solved the problem of lighting and special arrangement of equipment. Then the emergent researcher and the participant collaboratively worked through the software up until that point, when the two of them began to stray away from the original project. At that point, the experienced researcher re-directed both the participant and the emergent researcher, bringing them back on task.

In a project such as this one, we demonstrated that problems are dealt with as they arise and participants often play as much a part in resolving them as do the researchers.

Third, we explored a project conducted in a school setting. As video recording of minors needs to be carefully thought through, we demonstrated how this researcher used the video recorder to document drawing processes. In this case, the researcher focused the camera on the hands. While videotaping drawing processes, the researcher was free to take field notes and collect other relevant material.

However, while this section began with collecting video data, we soon moved into a broader area that is not limited to studies in which researchers collect video data. Here, we investigated the relationships that a researcher forms when conducting participant-ethnography. We incorporated this wider aspect, as relationships and the researcher role are always intertwined. Further, this was a nice example with which we could show that the more a researcher is involved in a project, the more likely it is that problems may arise. While such problems can be quite intense, these often ethical/moral problems force the researcher to contemplate not only the field and their research, but also, and most importantly, their very own ethical/moral beliefs.

In all three projects, the researchers were present when collecting video data. This is a particularly important aspect, we believe. While video cameras can record certain aspects of the environment and/or actions, there is a lot that a video camera cannot do (see Emmison and Smith 2000; Wagner 2002). A video camera does not record anything visual that it is not focused upon; it often misses whispers; never records smell, warmth/cold, touch, or tensions in the air that a researcher may subjectively feel. While this is clearly subjective knowledge, it does inform the data; and in this vein, we would like to make the point that there is no true objective data, anyway. All data, even the video recorded data, that allows us to analyse every lower-level action performed, is subjective-objective data.

Taking the process of drawing above as our example, we can say very much about each pencil stroke, and yet, what does it really mean to say a lot about a pencil stroke? As soon as we discuss individual pencil strokes, we subjectively enhance their meaning, a meaning that the pencil strokes as such did not have as they were embedded in the drawing and embedded in the classroom. While the pencil stroke has been recorded objectively, it has been focused upon quite subjectively.

Video records are immensely useful for analysis; yet, we need to make sure that we do not forget that the mere practice of collecting video data is just as subjective as walking into a classroom and feeling that it is very stuffy on a hot summer's day.

Further readings

Kress, Gunther. 2011. 'Partnerships in research': multimodality and ethnography. *Qualitative Research* 11(3): 239–260.

Pink, Sarah. 2007. Walking with video. *Visual Studies* 22(3): 240–252.

Project idea

Consider attempting to study a naturally occurring social interaction. This interaction could occur in a home, in a public space, or at an institution like a school or university. After choosing an interaction (this could be a conversation, a meal, a coffee order, a tutoring session), think about where this interaction takes place, who you will be studying and your existing relationship with them.

First, where would you place the camera(s)? Make a map of the location and identify the areas which you deem would be most advantageous for camera positioning. Also, make a list of why you think this position will be best suited to the interaction you will be studying (you may need multiple cameras, but explain why this is necessary).

Second, how will camera placement, and/or your relationship with the potential participants affect the data (recording of the interaction). Here, try to think about what the camera will not pick up, and also, how your presence as a researcher and camera operator during the unfolding of the interaction may affect the interaction itself. Will the camera have an effect on the interaction? In what ways? Is there some way to minimise the effect of the camera?

Finally, what considerations will you have to make when you begin your analysis? Try to be as explicit as possible and articulate exactly how your presence as a researcher might bear on the interaction itself. Also, what other data can you collect prior to or after the interaction which will provide some more empirical information about the nature of the interaction? For this, consider observational notes, interviews, focus groups and playback methodology.

References

Dicks, Bella, Rosie Flewitt, Lesley Lancaster and Kate Pahl. 2011. Multimodality and ethnography: working at the intersection. *Qualitative Research* 11(3): 227–237.
Michael Emmison and Philip Smith. 2000. *Researching the Visual*. Thousand Oaks, CA: Sage.
Jana Holsanova. 2012. New methods for studying visual communication and multimodal intergration. *Visual Communication* 11(3): 251–257.
Luff, Paul and Christian Heath. 2012. Some 'technical challenges' of video analysis: social actions, objects, material realities and the problems of perspective. *Qualitative Research* 12(3): 255–279.
Norris, Sigrid. 2004. *Analyzing Multimodal Interaction: A Methodological Framework*. London: Routledge.
Norris, Sigrid. 2011. *Identity in (Inter)action: Introducing Multimodal (Inter)action Analysis*. Berlin/New York: de Guyter Mouton.
Pink, Sarah. 2011. Multimodality, multisensoriality and ethnographic knowing: social semiotics and the phenomenology of perception. *Qualitative Research* 11(3): 261–276.
Wagner, John. 2002. Contrasting images, complementary trajectories: sociology, visual sociology and visual research. *Visual Studies* 17(2): 160–171.

Jesse Pirini, Sigrid Norris, Jarret Geenen and Tui Matelau
18 Studying social actors: Some thoughts on ethics

Introduction

We live in a country, in which ethical review boards have stringent expectations of what they believe ethical research is. While we certainly have a critical stance towards review boards' notions of ethics, as researchers, we are firmly grounded in research ethics.

Applying for, and receiving, ethical approval for research projects can be a challenging and drawn out process in any instance. Yet, this can be multiplied many times when researchers aim to study and video tape naturally occurring interactions, and/or want to work with children, youth, and populations that ethics boards consider vulnerable. Some of these considerations we agree with, such as young children; and some of these we disagree with, such as pregnant women. Notions of vulnerability and informed consent are discussed throughout this chapter.

In the worst-case scenario, researchers are put off from conducting research that involves applying for ethics approval. But, in the best-case scenario, the process of applying for ethics approval helps the researchers design a better research project, by considering issues from a participant perspective. Since we cannot evade ethical approval for our studies in New Zealand, we tend to take this time to work through true ethical dilemmas that could arise in the study that we are proposing.

This article outlines some of our thinking regarding a new project that we are embarking on, where we will investigate video conferencing between family members. For the families, we are looking at a young family with at least one Baby or very young child and their interaction with other family members via video conferencing.

Key terms: Ethics application, ethics review boards, research ethics.

What are ethical applications meant to accomplish?

The central thrust of ethics applications is to protect participants from harm or discomfort, and there is a primary focus on participants providing informed consent. However research ethics is not just – and in our view should not be – about gaining approval from an ethics review board, but rather should reflect the state of mind and the state of being of the researcher(s) during research. Guillemin and Gillam (2004) categorise ethics into *procedural ethics*, and *ethics in practice*. Procedural ethics refers to the ethics application and approval stage. Ethics in practice refers to ethical behaviour throughout the research project. Guillemin and Gillam (2004) suggest that a research project has moments of ethical importance and that reflexivity as an ethical tool can be useful here.

Other authors also take this approach to ethics in practice, suggesting that the mindset of the researcher during research is important for ethical conduct. Aluwihare-Samaranayake (2012) refers to a critical consciousness approach to both the procedural and ethics in practice phases in research.

However, due to the complex nature of sociocultural groups and interactions, perhaps a mindset and desire to act ethically cannot provide enough of an ethical framework for research in naturally occurring situations, where a moment of ethical importance may appear unforeseen and require an immediate response.

Miller and Scollon (2011) examine ethics during research on peace and security that has real outcomes for the practice of UN and development organizations in many countries. They believe that "the work of such personnel is sufficiently complicated that it cannot be solved by simple introspection on one's own behaviour and a general willingness to act ethically." (Miller and Scollon 2011: 112). They develop the beginnings of a model of ethics for cultural research and programme design on peace and security.

This model has two main features. Firstly individuals and communities involved in research are "recognized and positioned to be 'agentive' and hence are involved in establishing the meanings of engagements with community-external agencies and other stakeholders" (Miller and Scollon 2011: 130). Note here, how the procedural stage of ethics which generally has to be completed prior to participant recruitment creates a barrier to this type of approach. Secondly, engagements with these individuals and communities are "understood to be – and must function as – multilateral negotiations for ethical common ground in the pursuit of situated action towards common goals" (Miller and Scollon 2011:130). This model treats participants as co-researchers, and also makes it easier to act ethically with populations traditionally considered as vulnerable.

The standard discourse of ethics regarding so called vulnerable populations, contrary to what Miller and Scollon have proposed, presumes some people are unable to make choices about their involvement in research, and takes a paternalistic approach to "protect" them from harm. Rhodes (2010) lists some of those defined as *vulnerable* including the mentally ill, pregnant women, children and teenagers, prisoners, the elderly, economically and educationally disadvantaged and indigenous populations. However, Rhodes (2010) argues that classifying groups as vulnerable denies them respect, as they are not treated as autonomous individuals, who are capable of making their own choices. She further points out that this:

> '… becomes glaringly obvious when we stop to notice that pregnant women are presumed to have the capacity to make choices about child bearing, that the mentally ill are frequently allowed to make choices about their living arrangements, and that restrictions on the liberty of the elderly or the educationally or economically disadvantaged in any circumstances other than the consent to research would be branded unacceptable discrimination.'
>
> (Rhodes 2010: 23)

Similar to Miller and Scollon (2011), Rhodes (2010) argues that the focus of ethics needs to shift to view researchers and subjects as "cooperative partners engaged in and committed to socially important collaborative projects" (Rhodes 2010: 33). She also argues that the focus of ethics should shift from informed consent, to studies conducted to the highest ethical standards.

Informed consent, in the context of working with children, is discussed in the next section. We then consider how researchers can use the procedural ethics process to think through situations that may arise in the field, identify potential ethical sticking points, and ensure methods are congruent with research ethics.

Finally we look at examples from the field, and how the way that methods are applied can be used to ensure that research participants are treated as cooperative partners in research. Here, we demonstrate some ways that are more concrete than simply taking on a *mindset* or *striving for reflexivity*. Importantly we show that this requires the researcher to make sure control over the research project is distributed amongst themselves and participants as co-researchers.

Children as research participants

The United Nations Convention on the Rights of the Child was ratified in 1989 and is a document that guides nearly all countries in the world, in their dealings with children (Dillen 2006). The 54 different articles contained in this document have been summarised into three principles: protection, provision and participation rights (Marshall and Parvis as cited in Dillen 2006). An aspect of the participation rights of children evident in this document is "their right to information and freedom of association," (Dillen 2006: 239). The principle of participation rights opens up a space that highlights children's competencies and their right to "give voice to their own experiences, meanings, and interactions," (Trussel 2008: 166).

Yet, the autonomy of children is diminished by their vulnerable positioning in society and their need for protection. This protection extends into the field of research and stems from one key difference between children and adults: the ability to give or not give legal consent (Matutina 2009). Children are not able to give their consent to be involved in a research project. Instead their parents are required to provide consent for the child and where possible the child provides assent. The act of seeking assent from the child in an age appropriate way can help in creating a relationship between the researcher and the child (Trussel 2008).

There are several factors that contribute to the vulnerability of a child. As mentioned, their inability to provide informed consent is one. Other factors include the socioeconomic position of their family and the numerous power imbalances that exist between themselves and others (Matutina 2009). A child's level of cognitive ability and their parent's motivation to be involved in the research project can also contribute to their vulnerability.

Thinking of children as co-researchers ensures the above factors are considered in the design of a research project. Aluwhihare-Samaranayake (2012) states that no matter the participant, they should be involved in the research project as co-researchers because "participant and researcher equally contribute to the transparency of the ethical process," (Aluwhihare-Samaranayake 2012: 65). Before conducting research with children, this relationship between participant and researcher needs to exist in the researcher's mindset to inform ethical practice in the field.

Power imbalance between researcher and participant is a factor that the researcher should always consider. When the participant is a child this power imbalance could be magnified. However Matutina (2009) states that if the child is considered to be a co-researcher than the power imbalance between child and researcher is lessened. "In an effort to balance the power between the researcher and the child, the child should be included as a member of the research team. The child may be given control by allowing choices, valuing input and encouraging participation," (Matutina 2009: 44).

Considering data collection, and what ethical issues may arise

As touched upon above, one way to approach the idea of ethics in research is to compartmentalise research ethics into two distinct yet interrelated components: procedural ethics and ethics in practice. While admittedly, the two are intimately connected, the benefit of distinguishing between them is primarily for one's own clarity. In this section, we highlight some of the benefits of thoroughly articulating procedural components of the research process through specification of methods of data collection and how this can assist in exercising ethical behaviour while engaging with participants in the research site. In doing so, we introduce some concrete examples which have come to fruition through our own research project investigating video-conferencing, and its effect on the ways in which increasingly dispersed family populations interact.

A key component when considering ethics in relation to any research project is articulating one's own ethos regarding what the research process consists of and how method affects and influences one's behaviour in the field. We would contend that the ethics application process (depending on one's country of residence), and the strategic consideration of methods in relation to fieldwork can be employed as a useful tool, and can be conceptualised as affording the opportunity to engage in some fruitful and relevant procedural planning. Of course, what happens when one is in the field can vary drastically, and typically, never occurs as one would have imagined, however: through carefully considering how things might go in the field one can strategize and make plans for situations which might occur.

Planning and preparation for dealing with worst case scenarios (though these may never occur) can better prepare one for the complex situations that transpire when engaged in data collection. Many times, exercising ethical conduct and learning how to interact with participants while engaged in social science research is learned by jumping in the deep end. In most cases, you will not only survive, but invent unique new strokes that are both personally and professionally enriching. While jumping in the deep end has proven a useful strategy in the past, we hope to point out that there are floatation aids available, and knowing where they are can help alleviate stress and anxiety which will further contribute to positive experiences, better data and reflexively exercising ethical conduct during all stages of the research process.

Here, we argue for the utility of the procedural ethics process – a process that is necessary to undertake in many countries – as a tool which can assist researchers of varying experience levels in the application of ethics in practice.

The processes referred to herein as procedural comprise the requirements dictated by institutions in relation to ethics application and review. While the guidelines, stringencies and particularities of procedural ethics may vary somewhat between institutions, the considerations necessitated by the process can be employed to one's advantage.

The concerns in ethics application documentation traditionally relate to methods, i.e.: what exactly one will be doing in the field; and ethical consideration, i.e.: how do methods relate to the principles of partnership, participation and protection. As a result, the procedural ethics process is primarily a judgement of congruity between what one plans to do during fieldwork, and what considerations need to be made explicit to ensure the wellbeing of those who participate in the project.

In the design of ethnographically oriented projects, and/or endeavours in which the researcher seeks to study naturally occurring social interaction/phenomena, a central aspect of consideration should be: In what ways might my presence as a researcher affect or influence the behaviour of the individuals who I plan to study? And, in what ways might the structure of my intended observational protocol contribute to events which might require explicit ethical consideration? While a sociocultural approach to the research endeavour unequivocally recognises the centrality of participants as co-constructors of events and phenomena, an explicitly reflexive recognition of the possible negative effects of researcher presence can help one to strategize how to minimise the possibility. An example from one particular research project might help explicate this component in more detail.

An example

As mentioned above, we are currently embarking on a research project focused on how increasingly spatially dispersed families connect and interact through the employment of video-conferencing software. A central occupation of the research concerns the ways in which distant family members learn to interact with very young children and very young children learn to interact with distant family members through a screen. Resultantly, our recruitment strategies and data collection methods focus explicitly on families with very young children who use video-conferencing software to connect with overseas relatives. While intentions champion the observation and audio-video recording of naturally occurring conferencing sessions, the acuity of our empirical attention has brought forth a number of concerns.

First, we have had to explicitly consider the autonomy of young-child participants who will not be able to provide consent to participation. The authority will rest with their legal guardians who will also have considerable influence over the nature and extent of the child's participation. This has raised the question: In what ways might the legal guardian possibly override the autonomy of a child participant, forcing a child to interact because researchers are present? Answering this question brings to fruition the ways in which methods (what one intends to do in the field) might explicitly affect ethics in practice.

It is within the realm of possibility that the emotional and/or behavioural dispositions of young children might explicitly conflict with the intended observational protocol and the children's legal guardians' desires at that particular time. Parents might be more apt to disregard emotive dispositions of the child in favour of their inclusion in the video-conferencing session.

The legal guardians may be considerably less permissive of the child's conduct because "important" people are here to conduct "important research", or moreover, because the interactions are witnessed and/or video-taped. They might want to force the child to engage in the conferencing session and not concede to the child's emotional dispositions. Discussing this fictitious scenario made us ask the question: If this occurs, what role do we play as researchers; and how can we act so as to exemplify ethical conduct in relation to all participants in the research site; or what can we do to alleviate such a possibility in the first place?

Resultantly, the fictitious example above has led us to consider how we can minimise this possible problem from occurring in the field in the first place. This, in turn, has brought us back to the method and our theoretical notions that underlie our research practice: We intend to collect naturally occurring data – as much as that is possible with researchers being present. Therefore, we will highlight this aspect when speaking with parents and/or guardians about the project. While we do hope to see how young children interact and are interacted with via a screen, we have no interest in forcing the matter. In fact, forcing the matter would go against our desire to collect data of naturally occurring interactions. And, as we are interested in naturally occurring interactions, we may find that some children and adults do not readily interact with one another via the screen.

Through engagement in discussion of possible ethical problems arising in the field, we have been able to examine how our data collection methods influence the principles of partnership, participation and protection. This is a case of employing our ethical considerations to our empirical advantage. While this is one example of an issue that we have thought through, there are of course many more.

While many of these situations might never transpire while engaged in fieldwork, conceiving of their possibility can assist with preparation and planning. This may even contribute to considerably less stress and anxiety if researchers are confronted by such events while engaged in the field. As a result, they may be able to exercise better judgement, ethical consideration and reflexivity, contributing to more ethically sound conduct.

Considering situations that might arise also highlights what aspects of method might result in the aforementioned moments of ethical importance. In the next section we present real examples from moments in the field when *how* the method was executed became ethically important.

Real children, real research

Having conducted much research with young children of different age groups (Norris, 2002, 2004, 2011), we find what is of particular importance for the researcher(s) is to take children seriously. Children are small people. They have their own ideas about the world, ideas about others and ideas about the researcher, who may be walking around with camera in hand.

Children run on their own timelines. They engage when they feel like engaging and their timelines are often of quite a different kind than that of the researcher(s). As an example, one day in the field (Norris 2011) the researcher wanted to follow two adult participants in a large store, while five child participants began to take their co-researcher roles seriously and started to use the researcher as their film agent: The children were sitting on a large shopping trolley, and requested that the researcher film them while they sang a song; they then continued in their role, telling the researcher which signs and objects needed to be photographed; and generally, took on the role that they had been offered. The researcher accepted the children's point of view of the in-store data collection and spent very little time collecting the data that she had thought she would collect.

At a different time, the researcher (Norris 2011) followed one adult participant and a very young child into the city centre. A valuable data collection session arose in a book store. However, at that very same point, the Baby (about 2 years old), sitting in her stroller, asked the researcher to have a look into the camera. By the time the child had lost her interest, the adult participant had moved on, and the moment that the researcher thought she was interested in had passed.

The point here is that if you do wish to work with children, it is you the researcher who needs to be flexible. No researcher can expect a child to travel along a research timeline. No child can be expected to have the patience or the need to see what a researcher wants to collect. As soon as children are engaged, the research project intermittently is run by the children, and not the researcher.

Focusing on naturally occurring interaction in the field limits the possibility that children are coerced by their guardians to engage when they do not want to engage. Focusing on children as co-researchers allows for authentic interaction in the field that respects children and takes them seriously. In fact research projects that include children, make for an ever-interesting data collection. While you may not always collect just what you as researcher intended to collect, you will no doubt always collect most interesting and genuine data.

Conclusion

We have provided some strategies about *how to gather data ethically*, and illustrated these with examples from our own experience. Ethical approval for research is required in many countries, and the approval process can put off researchers from taking on projects focussing on naturally occurring situations, and working with populations traditionally defined as vulnerable. Ethics applications for projects like this can be difficult, due to conceptions of informed consent, and vulnerability. In our experience we have found that researchers can make the most of the ethics application process by using it to consider what issues might arise in their research, and how their execution of method can alleviate these.

Treating participants as co-researchers, with a real vested interest in how the research progresses, can overcome many of the issues associated with research ethics. This impacts on the methods selected, and the stance that the researcher takes throughout recruitment and data collection. Ethics in practice is about how a method is carried out. This provides for a more concrete basis for ethical research than *solely* relying on a mindset or desire to act ethically.

The examples presented above demonstrate the utility of discussing moments of ethical importance that may arise during research, and of treating participants as co-researchers, especially when working with children. Fundamentally, ethical research in naturally occurring situations requires *sharing control over what constitutes the research*, so that participants truly can take on a role of co-researcher. This positioning should flow through the research design, and will then be evident in the ethics application, and in the researcher's behaviour throughout the research project.

Further readings

Rhodes, R. 2010. Rethinking research ethics. *The American Journal of Bioethics*, 10(10), 19–36.
Laine, M. de. 2000. *Fieldwork, participation and practice: ethics and dilemmas in qualitative research*. London/California: SAGE.

Project idea

Choose an article or book chapter discussing a research project that interests you. Consider the types of ethical questions that may have arisen prior to undertaking the research. Is it clear how these were addressed in the project? If yes, how? If not, how would you overcome the ethical issues you raise?

References

Aluwihare-Samaranayake, D. 2012. Ethics in Qualitative research: A View of the Participants' and Researchers' World from a Critical Standpoint. *International Journal of Qualitative Methods*, 11(2), 64–81.
Guillemin, M., and Gillam, L. 2004. Ethics, Reflexivity, and "Ethically Important Moments" in Research. *Qualitative Inquiry*, 10(2), 261–280. doi:10.1177/1077800403262360
Miller, D. B. and Scollon, R. 2011. Cooperative ethics as a new model of cultural research on place and security. In Cramer, C., Hammond, L. and Pottier, J. (eds.), *Researching violence in Africa ethical and methodological challenges*. Leiden/Boston: Brill.
Rhodes, R. 2010. Rethinking research ethics. *The American Journal of Bioethics*, 10(10), 19–36.
Dillen, A. 2006. Children between liberation and care: ethical perspectives on the rights of children and parent–child relationships. *International Journal of Children's Spirituality* 11 (2), 237–250. DOI: 10.1080/13644360600797230
Matutina, R. 2009. Ethical issues in research with children and young people. *Paediatric Nursing*, 21 (8), 38–44.
Norris, Sigrid. 2011. *Identity in Interaction: Introducing Multimodal Interaction Analysis* (Vol. 4). Berlin, New York: Mouton De Gruyter.
Norris, Sigrid. 2004. *Analyzing multimodal interaction: a methodological framework*. London: Routledge.
Norris, Sigrid. 2002. The implication of visual research for discourse analysis: transcription beyond language. In B Dicks (Ed.), *Digital Qualitative Research Methods*. London, New Delhi: Sage.
Trussel, D. E. 2008. Unique ethical complexities and empowering youth in the research process. *Journal of Park and Recreation Administration*, 26 (2), 163–176.

Acknowledgements

Research for this chapter was made possible by Auckland University of Technology's *New Zealand Work Research Institute's Digital Mobility Research Group* Seed Funding.

derma
IV Sample analyses

Editors' introduction
19 Mediation as interrelationship: Example of kitesurfing

Topic

This chapter addresses researchers and students interested in the analysis of extreme sports. However, rather than taking a more common cultural studies approach, the author focuses on the real-time actions that participants take.

Key terms: Mediation, mediational interrelationship, kitesurfing.

Methodology

This chapter takes a mediated discourse approach, particularly investigating and advancing the notion of mediation as first discussed by Vygotsky, Wertsch and Scollon.

Thematic orientation

Thematically, this chapter has more of a theoretical theme, namely that of the interconnection of mediational means in action. The importance of these interconnections is illustrated through the examination of the life-style sports: kitesurfing.

Related chapters

Chapters 9, 17, 18, 20, and 26.

Jarret Geenen
Mediation as interrelationship: Example of kitesurfing

Introduction

In this chapter, I articulate the theoretical imperative of conceptualising mediation as primarily a property of interrelationship between multiple and interconnected cultural tools and/or mediational means. It has long been acknowledged that all mediated action occurs with or through multiple mediational means and/or cultural tools (Wertsch 1991, 1998; Scollon 1998, 2001; Norris 2004, 2011; Norris and Jones 2005). While this idea helps situate analytical orientation towards *multiple* mediational means and/or cultural tools, the analysis below posits that mediation is always a property of *interrelationship*. If analytical orientation is allocated to understanding the ways in which mediation occurs, we must simultaneously acknowledge that mediational means and cultural tools are multiple, interconnected and interrelated. In so doing, articulation of the mediating character of any cultural tool as a mediational means must unequivocally involve an articulation of the interconnections a single cultural tool has with a plethora of others.

The data referred to below comes from a year-long video ethnography investigating mediated actions and practices exemplified in the sport of Kitesurfing. The data comprises representative samples from over 60 hours of audio-video footage coupled with observational notes and interview transcripts. The analysis is guided by contemporary Multimodal Mediated Theory specifying the unit of analysis as the social action exemplified by the irreducible tension between social actor and mediational means.

Multimodal mediated theory

Multimodal Mediated Theory, in following Mediated Action Theory (Wertsch 1991, 1998) and Mediated Discourse Analysis (Scollon 1998, 2001; Norris and Jones 2005), takes the ecological unit of analysis as the mediated action which is the social actor acting with or through mediational means and/or cultural tools. The concepts of mediation and mediational means come from the work of Vygotsky (1978) and his contemporaries whose sociocultural approach to psychological functioning posited that all "higher mental functioning and human action in general are mediated by tools (or *technological tools*) and signs (or *psychological tools*) (Wertsch 1991: 28). Vygotsky's occupation with sign systems and the ways in which they function as part of, or as mediating various forms of human action was taken up by Wertsch in his development of Mediated Action Theory.

Wertsch explicitly articulates the utility of the mediated action as the ecological unit of analysis which maintains the irreducible tension between the agent (social actor) and mediational means (cultural tool). In doing so, analytical attention is simultaneously oriented towards individual, cultural, historical and institutional elements which manifest in and through mediated action. Scollon (2001) describes this as "cutting the Gordian knot of the individual – society antinomy" which finesses the debate regarding which component should hold analytical priority.

Paramount in discussions regarding mediational means as they manifest in and through social action is the idea that mediational means must always be conceived of in and through the action itself

> The claim that mediational means are inherently related to action is fundamental.... Only by being part of action do mediational means come into being and play their role. They have no magical power in and of themselves. The widespread tendency in several disciplines to focus on language and other sign systems in isolation from their mediational potential usually means that one is not focusing on mediation at all ...
> (Wertsch 1991: 119)

Scollon's (2001) work takes up this affirmation and further articulates the necessity of concentrating on the cultural tool and/or mediational means in-use and advances the notion through the analysis of the ways in which a crayon and kitchen items mediate multiple differentiated mediated actions. Scollon's (2001) discussion of mediational means reaffirms the concept of in-use as paramount by explicating the ways in which the same mediational means can mediate vastly different actions. His analysis shows how kitchen items can mediate the action of quieting an upset child as a form of pacification, and moments later, mediate the actions of noise making. In both cases, we see artefacts and objects employed as mediational means in two different ways, neither of which could be described as the intended use of the utensils themselves (normally for cooking).

Simultaneously, Scollon (2001) questions the ambiguity in the classification of mediational means which differ drastically in their material composition. There are highly semiotised mediational means like language, physical objects, the social actor's physical body etc. In doing so, he identifies multiple other categories of mediational means which are manifested as salient in the particular study (i.e. ambient objects as mediational means).

However, if we consider mediation as always and only a property of interrelationship, we are able to clarify a number of the ambiguities identified about how objects function as mediational means and we also bypass the necessity of classification. If mediation is always multiple interconnected mediational means, there is an inherent contradiction in attempts to describe categories because mediational means only "come into being and play their role" (Wertsch 1998: 119) in relation to multiple other mediational means. Second, conceptualising mediation as always a property of interrelationship forces the analyst to consider the complex ways in which multiple interconnected mediational means function in mediated action.

Mediational interrelationship

The 18 frame image sequence below comes from a 0:09:00 (m/s/ms) video clip. Each frame is a still image exemplifying an approximately 0.5 second lapse in time. The segmentation of the video in this manner has been done to suit the constraints imposed by attempting to represent real-time video in a segmented fashion while (hopefully) maintaining the phenomenological acuity of the multiple mediated actions themselves.

The sequence in Figure 1 exemplifies a kiter performing one of the more basic aerial manoeuvres typically associated with freestyle kitesurfing. Jumping is a specialised practice whereby the kiter generates lift in an upward direction through a constellation of materially and temporally interrelated mediated actions. Resultantly, the kiter is propelled skyward and floats in the air for a period of time before landing back on the surface of the water and continuing to ride. A salient component of this data excerpt, and characteristic of the practice of jumping in kitesurfing, is that the kiter jumps much higher than would ever be physically possible using one's legs alone. Therefore, there must be some other mediational means (apart from the social actors body) which mediated this particular action; and the analysis of the ways in which multiple mediational means function in this instance of jumping thoroughly exemplifies the methodological and theoretical necessity of conceptualising mediation as always and only a property of interrelationship.

There are a number of visually salient mediational means which are clearly identifiable in the frame sequence. Extending from the lower region of each individual image, there is a complex configuration of lines; two of which connect in a V formation and two others which extend in a linear trajectory towards

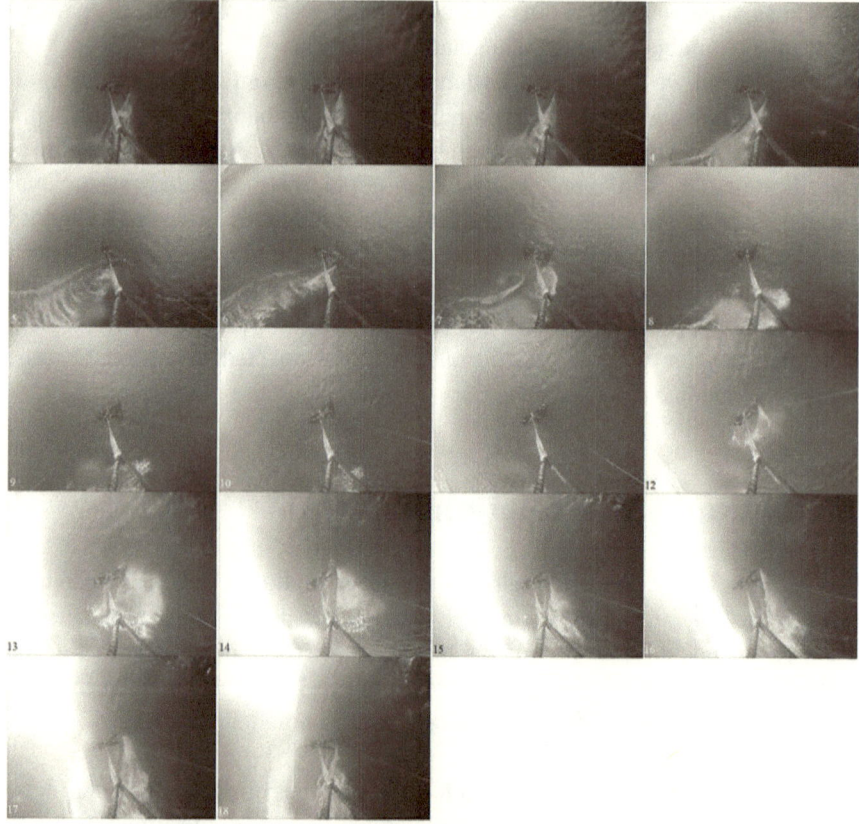

Figure 1: Kiter performing an aerial maneuver traditionally called *jumping*: Occasionally referred to as *getting-air*, *boosting* or a *sent-jump*

the kiter. The centre lines (which form the V) also extend in a linear fashion towards the kiter and these protrude through the middle of the control bar which is located in the kiter's hands. At the end of the front lines, there is a small loop (chicken loop) which is connected to a harness which is wrapped around the kiter's waist. The outside lines (steering lines) connect to the ends of the control bar. In the opposite direction and not visually represented in the sequence, the lines attach to a large LEI (Leading Edge Inflatable) kite which has a series of lines and pulleys called a bridal.

Simultaneously, the Kiter is standing on top of a board, which is rectangular in shape and on the top-side of the board is a combination of straps, pads and a handle. Water is also functioning as a mediational means in these mediated actions. There is a clearly visible trail of white wash wherein the surface continuity of the water has been disrupted by the board, and without the water, none of these mediated actions would be possible. Also, there is another integral mediational means; the wind. While it is not visually recognisable, it is clearly audible in the audio-video footage and it plays a central role in the mediational interrelationship.

When attention is allocated to describing the ways in which mediation is occurring in this particular example of jumping in kitesurfing, one is forced to draw upon the functionality of the mediational means mentioned above. However, if the project is to describe *jumping* as a mediated action, it becomes increasingly clear that discussion of a single mediational means provides little insight into mediation itself. Moving a step further, attempting to articulate how each mediational means functions, unequivocally involves a description of the mediational means *in relation* to multiple others.

Consider the kite for example. It seems quite obvious that the kite plays an important role in mediating the action of jumping. Without the kite, the social actor would not be able to jump nearly as high, or float in the air nearly as long. However, considering the ways in which the social actor accomplishes jumping through the kite as a mediational means unequivocally implicates another mediational means; the wind. The kite cannot mediate much of anything by itself, therefore, if one attempts to describe the kite as a mediational means, it is only possible by articulating the interrelationship between the kite and the wind. Without an adequate amount of wind, the kite would not propel the social actor across the surface of the water, nor would the kite propel the social actor skywards in the action of jumping.

At the same time, the kite and the wind as mediational means do not adequately articulate mediation as it is occurring in the action of jumping. The board and water play an equally integral role in the accomplishment of this action.

The social actor skilfully changes the flying trajectory of the kite which is realisable in the changing orientation of perspective in the frame sequence. Initially the kite is travelling in the same direction as the kiter, towards the kiter's left. In frames 1–6, there is a continuous changing of perspective which is a result of the social actor steering the kite to a position overhead. Once the kite is almost directly overhead, the kiter pulls in on the control bar creating more force, resultantly, the individual is propelled skyward. However, simultaneously there is a visually salient changing dispersion of bodyweight which can be seen in the disruption of the linear wash line created by the board in the water. Here, the kiter (while steering the kite overhead, and pulling in on the control bar) leans back aggressively so as to create a force in a direction which opposes that of the kite. This opposing force is primarily created through the board, water and changing dispersion of body weight. Without creating force in an opposite direction which is predominantly mediated by the board and the water, jumping would not be possible. As a result, it must be conceded that the board and water also play an important role in mediating the action of jumping. Without them, jumping would not be possible (at least in this particular way).

Interconnections and interrelations

Recognising mediation as always and only a property of interrelationship helps orient the analyst's attention towards the multiple, interconnected and interrelated mediational means which function in the undertaking of mediated action. Moving a step further, by conceding that mediation is a property of interrelationship, one may be directed to consider how mediational means and/cultural tools manifest through processes of production and design as explicitly coordinated with other mediational means and/or cultural tools. For instance, the design, construction and marketing of inflatable kites has occurred explicitly to suit employment on the water. Simultaneously, the material composition of boards, straps, pads, harnesses and control systems have manifested through complex interrelationships with practices which become regularised and so as to be employed with other mediational means and/or cultural tools in the undertaking of action. In this way, while mediation is always a property of interrelationship, the very material composition of the objects employed as mediational means are often engineered explicitly for employment as related to a complex of others.

Conclusion

By conceptualising mediation as primarily a property of interrelationship between multiple interconnected meditational means, one must unequivocally allocate analytical attention to the ways in which interrelationships manifest and how they affect the structure of phenomena itself. In applying the notion to other instances of mediated action like speaking or writing, one is forced to consider the relationships between the multiple and interconnected meditational means. In terms of multimodal phenomenon, this implies that considerable attention must not only be allocated to the multiple modes of communication that manifest, but how these multiple modes interrelate, are co-constitutive and function as meditational means only through the complex and dynamic relationships which manifest through mediated action.

Further readings

Norris, Sigrid. 2003. Multimodal discourse analysis: A conceptual framework. In Philip LeVine and Ron Scollon (eds.). *Discourse and Technology: Multimodal Discourse Analysis*, 101–115. Washington, DC: Georgetown University Press.
Norris, Sigrid. 2011. Teaching touch/response-feel: A first step to an analysis of touch from an (inter)active perspective. In Sigrid Norris, (ed.), *Multimodality in Practice: Investigating Theory-in-Practice-through-Methodology*. New York: Routledge.
Rowe, Shawn and James Kisiel. 2012. Family engagement at aquarium touch tanks – exploring interactions and the potential for learning. In Eva Davidsson and Anders Jakobsson (eds.) *Understanding Interactions at Science Centres and Museums: Approaching sociocultural perspectives*, 63–77. Rotterdam: Sense Publishers.
Wheaton, Belinda. 2004. Introduction: mapping the lifestyle sport-scape. In Belinda Wheaton (ed.), *Understanding Lifestyle Sports: consumption, identity and difference*, 1–29. New York: Routledge.

Project idea

Identify an object in the room which is regularly used in some active manner. Write down what the object is traditionally used for and/or identify a mediated action in which the object is employed as a mediational means (i.e. a pencil in the mediated action of writing). Next, write down what elements of the physical body contribute and interrelate in the undertaking of this mediated action (for the pencil, we might include hands and fingers, arms etc.). Now, what other objects or cultural tools contribute in the undertaking of this mediated action (paper, writing surface, chair, sufficient arms space etc.).

In what ways do the multiple mediational means through which the action is taken come into explicit interrelationship through that action? For instance, in the case of the pencil, we might have to discuss the relationship between the lead-like substance, its material composition and the paper itself. Paper of a certain finish might not enable writing through the mediational means of a pencil. Also, consider the writing surface, the body of the social actor, the chair (or lack thereof) which is also being employed in this mediated action.

Finally, make a flow chart identifying the mediated action in the middle, along with a list of all the other mediational means which simultaneously figure in the action itself. Now, draw a line between the mediational means which interrelate in some way. Here, we might draw a line between the pencil and the paper. Next, we might draw a line between the pencil and the writing surface, and in doing so, we could draw the line through the word paper.

Continue the exercise until you have connected all (or most of) the mediational means functioning in this mediated action. Finally, is there any mediational means which is employed in isolation (which cannot be connected to another)? Or, is there any mediational means which is characterisable in this action by itself?

In writing, we might be hard pressed to talk about how the pencil is mediating the action by itself, the paper seems equally important and any discussion of the pencil necessarily involves that of the paper. Simultaneously, if it is a sentence, we would have to concede that language is also playing an integral role in this mediated action.

References

Norris, Sigrid. 2004. *Analyzing Multimodal Interaction: A Methodological Framework*. London: Routledge.
Norris, Sigrid. 2011. *Identity in (Inter)action: Introducing Multimodal (Inter)action Analysis*. Berlin/New York: de Guyter Mouton.
Norris, Sigrid and Rodney H. Jones (eds.). 2005. *Discourse in Action: Introducing Mediated Discourse Analysis*. London: Routledge.
Scollon, Ron. 1998. *Mediated Discourse as Social Interaction: A study of News Discourse*. London: Addison Wesley Longman Limited.
Scollon, Ron. 2001. *Mediated Discourse: The Nexus of Practice*. London: Routledge.
Vygotsky, Lev S. 1978. *Mind in Society: The Development of Higher Psychological Processes*. Michael Cole, Vera John-Steiner, Sylvia Scribner, Ellen Souberman (eds.). Cambridge, MA: Harvard University Press.
Wertsch, J.V. 1991. *Voices of the Mind: A Sociocultural Approach to Mediated Action*. Cambridge, MA: Harvard University Press.
Wertsch, James V. 1998. *Mind as Action*. New York: Oxford University Press.

Editors' introduction
20 Vertical identity production and Māori identity

Topic

The chapter addresses students and researchers who are interested in studying identity production. While this study draws extensively on multimodal data, the author presents the findings regarding her participants' vertical identity production without showing multimodal data due to ethical concerns.

Key terms: Central layers of discourse, intermediary layers of discourse, outer layers of discourse, vertical identity production.

Methodology

Coming from an interactional perspective, the chapter grapples with the gaining of insights into participants' vertical identity production through a short-term, ethnographically informed study. The chapter takes a multimodal (inter)action analytical approach.

Thematic orientation

Thematically, the chapter focuses on indigenous identity production of Māori in New Zealand, discussing various aspects of what kind of ethnic identity is expected and enforced and what kind of identity production is valued by the particiapnts.

Related chapters

Chapters 3, 9, 18, 19, and 26.

Tui Matelau
Vertical identity production and Māori identity

Introduction

There continues to be a gap in the research into an inclusive Māori identity as the traditional Māori identity neglects to include a large number of Māori and the negative Māori identity is grounded in negative representations of Māori. The fluid Māori identity is more inclusive but is a relatively new concept and has yet to be adopted by intervention programmes that are aiming to increase the success of Māori. Instead, such intervention programmes utilise the traditional Māori identity which can leave some participants feeling 'not Māori enough.' In this chapter I illustrate the vertical identity construction of two Maori female tertiary students in order to demonstrate the need for intervention programmes to model a more inclusive Maori identity.

In this research project multimodal interaction analysis was used to examine the Māori identities of two female Māori participants: Kerry and Julia. I spent approximately a week with each participant conducting ethnographic observations and at the end of that week I conducted semi-structured sociolinguistic interviews with each of them. Vertical identity production was used in this research project to analyse how agentive the participants are in the construction of their Māori identity/ties. I had intended to utilise multimodal transcripts within this study in order to depict the way that the participants' construct their Māori identity elements multimodally. In order to achieve this, I had video recorded the participants in different settings. However, after analysing the data I felt that it would be more appropriate if the participants' identities were kept anonymous due to comments that were made about staff from the tertiary institute and from their place of employment. Unfortunately this meant that I could not use images of the participants. However, the analysis was greatly informed by my visual data.

Māori identity-traditional/*marae* Māori identity

The traditional/*marae* (Māori meeting place) Māori identity is the most commonly accepted and is the Māori identity that is most used within intervention programmes. The Māori identity is referred to by Meijl (2006) as *'marae'* identity.

He terms this *'marae'* identity because it is defined by knowing how to conduct oneself on a *marae*, how to take part in and follow *marae* protocol as well as having a firm grasp of the Māori language. McIntosh refers to this as traditional Māori identity and defines it as having knowledge of "*whakapapa* (genealogy), *matauranga Māori* (Māori worldview), proficiency in *te reo* (Māori language) and *tikanga* (Māori customs)" (McIntosh 2005: 43).

Within the traditional/*marae* identity cultural markers are used to indicate one's 'Māoriness'. These cultural markers usually reflect or are similar to cultural components of Māori life, pre-European contact. Borell explains this by stating "a person may be considered more or less Māori not only as a result of their genealogy but also their engagement and participation in a range of cultural activities that generally have their origin in pre-European tribal society" (Borell 2005: 194).

The nature of the traditional Māori identity can exclude many Māori who are unable to perform the cultural markers that are associated with this identity. A lack of proficiency in the Māori language means that an individual does not meet the required standards and has to endure "the shame of not knowing and the fear of being a poor learner" (McIntosh 2005: 45). This Māori identity does not meet the needs of most Māori youth who live in urban environments. Therefore when it is used within intervention programmes for youth, it is incongruent with the Māori identity held by the majority of the audience (Borell 2005; Meijl 2006). This can severely impact the success of such programmes.

Negative Māori identity

Although all identities are "forced from within and without" (McIntosh 2005: 48) the forced identity that McIntosh explores is mostly forced from without. This is where the issue of marginalisation impacts identity formation for Māori. A number of Māori inhabit the margins of society, both excluded from the mainstream and from Māori who identify with the traditional Māori identity. For this group "unemployment, illness, psychiatric conditions, poverty and prison life are marks of being Māori" (McIntosh 2005: 49). Moeke-Maxwell (2005) terms this an assimilated identity and/or a colonized identity. McIntosh (2005) states that this marginalisation results in the deformation of the 'within' which in turn strengthens the influence of the 'without.'

Fluid Māori identity

As identity changes over time, it is possible that a new and emerging Māori identity could become the more accepted Māori identity as opposed to the more rigid traditional/*marae* Māori identity. In contrast to the traditional/*marae* Māori identity, the fluid identities that McIntosh (2005) refers to are more inclusive as they combine more varied ideas about culture, language, tradition and the present social environment. Māori who live in urban areas frequently adopt these identities and absorb a Polynesian flavour due to intermarriage and the social make up of many urban areas. McIntosh (2005) cites Ormond to show that this occurs outside of urban areas as well. In most cases youth are a group who adopt fluid identities. McIntosh claims that fluid identity reflects the nature of identity overall as "it borrows and transforms many of the more fixed elements found in the traditional identity. It also challenges notions of authenticity and lays out new forms of claims making," (McIntosh 2005: 47). Kidman identifies positive future benefits if this occurs by stating "that Indigenous cultural identity then, is not a static creation locked in a frozen embrace with the past, rather it can be seen as an agentic articulation of selfhood that aids Māori young people in their navigation of an uncertain future," (Kidman: 2012: 198).

Vertical identity construction

There are three vertical layers of discourse that Norris (2011) identifies and these produce identity. They include the outer layers, the intermediary layers and the central layers of discourse. These layers of discourse "are viewed in multimodal interaction analysis as building three vertical layers of an identity element; and vertical identity element production is apparent in the levels of discourse that a social actor refers to and/or enacts simultaneously" (Norris 2011: 180). The three layers of discourse are interlinked and embedded within each other.

The outer layers of discourse for Julia and Kerry both include a Māori community that is not specific to any one physical place or time. This Māori community is a construct that has certain cultural markers associated with it, which Julia and Kerry either reject or adopt. However the Māori community that contributes to Kerry's continuous Māori identity element is dramatically different from the one that contributes to Julia's. The Māori community that Kerry perceives is one that is similar to the traditional/*marae* Māori identity. This Māori identity has cultural markers such as: proficiency in *Te Reo Māori* (the Māori language), capability to conduct oneself confidently on a *marae* (Māori meeting place) and knowledge of one's *whakapapa* (genealogy). Kerry indicated in her utterances from her first interview that this outer layer of discourse forces upon her the above cultural markers and she responds positively by attempting to adopt these cultural markers. For Julia, the Māori community that contributes to her outer layers of discourse is one that reflects a negative Māori identity which has characteristics and markers based on material disadvantage and over representation in negative statistics. In Julia's interview it became apparent that instead of adopting the markers associated with this Māori identity, Julia avoids them.

Within the intermediary layers of discourse that contribute to Julia's and Kerry's continuous Māori identity elements, there are again differences but there are also similarities. The Māori support staff at the tertiary institute in which they study is a network that contributes to both Julia's and Kerry's continuous Māori identity elements. This team of Māori staff aim to help Māori students at the tertiary institute to succeed. In order to do this they offer scholarships, mentoring programmes, academic workshops amongst other intervention strategies aimed at increasing success of Māori students at the tertiary institute. They frame their work within a traditional/*marae* Māori identity. For Kerry, this Māori identity is accepted and adopted. Other social actors who are immersed and proficient within this Māori identity are bench marks for Kerry as she attempts to become the same. However, for Julia, this Māori identity leads to a sense of exclusion. When social actors within this network question Julia's cultural identity, they are identifying her as different; and when they expect a Māori identity element that includes the cultural markers of traditional/*marae* Māori identity, they exclude her. It is this sense of difference and exclusion that Julia perceives and responds to. This feeling extends to parts of her extended family network as well.

There is a difference between Julia's and Kerry's continuous Māori identity element, in the outer layers of discourse that extend from the business network for Kerry and Julia's immediate family network. The business network forces upon Kerry the act of having to critically question her peers, as they fail to incorporate Te Reo Māori into their assessments, as encouraged by their lecturers. This critical questioning fits well within the Fluid Māori identity that is emerging in the research (McIntosh 2005; Moeke-Maxwell 2005). Whereas, in the past, members of Julia's family have acted in ways that suggest that they perceive a negative Māori identity. Due to this, acculturation into western society has been forced upon Julia. Her perception of the Māori community that contributes to her outer layers of discourse is a remnant of this historical intermediary layer of discourse.

The above historical intermediary layer of discourse also impacts upon the present central layers of discourse that contribute to Julia's immediate Māori identity element. One type of utterance continuously came up in Julia's first interview and this was an utterance that made claims about Julia's personal identity, whereby Māori culture was not incorporated.

Audio 1.1: Just Julia
(1184)   Julia   I guess I'm consciously trying to put it out there
(1185)   hey guess what I'm Julia (last name)
(1186)   I'm not nothing else

This utterance was the first of several that Julia made in her interview whereby, she is defining her own personal identity through excluding culture.

Audio 1.2: Just Julia
(1264)   Julia   I don't know I'm always being somebody else
(1265)   actually it's I'm just Julia

Audio 1.3: Just Julia
(1437)   Julia   you know sometimes I'll just get along with it
(1438)   and I'm just me

These 'just Julia' utterances indicate that the negative Māori identity that she rejects and the traditional/*marae* Māori identity from which she is excluded, are not included in her definition of her personal identity. Yet, the actions that Julia performs with her children are seemingly contradictory.

Audio 2: Julia's actions with her children
(1408)   Julia   and I speak to him in Māori as well
(1409)   and yeah (Son) went to (school)
(1410)   he was in the Māori bilingual unit
(1411)   when he first started primary school
(1412)   so I think he got a good grasp
(1413)   of the Māori language
(1415)   and man did I really yeah hammer into him
(1416)   the importance
(1417)   yeah Māori culture

With her children Julia performs actions in the hope of creating a positive Māori identity for them that incorporate markers associated with the traditional/*marae* Māori identity. Her actions with her children reflect more of a fluid Māori identity and the way that she is responding to these central layers of discourse also suggest that Julia is renegotiating her Māori identity element.

For Kerry, some of the central layers of discourse contributing to her immediate Māori identity element are in response to her outer and intermediary layers of discourse. Both, the Māori community that contributes to the outer layers of discourse and the Māori support network that contributes to the intermediary layers of discourse, adopt the traditional/*marae* Māori identity. This Māori identity enforces certain cultural characteristics that Kerry willingly adopts into her general, continuous and immediate Māori identity elements. Within these central layers of discourse is a continuum which Kerry utilises to measure 'Māoriness.'

Audio 3.1: Māori Māori

(2002) Kerry it was important
(2003)   because I was
(2004)   doing kind of Māori stuff
(2005)   on my own
(2006)   not just in Tertiary Institute
(2007)   yeah
(2008)   which is where I want to go too
(2009)   yeah
(2010)   so that was my first
(2011)   real Māori Māori experience

Audio 3.2: Half pie Māori

(2028) Kerry I hate yeah
(2029)   I just don't like
(2030)   being one of those
(2031)   half pie Māoris
(2032)   who don't really know
(2033)   what they're singing about or doing

On one side of the continuum is the construct 'half pie Māori' and on the other side of the continuum is the construct 'Māori Māori.' Where one sits in this continuum is dependent on whether or not one can perform the cultural markers associated with the traditional/*marae* Māori identity. Kerry also enacts a fluid Māori identity within these central layers of discourse in the way that she engages in trying to merge her Māori identity element with her other identity elements: her student identity element, her future business woman identity element, her friend identity element and others.

Figure 1 and figure 2 display the vertical identity production of both participants. The three layers of discourse are represented by the three circles and the networks and actions that contribute to each layer of discourse are listed within the relevant circle. The colours and patterns represent the type of Māori identity that is either forced upon each participant or is enacted by each participant and where more than one identity was evident the colours and/or patterns were mixed.

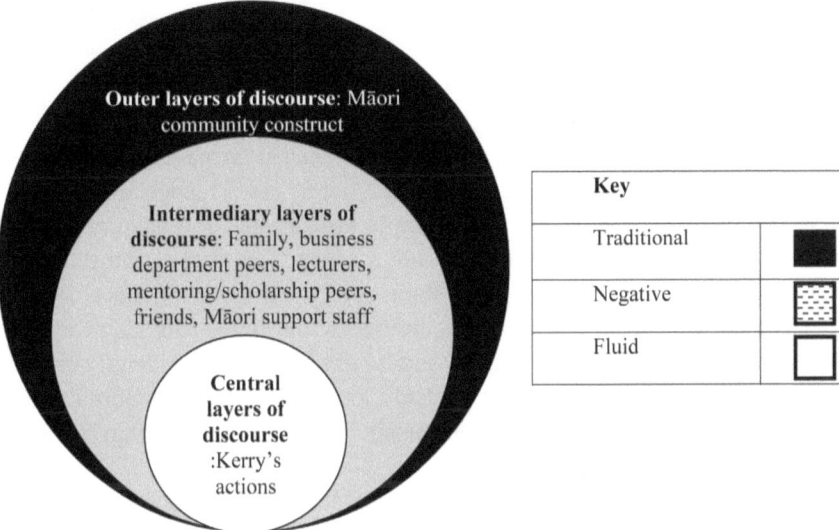

Figure 1: Kerry's vertical identity production

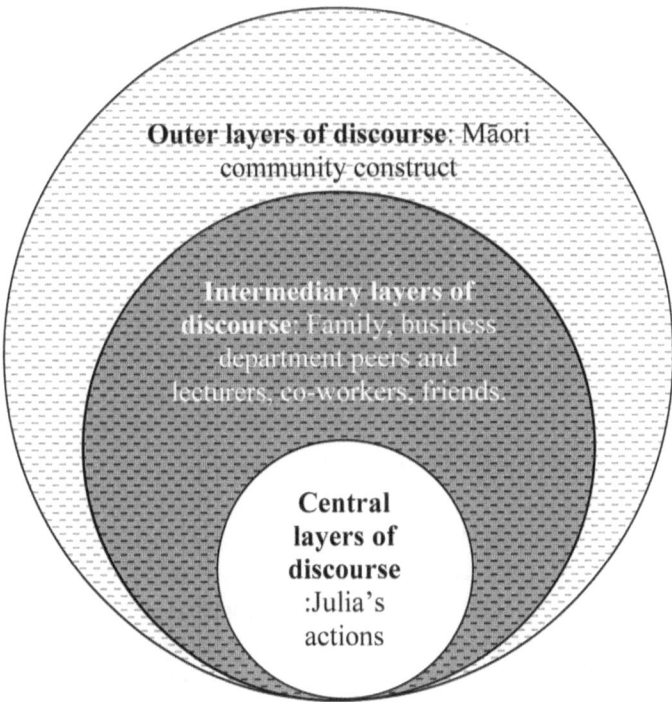

Figure 2: Julia's vertical identity production

Conclusion

For Kerry the traditional/*marae* Māori identity does not pose a problem. Kerry willingly and positively adopts the cultural markers associated with this Māori identity. Kerry responds positively to initiatives aimed at increasing Māori success due to her positive response to the traditional/*marae* Māori identity. However, for Julia the traditional/*marae* Māori identity is problematic. The cultural markers associated with this Māori identity create a sense of exclusion and difference for Julia as she does not enact this Māori identity. Instead the Māori identity that is most evident in her general, continuous and immediate Māori identity elements is a negative Māori identity. Due to this, Julia's Māori identity element is rarely in the foreground of her attention and instead, Julia is more comfortable foregrounding other identity elements and interacting within networks where she can be 'just Julia.'

Through exploring the vertical layers of discourse that contribute to the Maori identities of these two Maori females, it becomes clear that defining an inclusive Maori identity that intervention programmes can utilise is imperative. A more inclusive environment may on the one hand allow students like Julia to engage more with the programs, and on the other hand give students like Kerry the opportunity to be better able to interact comfortably with others outside the programme. In this way, the core of the programme, i.e. Māori identity, would be strengthened as even more Māori students could get involved, and it would build confidence in participants beyond Māori identity, focusing on inclusion rather than on a stark point of difference.

Further readings

McIntosh, Tracey. 2005. Māori identities: Fixed, Fluid, Forced. In James H. Liu, Tim McCreanor, Tracey McIntosh and Teresia Teaiwa (eds.), *New Zealand Identities, Departures and Destinations*, 38–51. Wellington: Victoria University Press.

Project idea

Choose someone and observe them for a day. Ensure to take detailed notes of their actions and interactions. Once you have collected all of your data, analyse it to see if you can determine where your participant enacted their continuous, intermediary and immediate identity elements. Once you have written up your results, show them to the person that you observed and see if they agree with what you have written.

References

Borell, Belinda. 2005. Living In the city aint so bad: Cultural Identity for Young Māori in South Auckland. In James H. Liu, Tim McCreanor, Tracey McIntosh and Teresia Teaiwa (eds.), *New Zealand Identities, Departures and Destinations*, 191–206. Wellington: Victoria University Press.

Kidman, Joanne. 2012. The land remains: Māori youth and the politics of belonging. *AlterNative: An International Journal of Indigenous Peoples* 8: 189–202.

McIntosh, Tracey. 2005. Māori identities: Fixed, Fluid, Forced. In James H. Liu, Tim McCreanor, Tracey McIntosh and Teresia Teaiwa (eds.), *New Zealand Identities, Departures and Destinations*, 38–51. Wellington: Victoria University Press.

Van Meijl, Toon. 2006. Multiple identifications and the dialogical self: urban Māori youngsters and the cultural renaissance. *Journal of Royal Anthropological Institute* 12: 917–933.

Moeke-Maxwell, Tess. 2005. Bi/Multicultural Māori women's hybridity in Aotearoa/New Zealand. *Discourse: Studies in the Cultural Politics of Education* 26: 497–510.

Norris, Sigrid. 2011. *Identity in (Inter)action: Introducing Multimodal Interaction Analysis*. Göttengin: De Gruyter Mouton.

Editor's introduction
21 The Matrix phenomenon

Topic

Chapter 21 will be of particular appeal to students and researchers who have an interest in film and film advertising, image text-correlations, and marketing/audience research in general.

Key terms: Experiential meaning, interactive meaning, mood, rheme, textual meaning.

Methodology

This chapter uses aspects of Halliday's functional grammar and the grammar of visual design as established by Kress and Van Leeuwen, where the grammar of visual design is also based on Halliday's functional grammar.

Thematic orientation

Generally, the chapter is situated in the study of texts and images and their relationships and more specifically, it is an example for the study of film advertising posters. Through in-depth analyses, Maiorani not only illustrates just how the analyses are conducted, but also establishes a strong link between the advertising agency's assumptions and intentions and the targeted consuming public that is addressed with the posters and the by-products of the film. With this, the author gives insight into a social and cultural phenomenon that is unpacked through the multimodal analyses of the posters.

Related chapters

Chapter 4, 10, and 22.

Arianna Maiorani
The Matrix phenomenon

Introduction

The Matrix film trilogy created a widespread commercial, social and cultural phenomenon that was promoted not only by the films themselves but also by its by-product market. The films' success was boosted by the introduction of incredibly innovative special effects and shooting techniques that merged film and Massive Multiplayer Online Role-Playing Games (henceforth MMORPG) technology, and by a clever re-interpretation of religious and philosophical *topoi* in the Internet era (Constable 2009). It was 1999, just at the turn of the third millennium, when the first episode of the trilogy was released, marking the beginning of a new trend in science fiction movies and also in the perception of motion pictures as interactive social and commercial events (Coates 2009 (1994)). The Matrix trilogy is a creature *of* and *for* the Internet era, created for and by a socio-cultural context where the possibility of accessing the Internet is part of everyday life and where Internet communities constantly trigger processes of cultural globalisation (Maiorani 2008, 2009). However, the expectations raised by the first movie were disappointed by the second: *The Matrix Reloaded* mainly relied on high technology performances and the characters' cult look rather than a strikingly catchy plot. The audience's curiosity was not raised enough and *The Matrix Revolutions* was relatively speaking a commercial flop (box office: *The Matrix* (1999) 456,500,000 $, *The Matrix Reloaded* (May 2003) 738,576,929 $, *The Matrix Revolutions* (October 2003) 424,259,759 $).

Ultimately, both sequels relied on the strong social impact and commercial success of the first film to develop and sell the range of by-products like accessories, clothes, gadgets, dvds, cds, video games, etc. The development of this huge market can be traced in the development of the promotional poster campaigns for the film trilogy.

Aims

The Matrix trilogy poster campaigns developed and changed with the Matrix market. The following analysis will show that after the success of the pilot film, the poster campaigns for the second and third episodes of the trilogy were aimed at advertising a whole market as well as the originating product, the trilogy itself.

Methodology

The posters have been analysed using Halliday's Functional Grammar model for the verbal semiotics realised by the slogans (Halliday 2004) and Kress and van Leeuwen's visual grammar model for the visual semiotics (Kress and van Leeuwen 2006). The posters used for the analysis were selected according to two main criteria: posters had to be distributed internationally (i.e. they were to be displayed in all countries where the films were distributed) and slogans had to be in English (not translated into local languages). The selection was composed as follows:

- *The Matrix*: two posters featuring at least the three main characters;
- *The Matrix Reloaded*: single characters against blank background series; close-up-on-clothes series; sunglasses series; slogan series;
- *The Matrix Revolution*: characters series; slogan series.

The posters created for the first film clearly had to provide a potential audience with catchy hints and try to raise the interest in as many people as possible but without revealing the core of the film plot: the fact that the Matrix is actually a very sophisticated computer programme where human beings are unconsciously connected under the illusion of living a real life. Hints had to provide information about the film genre, locations, characters' salience and affiliations, and recurring/distinctive features.

Analysis

The visual/verbal analysis performed on the first poster (Figure 1) provided the following results:

Visual Experiential meanings: some very little action is suggested by the attitude of participants, analytical processes suggest the main features and function of each character through attributes (clothing, weapons, accessories), classificational processes indicate a hierarchy. The catchiest feature is the constant presence of concealed reaction processes realised (supposedly) behind mysterious sunglasses. The location is also mysterious: it looks like a rainy alley from a distance but it is actually made by a backdrop of tiny little figures.

Visual Interactive meanings: the concealed looks make it impossible to distinguish whether the poster realises a demand or an offer but it certainly captures the attention; the scene looks pretty naturalistic, the viewer is mainly

The Matrix

Experiential Meanings: concealed non transactional reaction; non transactional action; analytical and classificational structures. Locative circumstance.

Interactive meanings: dubious demand/offer; impersonal distance; involvement; power equality; naturalistic coding orientation.

Textual meanings: mainly centralised image; no framing. main character salient by focus, position and sharpness.

Figure 1: *The Matrix* sample poster A

involved with the central/presumably main character through a full frontal horizontal angle. An eye-level vertical angle and the long shot suggest equality of power and impersonal distance between the viewer and the represented participants. The medium/medium high values of modality markers such as light, colour, and detail quality suggest a realistic coding orientation.

Visual Textual meanings: the whole scene seems to rotate around what is presumably the main character, the man in the centre holding a big gun (maybe a means for some action? The fight about which we will read in the slogan?), made salient by focus and sharpness and by his position.

The analysis of the second poster in the series (Figure 2) provides more or less the same results: the only difference in the visual semiotics is an enhanced focus on the trinity of main characters at the centre of the composition, realised by the analytical and classificational structures, the more approachable social distance realised by the medium close shot, and the ever present concealed reaction processes.

The Matrix

Experiential Meanings: concealed non transactional reaction; analytical and classificational structures. Locative circumstance.

Interactive meanings: dubious demand/offer; social distance; involvement; power equality; naturalistic coding orientation.

Textual meanings: mainly centralised image; no framing, main character salient by position.

Figure 2: *The Matrix* sample poster B

In terms of verbal semiotics, the analysis of the two slogans is as follows:

Table 1: slogan analysis – *The Matrix* sample poster A

On April 2nd	the fight for the future	begins
Circumstance of Location/Time	Actor (inanimate)	Process: Material
	Subject	Finite
	Mood Block	
	Residue	
Theme	Rheme	

Table 2: slogan analysis – *The Matrix* sample poster B

Believe	the unbelievable
Process: Mental/cognition	Phenomenon
Predicator	Residue
Theme	Rheme

The slogan for poster A is a declarative clause foregrounding the date of release of the film and it announces a fight but remains mysterious about who is going to fight (maybe the people in the poster, who all hold guns?) and where, while the slogan for poster B strongly invites the viewer to believe in something that is not specified: is the trinity of characters unbelievable? Or does the slogan hint at the mysterious tiny figures once more surrounding them?

The interplay: visual and verbal semiotics in these first posters work to emphasize three main features: 1) that the film plot involves human beings fighting an 'unbelievable' fight; 2) that there is a hierarchy among characters and that there is a 'trinity' that is more important than the rest; 3) that the Matrix is something mysterious and maybe the sunglasses all characters are wearing – in the total absence of sun but in the presence of puzzling little code-figures – has to do with it. Posters do focus on the film.

The character series of posters for *The Matrix Reloaded* were quite different, as shown by the samples in Figure 3:

Figure 3: *The Matrix Reloaded* sample posters

The visual analysis shows some striking differences with respect to the first film posters: no action process is performed in any series, only the typical concealed reaction processes (when faces are visible) and analytical processes are

Figure 4: *The Matrix Reloaded* slogan poster samples

realised, and they draw the viewer's attention to the look of the characters (represented singularly) and in particular to their sunglasses (a different model for each character). Participants are displayed against a blank background, suspended in time and space, frontally in order to get the viewer involved with the representation. The little tiny figures forming the background in the first campaign and some slogans have now been reserved for the posters announcing the date of release in Imax theatres (Figure 4). The dubious demand/offer type of contact remains but it becomes just an offer in the series that does not portray the face of the characters (realising non-exhaustive analytical processes). The participants are represented from a slight low angle thus in a slight overpowering position with respect to the viewer. Coding orientation is naturalistic and all figures have the colour and light quality that enhances the quality of clothes in fashion photos. All the posters actually look like fashion photos advertising a brand called "Matrix Reloaded": the absence of a slogan makes it even more difficult to identify these posters with a film campaign, unless you have seen the first film. Unless you are already a 'Matrix customer' and you know what the film is about, who the characters are and why they wear those sunglasses (that embed images of the film in the sunglasses series of posters). The whole campaign relies on the existence of an eager audience of fans who are inclined to buy the by-products of the market as well as seeing the second film of the trilogy. The only slogans featured by the *Reloaded* (Figure 4) campaign appeared in a few posters representing just the Matrix tiny figures as a background and advertising the date of release in each different country and the Imax theatres where the film was shown.

They all feature imperative clauses demanding action in terms of choosing Imax theatres to see the film and enjoying a specific new type of technology: the Imax market joins forces with the Matrix market.

Table 3: example of *Reloaded* slogan analysis on 'only date posters'

Free	your mind
Process: Material	Goal
Predicator	Residue
Theme	Rheme

Table 4: example of *Reloaded* slogan analysis on 'Imax posters'

Reload	in Imax
Process: Material	Circumstance: Location/Space
Predicator	Residue
Theme	Rheme

The Interplay: in the poster campaign for the second film of the trilogy, visual and verbal semiotics work in interplay across the poster series. Poster series featuring characters are clearly visually oriented and they focus on characters' looks and accessories. The film core plot is taken for granted. Character posters seem to rely on the existence of slogan posters for a catchy verbal message to the audience of old and new fans: slogan posters, however, exploit the well-known Matrix background to highlight just the film date of release, and when a message is sent it focuses on another 'product', the Imax theatre where films are screened. Character and slogan poster series work complementarily but always focusing on the film franchise by-products rather than on the film itself. This strategy shows that advertisers are confident that the film will exploit the success of the first episode and attract an audience of fans, and that the advertising campaign must therefore boost the by-product market that has grown around *The Matrix*.

The Matrix Revolutions poster campaign only features a main series of posters with characters (Figure 4), accompanied by some 'slogan posters' featuring the same slogan that is used for the characters' series and the date of release of each country. In terms of visual semiotics, they seem to propose a synthesis of the campaigns created for the first two films of the trilogy. All posters realise the characteristic non-transactional reaction and analytical structures, common to both previous campaigns. The Matrix tiny figures reappear as a locative circumstance but they construe a more atmospheric and less detailed location due to the light source of the images. The dubious type of contact is common to all campaigns, as well as the mainly naturalistic coding orientation. Characters are again placed centrally and represented either singularly or in meaningful couples (on the basis of the trilogy plot).

The Matrix Revolutions

Experiential Meanings: concealed non transactional reaction; analytical structure. Locative circumstance.

Intercative meanings: dubious demand/offer; social distance; involvement; power equality; mainly naturalistic coding orientation.

Textual meanings: centralised image; no framing.

Figure 5: *The Matrix Reloaded* poster sample

All posters (the characters posters, like in *The Matrix* campaign, and the slogan/date posters, like in *The Matrix Reloaded* campaign) feature the same slogan. Even the slogan poster synthesizes information featuring the slogan and the date of release together instead of diversifying the verbal messages in different issues (Figure 6). The slogan is analysed in the table below:

Table 5: *The Matrix Revolutions* slogan analysis

Everything that has a beginning	has	an end
Carrier/Possessor	Process: Relational/Possessive	Attribute Possessed
Subject	Finite	Residue
Theme	Rheme	

The declarative clause realises a Relational Possessive Process that builds a link between the Carrier containing an embedded clause that points at the previous films and the end of the trilogy as an Attribute. This is a slogan advertising not only the last episode but also – and mainly – the Matrix trilogy.

The Interplay: visual and verbal semiotics, in this third film campaign, work in interplay across campaigns. Visual and verbal features are equally referring

Figure 6: *The Matrix Revolutions* slogan poster

to past campaigns and focusing on the end of the trilogy. Posters exploit and combine the visual characteristics of the first and second film campaigns by focusing on characters and their relationships while the slogan constantly refers to 'the end', reminding the potential audience that this is the episode that ends the trilogy (and that therefore it cannot be missed). Advertisers are clearly turning full circle by pointing again at the mystery of the Matrix but relying at the same time on the 'Matrix culture' created by the by-products that spawned from the franchise between 1999 and 2003: videogames, MMORPG, website applications, accessories, DVDs, comic books, books, branded gadgets. The focus on the end of this franchise also subtly suggests that all the items involved in it will become collectibles, thus opening a completely new market for the 'Matrix phenomenon'. The Matrix franchise will therefore exploit also its very end as a new beginning.

Conclusion

The multimodal analysis performed on the three poster campaigns for *The Matrix* film trilogy shows not only how the films were progressively advertised but also how they became a commercial phenomenon of consistent social impact, so much that the second and third film campaigns relied on the audience's knowledge of and loyalty to the Matrix brand. It also shows how the films are not the exclusive focus of the second and third campaigns anymore but rather the original product that spawned a quite diversified market and that is progressively packaged as a showcase. The poster campaigns took the Matrix into the real world of film franchising and created a market through which the 'Matrix community' of film fans and collectors could find a large variety of by-products. Many other advertising campaigns were inspired by the features and impact of The Matrix advertising campaigns (Margolis et al. 2012). The multimodal analysis of the poster campaigns provides evidence of the birth and development of this phenomenon in that it highlights how the strategies of advertising communication relied on the creation and growth of a 'Matrix culture' that turned a film into a commercial and socio-cultural phenomenon right at the turn of the second millennium.

Further readings

Beasley, Ron and Marcel Danesi. 2002. *Persuasive Signs: the Semiotics of Advertising*. Berlin-Berlin/New York: Mouton de Gruyter.
Maiorani, Arianna. 2009. *The Matrix Phenomenon: a linguistic and multimodal analysis*. Saarbrücken, VDM.
Eija Ventola and Arsenio Jesús Moya Guijarro (eds.). 2009. *The World Told and the World Shown*. London/New York: Palgrave Macmillan.

Project idea

Try to analyse in the same way the poster campaigns for *The Lord of the Rings* film trilogy and answer the following questions:
- do the campaigns try to advertise anything more than the films?
- How do you explain your results?
- How does the existence of a book trilogy prior to the films influence the advertising of the product?
- Can you find any similar example of an advertising campaign?
- What type of social insight does this type of analysis provide?

References

Coates, Paul. 2009 (1994). *Film at the Intersection of High and Mass Culture*. Cambridge: Cambridge University Press.
Constable, Catherine. 2009. *Adapting Philosophy: Jean Baudrillard and The Matrix Trilogy*. Manchester: Manchester University Press.
Halliday, Michael A.K. 2004. *An Introduction to Functional Grammar*. London: Hodder Education.
Kress, Gunther and Theo van Leeuwen. 2006. *Reading Images: The Grammar of Visual Design*. London/New York: Routledge.
Maiorani, Arianna. 2008. "Movies 'reloaded' into commercial reality: representational structures in "The Matrix" trilogy promotional posters". In Carys Jones and Eija Ventola (eds.), *From Language to Multimodality: New Developments in the Study of Ideational Meaning*, 275–296. London: Equinox.
Maiorani, Arianna. 2009. *The Matrix Phenomenon: A Linguistic and Multimodal Analysis*, Saarbrücken, VDM.
Margolis, Harriet, Sean Cubitt, Barry King, and Thierry Jutel. 2012. *Studying the Event Film. The Lord of the Rings*. Manchester: Manchester University Press.

Editors' introduction
22 Typography

Topic

The chapter addresses students and researchers who are interested in multi-modal aspects of typography and possible ways of analyzing complex context-dependent typographical meanings. In this chapter, the advertising genre provides the series of examples to illustrate the approach. Each analysis is conducted at the micro, meso and macro level in terms of design features and patterns.

Key terms: Connotation, intermodal harmony, metaphor/metonymy, semiotic mode, typographic configuration, typography/typographic.

Methodology

Coming from a combined perspective which originates in three paradigms – sociolinguistic, pragmatic-cognitive and (social semiotic) multimodality – the chapter introduces some key characteristics of typography as a semiotic mode, focusing on its resources, meanings and functions. The chapter highlights the in-between status of typography revealing how it is a combination of language and image. In this vein, the meaning-making relation of typography with other semiotic modes is also discussed.

Methodologically, this chapter takes a multimodal approach most closely aligned with a social semiotic approach.

Thematic orientation

The chapter is widely applicable to all media using static typography as a semiotic practice. In this chapter, the author illustrates the usefulness of this approach by investigating typography in print advertising. He demonstrates how an analysis of typography includes linear and spatial dimensions of print (such as words, lines and text blocks) as well as type-faces. Further, the author gives insight into the genre-identifying function of typographic conventions.

Related chapters

Chapters 4, 10, 12, 15 21, and 25.

Hartmut Stöckl
Typography

Visual language and multimodality

If a semiotic mode is defined as a "socially shared and culturally given resource for making meaning" (Kress 2009: 54), then typography, i.e. the shape of type and the overall graphic and spatial design as well as the materiality of text (cf. Stöckl 2004: 12) must clearly count as one. As Fix (2001: 115) and Stöckl (2005: 213) suggest, typography or the 'new writing' (van Leeuwen 2011: 567–568) has been moving into the centre of the semiosphere. Whereas in the past type and graphic design were the domain of the expert, they have now – thanks to digital technology – become a layman semiotic activity, which forms part and parcel of writing. Paraverbal typography is in this account and analysis seen to be capable of producing its own typical meanings and contributing to a multimodal text's message in close cooperation with all other modes.

The samples will mainly be drawn from advertising (Stöckl 2008, Gaede 2002: 501–617), a genre known to exploit every possible semiotic resource to maximum effect. They are to demonstrate the richness of typographic structures and their flexible functionality. The strategic choice of examples also aims to illustrate the genre-typical use of typography and its potential for multimodal meaning-making. Every analysis will follow three guiding principles. First, I will identify the kind of typographic forms or techniques at issue. They generally belong in four interconnected domains of typographic work (Stöckl 2005: 210, for inventories of typographic forms cf. also van Leeuwen 2011: 564–566, Pauwels 2011: 578, Lim 2004: 235) and range from fonts (microtypography) over lines and text blocks (mesotypography) to page/document (macrotypography) and materiality (paratypography). Secondly, I will look at how the typographic means employed relate to the meanings made in other modes, e.g. language and picture, and how multimodal meaning is constructed. Third, I will inspect the contribution of typography to the overall text and reflect on its major functions.

Resources, meaning potentials and functions of typography

Before advertising started to become verbally minimalist its long copies in many ways resembled the typography of book pages. Type faces and their sizes, the

156 DIE NATUR: ZU FREIEN FARBEN UND FORMEN

EIN DORF WIRD AUFGELÖST. – IN FORM UND FARBE!

Ist das überhaupt ein Landschaftsbild? Ja: vorne rechts ist eine **Allee** zu sehen, darüber das rote Dach und der helle **Turm einer Kirche** und etwas links unterhalb der Kirche noch ein weiteres **rotes Dach**. Oder doch nicht? Das Bild besteht ja fast nur aus verschiedenen FARBFLECKEN, großen Formen neben kleinen Farbtupfen! Die Farben sind **leuchtend bunt**, ja heiter. Sie strahlen Fröhlichkeit und Lebensfreude aus. Die Formen haben **Schwung**. Bildgegenstände mit Volumen, also Körperformen, gibt es nicht, kein Vorne und Hinten: Alles bleibt in der Fläche. Man muss **Farben und Formen** einfach als solche auf sich wirken lassen und nicht auf das warten, was sie uns über das Aussehen der Dinge erzählen.

Der Maler WASSILY KANDINSKY hat für dieses Bild einen Blick von seinem Haus auf die Kirche von Murnau am Staffelsee als Grundlage genommen. Doch die Formen und Farben haben angefangen, sich von den Gegenständen zu lösen. Später werden in Kandinskys Bildern gar keine Gegenstände mehr zu erkennen sein. *Die abstrakte Malerei entsteht.*

> **INFO**
>
> **Wassily Kandinsky (1866–1944)** war Russe. Musisch sehr begabt, entschloss er sich nach einem Rechtsstudium, Maler zu werden. Ein Bild von Claude Monet hatte ihn in einer Moskauer Ausstellung zutiefst beeindruckt. Kandinsky studierte Malerei in München und lebte bis zum Ersten Weltkrieg und wieder ab 1921 in Deutschland.
> In München gehörte er zu den Gründern der Künstlergruppe »Der Blaue Reiter«, später war er Lehrer am Bauhaus, einer Schule für Kunst und Design. 1933 emigrierte er nach Frankreich. Kandinsky ist einer der wichtigsten Maler des 20. Jahrhunderts und verfasste auch theoretische Schriften zur Kunst. Er gilt als einer der Erfinder der abstrakten (gegenstandslosen) Malerei.
>
>

RECHTE SEITE
WASSILY KANDINSKY · *Kirche in Murnau* · 1910

Figure 1: p. 156 from Kretschmer, H. (2010): *Das Abenteuer Kunst.* München etc.: Prestel

Figure 2: Ad for *Lorenzini* shirts, Claus A. Froh (Weidemann 1994: 151)

alignment of the print, and the use of italic or bold fonts were meant to guarantee smooth readability and provide a strategic organization of a text's content. This can easily be illustrated with the help of Figure 1, a page from a junior book on art. Here, running heads and sub-headline are marked in stencilled, green bold caps to indicate a kind of meta- or para-text. The same typography is used for the special art terminology, i.e. artists, styles (e.g. *Farbflecken, Wassily Kandinsky*). Bold black of the standard type-face in contrast pinpoints words related to what can be seen in the pictures. Finally, colour-highlighted italics of the standard font emphasize full-sentence references to movements and periods in art history. Add to this the outsourced *info* about the artist on the stylized note-card and the fixed typographic format for the captions and you end up with a neatly coded system for the graphic organization of text. The same can be seen at work in a 1960ies ad for men's shirts (Figure 2), where similar *micro- and macrostructural resources* (small caps, italics, bold, margins) are used to create legible print that visually helps organize textual content.

As ads are being reduced to single lines of print in the form of headlines, claims or slogans, it is important to compact paraverbal and pictorial meaning into them that reinforces the utterances made. This central design principle is based on the metaphorical or connotative qualities (van Leeuwen 2005: 139–141) of mainly *micro-typographic features*. It can have various meanings and effects but usually indicates the character of the sender, establishes semantic parallels to the product type or marks an affiliation with certain time periods or cultural practices. In Figure 3 – an ad for hair-care products – the curvy and overlong endings of the fine lines in some of the letters (e.g. l, b, f, g in *long is beautiful*) literally represent length and evoke associations of elegance and delicateness. In turn this design allows for calculated semantic parallels to the content of slogan and picture.

Figure 3: *Pantene*, Haircare, Wing, New York, Typographer: Arturo Macouzet (LA 4/11: 66, 4.1117)

If hairline-print representing hair and its elegance is a metonymic-metaphorical reading of type (cf. *experiential meaning potential*, Kress and van Leeuwen 2001: 10, 22), the next example (Figure 4) shows the connotative powers of micro-typographic resources – something Kress and van Leeuwen (2001: 10, 22) call *provenance*. The ad for a German motorcycle sets its claim and slogan (*Designed with the usual madcap German sense of humour. Proudly German*) in a Gothic type-face. As these kinds of fonts were widely used in Germany up until the 1930ies they came to acquire strong connotations of Germanness (Spitzmüller 2012), which remain intact when the script is imported into a very different context. Trusting in such connotative potential, which derives from conventional associations of script-design with domains of usage, culture or time, is a very

Figure 4: *MZ*, Motorbikes, Y&R Malaysia, 2004 (Wiedemann 2006: 636)

Figure 5: *Prialt*, Painkiller, Saatchi & Saatchi, London (LA 4/11: 108, 4.1114)

frequent and fruitful device in advertising. Advertising itself is a meaning-making practice that has a robust authority to design new fonts, which – either as logotypes or corporate typography – must stand for whole brands and associate their personalities.

Typography is not restricted to type-faces, it also concerns the linear and spatial dimensions of print (words, lines, text blocks) on the page. This is the level of *meso-typography*, which also creates meaning potential to be activated in a multimodal interplay. Consider Figure 5 – an ad for a strong, morphine-like painkiller that promises not to numb patients. Its copy, a poem with an internal monologue of a woman depicted sitting under water, uses curvy lines. Given the contextual knowledge, the wavy text block (*Drown my pain not my spirit [...] and here this distorted reflection of me [...] not burning not drowning just one more time free*) can symbolize the muted sensations of people in heavy pain and muted pain itself, meanings the picture also tries to convey. So the function of meso-typography here is to support the verbal and pictorial interpretations and to make the print tie in with the overall tone of the piece of communication – a phenomenon that could be called *inter-modal harmony*.

The ad in Figure 6 promoting a camera with an especially powerful zoom demonstrates that meso-typographic features may also be instrumental in explaining a product message. Contrary to convention, the words (*River, Crocodile, Fangs, Fish, No. A Hand*) are superimposed on one another so as to make reading them difficult. Once deciphered they suggest a scenario of someone zooming objects with a camera and finally spotting something unexpected – this scenario is to prove the quality of the zoom in the advertised camera. It is the arrangement of type and the adjustment of colour and size that make these semantic effects possible in the first place. Here, typography has already considerably emulated pictorial qualities – the words virtually replace the elements of an image visible through a viewfinder.

Figure 6: *Canon*, Powershot SX 210is, Athos/TBWA, Santa Cruz, Bolivien (LA 4/11: 112, 4.1104)

Figure 7: *Australian Navy Recruitment*, George Patterson Y&R, Melbourne (LA 2/12: 85, 2.1202)

Typography is often said to stand midway between language and image (Stöckl 2005: 206–208). This implies two phenomena: type assumes picture-like qualities and type mingles and combines with pictorial elements and contents. Typographic design aimed at such pictorial qualities may be labelled *typopictoriality* (Weidemann 1994) and may concern all domains of typographic work, mainly the meso- and macro-typographic.

Figure 7 is an advert for the Australian navy; it asks *Have you got what it takes to be a submariner?* and specifies the quality sought by representing a submarine composed of the line *determination*. Here the delicate lettering constitutes the picture to a large extent – it takes a while for the eyes to spot the word, as its graphic shape comes part and parcel of the picture. The subtlety of this typographic solution results from the fine merging of graphic and pictorial elements. Its communicative effect is that determination and submarines are literally equated and therefore semantically likened to each other, even though this connection is not self-evident. A reverse case, i.e. pictures constituting letters is also common in advertising (cf. Figure 8). It has, perhaps, a less striking visual impact but the same semantic effect: the meaning of both modes is closely tied to each other. In the example the design visualizes the claim that the articles in the advertised magazine truly represent the artist Madonna.

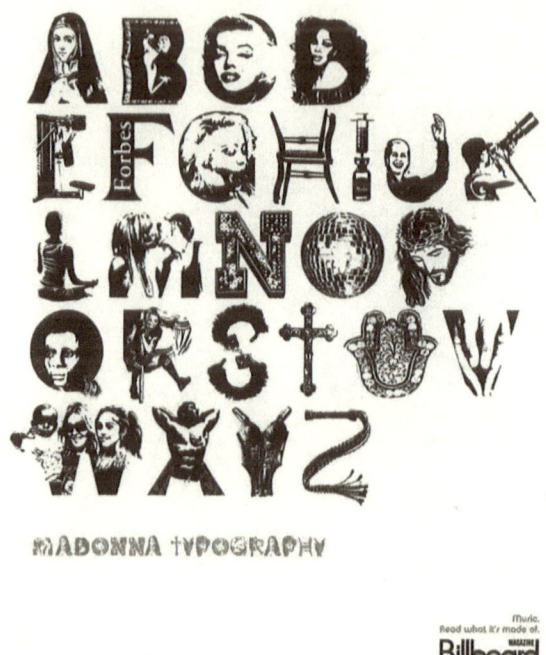

Figure 8: *Billboard Magazine*, Almap BBDO, Buenos Aires (LA 4/11: 116)

The analyses so far have shown the meanings of typography to be determined by many interrelated design features on diverse levels. The practice of signing through type would be unthinkable, however, without a consideration of the materials and the techniques that go into the making of type (Stötzner 2003: 298–299). They may crucially add to its meaning potential and are subsumed under *para-typography* (Stöckl 2004: 37–38).

A poster for the film *Contagion* about a viral pandemic (Figure 9) produced the type by having fungi and bacteria grow to form the lettering of the title. The typographic surface, even though still paper, communicates the nature of the film with an apt immediacy as it is literally composed of the stuff the film is about. Rather than "just" reinforce verbal meaning, a text's materiality (Fix 2008: 347–348) may also add connotations not present in the language. This can be seen in the bike catalogue page (Figure 10) where the worn look of the paper and the torn pages signify frequent use and, therefore, timeless value.

Finally, a whole set of typographic resources forms what Wehde (2000: 119–126) calls *typographische Dispositive*, i.e. conventional configurations or patterns

Figure 9: *Contagion* (Film Poster), Lowe Roche/Amuse, Toronto (LA 1/12: 83, 1.1205)

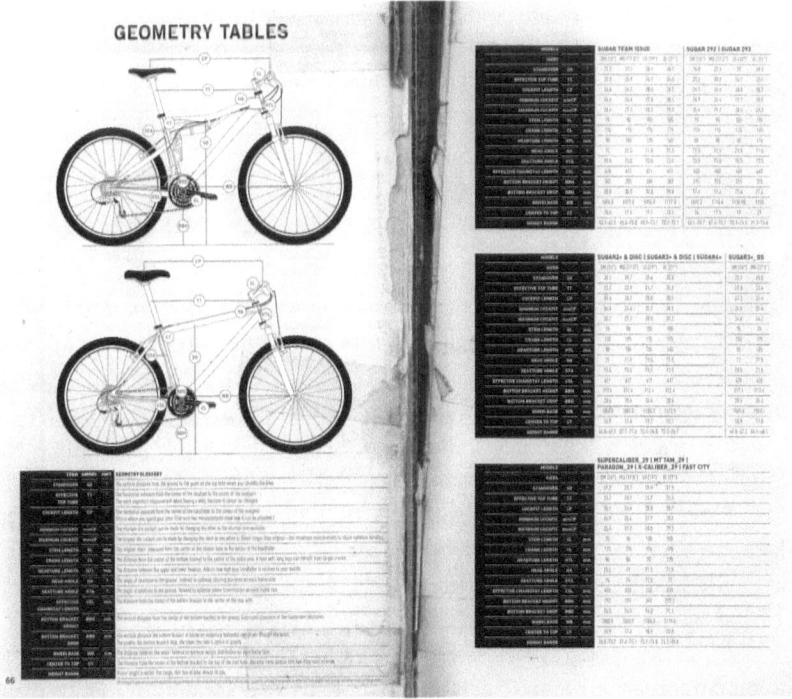

Figure 10: *Gary Fisher Bikes* (Catalogue 2003) (private collection)

Figure 11: *Cepia*, Safe Driving Campaign, Africa, São Paulo (LA 1/12: 110, 1.1204)

of graphic design which mark texts as belonging to a certain genre. Advertising employs the genre-identifying function of those larger typographic patterns in order to dress promotional messages in other guises or to play with the patterns for semantic and argumentative effect (Bhatia 1997 calls this *genre embedding* or *mixing*).

Such a playful use is illustrated in a social ad that warns not to text while you are driving (Figure 11). Here, the typographic conventions of texting (i.e. plain print with punctuation and emoticons only) and road signs (large bold print on rectangular plates) converge in one message, which is to highlight the dangers of combining the two activities. This argument could not be construed without the typographic resources.

The nature of typography

The analyses have shown that print ads strategically design typographic forms with a keen eye to the meanings made in text and picture and the overall communicative effects envisaged. Advertising, therefore, can be seen as a semiotic practice, which treats typography as a full-blown mode, albeit one that is inherently tied to written language and graphic space. If we generalize from the diversity of uses illustrated in the samples, three major typographic functions emerge. First, shape and structure of visual language help to reinforce the product message or create visual evidence for an argument constructed (cf. Figure 3, 6). Second, typographic design evokes and emphasizes material qualities of the medium – it stylizes print as a material object or as a picture (cf. Figure 7, 9). Third, typographic resources seek to create inter-semiotic harmony, i.e. a semantic and structural balance that lends the ad uniform texture (cf. Figure 5, 11). In the analyses we have also seen the varied levels and types of typographic forms and their tendency to integrate into one another to form complex configurations. Typographic meaning, therefore, is not made through simple form-meaning correspondences. Instead it is inter-modal, context-dependent and relative to culture and communicative knowledge.

The analyses can be framed within three larger paradigms (Spitzmüller 2010: 104–118). First, in a sociolinguistic light, typography is a socially relevant stylistic choice in communicative processes, which responds to register, the identities and values of text producers and the anticipated expectations of recipients (Androutsopoulos 2004; Jaffe, Androutsopoulos, and Sebba 2012). Second, in a pragmatic-cognitive light, interpretations of typography hinge on the shared semiotic and graphic knowledge of the communicators. In this sense typography functions as 'contextualization cues' to this knowledge. Depending on the amount of knowledge available, typography makes meaning to varying degrees. Finally, in the light of multimodality, typography is tied to both modes and media used in the semiotic product. Consequently, typographic meaning needs to be modelled in its coherent ties to other modes and will essentially reflect the potential of the medium.

Further readings

Van Leeuwen (2005, 2006) is a good starting point for exploring a multimodal view of typography that provides some theoretical footing and analytical criteria.

Stöckl (2005) provides a systematic theoretical and practical framework for textual interpretations of typography – it is good back-up reading for the present analysis. Stöckl (2004) would be a more comprehensive treatment of the same issues written in German. Stöckl (2008) – also in German – treats advertising typography and provides plenty of examples.

Stötzner (2003) is a somewhat broader, essentially semiotic and very profound account of the graphic sign written from a typographer's perspective. It is also available in German.

Walker (2001) is a sociolinguistically informed textbook exploration of typography, which especially highlights conventional uses of typography.

Project idea

Make a small collection of wine labels. Identify the typographic resources at work and describe what kinds of meanings they make in which way. Pay particular attention to how typographic forms integrate to form larger patterns. Is there something like a conventional, genre-typical configuration of typographic features? Also take care to specify how type builds inter-modal harmony with pictorial elements and the verbal messages conveyed. How does the materiality of the labels affect the meanings they make? Which communicative effects or functions seem typical of the genre 'wine label'? If you happen to find older wine labels, you should also be able to notice diachronic changes in the uses of typography. A similar project would also work well with CD sleeves/artwork (cf. Machin 2010: 58–76).

References

Androutsopoulos, Jannis. 2004. Typography as a resource of media style. Cases from music youth culture. In Klimis Mastoridis (ed.), *Proceedings of the 1st international conference on typography and visual communication*, 381–392. Thessaloniki: University of Macedonia Press.

Bhatia, Vijay K. 1997. Genre-mixing in academic introductions. *English for Specific Purposes* 16: 181–195.

Fix, Ulla. 2001. Zugänge zu Stil als semiotisch komplexer Einheit. Thesen, Erläuterungen und Beispiele. In Eva-Maria Jakobs and Annely Rothkegel (eds.), *Perspektiven auf Stil*, 113–126. Tübingen: Niemeyer.

Fix, Ulla. 2008. Nichtsprachliches als Textfaktor: Medialität, Materialität, Lokalität. *Zeitschrift für germanistische Linguistik* 36 (3): 343–354.

Gaede, Werner. 2002. *Abweichen von der Norm. Enzyklopädie kreativer Werbung*. München: Langen Müller/Herbig.

Jaffe, Alexandra, Androutsopoulos, Jannis, and Sebba, Mark (eds.). 2012. Orthography as social action. Scripts, spelling, identity and power. Berlin/New York: de Gruyter.

Kress, Gunther. 2009. What is a mode? In Carey Jewitt (ed.), *The Routledge handbook of multimodal analysis*, 54–67. London/New York: Routledge.

Kress, Gunther and Theo van Leeuwen. 2001. *Multimodal discourse. The modes and media of contemporary communication*. London: Arnold.

Lim, Fei Victor. 2014. Developing and integrative multi-semiotic model. In Kay L. O'Halloran (ed.), *Multimodal discourse analysis. Systemic-functional perspectives*, 220–246. London/New York.

Lürzer's Int'l Archive. Advertising Worldwide. European Edition (LA). Vol. 4/11, 1/12, 2/12.

Machin, David. 2010. *Analysing popular music. Image, sound, text*. Los Angeles etc.: Sage.

Pauwels, Luc. 2011. Researching websites as social and cultural expressions. Methodological predicaments and a multimodal model for analysis. In Eric Margolis and Luc Pauwels (eds.), *The Sage handbook of visual research methods*, 570–589. London/Los Angeles: Sage.

Spitzmüller, Jürgen. 2012. Floating ideologies. Metamorphoses of graphic 'Germanness'. In Alexander Jaffe, Jannis Androutsopoulos, and Mark Sebba (eds.), *Orthography as social action. Scripts, spelling, identity and power*, 255–288. Berlin/New York: de Gruyter.

Spitzmüller, Jürgen. 2010. Typografische Variation und (Inter-)Medialität. Zur kommunikativen Relevanz skripturaler Sichtbarkeit. In Arnulf Deppermann and Angelika Linke (eds.), *Sprache intermedial. Stimme und Schrift, Bild und Ton*, 97–126. Berlin: de Gruyter.

Stöckl, Hartmut. 2008. Werbetypographie – Formen und Funktionen. In Gudrun Held and Sylvia Bendel (eds.), *Werbung – grenzenlos. Multimodale Werbetexte im interkulturellen Vergleich*, 13–36. Frankfurt/Main: Lang.
Stöckl, Hartmut. 2005. Typgraphy: body and dress of a text – A signing mode between language and image. *Visual Communication (The new typography)* 4 (2): 205–214.
Stöckl, Hartmut. 2004. Typographie: Gewand und Körper des Textes – Linguistische Überlegungen zu typographischer Gestaltung. *Zeitschrift für Angewandte Linguistik* 41: 5–48.
Stötzner, Andreas. 2003. Signography as a subject in its own right [transl. from the German, Signographie als eigenständiges Fach. *Signa* 1 (2000): 23–36 by Hartmut Stöckl]. *Visual Communication* 2 (3): 285–302.
Van Leeuwen, Theo. 2011. Multimodality and multimodal research. In Eric Margolis and Luc Pauwels (eds.), *The Sage handbook of visual research methods*, 549–569. London/Los Angeles: Sage.
Van Leeuwen, Theo. 2006. Towards a semiotics of typography. *Information Design Journal* 14/2: 139–155.
Van Leeuwen, Theo. 2005. Typographic meaning. *Visual Communication (The new typography)*. 4 (2): 137–143.
Walker, Sue. 2001. *Typography and language in everyday life. Prescriptions and practices.* Harlow: Pearson.
Wehde, Susanne. 2000. *Typographische Kultur. Eine zeichentheoretische und kulturgeschichtliche Studie zur Typographie und ihrer Entwicklung.* Tübingen: Niemeyer.
Weidemann, Kurt. 1994. *Wo der Buchstabe das Wort führt. Ansichten über Schrift Typographie.* Ostfildern: Cantz.
Weidemann, Julius (ed). 2006 Advertising now Print. Koln: Taschen.

Editors' introduction
23 Multimodal constructions of factuality and authenticity in TV-news bulletins

Topic

The chapter addresses students and researchers who are interested in the analysis of television news.

Key terms: Audience address, authenticity, factuality.

Methodology

This chapter takes a social semiotics approach. The author introduces the main characteristics of news opening sequences of hourly television news bulletins as a complex semiotic text focusing on its resources, meanings and functions. She highlights the importance of semiotic modes other than language in the dynamic structure of the televisual news discourse; and focuses on the multimodal constructions of factuality, truthfulness and authenticity through which this type of news conveys various events and engages the viewers.

Thematic orientation

The chapter is thematically situated in the study of news discourse, giving insight into the ever-growing array of multimodal strategies and resources that are employed by news networks. In order to illustrate this, the author investigate aspects such as the anchor's appearance and style, the viewer's address and positioning, the cinematographic devices, and the theme music.

Related chapters

Chapters 11, 13, and 15.

Sabine Tan
Multimodal constructions of factuality and authenticity in TV-news bulletins

Introduction

The news is probably one of the most widely researched discourse types in a variety of disciplines, especially from text-linguistic perspectives. In the past, approaches to television news traditionally tended to foreground the importance of linguistic data. Following the highly visual presentational style introduced by cable news networks in the 1980s, however, analytic approaches to televisual news discourse have begun to recognize the importance of semiotic resources other than language. By exploiting the affordances of modern technology, television news displays an increasing "appreciation for multiple electronic feeds, image-text combinations, videographics, and studios with banks of monitors that evoke video installations" (Caldwell 1995: 13). Owing to advances in technology, television news in the 21st century utilizes an ever-growing array of multimodal resources in presenting news events to their audiences.

The analysis presented in this chapter explores how television news bulletins convey events and engage viewers through multimodal constructions of factuality, truthfulness and authenticity. Following Graddol (1994), the concept of televisual 'factuality' must not be understood simply in terms of apparent truth-values, but rather as a complex multimodal semiotic system, which provides for varying degrees of "authority, certainty and appropriateness to be allocated to particular representations of the world" (Graddol 1994: 137). The dynamism that exists between visual and verbal resources contributes significantly to the effect that television news appears credible and authentic, and functions as a crucial element in engaging audiences.

The following analysis of an approximately two minute-long opening segment, extracted from an hourly news bulletin screened on BBC World News, aired on 16 September 2004 at 11:00 pm Singapore Time, offers a brief example of how television news conveys instances of televisual factuality and authenticity as authoritative, credible, and appealing to audiences, through the dynamic interplay of multimodal resources, such as conveyed by videographic displays, on-screen text, sound and verbal discourse (see Table 1.1).

Table 1: Excerpt of BBC World News Bulletin, aired on 16 September 2004 at 11:00

Row	Time	VISUAL ELEMENTS		AURAL ELEMENTS	Verbal Discourse	
		Videographic Display	On-Screen Text	Sound	Anchor	Correspondent
1.	00:00	Brightly colored computer animated graphics of spinning globe encircled by swirling red and orange bands, overlaid with countdown digital clock display		Rhythmic, pulsating theme music (loud)		
2.	00:05	Brightly colored computer animated graphics of spinning globe encircled by swirling red and orange bands	"BBC WORLD" logo appears at bottom of the screen	Rhythmic, pulsating theme music (loud)		
3.	00:09	Medium close-up of male anchor in direct address to viewer, seated in the studio against the backdrop of multiple TV-screens	"BBC-Word" logo displayed in lower left-hand corner of screen	Rhythmic, pulsating theme music at lower volume in the background	Hurricane Ivan *now* batters the Southern US with fierce winds and heavy rain (.)	
4.	00:13	Night-time shot of street lined with trees swaying violently in the wind and rain	"HEADLINES" "Hurricane Ivan hits southern US"	Rhythmic, pulsating theme music at lower volume in the background	The Hurricane is hitting a 600 kilometer stretch of the Gulf Coast (.)	
5.	00:18	Quick succession of video footage showing Chinese parliament assembly, Chinese leaders mingling, walking towards the camera	"HEADLINES" "China Communist Annual meeting"	Rhythmic, pulsating theme music at lower volume in the background	China's ruling communist party meets with rumors of power struggles and internal corruption (.)	

Table 1: *Continued*

		VISUAL ELEMENTS		AURAL ELEMENTS	Verbal Discourse	
Row	Time	Videographic Display	On-Screen Text	Sound	Anchor	Correspondent
6.	00:24	Video footage of US Secretary General shaking hands with presumably Australian and/or British officials	"HEADLINES" "Annan Iraq War 'Illegal' claim rejected"	Rhythmic, pulsating theme music at low volume in the background	And Australia and Britain reject the UN Secretary General's assertion that last year's invasion of Iraq was illegal	
7.	00:32	Brightly colored computer animated graphics of spinning globe encircled by swirling red and orange bands, and crisscrossed streaks of headline-like bands of text	Large display of "BBC NEWS" logo appears at center and in smaller letters at the bottom of the screen	Rhythmic, pulsating theme music (loud)		
8.	00:43	Cut to far, high angle shot of the news studio				
9.	00:45	Medium close-up of male anchor in direct address to viewer, seated in the studio against the backdrop of multiple TV-screens	"NIK GOWING"		A warm welcome (.) I'm Nik Gowing *here* on BBC World.	
10.	00:47	Graphic image of brightly colored blue and orange globe against black backdrop, rotating clockwise toward United States of America.			After battering Granada, Jamaica, the Cayman Islands and Western Cuba, Hurricane Ivan is *now* bombarding the Southern Gulf Coast of the United States (.)	

Table 1: Continued

		VISUAL ELEMENTS		AURAL ELEMENTS		VERBAL DISCOURSE	
Row	Time	Videographic Display	On-Screen Text	Sound		Anchor	Correspondent
11.	00:56	Zoom-in on brightly colored graphic map of Florida and US Gulf Coast	"HURRICANE IVAN"			Two people are reported to have been killed in Florida. In Louisiana, Mississippi, Alabama and Florida, two million people have fled the coastal areas. Power lines are down, emergency shelters are full, and winds are forecast of more than 200 kilometers an hour.	
12.	01:10	Night-time video footage of rain-swept road, filmed from inside a moving car	"MATT FREI" "MOBILE, ALABAMA"	Rushing sound			Every Hurricane has a name, and this one has a well deserved nickname (.) Ivan the Terrible (.)
13.	01:19	Quick succession of video footage showing palm trees, traffic signs, and traffic lights swaying violently in the wind		Rushing sound			*Nine in the evening*, and everything is dancing to the storm's tune (.) It's eye is still 80 miles away (.)
14.	01:28	Video footage of deserted parking lot in front of what is presumably a shopping mall					but the shopping malls along the Alabama coast are deserted (.)

Table 1: *Continued*

		VISUAL ELEMENTS		AURAL ELEMENTS	Verbal Discourse	
Row	Time	Videographic Display	On-Screen Text	Sound	Anchor	Correspondent
15.	01:31	Video footage of police car cruising along street in front of shopping mall				The only sign of life a police car looking for looters (.) There are none of course.
16.	01:38	Cut to live footage of correspondent in the rain in empty parking lot in front of shopping mall		Rushing sound		[hurried, excited] The winds are already gusting about 60 to 70 kilometers an hour (.) and this is just the beginning (.) We are still three hours away [reporter looks away from camera] from the eye of the storm, which will pass (.) over [reporter ducks] (.) Mobile city at some stage in the middle of the night (.) *Then* it will be far too dangerous *out here*.

Analysis and discussion

The news opening sequence

News opening sequences of hourly television news bulletins signal not only the beginning of the program, they also fulfill the crucial function of engaging viewers by utilizing a wide range of multimodal resources. As illustrated in Table 1.1 (Rows 1–2), the opening sequence of the analyzed segment of a BBC World news bulletin commences with a brief display of brightly colored computer animated graphics which depict a spinning globe encircled by swirling red and orange bands, overlaid with a countdown digital clock display and the news network's logo. These animated graphic images are accompanied by rhythmic, pulsating theme music, which convey a sense of upbeat urgency and excitement. According to Allan (1998), ticking clocks and swirling globes – common resources graphic features employed in hourly news bulletins – function to "signal the up-to-the minuteness of the news coverage" (Allan 1998: 123). At the same time, it can be argued that these brightly colored animated digital graphics, which represent the news program's signature theme, also function to attract and hold the viewer's attention. As Graddol (1994) observes, such appealing news opening sequences "ensure that the boundary with other programmes is strongly maintained whilst simultaneously signifying drama and urgency... they create a space within which the business of factual reporting can be accomplished" (Graddol 1994: 147).

The opening graphics in the analyzed segment of the BBC World news bulletin are then followed by a medium close shot of a conservatively dressed middle-aged male anchor seated behind a desk in the news studio, who delivers a quick summary of the top headlines of the hour in direct address to camera, and by extension, the audience (Table 1.1, Row 3). These news headline are specifically designated as such in the form of on-screen text (Table 1.1, Rows 4–6). The hour's top verbal headline "Hurricane Ivan now batters the Southern US with fierce winds and heavy rain" Table 1.1, Row 3) is succeeded by actual footage of a wind and rain-swept streetscape, which is closely synchronized with the anchor's voice-over narration (Table 1.1, Row 4). In this manner, the anchor's voice-over narration outlines the main focal point for each of the selected top stories, which is to be focused on in greater detail in the main section of the news bulletin.

Anchor authenticity and audience address

Apart from delivering a factual and truthful account of the day's noteworthy events, television news has the obligation to present these events as credible and authentic (see also Coupland 2001: 416). Naturally, this involves utilizing multimodal semiotic resources other than language, and extends to the projected integrity and credibility of the anchor/presenter (see also Allan 1998). In fact, the portrayal of the anchor or presenter is highly significant. According to Budd, Craig and Steinman (1999), it "condenses the key news values of responsibility, seriousness, and objectivity so crucial to the credibility of the impersonal news institution" (Budd, Craig and Steinman 1999: 125). In the hierarchy of television news networks, anchors alone are tasked to establish a "pseudopersonal" rapport with the viewer (Budd, Craig and Steinman 1999: 124–125). For Budd, Craig and Steinman (1999), the power of viewer address is crucial for conveying television news' symbolic power and authority: "Whatever else network news may tell us, its very way of presenting itself – and of hailing or positioning us – reinforces its hierarchy of authority and its deliberate confusion of the gravity of the news with the constructed personality of its anchors and correspondents" (Budd, Craig and Steinman 1999: 124).

Following the opening sequence of the analyzed excerpt of the BBC World news bulletin, and before presenting the top headline news event, the anchor takes care to establish a relationship of solidarity with the viewer by introducing himself and his news organization by name ("I'm Nik Gowing here on BBC World") and by extending "A warm welcome" to the viewing audience while looking straight at the camera (Table 1.1, Row 9). By addressing the viewer directly, visually as well as verbally, the illusion of a shared co-presence with the audience is thus achieved. It not only functions to personalize the interaction with the audience but effectively manages to conflate "the seriousness and prestige of the news with those who read it " (Budd, Craig and Steinman 1999: 124).

Goodman and Manners (1997) maintain that an anchor's style of delivery, intonation and pace are equally important. They believe that a news story which is presented well affects how viewers respond to the news (see Goodman and Manners 1997: 56). Together with the visual display of an anchor's authority, as expressed through his formal and conventional attire (see also Tan and Owyong 2009), measured and reserved body language, these multimodal resources contribute significantly to impressions of personal integrity and trustworthiness, which symbiotically serve to uphold the "authenticity and truth value of the newscast" (Allan 1998: 125).

Expressions of verbal and visual factuality

Television news is a discourse domain where facts and truth-values tend to be particularly foregrounded. Dialogically, this is often achieved by frequent references to figures and numbers, and other linguistic devices which enhance the appearance of precision and truthfulness, such as temporal and spatial references, such as place names, for instance (see Bell 1998; see also van Dijk 1988).

This proclivity for numbers as well as temporal and spatial references can also be observed in the analyzed excerpt of the BBC World news bulletin. In delivering the top news event of the hour, the anchor relays emphatically that "two people are reported to have been killed in Florida. In Louisiana, Mississippi, Alabama and Florida, two million people have fled the coastal areas. Power lines are down, emergency shelters are full, and winds are forecast of more than 200 kilometers an hour" (Table 1.1, Row 11). However, as van Dijk (1998) emphasizes, "it is not so much the precision of the numbers that is relevant but rather the fact that numbers are given at all. They are predominantly meant as signals of precision and hence of truthfulness" (van Dijk 1988: 87).

In addition, television news simultaneously seeks to engage viewers by creating the illusion of a shared co-presence, which goes beyond simple viewer address. According to Allan (1998), televisual news discourse aims to provide an "up-to-the minute (now) narrative which, in turn, projects for the viewer a particular place (here) from which she or he may 'make sense' of the significance of certain 'newsworthy' events" (Allan 1998: 105). Linguistically, this is signaled through the use of temporal and spatial deictic references (e.g. *'here'*, *'now'*), which help to create the impression of a shared frame of reference for the audience (see Table 1.1, Column 'Verbal Discourse', text in italics).

However, in order to convince viewers of the truth-value and credibility of the events it portrays, television news also needs to "accommodate immediacy, geographical and temporal location" (Graddol 1994: 140) by means of visual resources and other cinematographic conventions. Television news routinely relies on videographic news footage to locate events in the 'here' and 'now'.

In the analyzed segment of the BBC World news bulletin we observe for example that the voice-over narrative is synchronized closely with actuality video footage and graphic images, which help to orientate viewers spatially and temporally. For instance, in synchrony with the anchor's verbal delivery of the headline news story "Hurricane Ivan is *now* bombarding the Southern Gulf Coast of the United States", a brightly colored globe rotates clockwise toward the United States of America and zooms-in on a brightly colored map of Florida and the US Gulf Coast (Table 1.1, Rows 10–11). In other words, it moves from the locale of the news network (the BBC studio) towards the locale of the news event in question.

Similarly, night-time video footage of rain-swept roads, violently swaying trees and traffic lights, and empty parking lots in front of deserted shopping malls are synchronized with the correspondent's verbal proclamations "*Nine in the evening*, and everything is dancing to the storm's tune. Its eye is still 80 miles away, but the shopping malls along the Alabama coast are deserted" (Table 1.1, Rows 12–15). Coupled with the correspondent's use of the inclusive pronoun '*we*' ("We are still three hours away from the eye of the storm, which will pass over Mobile city at some stage in the middle of the night"), these temporal and spatial co-relations, which are established visually as well as verbally, all help to create the illusion of shared time and space for the audience, and – at the same time – function to situate the viewer as a direct onlooker to the events portrayed on the screen.

Additionally, the cinematographic effects produced by the hand-held camera, such as the shaky images taken from the inside of a moving car, the quick succession of night-time scenes, the over- and underexposed lighting, the audible ambient sounds such as the gushing wind (Table 1.1, Rows 12–15), together with the breathless and rushed narrative delivered by the correspondent on the ground, all help to further deepen the impression of reality and authenticity of the televised event (see Budd, Craig and Steinmann 1999; Coupland 2001; Goodman and Manners 1997). As Allan (1998) notes, these cinematographic conventions, which are "far from being a neutral reflection of the world out there" (Allan 1994: 150) work to construct a specific relationship for the viewer. The viewer is positioned not as a disinterred observer or spectator in front of the television, but rather as direct onlooker or witness to the events portrayed on the scene.

Conclusion

The above analysis of an excerpt from a BBC World news bulletin has shown how television news creates the impression of factuality, truthfulness and authenticity, through the dynamic interplay of multimodal resources, such as videographic displays, on-screen text, sound and linguistic devices. The analysis has highlighted the importance of animated graphic images and theme music to entice viewers to the program. It has emphasized the significance of an anchor's personal appearance and style of delivery, and stressed the power of viewer address and artful manipulation of cinematographic devices as crucial factors in engaging and situating audiences.

While past approaches to television news tended to privilege linguistic data, the above analysis has shown that impressions of televisual factuality and authenticity are not created by words alone. For example, as Turner (1994) notes, "[w]hen we deal with images it is especially apparent that we are not only dealing with the object or the concept they represent, but we are also dealing with *the way in which they are represented*" (Turner 1994: 121; original emphasis). Turner (1994) advocates that a multimodal semiotic perspective can yield insight into such activity "because it allows us to separate ideas from the representation (at least theoretically) in order to see how our view of the world, or a film, is constructed" (Turner 1994: 122).

Consequently, in order to sufficiently account for these multimodal versions of televisual factuality and authenticity, due consideration must be given to the strategies and resources that are drawn upon by news networks for conveying events and positioning viewers through the dynamic interplay of graphic images, logos, sound effects, on-screen characters, studio props and settings, etc., to aid our understanding of how these function – often simultaneously – to convey multiple meanings about events in the world and how we are to perceive them.

Further readings

Allan, Stuart. 1998. News from NowHere: Televisual news discourse and the construction of hegemony. In Allan Bell and Peter Garrett (eds.), *Approaches To Media Discourse*, 105–141. Oxford: Blackwell.

Goodman, Sharon and Paul Manners. 1997. Making It 'Real': Words and Pictures in Television News. *Language & Communication* 17(1): 53–66.

Graddol, David. 1994. The visual accomplishment of factuality. In David Graddol and Oliver Boyd-Barrett (eds.), *Media Texts, Authors and Readers: A Reader*, 136–160. Clevedon, England; Philadelphia: Multilingual Matters in association with The Open University.

Project idea

To investigate the ways in which television news operates to convey instances of televisual factuality and authenticity to their audiences, compare and contrast how different English language news bulletins in your country present current news events – specifically hard news stories that are grounded in a material event, such as serious accidents, natural disasters, riots or terrorist attacks – to their audiences.

Consider how these events are introduced in the opening sequences of the news programs, and how they are represented multimodally through videographic displays, on-screen text, sound and verbal discourse.

Take into account the anchors' body language, voice quality, style and delivery, and forms of audience address.

Identify the linguistic resources that are used to create impressions of exactness and precision, such as references to figures and numbers, places and time, and observe whether they are augmented visually in the form of tables, charts, maps, and other forms of graphic display.

Examine how the factual nature of the events is established dialogically, e. g. by direct "on-the-ground" reportage of the ongoing event, evidence from eyewitnesses or other reliable sources, such as authority figures or professionals, or other persons that are directly involved in or affected by the event.

Reflect on at the cinematographic devices that are drawn upon to represent these events, e.g. camera angle, perspective, subjective framing, point of view, etc., and take into account the sound effects that accompany these videographic representations.

Finally, take note of any distinctive patterns, similarities and differences in the particular ways in which these news channels engage and situate their audiences.

References

Allan, Stuart. 1998. News from NowHere: Televisual news discourse and the construction of hegemony. In Allan Bell and Peter Garrett (eds.), *Approaches To Media Discourse*, 105–141. Oxford; Malden, Mass.: Blackwell.

Bell, Allan. 1998. The discourse structure of news stories. In Allan Bell and Peter Garrett (eds.), *Approaches To Media Discourse*, 64–104. Oxford; Malden, Mass.: Blackwell.

Budd, Mike, Steve Craig and Clay Steinman. 1999. *Consuming Environments: Television and Commercial Culture*. New Brunswick, New Jersey: Rutgers University Press.

Caldwell, John T. 1995. *Televisuality: Style, Crisis, and Authority in American Television*. New Brunswick, NJ: Rutgers University Press.

Coupland, Nikolas. 2001. Stylization, Authenticity and TV News Review. *Discourse Studies* 3(4): 413–442.

Goodman, Sharon and Paul Manners. 1997. Making it 'real': Words and pictures in television news. *Language & Communication* 17(1): 53–66.

Graddol, David. 1994. The visual accomplishment of factuality. In David Graddol and Oliver Boyd-Barrett (eds.), *Media Texts, Authors and Readers: A Reader*, 136–160. Clevedon, England; Philadelphia: Multilingual Matters in association with The Open University.

Tan, Sabine and Yuet See Monica Owyong. 2009. The semiotic function of clothing and gender roles on broadcast business news. *Business Communication Quarterly*, 72 (3): 368–372.

Turner, Graeme. 1994. Film languages. In David Graddol and Oliver Boyd-Barrett (eds.), *Media Texts, Authors and Readers: A Reader*, 119–135. Clevedon, England; Philadelphia: Multilingual Matters in association with The Open University.

Van Dijk, Teun A. 1988. *News as Discourse*. Hillsdale, New Jersey: Lawrence Erlbaum Associates.

Editors' introduction
24 Facebook: A multimodal discourse analysis of (semi-)automated communicative modes

Topic

The chapter addresses students and researchers who are interested in the analysis of social media, and in particular Facebook.

Key terms: (Semi-)automated communicative modes, Social Network Sites (SNS), user text actions

Methodology

The chapter combines pragmatics and insights from various multimodal methodologies.

Thematic orientation

The chapter reveals the impact of Facebook on users' text generation practices focusing on its text automation processes; and highlights the disempowering effects of the standardized options of the online environment upon its users.

Volker Eisenlauer
Facebook: A multimodal discourse analysis of (semi-)automated communicative modes

Multimodality in Social Network Sites

With one billion monthly active users[1], Facebook has become the world's largest Social Network Site. Like other types of Social Media (Kaplan and Haenlein 2010) such as blogs (cf. Blogger), content communities (cf. YouTube) or collaborative sites (cf. Wikipedia), the Social Network Site Facebook offers many possibilities for composing multimodal texts. When members connect with other members and/or tell their life stories on the platform, they seldom limit their communicative acts to the verbal, but upload and share photos/videos or embed multimodal content that is stored on external servers[2]. Unlike many other types of Social Media, Facebook does not only facilitate the creation of multimodal content, but also provides *(semi-)automated modes of expression* that affect or even replace authors when creating texts. In order to explore and understand meaning creation through the strategic deployment and activation of automated text processes, this analysis focuses on software-biased semiotic practices performed via and within Facebook. More precisely, it uncovers the subtle connections between the users' mediated actions (Norris 2004) and the software environment in which they are performed.

The used example was drawn from the profile *Timeline* of a male student Facebooker, whose text actions were observed and collected over a period of four months to conduct a larger study on the options pre-set by Facebook and the users' individual semiotic practices (see Eisenlauer 2013).

Social Network Sites and (Semi-)Automated Communicative Modes

In comparison to other online environments, where users gather around certain subjects and individual themes play a crucial role, Social Network Sites (SNS)

---
[1] See http://newsroom.fb.com/Key-Facts
[2] Such as songs on SoundCloud or films on YouTube.

primarily stand out through the formation of social ties and the interaction among users. There are many different types of SNS, among them business SNS (cf. Xing), dating SNS (cf. Match) or travelling SNS (cf. Couchsurfing), but at the very heart of all these services is, firstly, the creation and upload of personal profiles and, secondly, the formation and maintenance of online communities (Gross and Acquisti 2005, boyd[3] and Ellison 2007, Eisenlauer 2013). As a so-called friendship SNS Facebook is used to manage and maintain ties of friendship. The displayed connections primarily result from previous established offline contacts (Ellison, Steinfield and Lampe 2007) and the data that Facebook members disclose can be commonly connected to their offline identities (Zhao et al. 2008). When presenting themselves and connecting with others, members employ diverse representational formats to give information concerning their current whereabouts, actions, or thoughts. Moreover and from the perspective of multimodality of particular interest, Facebook members gradually outsource the creation and/or distribution of their texts to standardized algorithmic processes of the software environment.

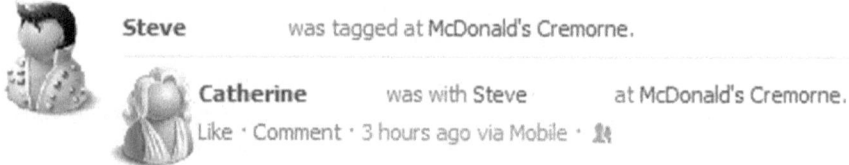

Figure 1: Facebook's *Location Service*

Figure 1 displays a post that was generated with the help of Facebook's so-called *Location Service* – an automatic text generation device that provides information on someone's current location. With a profile picture and the name of the profile owners being automatically added to the post, the disclosed information contributes to the offline anchorage of user data. The so called *Tag Function* supports the maintenance of network connections: Profile owners may easily incorporate information on who they are with by clicking on the name of a befriended member. As we can see, (semi-)automated texts provide not only new semiotic resources for self-presentation, but also restructure social interaction and discursive behavior in online environments. As a site of engagement (Scollon 2001, Jones 2005) the electronic platform enables and constricts particular actions and has great impact on the semiotic shape of the actions being

---

[3] Note that danah m. boyd spells her name using lowercase letters.

performed. The complex interrelations between the actions members perform and the employed semiotic forms can be best explained by looking at key issues in language philosophy and pragmatics: We know from pragmaticians such as Austin (1962) and Searle (1969) that on a semiotic plane a text producer's intention is realized through a speech act. The performance of a speech act can be related to four different levels, i.e. the *utterance act* that refers to the uttering and/or animation of texts, the *propositional act* that refers to the selection of a text's proposition, the *illocutionary act* that points to the text's communicative function and the *perlocutionary act* that involves the consequential effects of the text upon feelings, thoughts, or actions. When operating the Facebook platform, members may delegate the propositional act and the utterance act to varying degrees to algorithmic text generation processes.

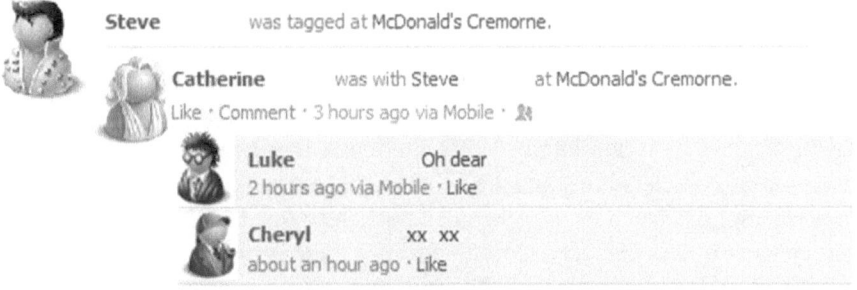

Figure 2: User-generated Comments following Software-generated Posts

In relation to the comment section (in Figure 2), Luke and Cheryl performed the utterance act, when typing the letters, and carried out the propositional act when choosing the comments' propositions. In relation to the post section, Catherine delegated the selection and animation of her posts at least partially to pre-set software algorithms: In order to provide information on her current whereabouts and who she is with, Catherine pressed Facebook's *Check-In Button*[4] and could choose from a list of Facebook friends and places near her. After checking in and tagging Steve, the software created two posts and distributed them in Chaterine's and Steve's friends' News Feeds. Catherine partially outsourced the creation and distribution of the text material to the platform's default algorithms, when employing Facebook's automated communicative modes. Nevertheless, we can suppose that she assigned particular communicative functions to her platform operations (illocutionary act) and that her posts

---

[4] By pressing the *Check-In Button* on Facebook's *Location Service*, members may share their current location.

will generate all kinds of effects and/or changes in the interlocutors' thoughts and feelings (perlocutionary act). With regard to the utterance and the propositional act, we can distinguish two types of Facebook operations which are fundamentally different in nature, i.e. *Creative Text Actions* and *Automated Text Actions*.

Table 1: Creative Text Actions and Automated Text Actions

Creative Text Actions (CTA)	Automated Text Actions (ATA)
– user-authored: – selection and alignment of text propositions mastered by a human agent	– machine-authored: – selection and alignment of text propositions mastered by the software service

Creative Text Actions (CTAs) are *user-authored* and involve a human agent who selects and aligns individual semiotic signs. As opposed to this, Automated Text Actions (ATAs) are *machine-authored*. Here, the selection and alignment of semiotic signs is largely controlled by the software service. From a practical point of view, CTAs are afforded through 'blank text templates' – empty text boxes to be completed individually by users. In contrast, ATAs can be activated by clicking links (such as the Like, the Check-In or the Add Friend Button) and set up more or less distinct actions in advance for the users to perform.

Facebook's text automation becomes not only apparent in the software supporting the generation of text material, but also in the (semi-)automated distribution of user data. The platform's status as a 'Meso Medium' – that can neither be captured by the traditional concept of mass media nor by that of private media (Zerdick et al. 2004) – makes it difficult for users to estimate who and/or how many other members will ascribe meaning to their textual performances. While in unmediated physical spaces 'social scripts' are provided by the individual situation and/or conventional setting (e.g. a wedding, a consultation, a workplace conversation), contextual cues in online situations are far more complex: Social norms bound to SNS are commonly based on a certain, more or less heterogenic group of users. An individual member's text actions are, by design, distributed in the News Feed streams of their network of friends. In particular members with large and divergent lists of friends have great difficulties anticipating the diverse social contexts to which their data is automatically distributed. While a particular set of semiotic choices, such as the display of last night's party pictures, might be an appropriate 'semiotic register' (see Halliday 1978, van Leeuwen 2005) among some Facebook friends, the same semiotic choice might be totally out of place for other network contexts. Although Facebook introduced a tool that lets members distinguish between close friends, acquaintances and others, such a categorization involves extra effort and does not meet the changeability, variability and complexity of social contexts. Given that software algorithms intervene in the generation and distribution of users' texts, the question arises to what extent members stay in control of actions.

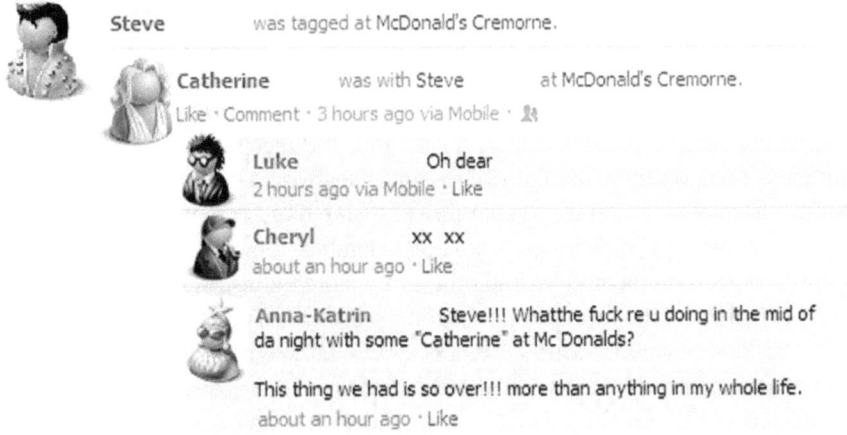

Figure 3: The Perlocutionary Effects of Software-generated Posts

Figure 3 displays how Steve's girlfriend, Anna, reacted to the computer-generated posts (see comment section) and helps to consider the question of user control in more detail. We can assume that Catherine has disclosed the information deliberately to be read by some of her and maybe also by Steve's friends. She might even have created the posts deliberately to be read by Anna or she might not have foreseen it. Likewise, we are lacking insight into the extent Steve anticipated the creation and distribution of his location in certain contexts. Whatsoever Catherine's and Steve's communicative aims were, what this example shows is that (semi-)automated modes can support and/or interfere with the communicative aims of individual members. We can see that member actions are significantly influenced by the communicative settings of the platform. The platform's functional settings shape the structure and, in some cases, even the content of the respective discourse. The electronic environment has a great impact on the contexts in which user- and software generated texts are presented and intervenes in the communicative action of profile owners and recipients.

Such a software bias entails positive and negative consequences for users when presenting themselves and connecting with others: Users may benefit from Facebook's automated modes as they are offered new semiotic resources and discursive spaces for identity creation. The efficient creation and distribution of software-generated texts via and within Facebook does by no means effect in the creation of "alternate spaces into which people escape from the 'real world', [but] help to reveal the layered simultaneity of space and time that has always been there" (Jones 2013: online). In this sense, Facebook offers members a tool that enables them to layer the simultaneity of multiple social contexts and creates new ways of being present to one another. From an identity theoretical perspective (cf. Davies and Harré 1990, Lucius-Hoene and Deppermann 2000) Facebook's automated modes allow members to disclose things about themselves and/or other members in a more indirect fashion. Whereas self-authored texts on individual attributes and likes would always run the risk of being interpreted as rather straightforward and blunt identity performances, the employment of software generated texts enables a member to claim various identity aspects on themselves and others in a more indirect way. Without typing a single word, Catherine could position herself as 'having ended up with Steve at a fast food restaurant after a big night out'. Although she was, at the most, partially responsible for the individual wording of the posts, her actions had significant effects on the members' social identities and even resulted in the breakup of couple Anna and Steve.

Negative consequences of automated modes arise from cases where members are not even aware to have set off text generation processes or where they misjudge the contexts in which their texts are dispersed and re-displayed. Such user performances can be referred to as 'Non-Intended Text Actions'. In relation to the example, a 'Non-Intended Text Action' would apply, if Catherine (and/or Steve) did neither foresee nor intend the reproduction of their location on Anna's News Feed. Most obviously, such Non-Intended Text Actions cannot be assessed solely from text data, but call for an integration of qualitative information, i.e. through personal interviews or questionnaires.

A Critical and Multimodal Discourse Analytical Approach to Text Automation

As this analysis piece showed, doing things with and within Facebook is conditioned in various ways by text automation processes. Discursive acts of self-portrayal and maintaining friendship are inevitably bound to pre-set templates and automatically linked fragments of texts. When using Facebook, members may outsource their text actions (or parts thereof) to the service. The platform's pre-set semiotic choices gradually define and standardize user texts. The here proposed analytical framework contributes to a reflective evaluation and enhanced critical understanding of software-directedness in new media texts. While established critical approaches to media commonly emphasize the role of the media in the dispersion of certain ideologies (Kellner and Share 2005) or question the ownership of media (Bagdikian 2004), a critical and multimodal investigation is interested in how the media in services, such as Facebook, can mould the choices and actions of media users. The identification of Facebook-specific modes, such as ATAs, CTAs and Non-Intended Text Actions, provides a convenient and tangible methodological access to the media bias of user-generated texts. While the framework was developed to reflect on Facebook, the model is likewise well-suited for a critical investigation of other services supporting automatic text generation/distribution. Social spaces allocated by Web 2.0 technologies are by no means 'neutral environments', but may epitomize the hidden agendas of their developers and/or the person who runs the website. This idea of disempowerment and user standardisation has already been appropriated by network artists, such as Tobias Leingruber and Esben Hardenberg. In their Facebook Resistance project they developed ideas such as the 'Facebook co-creation identity game', in which "everyone can edit your information, except yourself" (Facebookresistance.com).

Further Reading

Boyd and Ellison (2007) provide a good insight into existing scholarship on SNS and discuss the history and key characteristics of such sites.

Gross and Acquisti (2005) study a large data sample of Facebook profiles to reflect on patterns of information revelation and privacy issues. Livingstone (2008) takes a more qualitative approach to privacy issues in SNS and also contrasts teenagers' graded conception of 'friends' with the binary classification provided by the software.

Eisenlauer (2013) reflects on the interlacing of templates pre-set by Facebook and the users' individual semiotic practices. Eisenlauer (2011) applies a diachronic perspective on SNS and shows the continuities and also the differences between new and old forms of textual networking.

Jones and Hafner (2012) offer a timely introduction to new media literacies and discuss diverse types of Social Media from a multimodal and critical media perspective.

Project Idea

Compile a small corpus of text actions from the profile Timelines of befriended Facebook users. Categorize the Facebook operations at work (CTA/ATA) and discuss in what sense the employed automatic modes support and/or contradict with the members' individual communicative aims. What kinds of meanings are made by employing software-generated texts? In what sense do they reiterate or contradict with meanings provided by other communicative modes (i.e. self-selected texts, photos, films)? Pay particular attention to how different social variables (gender, age, class and ethnicity) shape and are evoked through the employment of individual creative and automatic communicative modes!

References

Austin, John Langshaw. 1962. *How to Do Things With Words*. Cambridge (Mass.): Harvard University Press.
Bagdikian, Ben. 2004. *The New Media Monopoly*. Boston: Beacon.
boyd, danah and Nicole Ellison. 2007. "Social Network Sites: Definition, history, and scholarship." *Journal of Computer-Mediated Communication*, 13/1. URL: http://jcmc.indiana.edu/vol13/issue1/boyd.ellison.html (last accessed May 18, 2013).
Davies, Bronwyn and Rom Harré. 1990. 'Positioning: The discursive production of selves'. Journal for the Theory of Social Behaviour, 20/1: 43–63.
Eisenlauer, Volker. 2013. *A Critical Hypertext Analysis of Social Media. The True Colours of Facebook*. London/New York: Continuum.
Eisenlauer, Volker. 2011. 'Multimodality and social actions in personal publishing texts: From the German "poetry album" to Web 2.0 social network sites'. In Kay L. O'Halloran and Bradley A. Smith (eds). *Multimodal Studies. Exploring Issues and Domains*, 131–52. London: Routledge.
Ellison, Nicole, Charles Steinfield and Cliff Lampe. 2007. 'The benefits of Facebook "friends": Social capital and college students' use of online Social Network Sites'. *Journal of Computer-Mediated Communication*, 12/4. URL: http://jcmc.indiana.edu/vol12/issue4/ellison.html (last accessed May 18, 2013).
Gross, Ralph and Alessandro Acquisti. 2005. *Information Revelation and Privacy in Online Social Networks*. Proceedings of WPES'05, 71–80. Alexandria, VA: Association of Computing Machinery.
Halliday, Michael. 1978. *Language as Social Semiotic. The Social Interpretation of Language and Meaning*. London: Arnold.
Jones, Rodney. 2005. 'Sites of engagement as sites of attention: time, space and culture in electronic discourse'. In Sigrid Norris and Rodney Jones (eds). *Discourse in Action: Introducing Mediated Discourse Analysis*, 144–154. London: Routledge.

Jones, Rodney. 2013. 'Space, technology, and attention structures'. *Semiotix XN* 10/12. URL: http://semioticon.com/semiotix/2013/05/space-technology-and-attention-structures/. (last accessed June 12, 2013).

Jones, Rodney and Christoph Hafner. 2012. *Understanding Digital Literacies: A Practical Introduction*. London/New York: Routledge.

Kaplan, Andreas and Michael Haenlein. 2010. 'Users of the world, unite! The challenges and opportunities of Social Media'. *Business Horizons*, 53(1): 59–68.

Kellner, Douglas and Jeff Share. 2005. 'Toward Critical Media Literacy: Core concepts, debates, organizations and policies'. *Discourse: Studies in the Cultural Politics of Education*, 26(3): 369–386.

Livingstone, Sonia. 2008. 'Taking Risky Opportunities in Youthful Content Creation: Teenagers' Use of Social Networking Sites for Intimacy, Privacy and Self-Expression'. *New Media and Society*, 10(3): 459–477.

Lucius-Hoene, Gabriele and Arnulf Deppermann. 2000. 'Narrative identity empiricized. A dialogical and positioning approach to autobiographical research interviews'. *Narrative Inquiry*, 10(1): 199–222.

Norris, Sigrid. 2004. *Analyzing Multimodal Interaction*. London/New York: Routledge.

Scollon, Ron. 2001. *Mediated Discourse: The Nexus of Practice*. London/New York: Routledge.

Searle, John. 1969. *Speech Acts*. Cambridge: Cambridge University Press.

van Leeuwen, Theo. 2005. *Introducing Social Semiotics*. London/New York: Routledge.

Zerdick, Axel et al. (eds). 2004. *E-merging media. Communication and the Media Economy of the Future*. Berlin: Springer.

Zhao, Shanyang, Sherri Grasmuck and Jason Martin. 2008. 'Identity construction on Facebook: Digital empowerment in anchored relationships'. Computers in Human Behavior, 24(5): 1816–36.

Editors' introduction
25 3-D realisation of discourse: The case of war monuments

Topic

This chapter addresses students and researchers that are interested in discourses of war.

Key terms: Critical discourse analysis, material culture, war monuments

Methodology

The chapter takes an approach similar to Kress and Van Leeuwen's Reading Images by discussing 3-D artefacts.

Thematic orientation

Thematically, the chapter, as its topic suggests, is situated in the study of war discourses. It illustrates how 3-D artefacts can be analysed in terms of semiotic choices which in turn communicate specific ideas, attitude and identities.

Related chapters

Chapters 10 and 15.

Gill Abousnnouga and David Machin
3-D realisation of discourse: The case of war monuments

Introduction

Discourses of war are disseminated not only linguistically through speeches and written texts but through other semiotic resources such as the visual and material. One such case of this is the war monument. These designs deploy specific choices in materials, shape, form and iconography to communicate specific ideas, attitudes and values about the meaning of war. In doing so these monuments play an important role in justifying and legitimising the practice of warfare in our societies: by helping to suppress much of what comprises war – pain, maiming, humiliation, shattered families, displaced populations, disease, hunger, profit from the weapons industry – they instead foster celebratory discourses of nation, protection and noble sacrifice. The positioning of war monuments in everyday public locations allows them to act as banal reminders of the more positive meanings of discourses of war as they sit alongside other monuments and civic buildings that also claim to house our most cherished values and historical identities, yet which are all infused with dominant ideologies.

We have carried out a number of studies on the way that these war monuments communicate their discourses (see Abousnnouga and Machin 2013). In our original analysis we carried out interviews with designers and examined commissioning and planning documents in order to plot the motivations that lie behind the erection of these objects. What is clear is that authorities have continually used monuments to gain support for and naturalise war and promote nationalism as a distraction from left wing ideologies. Our study also involved a social semiotic analysis of the precise way that these objects communicate. It is this part of our analysis for which we provide an introduction in this chapter. In this kind of social semiotic analysis we ask a number of questions:
- What kind of communicative resources are available to designers of such material objects?
- Which precise semiotic choices are deployed to communicate specific meanings about war, why it was fought, by whom and how?
- How is the observer encouraged to relate to these semiotic choices?

Below we illustrate how we can approach answering these questions in the case of a number of war monuments and we provide a number of meaning potentials that can be deployed by monument designers, and those of other material objects. The meaning potential comes here both from provenance, which is the accumulated meaning an element, feature, or form, can carry in a culture over time (Barthes 1977) and from metaphorical association (Arnheim 1969), which is where humans attribute meanings through association with their physical experiences of other objects in the world.

Material meaning potentials for monuments

Elevation

The Figures of soldiers that stand on monuments can be positioned at the same height as the viewer, raised up on a pedestal to different degrees, or lowered. Such a design choice has important meaning potential. Height can have metaphorical associations as in 'upper class' and as in 'high ideals', although it can have the opposite meaning where we say someone has their head in the clouds. Lack of height can mean 'heaving ones feet on the ground'. Kress and van Leeuwen describe such associations in terms of that which is placed at the top of visual compositions as the "ideal" and that placed at the bottom is the "real" (Kress and van Leeuwen 1996: 193). In the case of monuments those placed below ground level tend to have the connotative meaning of "the organic" and "of the earth". The Figures of WW1 soldiers tend to be raised up on a pedestal (Figure 1). This is often so that their feet stand at about shoulder height. Clearly being placed on a much higher pedestal, such as of 100 m would be excessively idealising and is something reserved more for national, or "cult", figures. In contrast, more recent statues find soldiers closer to the ground (Figure 2). These soldiers are therefore more "like us" and less "ideal". This is part of a broader discourse of the humanisation of the soldier. More recently, soldiers have become represented across the media as more human and often even the very victims of war itself as actual reasons for conflict and even identification of the actual identities of enemy have become obscured.

Size

Size of the Figure on the monument itself carries meaning potential. We can imagine the meaning potential if a soldier was represented in the size of a giant or conversely as the size of a doll. If we look around the world at very large statues we find these generally represent dictators. In contrast, WWI Figures

Figure 1: 'Abertillery monument with soldier raised on pedestal'

tend to be larger than an average human by about half a meter. As well as being idealised, therefore, they are also slightly larger than life. More recent statues show soldiers represented on a much more human scale, again part of the process of the humanisation of the soldier. In British monuments we do find some exceptions to this pattern such as the 4m tall "Yomper" monument in Portsmouth (Figure 3) commemorating the soldiers that died in the Falklands war, an ambiguous nationalism-fuelled battle over territory off the shore of Argentina. At this time there was a temporary cult of the soldier as the war was used for nationalist purposes by the right wing government at a time of social upheaval. Yet this remains modest in comparison to the massive 52 m 'Motherland Calls' monument at Volgograd commemorating those who fought for Stalingrad.

Angle of interaction

It is also useful to ask just how viewers are encouraged to interact with a monument. Can they walk around it, through it, or simply look at it from one side? All

Figure 2: 'Portsmouth WW2 monument erected in 1997. There is still a pedestal but lower'

Figure 3: 'The Yomper' around here

these have important meaning potentials that relate to social distance and personal relations. Some monuments can communicate their discourses through 'learning', 'homage', or the pleasure of heritage tourism. One particular semiotic resource for setting up interpersonal relations is elevation. Along with size, elevation can point to relative power and status. As regards the WW1 monuments the viewers were positioned looking up at them. This could have the effect of making the viewer 'look up to them' with respect or have a sense of being beneath them and humbled or weaker. In most contemporary monuments, since the soldiers are positioned at the same height, there is a sense of equality – although even here other design features, such as borders and other boundaries may maintain social distance.

Solidity/hollowness

Solidity or hollowness can be used by designers due to their meaning potential. Hollowness can suggest openness, transparency or even vulnerability and complexity, or encouraging us to look beneath the surface. Most statues of soldiers are represented as solid and so not vulnerable and we are not, therefore, encouraged to look beneath the surface. They are to indicate solidity of character and suggest something uncomplicated. We can imagine the difference had these boys who were killed been represented as hollow or somehow transparent. Immediately something more problematic would be indicated.

Modality

We can think about the ways that monuments represent soldiers realistically or not, whether there is high or low modality, in the fashion described by Kress and Van Leeuwen (1996). We can ask what kinds of features have their details increased, and which have them decreased or even enhanced. Reduction of detail on statues can occur through subtle reductions in surface details or in shifts into complete abstractions where communication is at a sensory level. On the Welsh monument (Figure 4) details of the soldiers have been reduced in term of the articulation of the detail of surface realisation. It is typical to find faces represented without the finer details of features and with complete symmetry, as was common in classical statues.

The clothing on the Welsh monument too is represented without detail and without colour. The opposite of this would create more of a sense of documenting rather than symbolising which was not the aim of these statues. The clean,

Figure 4: 'Welsh monument'

Figure 5: 'The New Zealand monument Hyde Park London'

smooth simplified details also help to simplify and idealise the soldier. Other statutes use even lower modality as the surfaces are roughened, even blurred as is the case in the Will Lambert project to commemorate concentration camp victims. Clearly something other than certainty and truth is being communicated in this case.

Many more recent monuments have modality reduced further shifting into abstraction. The Figureures in the New Zealand monument (Figure 5) are represented by oblique iron poles in the shape of the Christian cross. On the one hand here naturalistic truth is reduced. On the other, we move into sensory truth where it is the certain, organised, forward force of movement that is symbolised rather than any attempt to document actual persons and events. The same monument also carries detailed indigenous Maori designs and other cultural references. Moreover, the poles stand in the precise formation for Haka performed by the national rugby team. These contain high naturalistic truth claims and communicate the 'truth' of cultural heritage, history and 'learning'. Here war seamlessly blends with culture, tourism, and sport.

Materials

The meaning of materials used in the monuments also carries important meaning potential. Most war monuments are marble or bronze. Marble is important for its connotations of the classical civilisations of Rome and Greece and the high ideals we now associate with them. Since statues from this time still stand, this also brings a sense of something timeless and enduring. Bronze is also enduring, heavy and solid. We can bring out the meaning potentials of these materials by thinking about what materials would not be suitable for war memorials. Clearly plastic would not do due to its associations with cheapness and lightness, even though it would be long lasting. Other metals such as iron might be viewed as cheaper and more everyday than bronze. Aluminium and titanium would bring connotations of technology – and also metaphorical associations of lightness and solidity come into play here. What is also important here are associations of the handmade, personal processes of forging bronze, as opposed to the impersonal industrial associations of aluminium. Like marble and other stones, bronze can also bring associations of the naturalistic. The sacrifice of these soldiers is intertwined with the mythology of nation and landscape.

Soft/hard

It seems obvious that monuments should be hard as opposed to soft. But this should not mean that we underestimate this as a meaning potential. Surfaces can be made to invite physical contact and be comforting or the opposite. Or they can be made to feel hardwearing and durable or the opposite. Monuments could theoretically feature soldiers that were soft and invited squeezing and with surfaces that appeared not so durable. Softness can also be communicated through lack of rigidity. So if we pressed the surface it could give to different degrees. The dashboard of a car will do this if we press our finger against it communicating a sense of comfort, ease and accommodation rather than resistance. If a Figure of a soldier gave when we pressed it in this manner such accommodation could suggest a sense of pliability or weakness – a more sensitive soldier who was easily affected by events. In fact, more contemporary monuments are designed for interaction and engagement in a way that older ones were not, but this is certainly not in terms of tactility, comfort, nor accommodation. Of course there are degrees of softness and this is utilised in the design of monuments. Different kinds of stone can communicate different degrees of hardness and softness.

Conclusion

What we have indicated here is that the 3-D artefact can also be analysed in terms of a set of available semiotic choices that can be harnessed by communicators to do a particular job, to communicate a specific set of ideas, attitude and identities. These can be documented and inventorized to create a predictive framework. In this case it allows us to think about the way that war monuments use specific semiotic resources to communicate particular kinds of ideas, attitudes and values about war. The actual process and participants in war are recontextualised to suggest respect, eternity and to symbolise the commitment of the soldiers themselves and at the same time our changing relationship with them. And importantly these are one way by which discourses can be placed into public spaces claiming to house our collective feelings and memories.

Further readings

Abousnnouga, Gill and David Machin 2010 War Monuments and the Changing Discourses of Nation and Soldiery. In Adam Jaworski and CrispinThurlow (eds) *Semiotic Landscapes*, 219–240. London: Continuum.

Abousnnouga, Gill and David Machin 2011 Visual discourses of the role of women in war commemoration: a multimodal analysis of British war monuments *Journal of Language and Politics* 10(3): 322–346.

Project idea

Select two monuments from your own locality. Find out about their background, who commissioned them and why. Then look at the semiotic resources they use to communicate ideas, values, attitudes and identities- do they suggest lightness or weight, do they document or symbolise etc? Consider how these semiotic resources communicate specific ideologies.

References

Abousnnouga, Gill and Machin, David. 2013. *The Language of War Monuments*. London: Bloomsburg.
Arnheim, Rudolf. 1969. *Visual Thinking*. Berkeley C.A.: University of California Press.
Barthes, Roland. 1977. *Image, Music, Text*, New York: Hill and Wang.
Kress, Gunther and TheoVan Leeuwen. 1996. *Reading Images. The Grammar of Visual Design*. London: Routledge.

Editors' introduction
26 Multimodality and space exploration: Communicative space in action

Topic

This chapter illustrates how the notion of a communicative space (White 2012a) can be used in order to analyse communications around billboards and other advertising posters.

Key terms: Communicative space, modal density, site of engagement.

Methodology

This chapter takes an approach that combines mediated discourse and multimodal (inter)action analysis with social semiotics.

Thematic orientation

Coming from an advertising perspective, the chapter introduces some key characteristics of communicative space. The chapter highlights how this notion has a demonstrable effect upon the times, places and modes involved in a particular interaction.

Related chapters

Chapters 6. 8, 9, and 19.

Paul White
Multimodality and space exploration: Communicative space in action

Introduction

The purpose of this chapter is to present an explanation and a working example of a new tool in multimodal and mediated discourse analysis – the *communicative space* (White 2012a). Communicative space is a collective term defining as a single semiotic unit all spaces that are essential to a site of engagement within which a message is mediated. The concept of a communicative space arises from Scollon's (2005) assessment of spatial entrainments and Van Leeuwen's (2005) contention that semiotic modes "fuse" to create a single communicative action.

The data presented is an analysis of social interactions with a billboard for the confectionary brand, Pascall Fruitburst, which was set up in Auckland, New Zealand in 2009. I have chosen an interaction with a billboard as the example data because people interact with billboards on roads or streets, as they drive or walk by and, as the data reveals, via a computer screen or TV. Thus, we can identify more than one communicative space associated with the same message mediated via the same meditational means.

In essence, the communicative space affects the times, locations, communicative modes and actions involved in the successful mediation of a particular message at a particular site of engagement (Scollon 1998).

Background

The term communicative space has its roots in Scollon's (2005) consideration of *spatial entrainments* and Van Leeuwen's (2005) assertion that semiotic modes "fuse" to produce a single communicative action.

Spatial entrainments develop when actions take place in a space that is confined in some way. Scollon (2005) identifies three types of spatial entrainment: *bounded spaces*, such as rooms and spaces with walls or fences; *permeable spaces*, afforded by doors and windows that can be opened or closed; *unbounded spaces*, such as a city street on which a charity worker stands, rattling a donation bucket. Scollon's aim in describing spatial entrainment is to scrutinize the range of spaces within which a single action is included. Bounded spaces may serve to constrain actions, affect how they are carried out and determining how many people can be involved. Permeable spaces can reduce such constraints or give rise to even more restraints; e.g. opening a window can allow a social actor to lean out but might also cause rain to blow in. Unbounded spaces allow actions to take place without unnecessary regard for any boundaries.

In explaining how image and text work together on the page, Van Leeuwen points out that communication involves more than a "concatenation of interrelated parts" (Van Leeuwen 2005: 79). Instead he proposes that there is no clear sequence of individual semiotic modes involved that occurs when we read a text: the semiotic sequence is identifiable but all modes "fuse" creating a single, multimodal communicative action (Van Leeuwen, 2005).

Similarly, if we study the social actions that combine to create a higher-level action (e.g. reading a billboard) and that results in a social actor focusing their attention in order to interact with a message, we are able to identify a series of social actions. While we might distinguish the space each action takes place in, however, I identified a need to describe the various spaces that are collectively essential for a social actor to successfully interact with that message. Thus, while Van Leeuwen (2005) portrays modes as fusing to create a single communicative action, I proposed the concept of a communicative space (White 2012a), which arises from the need to describe all the spaces that "fuse" in the mediation of any single communicative action. All spaces that are an essential part of any single site of engagement therefore can be described as coalescing to form as a collective semiotic unit – the communicative space.

The other key concept employed in this study is that of *modal density* (Norris 2004). Modal density involves the communicative modes a social actor employs within a site of engagement in order to construct a higher-level action. A mode that completely changes the nature of a higher-level action if it is discontinued is assigned high modal density. A mode that slightly alters the nature of a higher-level action if it discontinued is allocated medium modal intensity. Modal density also "indicates the level of attention/awareness that a social actor places on a certain higher-level action" (Norris 2004: 92). Furthermore, Norris (2004) designates three levels of attention/awareness: foreground, mid-ground and background. This heuristic model enables the researcher to focus on relevant, simultaneously performed, higher-level actions. In reality, social actors are capable of and often do participate in several higher-level actions simultaneously.

Data and Analysis

On May 1 2009 advertising agency DDB in New Zealand created a billboard, asking the question, "When Will the Fruit Burst?" A giant pin and a giant strawberry-shaped balloon, filled with ten thousand Fruit Burst Jellies, were attached to a conventional billboard measuring 9 × 6 metres, on the corner of Victoria Street and Albert Street in the Auckland CBD. A camera was set up to provide 24 hour live streaming of the gradually expanding strawberry. It could be viewed online at *whenwillthefuitburst.co.nz* – a website created especially for the campaign. As the balloon slowly filled with air, it moved closer and closer to the pin. Over the course of thirty-one days members of the public were invited to win $5,000 by guessing when the strawberry balloon would burst. On May 31, at 13.33.11 hours precisely the strawberry finally touched the pin and duly burst. Thousands of wrapped sweets rained down on to the parking lot below the billboard site. These were eagerly gathered up by hundreds of passers-by.

A message was mediated via the cultural tool of one billboard site through one of these two sites of engagement: either inside a car on the street or on the pavement as a social actor walks by. Marketing theory suggests that, "Outdoor advertising is generally viewed from 100 to 500 feet away by people in motion"

Figure 1: Fruitburst billboard, week one: 1–6 May 2009

Figure 2: Fruitburst billboard, week four: 31 May 2009

(Arenas 2004: 585). Thus we can say that the communicative space associated with the physical Fruitburst billboard extends between 100 and 500 feet, or 30 and 150 metres.

Within this particular communicative space the mode of proxemics plays a key roll in constructing both a site of engagement and the higher-level action of reading the billboard. It is reasonable to suggest that an interaction is initiated during the first week of the billboard's existence when a social actor's attention becomes focused on the giant pin, which at this stage is the most salient semiotic feature of the billboard (Kress and Van Leeuwen 1996).

If we now look at a social actor interacting with the Fruitburst billboard as he or she walks along the street, following Scollon's (2005) description of spatial entrainments, we can say that within this particular communicative space the Fruitburst billboard occupies an *unbounded space*. It also occupies a communicatively unbounded space because its position on the road is not essential to the mediation of its message.

Now let us consider an interaction with the same billboard on May 31 2009 at precisely 13.33.11 hours. The location of the billboard – directly above a car park where 10,000 Jelly Fruit Bursts were dispersed by the big bang – is an essential component of the message it is mediating on that day, at that time and in that place. In other words, at that particular site of engagement in that particular communicative space occupied by the social actors in the car park who are constructing the higher-level action of reading the billboard as the strawberry balloon explodes the Fruitburst billboard occupies a communicatively bounded space.

Thus, a communicative space comprises either communicative unbounded spaces or bounded spaces, depending on the specific site of engagement.

Similarly, in the case of a social actor walking passed the Fruitburst billboard, both the billboard and the social actor occupy unbounded spaces within the communicative space. Whereas, in the case of a social actor who is the driver of or a passenger in a car, the billboard occupies an unbounded space but the social actor occupies a permeable space (provided by the car window which may or may not be open).

Moreover, the Fruitburst billboard mediates its messages within these sites of engagement and various social actors are able to construct other distinct sites of attention (Jones 2005) while interacting with the message mediated via the billboard, each one defined by the individual social actors participating in the interaction:

1. Car passing by on the street (drivers)
2. Car passing by on the street (passengers)
3. Pavement (passers-by)
4. Pavement at the time of the burst (gathered crowd)
5. Car park (passers-by)
6. TV screen – news programmes (viewers)
7. Computer screen before the burst – live-streaming (viewers)
8. Computer screen after the burst – YouTube (viewers)
9. Computer screen (bloggers/blog readers)

So far we have examined a communicative space that extends between 30 and 150 metres from the physical location of the primary meditational means – the billboard site. The camera set up to live stream the expanding strawberry, though, created a virtual location, constructed a different communicative space and afforded four more sites of engagement (numbers 6, 7, 8 and 9 in the list above).

In a communicative space constructed around a screen (TV, computer, tablet or phone) the mode of proxemics takes on a different role. That is to say, the social actor's physical distance from the billboard itself does not determine whether he or she is able to construct the higher-level action of reading the billboard. "Indeed, whereas the distance a social actor can be positioned from the physical location of the billboard and still successfully receive its messages can expand to thousands of miles, the communicative space ... shrinks to mere centimetres" (White 2012a: 148). It is crucial to note that the billboard remains

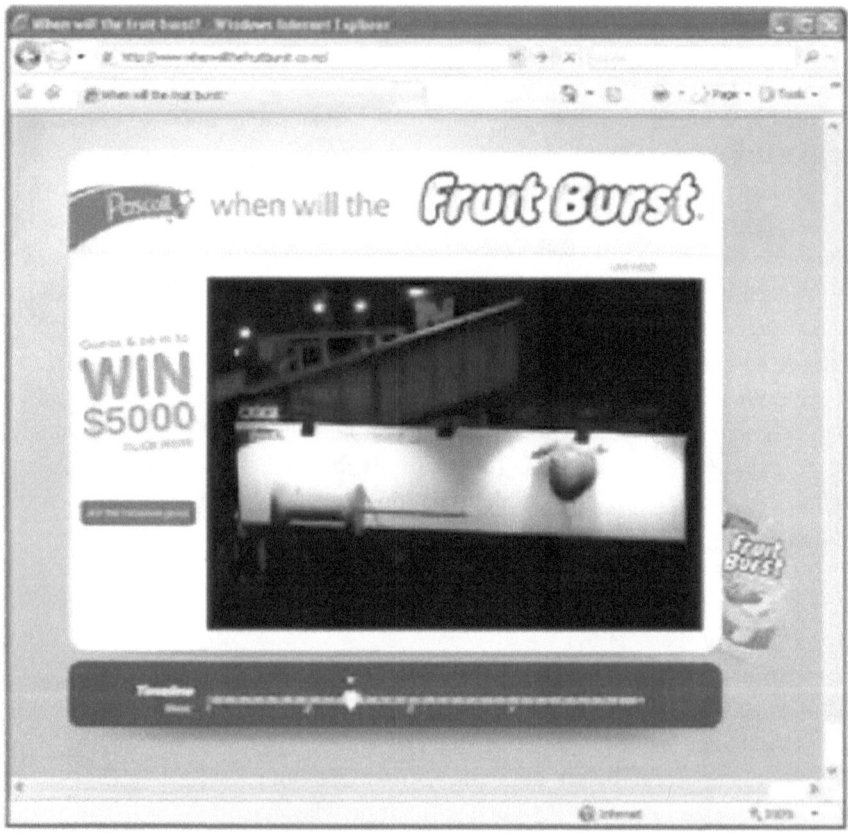

Figure 3: Fruitburst billboard website *whenwillthefruitburst.co.nz*

the site of engagement because, as Jones (2005) has pointed out, it is the content displayed and the not screen itself on which the social actor focuses attention.

An important aspect of identifying each communicative space associated with a particular cultural tool or mediational means is that by employing Norris's (2004) concept of modal density we can discover if attention varies in different communicative spaces. This becomes clear when we compare the case of a social actor who is the driver of a car interacting with the Fruitburst billboard with that of a social actor who interacts with the billboard via a computer screen.

In theory a social actor driving past the Fruitburst billboard is focused on the higher-level action of driving: employing high modal density to carry out

Table 1: Fruitburst billboard modal density graph A

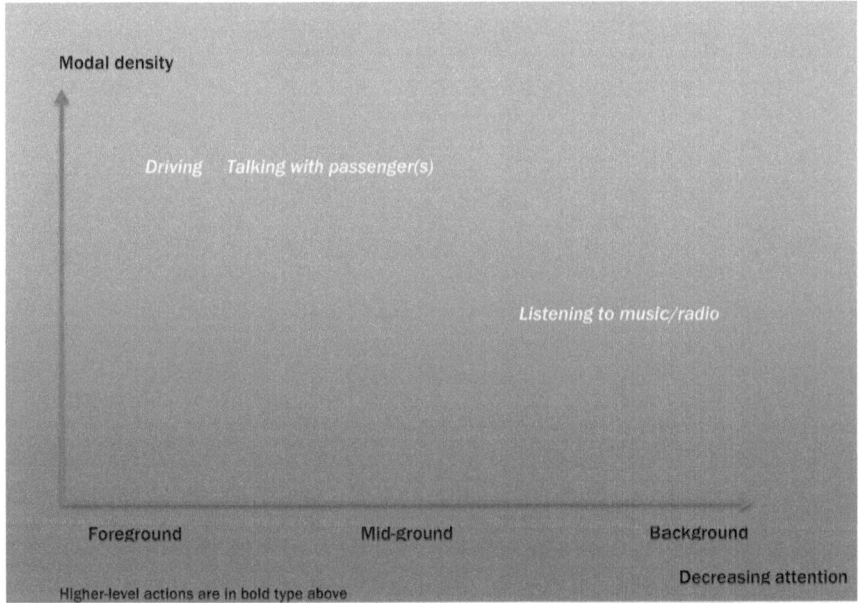

this action. In reality, that driver may also be listening to a radio, CD or mp3 player, talking to passengers or being distracted by passengers in the car. Hence, he or she may well employ less than the highest level of modal density to focus on the action of driving. Thus the high-level action of driving may well be mid-grounded by the social actor. Equally, the higher-level action of reading the billboard may also occupy the mid-ground of focus or share some of the foreground of the social actor's focus with the higher-level action of driving the car (see Table 1). Thus we can say that a social actor interacting with the billboard in this particular communicative space, which extends between 30 and 150 metres from the billboard site, is not likely to be paying the highest level of attention to the billboard and the message it is mediating.

Turning now to someone who interacts with the billboard via a computer screen (Figure 3): although the social actor may be physically much further away from the billboard itself, the communicative space within which the billboard mediates its message contains fewer if any distractions. As I noted in a previous study with regard to people interacting with messages via computer screens, "although Scollon (1998) has shown that a TV is as likely to be peripheral to the social actions going on in a room as it is to be fundamental, I would argue that the social actor who clicks on a YouTube clip ... is more likely

Table 2: Fruitburst billboard modal density graph B

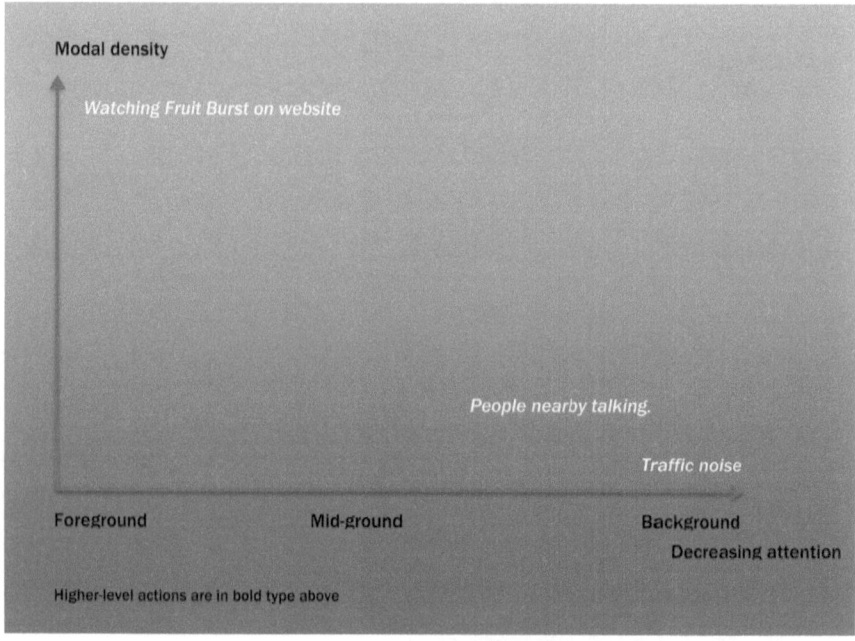

to be foregrounding the watching of the clip for the duration of that clip" (White 2012: 148). The same goes for someone who logs on to a particular website to view a live-stream video. Thus we can say that a social actor interacting with the billboard in this particular communicative space, located miles from the actual billboard site itself, is more likely to be paying the highest level of attention to the billboard and the message it is mediating (see Table 2).

Conclusion

This working example of multimodal and mediated discourse analysis using the communicative space tool highlights five key findings. First, it shows that more than one *communicative space* can be associated with the same meditational means mediating the same message(s). Second, once correctly identified, a communicative space has a demonstrable effect upon the times, places and modes involved in a particular interaction. Third, a social actor's focus of attention varies in different communicative spaces, even when those communicative spaces are associated with the same communication and the same primary mediational means. Fourth, a communicative space does not necessarily arise around the physical location of the primary meditational means. Fifth, and specifically with regard to billboard interactions, a communicative space is not limited to the physical dimensions suggested by conventional marketing theory. This finding corroborates my suggestion made in a previous article (White 2012b).

Notes

Figures subsequently released by the advertising agency, DDB state that during the thirty-one days of May 2009 there were 81,000 viewers of the website and 12,000 unique visitors to the site. Of those 12,000 visitors, 6,000 entered the competition online[1]. The audiences of local television channels TV3 and Juice TV also saw the bursting of the fruit, during news broadcasts on the May 31, 3009. Finally, to date there have been 9,495 views on YouTube[1].

Further readings

Scollon, Ron. 2005. The rhythmic integration of action and discourse: work, the body and the earth. In Sigrid Norris and Rodney H. Jones (eds.), *Discourse in Action: Introducing Mediated Discourse Analysis*, 20–32. London and New York: Routledge.

White, Paul. 2010. Grabbing attention: The importance of modal density in advertising. *Visual Communication* 9(4): 371–397.

White, Paul. 2012. Reception as social action: The case of marketing. In Sigrid Norris (ed.), *Multimodality in practice: Investigating theory-in-practice-through-Methodology*, 138–152. New York: Routledge.

White, Paul. 2012. Multimodality's challenge to marketing theory: A discussion. *Multimodal Communication*, 1(3): 305–323.

Project idea

Imagine a conversation between two friends. Now describe the communicative spaces if they are a) speaking in a cafe b) communicating via video Skype c) having a phone conversation. How might the focus of attention of the conversation vary at each site of engagement?

---

1 Sources: http://adsoftheworld.com/media/ambient/pascall_fruit_burst; http://www.youtube.com/watch?v=JZlhHsMXl6Y; http://www.youtube.com/watch?v=pMMj-_ipbzw

References

Norris, Sigrid. 2004. *Analyzing Multimodal Interaction: A Methodological Framework*. New York: Routledge.

Jones, Rodney. H. 2005. Sites of engagement as sites of attention: Time, space and culture in electronic discourse. In Sigrid Norris and Rodney H. Jones, (eds.), *Discourse in Action: Introducing Mediated Discourse Analysis*, 141–154. London and New York: Routledge.

Kress, Gunter and Theo Van Leeuwen. 1996. *Reading Images. The Grammar of Visual Design*. London: Routledge.

Scollon, Ron. 2005. The rhythmic integration of action and discourse: Work, the body and the earth. In Sigrid Norris and Rodney H. Jones (eds.), *Discourse in Action: Introducing Mediated Discourse Analysis*, 20–31. London and New York: Routledge.

White, Paul. 2012a. Reception as social action: The case of marketing. In Sigrid Norris (ed.), *Multimodality in Practice: Investigating Theory-in-Practice-through-Methodology*, 138–152. New York: Routledge.

White, Paul. 2012b. Multimodality's challenge to marketing theory: A discussion. *Multimodal Communication*, 1(3): 305–323.

Van Leeuwen, Theo. 2005. Multimodality, genre and design. In Sigrid Norris and Rodney H. Jones (eds.), *Discourse in Action: Introducing Mediated Discourse Analysis*, 73–94. London and New York: Routledge.

Editors' introduction
27 Mediated discourse analysis, 'embodied learning' and emerging social and professional identities

Topic

The chapter is of particular interest to students and researchers interested in workplace practices and learning.

Key terms: Embodied learning, geography of discourse, nexus of practice.

Methodology

The chapter takes a mediated discourse approach, showing how the engagement in action also commits the learner to enter a certain nexus of practices with associated worldviews.

Thematic orientation

Generally, the chapter is situated in the area of learning workplace practices; and more narrowly, the chapter addresses the learning of being a car mechanic. In this sense, the author demonstrates that the actions that learners take also imbue them with a new kind of identity.

Related chapters

Chapters 6, 7, 8, 19, and 26.

Ingrid de Saint-Georges
Mediated discourse analysis, 'embodied learning' and emerging social and professional identities

Apprenticeship and embodied learning

From 2005 to 2010, together with colleagues[1], I became engaged in a study of apprenticeship learning in the field of car mechanics. We followed learners at school and work, gathering data through fieldnotes, video-recordings, our own sensory experiences, and formal and informal interviews. We were particularly interested in finding out what roles discourse and other modes (e.g. gestures, visuals, touch) played in learning new skills. We were also curious to investigate whether appropriating new skills and values influenced over time the development of new social and professional identities. In the sample analysis presented here, drawn from this larger project, I attempt to show how learning not only extends capabilities, but also often inextricably commits the learner to engage with certain worldviews and practices. I make the hypothesis that, once appropriated, these worldviews and practices often 'congeal' into habits (Norris 2004), and are difficult to see or to contest as they become part of the 'historical bodies' (Scollon & Scollon 2004) of the individuals.

Tracking workplace learning and emerging identities through mediated discourse analysis

Situations of vocational training are interesting to study because they are often moments when more experienced peers disclose and model views and practices that otherwise would be invisible to the newcomer. The practical challenge is to figure out how to study the construction/appropriation of these discourses and practices. In my case, I have found the framework of MDA particularly useful

---

1 This project was funded by the Swiss National Science Fundation (PP001-106603 & PP00P1-124650, L. Filliettaz (PI), B. Duc and myself (co-investigators).

(Scollon and Scollon 2004). MDA, contrary to most discourse analytical frameworks, takes actions and not discourse as its starting point. Only when the analyst has identified actions crucial for a specific set of actors does she start looking at which discourses or texts might figure in producing – or 'mediating' – these actions (Norris and Jones 2005). MDA analysts consider that broad social discourses of contemporary life circulate through any moment of action. Studying mediated actions is one way to work at disentangling 'taken-for-granted' discourses and 'commonplace practices' that would otherwise be invisible in the situation (Wohlwend 2013).

Methodologically, two propositions are made to recover these 'taken-for-granted discourses'. The first is that these discourses and commonplace practices can be empirically studied by looking at four kinds of 'entities' that come together in the mediated action: the *mediational means* used to carry out the action, the sociohistorical institutions and discourses that constrain the action (*discourses in place*), the interactional organization that regulates the encounter in which the action takes place (*the interaction order*) and the individual histories and biographical trajectories of the actors involved in the action (*the historical body*). The second proposition is that the research should not be 'obsessively narrowed to single moments, speech acts of events, or participants, but always strive to see 'how these connect to other moments, acts, events, and participants which make up the full nexus' (Scollon and Scollon 2004: 9). MDA thus encourages the researcher to determine the broad social, cultural and geographical histories of an action – its 'lineage and pedigree' (Blommaert 2010) – as well as its future trajectories (Scollon & Scollon 2004).

The focus of MDA on actions, histories, trajectories and genesis makes it a particularly interesting theory for studying 'learning', as both a process and a springboard for new possibilities of action, discourses and dispositions. MDA's interest in the body and concrete, physical practice makes it also particularly adapted to the study of 'apprentice style' and 'embodied kinds of learning' where knowledge is often communicated through touch, gaze, and engagement of the whole body in action, rather than through words.

What is learned when one learns to diagnose a breakdown?

The starting point for MDA is to identify a mediated action and to explore what processes or 'cycles' interconnect within the space of that action. In this brief sample analysis, I focus on one very common practice at the heart of the work of car mechanics: the action of diagnosing a breakdown. Fifteen years ago, such an action was a rather concrete, physical endeavor. The mechanic would try out some action and the way the car reacted to this action would prompt him to carry out other actions. Coming to a diagnosis required analysis of competing and sometimes contradictory information received through the senses as well as processes of induction and deduction. The introduction of electronics into the car industry has profoundly transformed this activity, requiring a new set of skills, in particular *computer literacy skills*. Indeed, the diagnosis now resembles 'distributed cognition'. The mechanic now plugs a computerised device into the car. The software analyses various parameters and prompts the mechanic to take a number of steps until the problem is resolved (see Pict. 1 and 2)

My interest is in this action as it occurs in the context of a medium-sized Jaguar repair shop in Geneva. The interaction order includes a mechanic (M) with almost 20 years experience with this brand of car, a young and confident apprentice (A) who had just started a one-month internship with the repair shop as part of his training, and myself, the researcher (R) filming the situation.

A mediated discourse analysis can look at this action of diagnosis from many perspectives (how it is mediated, participants' motivations for acting, how the action signals expertise and professional identity, etc.). My focus will be to examine how, from the perspective of the learner, this routine task of diagnosis connects workers to larger more complex social and economic 'geographies' (Scollon 2013).

In apprenticeship, learners usually enter a nexus of practices 'from the side' (Pict. 3). Working under the tutelage of a more experienced worker, they spend substantial periods observing, imitating, and repeating actions (Marchand 2008). They 'rely on the intercourse of visual, auditory and semiotic information' (Marchand 2008: 249) to access professional practices. But this posture of side-to-side working is more often than not also an opportunity to learn the 'social politics' of the work (Merchand 2008: 252) as the apprentice listens to exchanges and negotiations between team members, with clients, etc. Such exchanges can become 'prompts' (Kress 2013) for the learner to understand what adequate participation in work consists of or what is valued in the context. In the course of the one hour that the diagnosis action roughly lasts, there is in fact exposure of the apprentice to many such aspects of the social politics of work. As the mechanic scrolls down the screen and performs a series of actions on the car, many discourses emerge, having to do, among other things, with ethnic socialization, the construction of masculinity, the commodity discourse of advertisement, care of the worker for his tools, and even the porn movie industry.

Pict. 1: Using the diagnosis device

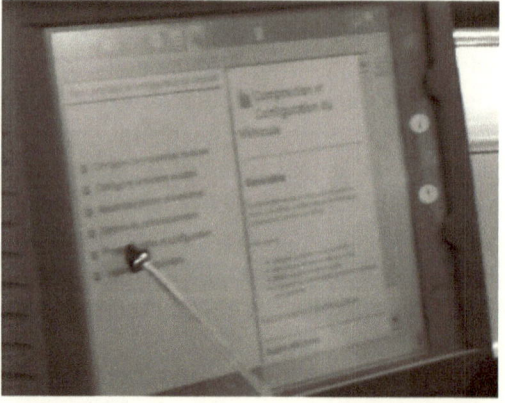

Pict. 2: Interacting with the software

Pict. 3: Displaying readiness and involvement in learning

Figure 1: Diagnosing a breakdown

Here, I give one example of how 'from the side' the learner gets engaged with worldviews as part of his learning experience. Obviously a full mediated discourse analysis would require a much more complex argument.

In this example, M. is scrolling down the screen of the diagnosis device, using an old antenna to click on links (Pict. 2), and reading instructions. At one point he starts telling us (A and myself, at his side) about the place electronics has taken in the trade and the kind of re-training involved:

> M: (1) So\on the whole/ we receive training despite the fact that I got my degree a very long time ago\ we get trained\ (...) depending on the models the new engines coming out we get trained 3 times or four times two days\
>
> [...]
>
> (2) So it is super important to detail/to detail that\ it's electronics- it forms an entire part of car mechanics/it is not like before/ when you just needed to repair engines that's over \electronic really forms a part of car mechanics of today and of the future

Here, speaking is not the instrument for carrying out the action. It does not serve either to teach the use of the diagnostic tool. Rather it intersects with the action of conducting the diagnostic process and serves to communicate knowledge about professional practice. It also signals to the apprentice certain features of a mechanic's identity. To unpack this action, it is interesting to uncover the connections between these practices of clicking and tapping on the screen and larger socioeconomic meanings and practices. One may best do this by retrieving the discourses that circulate in car repair shops about the use of such electronic devices.

In this respect we learned, from informal fieldwork interviews in various shops, firstly, that electronics has tended to make it more difficult for small car repair shops to be 'multibrand' or 'generalist'. Most car models now require specific diagnostic devices, with their associated software, and these are not compatible across brands. The cost of these machines is very high and the investment thus ties the shop more and more to specific car brands.

Secondly, electronics has also transformed the nature of car mechanics' work. Once mainly a manual activity, today it involves much more symbolic manipulation and computer literacy knowledge. For older generations of workers, the conversion is often difficult to manage and they find their expertise downgraded. For the youth entering the trade without much literacy or numeracy, the change is also creating hurdles, so much so, that in recent years, the education authorities chose to rethink certification and track organization, for example, by offering a certification as 'assistant in motor-vehicle maintenance' (2 years) on the low qualification side, as opposed to a 'mechatronics engineers' (4 years) certification with bridges to higher education.

Thirdly, as we see illustrated also in excerpt 1, learning to use these diagnostic tools often requires repeated re-training over a career as tools and engines evolve. Viewed as a part of a continuing education discourse, this has the advantage of opening up new perspectives in an evolving work environment. On the other hand, the cost of retraining falls on the shop owners, reinforcing their allegiance to a single brand.

This account shows the extent to which this new social practice of tapping on a screen connects the actions of the worker to a host of wider economic, political, social and educational practices. Learning to operate such a device and repeatedly using it over time obliges the worker to engage this nexus of practices which in turn seems to impact the car mechanic's identity. At least this is what the choice of words by M in (1) seem to suggest. By proposing that 'electronics forms an entire part of car mechanics', he seems to be saying that electronics is not just changing the trade, but changing the worker – possibly transforming him into a 'technoworker'. In manual trades, tools have always been inseparable from the worker. They shape his work and perceptions, as well as become shaped to his hands. In the same way, electronics seems here to be seen as becoming more and more one with the worker, the separation with his body becoming blurred.

Conclusion

With this brief sample analysis, I have tried to show that engaging in action commits the learner to enter a certain nexus of practices with associated worldviews. I have also tried to show how a mediated discourse analysis, even done as briefly as in this case, opens a window that helps make visible these worldviews and practices. For MDA, small actions such as touching a computer screen at a worksite are interesting to study because they are the point where individual biographies and much larger activity system come into contact and start to interact. Vocational education is a place where apprentices learn the multiple practices and discourses of their trade, and learn also to couple their action to a broader nexus of practices. Building on Scollon (2013), we could say that in that sense education is powerful because it connects the learner to a new class of actions. A mediated discourse analysis would probably also say education is powerful when it helps the learner be critical of the couplings and discourses circulating in the milieux he navigates so that s/he can then choose knowingly to ratify or contest them.

Further readings

Jones, Rodney H. 2012. Mediated Discourse Analysis. In *Discourse Analysis: A Resource Book for Students*, 32–35. New York: Routledge.
Jones, Rodney H. 2011. Sport and re/creation: What skateboarders can teach us about learning. *Sport, Education and Society* 16 (4): 593–611.
Scollon, Ron. 2001. *Mediated Discourse: The Nexus of Practice*. London: Routledge.
Scollon, Suzie Wong and Ingrid de Saint-Georges. 2011. Mediated Discourse Analysis. In James Paul Gee and Michael Handford (eds), *The Routledge Handbook of Discourse Analysis*, 66–78. New York : Routledge.

Project idea

Choose a learning situation that involves bodily engagement in some practice. Try to unpack the discourses that circulate through this learning situation. What kinds of texts are used in the situation, if any? What forms of talk are involved? Are there discourses that are hidden/submerged in the built environment, the layout of the physical space, the conventions that regulate the interaction? To what extent are the actions of the participants connecting them to larger socioeconomic meanings and practices (geographies of discourse)? How do you know? To what extent does engaging in the learning process commit the learner to engage with specific values and norms? What procedures did you use to unpack these 'taken-for-granted' norms and values?

References

Blommaert, Jan. 2010. Historical bodies and historical space. *Working papers in Urban langage and Literacies*, Paper 57.
Kress, Gunther. 2013. Recognizing Learning : A perspective from a Social Semiotic Theory of Multimodality. In Ingrid de Saint-Georges and Jean-Jacques Weber (eds), *Multilingualism and Multimodality: Current Challenges for Educational Studies*, 119–140. Rotterdam: SensePublishers.
Marchand, Trevor H. J. 2008. Muscles, morals and mind: craft apprenticeship and the formation of person. *British Journal of Educational Studies*, 56 (3): 245–271.
Norris, Sigrid. 2004. *Analyzing Multimodal Interaction: A methodological framework*. New York: Routledge.
Norris, Sigrid and Rodney H. Jones. 2005. *Discourse in Action. Introducing Mediated Discourse Analysis*. London: Routledge.

Scollon, Ron. 2013. Geographies of discourse: Action across layered spaces. In Ingrid de Saint-Georges and Jean-Jacques Weber (eds.), *Multilingualism and Multimodality: Current Challenges for Educational Studie*s, 183–198. Rotterdam: SensePublishers.

Scollon, Ron and Suzie Wong Scollon. 2004. *Nexus Analysis: Discourse and the emerging Internet*. London: Routledge.

Wohlwend, Karen E. 2013. Mediated Discourse Analysis: Tracking discourse in action. In Peggy Albers, Teri Holbrook and Amy Flint (eds.), *New Methods in Literacy Research*. London: Routledge.

Editors' introduction
28 Comic books

Topic

The chapter addresses students and researchers who are interested in the analysis of comic books.

Key terms: Balloon, caption, comic book, motion line, multimodality.

Methodology

The chapter explores the main characteristics and roles of the visual elements in a comic book, focusing on their capacity to develop specific metaphors; and highlights the visual stylistic conventions that are drawn upon in order to convey sequential narrative and speech while also evoking emotional or sensory responses.

Thematic orientation

Generally, the chapter is situated in the study of texts and images and their relationships and, more specifically, this chapter is an example for the study of these issues in comic books.

Related chapters

Chapter 8, 9, and 29.

Maria Jesus Pinar
Comic books

Introduction

The aim of this chapter is to analyse the visual elements that help develop the metaphor LIFE IS A JOURNEY in the comic book *Ug, Boy Genius of the Stone Age and his Search for Soft Trousers* by Raymond Briggs. LIFE IS A STRUGGLE TO CHANGE, LIFE IS A BATTLE AND LIFE IS A STRUGGLE TO SURVIVE are also metaphors which derive from the main one. The way the characters are depicted and the visual conventions used to transmit meaning will be the focus of this chapter.

The story

The story is set in The Stone Age, where Ug, a deep-thinking character, lives with his parents in a cave. He dreams of finding a soft pair of trousers and imagines a world where things are nice, soft and warm as opposed to cold, hard and dreary. His search fails, however, as almost everything surrounding him is made of stone. Meanwhile, Ug questions the world around him, trying to find solutions to the problems he observes (irrigation, cooking and heating using fire, boats and the wheel). The most difficult problem Ug has to struggle with is his mother, who is very set in her ways. Finally, his father helps him search for the trousers, but both fail in the attempt.

Research into comic books

Work in the field of comic books is becoming increasingly popular. It includes graphic novels, web comics (Zanfei 2008; Goggin and Hassler-Forest 2010), and autobiographical comics (El Refaie 2013). They can be considered a genuine multimodal genre whose meaning is constructed out of combinations of different modes and where each mode has a specific task and function. Modes are seen to enhance, reinforce or, in some cases, contradict each other. According to Kress, these modes form modal ensembles "based on designs or selections and arrangements of resources for making a specific message about a particular issue for a particular audience" (Kress 2010: 28). In comics, most of these modes are used for meaning-making, either in monomodal or multimodal combination, in order to convey a sequential narrative and to produce an aesthetic response in the viewer (Eisner 1985; McCloud 1993: 9).

Comics avoid the use of extended texts, which allows them to be extremely inventive in developing techniques to denote emotional status or changes, or emotions in general, such as surprise, disappointment, despair, anger or happiness (Pinar 2012). These techniques become conventions used in order to convey narration and speech and evoke emotional or sensuous responses. The conventions used to convey narration and speech include panels, motion lines, balloons, captions and gutters. Panels are the borders or edges around images. The borders are called frames and are normally rectangular in shape. Motion lines are used to indicate smell or movement. Balloons are containers of verbal and non-verbal communication (Forceville et al. 2010) and they are usually cloud-like shaped even though the author can change this depending on his specific needs. The gutter is the blank space between panels. Captions normally represent the narrator's voice and may also convey information "such as time or place, to set a mood or to convey additional non-visual information such as a sound or smell" (Marx 2007: 91) (for further details, see Pinar 2012; McCloud 1993; Forceville et al. 2010).

The repertoire of means of expression in comics include verbal, pictorial, and typographic signs which combine in a monosensory medium (the comic, which relies on only one of the senses – the eyes- to convey a world of experience) in order to transmit multimodal meanings. Following Norris (2004), these sign systems or modes should be considered as "embodied modes", implying that they may have a superordinate or equal value with respect to language. In fact, as Zanfei (2008: 60) points out, language and images are independently organized and structured messages whose codeployment and interplay make the whole meaning of the composition of the page. Visual elements can convey aural stimuli and readers/viewers are forced to "hear" with their eyes.

Ug: Life is a journey

As Saraceni (2003: 28) points out, "words and pictures are far from being redundant [...] words and pictures don't just mirror one another but interact in many different ways, and each of the two contributes its own share in the interpretation of the text". Even though words have a crucial role in the transmission of information in this comic book, the aim of the chapter is to analyse the visual elements surrounding the metaphor LIFE IS A JOURNEY, which can be studied in terms of participants, goals and processes. The participants are people/travelers, in this case Ug and his parents. The goal is to reach a destination: in Ug's case, to find soft trousers and create new objects in order to live more comfortably; in Ug's mother's case, to make her son change his attitude. The processes are the problems/crossroads that the participants have to face to achieve their goals: Ug's mother's complaints and the circumstances in which they are living.

LIFE IS A JOURNEY is related to LIFE IS A STRUGGLE TO CHANGE. The difficulties in the journey are caused by the obstacles Ug finds when he wants to "change" his habits. The first thing he has to fight against is his mother who can't see the point in using "soft" materials. Living in the Stone Age is another difficulty as they lack materials, fire or wheels to move objects. Ug tries to produce inventions to change his lifestyle but these always fail. He does as much as he can to change but his struggle is worthless.

Ug is identified with change whereas his mother is "the struggle against change". Ug's father is in the middle. Ug is a hieratic character as his face does not express too much apart from the fact that he is afraid of his mother: his mouth becomes a straight line (sadness) or a circle (fear) when he is talking to her. Acts like running away (see Figure 1) or protecting himself with his arms when he is close to his mother are some clues that indicate that they do not have a good relationship. Disappointment and failure are represented with both Ug's and his dad's head down (see Figure 4), when he fails to perform the tasks he involves in (making a boat, rolling a stone or cutting the trousers).

Ug's father's attitude changes in parallel to the story and is the character who best represents the metaphor LIFE IS A STRUGGLE TO CHANGE. This change is appreciated in the pictures. The good relationship he has towards his son is portrayed right from the beginning when he touches his son's head. However, this affection does not disguise the differences between them. The reader can see it when Ug shows his father a mammoth skin and his father's posture shows that he disagrees with him about it. Figure 2 shows Ug's father in a dubitative position, touching his head with his hand. Ug and his father are often represented with their heads down (see Figure 4), which indicates disappointment. The fact that Ug's father is ready for a change influences the relationship with his wife, who threatens him as if he were a child (see Figure 3).

Ug's mother's images transmit a great deal of information. She is always depicted showing annoyance through the position of her mouth and her diagonal eyebrows (Figures 1 and 3, to name only a few). Her skin contains more red than the rest of her family, which indicates anger and fury. Her finger pointing upwards shows superiority and power (Figures 3 and 7). She is also the key element in the metaphor LIFE IS A BATTLE. Ug has to fight against his mother to

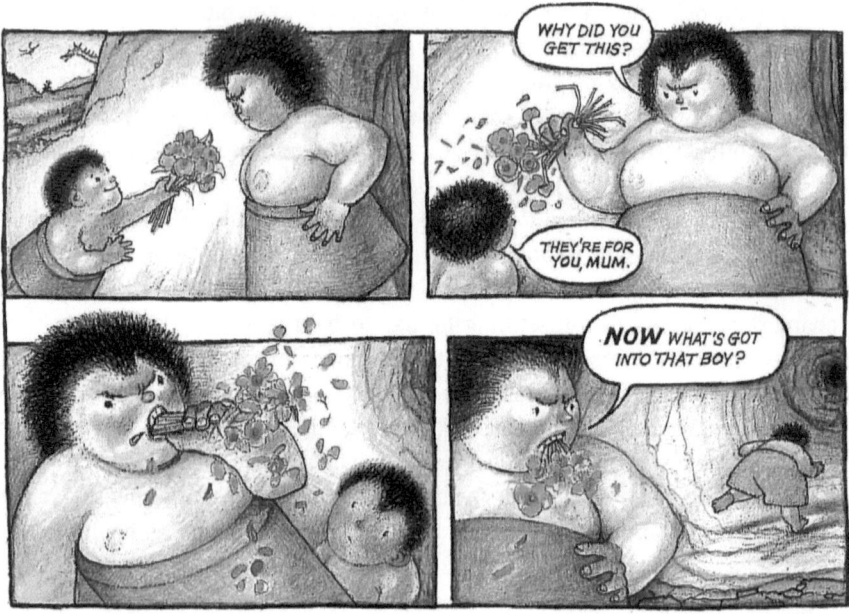

Figure 1: Relationship between Ug and his mother

Figure 2: Balloons and typography depicting characters

Figure 3: Ug's mother's characteristics

Figure 4: Representing emotions: failure and disappointment

Figure 5: Motion lines

achieve what he is looking for: a pair of soft trousers. From the mother's point of view, the purpose of the battle is another: she wants her son to be strong and tough so he can survive in hard times.

Apart from pictures, there are other visual devices used to express meanings such as "balloons", "typeface" or "motion lines". Balloons not only transmit narrative information but also make the reader "feel" the message, providing clues about how people behave or react. They are a visual unit that conveys dialogue, either spoken or thought. Balloons are usually rounded although the shape can change according to their purpose (see Forceville et al. 2010: 57 ff. for further information). The balloons used in this story are mainly "strict" (Forceville et al. 2010: 58) as they are virtually identical to what is regarded as the standard and of two types mainly: (i) a smooth oval circle that sometimes forms connected sub-balloons and (ii) rectangular rounded. When the author wants to change the rhythm of the story or add some extra information, he changes the shape of the balloons. This is especially true in the case of the balloons containing Ug's mother's speech, which are always serrated contour balloons. They are both strict and extended, according to her temper. They never contain Ug's or Ug's dad's words. Serrated balloons illustrate that the character is shouting (see Figures 3 and 6). The irregular shape of the balloon shows that

Figure 6: Example of serrated balloons

the tone of the speaker is different and higher than usual. This could be related to anger, annoyance or even to happiness and surprise. However, "happiness" is not visible in Ug's mum's face, so this specific use of the balloon is carefully chosen to show irritation and maybe her power over the family. Briggs adds extra information using corrugated balloons, which suggest that the characters are cold, as Figure 5 shows.

The use of thought balloons in this story is significant. According to Forceville et al (2010: 67) they are often the equivalent of interior monologue, conveying information that a character may suppress. The information in thought

Figure 7: Example of thought balloons

balloons is unavailable to fellow characters, but never to the reader. Both Ug and his mum make use of interior monologue. The former, when he is thinking of ways to change the world, the second when she gets exasperated with Ug's ideas. One example can be found in Figure 7, where the mother answers in a polite way, but thanks to the thought balloon the reader appreciates that she is bored of her son. Another example is Figure 8, where Ug's mum complains about Ug's thoughts.

Typeface is another visual device used to transmit meaning. As McCloud (1993: 8) points out, letters are static images arranged in a deliberate sequence that transmit meaning depending on the way they look. Bold is used for glossed terms and sometimes these words are underlined to catch the reader's attention (See Figure 8). Another typographical technique is to enlarge letters "in order to convey loud speech or noises" (Saraceni 2003: 20), such as "WHEEEEEE!" (see Figure 9), to show excitement. The irregular shapes of letters, Saraceni argues, resemble the irregular patterns in the way the people speak. This applies to Ug's mother, whose bad temper is clearly conveyed both through the irregular shapes and letters and the use of bold typeface. Together with the use of serrated

Figure 8: Typeface: Bold and underline

Figure 9: Letters enlargement

Figure 10: Introducing anachronisms

balloons and the way she is visually depicted, typography helps create Ug's mum identity.

Motion lines are used to represent movement and to show moods and feelings. They can only be understood in context, since they do not have any meanings on their own. In Figure 5 parallel short lines are around the characters, showing their state of coldness and how they are shivering. Figure 9 shows motion lines around Ug expressing happiness and excitement and also to depict that the stone ball is rolling.

Captions are generally reserved for narration rather than dialogue and take the form of squares of text attached above or below the panel. Captions can be used in place of thought balloons, can be in the first, second or third person, and can either be assigned to an independent narrator or one of the comic's characters. The importance of captions in this story is that they are used as a story within a story to explain the anachronisms the author has introduced. Thus, Figure 11 explains the anachronisms the characters have mentioned in Figure 10. The captions do not represent the narrator's voice conveying information about time, place or mood but introduce a completely different turn in the story.

Colours can give subtle clues about feelings. In this story, grey is the predominant colour, associated to Ug's mother (see Figure 3). This colour is typi-

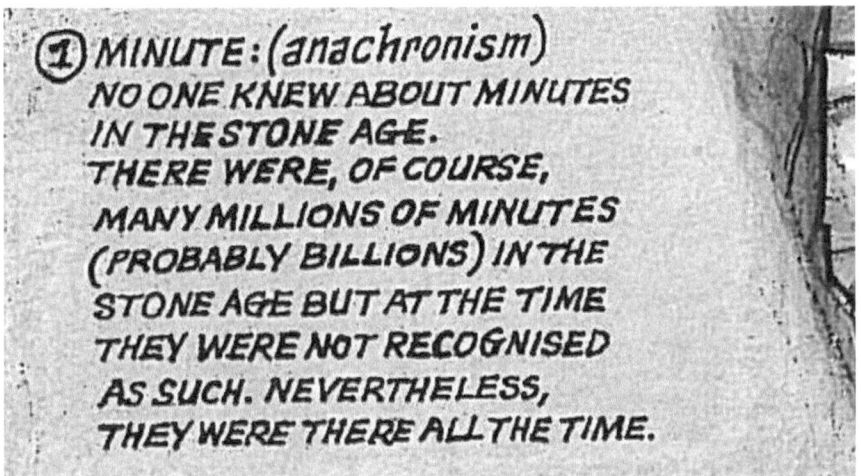

Figure 11: Captions

cally related to sadness. There are other panels that contain dark tonalities (see Figure 5) but in these cases the reader relates the colours to fear or coldness due to the presence of corrugated balloons whose waves are conventionally used to express shivers.

Conclusion

This study has shown the visual conventions used in the transmission of the metaphors LIFE IS A JOURNEY and LIFE IS A STRUGGLE TO CHANGE. Attention has also been focused on the analysis of balloons, typography, motion lines and captions. Visuals give us information about the depicted characters: we get to know the main characters both through images and also through the use of a specific type of balloon and typography. Visuals are useful for the comprehension of the whole story as they transmit character's feelings better than words do. Their role is to enhance and reinforce what verbal communication transmits, but are not essential to understand the plot. However, visuals on their own are not enough to get the full meaning potential in the comic book, so it would also be necessary to study how this relates to the verbal part. This opens up an interesting field of study where the verbo-visual relationship in comics can be studied from different perspectives, being McCloud's categories (McCloud 1993: 153–63) the most popular word/image combination in comics.

Further Readings

El Refaie, Elisabeth. 2012. *Autobiographical Comics: Life Writing in Pictures*. Jackson: University Press of Mississippi.
Harvey, Robert C. 1996. *The Art of the Comic Book: An Aesthetic History*. Jackson: University Press of Mississippi.
Wolk, Douglas 2008. *Reading Comics: How Graphic Novels Work and What They Mean*. Cambridge, MA: Da Capo Press.

Project idea

Kafka's *The Metamorphosis* has been adapted by Kuper to the format of a graphic novel. An interesting project would be the analysis of visual devices in this graphic novel, taking emotions into account.

References

Eisner, Will. 1985. *Comics and Sequential Art*. Tamarac, FL: Poorhouse Press.
El Refaie, Elisabeth. 2013. *Autobiographical comics: Life writing in pictures*. Jackson: University Press of Mississippi.
Forceville, Charles, Tony Veale and Kurt Feyaerts. 2010. Balloonics : The visuals of balloons in comics. In Joyce Goggin and Dan Hassler-Forest (eds.), *The Rise and Reason of Comics and Graphic Literature: Critical Essays on the Form*, 56–73. Jefferson, North Carolina, London: McFarland & Company.
Joyce Goggin and Dan Hassler-Forest (eds.), *The Rise and Reason of Comics and Graphic Literature: Critical Essays on the Form*. Jefferson, North Carolina, London: McFarland & Company.
Kress, Gunther. 2010. *Multimodality. A Social Semiotic Approach to Contemporary Communication*. London, England: Routledge.
McCloud, Scott. 1993. *Understanding Comics: The Invisible Art*. New York, USA: Harper Perennial.
Marx, Christy. 2007. *Writing for Animation, Comics, and Games*. Oxford: Focal Press.
Norris, Sigrid. 2004. *Analysing Multimodal Interaction*. London, England: Routledge.
Pinar, Maria J. 2012. Multimodality and comic books. In Carol C. Chapelle (ed.) *The Encyclopedia of Applied Linguistics*. New Jersey: Wiley-Blackwell.
Saraceni, Mario. 2003. *The Language of Comics*. London, New York: Routledge.
Zanfei, Anna. 2008. Defining webcomics and graphic novels. *International Journal of Comic Art* 10 (1): 55–61.

Acknowledgement

Most sincere gratitude to Patricia Barba, who introduced the author to Ug.

Editors' introduction
29 Multimodality in literature: An analysis of Jonathan Safran Foer's *A Primer for the Punctuation of Heart Disease*

Topic

The chapter addresses students and researchers who are interested in the analysis of literature.

Key terms: Cognitive poetics, conceptual metaphor, metonymy, stylistics, syntactic parallelism.

Methodology

Taking a multimodal cognitive approach to literature, the author presents in detail how narrative goals are achieved multimodally.

Thematic orientation

Generally, the chapter is situated in the study of semiotic modes and their relationships and, more specifically, this chapter is an example for the study of these issues in contemporary literature.

Related chapters

Chapter 28.

Alison Gibbons
Multimodality in literature: An analysis of Jonathan Safran Foer's *A Primer for the Punctuation of Heart Disease*

Introduction

Since the turn of the millennium, readers of literature may have noticed an increase in the inclusion of images, typographical variation, and exploration of page space within works of fiction. This is, in part, a response to the rapid technological developments of the period, which have improved the digital process of design while simultaneously reducing production costs. Pressman (2009) similarly points to the year 2000 as a turning point in literary sensibilities, advocating an "aesthetic of bookishness" whereby many authors strategically experiment with the material possibilities of the book in the face of digital take-over. Twenty-first century literature is therefore rich terrain for multimodal analysis.

This chapter combines multimodal analysis (Kress and van Leeuwen 2006 [1996]) with stylistic and cognitive-poetic analysis (Stockwell 2002). That is, it considers form, style, and language in context. It presents an integrated understanding of the way in which the different modes work together as well as a consideration of the cognitive processes by which readers deduce literary meaning and affect. This is the approach taken to Jonathan Safran Foer's (2003) short story 'A Primer for the Punctuation of Heart Disease'. The story is housed in a collection unified by its aim to capture contemporary American experience, itself viewed as an internalised collective sadness. What is remarkable about Foer's story, though, is that it achieves this narrative goal through multimodal means, offering a system of visual punctuation that represents the unsaid utterances in family discourse. As such, the text alternates between taxonomic definitions of punctuation symbols and narrative vignettes which exemplify the symbols' usages.

Analysis

Foer's story begins, "☐ The 'silence mark' signifies an absence of language, and there is at least one on every page of the story of my family life" (Foer 2003:

283). The opening sentence serves an explanatory purpose, informing readers how to interpret what Foer has named the silence mark: ☐. In some ways, Foer's pictorial choice is self-evident, the visual white space enclosed within the square iconically suggesting silence. In other words, ☐ enacts a metaphorical rendering in which visuality offers an impression of silence that the reader must interpret. Cognitively, then, literal visual emptiness is mapped onto inferred sonic silence.

There is an additional textual metaphor at work in the opening sentence, encapsulated in the phrase 'every page of the story of my family life', though this metaphor is not multimodal but realised through words alone. Underwriting this phrase is what is known in cognitive poetics as a conceptual metaphor, an underlying thought pattern in which one conceptual entity is mapped onto another. Such patterns of thought enable humans to understand complex abstractions such as LIFE and DEATH via reference to more physical or experiential items. Here, we have LIFE IS A BOOK: the physicality of books and their potential division into pages and chapters is used as a vehicle with which to understand the stages and development of life and particularly the evolution of family relationships.

With this first line, Foer's story instantly communicates the sadness of contemporary American experience at the heart of the short story collection. The affective force of Foer's narrative aperture stems from the reader's cognitive ability to comprehend both of the metaphors at work here: a textual symbol upon a page is the silence in a relationship, the narrator's family life is characterised by what he and his relatives do not say to each other.

In the opening paragraph, the narrator Jonathan discloses the family predisposition for heart attacks, with his father being the most-affected (it is claimed he has had twenty-two heart attacks). This life-threatening condition, it is intimated, is perhaps the reason for the difficulty of communication the family face since they struggle to articulate their love for each other and fears for their own and each other's mortalities. The first narrative vignette exemplifies the use of ☐ in a telephone conversation between the narrator and his father before the latter has to undergo an anglioplasty (a serious coronary operation for widening obstructed blood vessels) (Foer 2003: 283):

'Listen,' he said, and then surrendered to a long pause, as if the pause were what I was supposed to listen to. 'I'm sure everything's gonna be fine, but I just wanted to let you know – '

'I already know,' I said.
'☐'
'☐'
'☐'
'☐'
'OK,' he said.

Foer leaves implicit here that the delicate nature of the subject matter, the unsaid possibilities of what could happen during the operation and particularly what could go wrong, are the cause of the gaps of conversation between the characters. However, it is Foer's multimodal rendering of these gaps that make the scene poignant for readers. Not only do readers have to use their recently gained knowledge of the symbol to interpret its meaning, but the conceptual process of metaphorical transfer from visual literalisation to sonic inference renders a sensory dimension to the scene within readers' imaginations. In the mind's eye, readers experience the poignant chain of silences in this conversation in a way they would not had Foer chosen a different mode of representation.

As the story continues, the reader accrues further taxonomic understanding of the punctuation symbols, each time being offered a narrative anecdote which presents a moving illustration of Jonathan's and his family's dysfunctional communications. Their inability to express their true emotions is perhaps most keenly felt when Jonathan introduces what he calls the Barely Tolerable Substitutes (Foer 2003: 289):

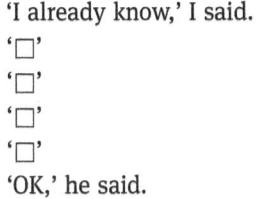 The 'severed web' is a Barely Tolerable Substitute, whose meaning approximates 'I love you,' and which can be used in place of 'I love you.' Other Barely Tolerable Substitutes include, but are not limited to:

→|←, which approximates 'I love you.'
🌀☐, which approximates 'I love you.'
🔒, which approximates 'I love you.'
✕↦, which approximates 'I love you.'

I don't know how many Barely Tolerable Substitutes there are, but often if feels as if they are everywhere [...]

Once again, as with the ☐ silence mark, readers must find a way to match the given definition of the symbol with its visual composition. Thus they engage in acts of visual-semantic interpretation. Some of the Barely Tolerable Substitutes are more transparent in visual meaning-making than others. '→|←', for instance, uses the directionality of the arrows into a central meeting point to suggest a relationship of reciprocity, thus readers might infer that the family love communicated by →|← is mutual. Others, when decoded, imply a poignant pathos: 🔒, 🕸, and ✂🕸, for example. The first, a lock, suggests that the relationship is closed in some way; the severed web indicates a network being cut or perhaps through contextual semantic inference family ties being broken; 🕸 uses the silence mark already introduced to readers, while the ear metonymically (through semantic association) suggests the act of listening, thus loving someone involves listening to their silences. Moreover, the fact that the narrator suggests that there are a plethora of Barely Tolerable Substitutes is, in itself, a source of despondency: It is as though Jonathan's family is continually attempting to find ways to say 'I love you' to each other, but such surrogate articulations are always inadequate.

In the final narrative vignette of the story, the reader is privy to another conversation between Jonathan and his father. This conversation uses most of the symbols presented in the course of the narrative. It is, therefore, worth providing a key to the symbols presented by the narrator in 'A Primer for the Punctuation of Heart Disease' (see Table 1).

Table 1: Taxonomy of symbols from Foer's (2003) 'A Primer for the Punctuation of Heart Disease'

Symbol	Symbol Name	Given Meaning
☐	Silence Mark	Silence; an absence of language.
■	Willed Silence Mark	An intentional silence.
??	Insistent Question Mark	Refusal to yield to a willed silence.
¡	Unxclamation Point	A whisper.
¡¡	Extraunxclamation Points	A silence that might have been an articulation spoken to quietly to hear.
!!	Extraexclamation Points	Agitated yelling in heated arguments.
~	Pedal Point	Placed at the end of a sentences to indicate a train of thought that has dissolved into a suggestive silence.
↓	Low Point	An emotional low point.
☐	Snowflake	A unique and previously unusued phrase in family communication.
☺	Corroboration Mark	A form of agreement or affirmation.
✂🕸→|←🕸☐🔒✗→ etc.	Barely Tolerable Substitutes	Approximation of 'I love you'.
::	Reversible Colon	What follows is an elaboration, summation, implication.
←	Backup	An attempt to understand an intended, but not fully or clearly communicated implied meaning.
{ }	Should-have Brackets	Words that haven't been spoken but should have been.

Many of these symbols are found in the final narrative vignette. However, it also contains symbols and combinations that have not been presented to the reader. As such, readers must use *both* the knowledge they have gained through the course of the short story as well as their own interpretive skills. The conversation between Jonathan and his father is as follows (Foer 2003: 291–2):

'Are you hearing static?'
'{I'm crying into the phone.}'
'Jonathan?'
'□'
'Jonathan~'
'■'
'??'
'I::not myself~'
'{A child's sadness is a parent's sadness.}'
'{A parent's sadness is a child's sadness.}'
'←'
'I'm probably just tired¡'
'{I never told you this, because I thought it might hurt you, but in my dreams it was *you*. Not me. *You* were pulling the weeds from my chest.}'
'{I want to love and be loved.}'
'☺'
'☺'
'↓'
'↓'
'⚇'
'☺'
'□↔□↔■'
'↓'
'↓'
'⏭○⏭'
'■ + ■ ⟶ ■'
'☺'
'👂□'
'⊠⊠'
'◎□❖'
'○⏭◉♦○○□♦•●'
'■'
'{I love you.}'
'{I love you, too. So much.}'

In this extended conversation, written as being composed of 33 utterances, there are in fact only five conversational turns which are apparently spoken aloud, thus showing how the majority of communication in Jonathan's family is, in fact, not actually communicated. That is, their conversations are characterised by their lack rather than by exchange. Even the spoken utterances ('Are you hearing static?', 'Jonathan?', 'Jonathan~', 'I::not myself~', 'I'm probably just tired¡') are not, actually, met with verbalised responses. Rather there is an abundance of unspoken or silently communicated signifieds in the form of symbols and should-have brackets.

As with the silence mark discussed at the start of this analysis, some of the symbols Foer uses work to add a sensory quality to the passage; namely □, ■, ~ and ¡. Thus the imagined realisation of the conversation has greater sonic clarity for readers. In the plethora of symbols towards the end of the discourse, there are many symbols and combinations of symbols that are new to readers. While any exact meaning cannot by ascertained unerringly, readers will probably assume that these are Barely Tolerable Substitutes, standing in for 'I love you's. As such, the dialogue presents numerous failed attempts to verbalise the most vital and heartfelt meaning. The poignancy of this, felt keenly by readers in imagined sonic silences is enhanced by the should-have said dialogue. Touchingly, there is a notable reciprocity in the should-have-said adjacency pairs: '{A child's sadness is a parent's sadness.}' ↔ '{A parent's sadness is a child's sadness.}' features syntactic parallelism with lexical substitutions (parent ↔ child) suggesting sadness shared because of emotional connection, while the closing '{I love you.}' is met with '{I love you, too. So much.}'. As such, while ultimately 'A Primer for the Punctuation of Heart Disease' is a story about deeply engrained family sadness and a failure to communicate, it is also about shared emotions and how, spoken or unspoken, they bind us together.

Conclusion

This chapter has presented an analysis of Jonathan Safran Foer's (2003) multimodal short story 'A Primer for the Punctuation of Heart Disease'. The multimodal analysis considered the visual nature of the symbols used and how they relate to their given meaning through iconic and semantic relation. The stylistic and cognitive-poetic approach enabled reflection of the linguistic composition of the text as well as the reader's cognitive efforts in literary interpretation and experiential affect.

Multimodality in literature takes various forms: images and photographs that accompany narrative text, words arranged on the page in concrete-poetic design, symbols and typographical variation, as well as other modes. Whatever form it takes, multimodality in literature has the capacity to produce vivid narrative worlds. 'A Primer for the Punctuation of Heart Disease' could indeed have been told through words alone, but in choosing to render dialogic scenes through multimodal means, Foer offers the reader a literary experience with greater sensory intensity and enhanced emotional poignancy.

Further Readings

Gibbons, Alison. 2012. *Multimodality, Cognition, and Experimental Literature*. London/New York: Routledge.

Hallet, Wolfgang. 2009. The Multimodal Novel: The integration of modes and media in novelistic narration. In Sandra Heinen and Roy Sommer (eds.), *Narratology in the Age of Cross-Disciplinary Narrative Research*, 129–153. Berlin: Walter de Gruyter.

Nørgaard, Nina. 2010. Multimodality and the Literary Text: Making Sense of Safran Foer's *Extremely Loud and Incredibly Close*. In Ruth Page (ed.) *New Perspectives on Narrative and Multimodality*, 115–126. London/New York: Routledge.

Project Idea

Choose a short extract of multimodal literature. You might for instance like to choose a concrete poem such as '40-Love' by Roger McGough, a concrete-poetic rendering of text within a fiction such as the Mouse's Tail/Tale in Lewis Carroll's *Alice in Wonderland*, a short story like Foer's 'A Primer for the Punctuation of Heart Disease' or extract from a novel such as Chapter 12 from Jennifer Egan's (2010) *A Visit from the Goon Squad* which is designed as a power point.

1. Composition: Make a list of the different modes that your chosen extract uses (e.g. words, colour, typography, images, visual space).
2. Compare and Contrast: Write out your extract (or some of it depending on length) in the format of traditional text. How does this change the effect of the text? What is missing in the 'monomodal' version? What does the text gain in its multimodal form?
3. Consequences: Why do you think the writer has chosen to present the text multimodally? How do you experience it as a reader?

References

Foer, Jonathan Safran. 2003. A Primer for the Punctuation of Heart Disease. In Marco Cassini and Martina Testa (eds.) *The Burned Children of America*, 283–292. London: Hamish Hamilton.

Kress, Gunther and van Leeuwen, Theo. 2006 (1996). *Reading Images: The Grammar of Visual Design*. London: Routledge.

Pressman, Jessica. 2009. The Aesthetic of Bookishness in Twenty-First Century Literature. *Michigan Quarterly Review* 48(4): 465–482.

Stockwell, Peter. 2002. *Cognitive Poetics: An Introduction*. London: Routledge.

Sigrid Norris and Carmen Daniela Maier
30 Concluding remarks

Editing *Interactions, images and texts: A reader in multimodality* has been a long, but in our view, highly fruitful endeavour. In fact, it is a joy to see so many different chapters coming from different approaches and/or mixes of approaches.

At the end of this book, we would like to thank our contributors from all over the world for making possible the publication of a Reader capable to illustrate the state of multimodality research today. From personal accounts revealing the birth of various multimodal approaches, and chapters elaborating on key concepts and methods from diverse positions, to the analyses that highlight what multimodal approaches can achieve when adopted in a wide range of contexts, all the contributions put together in this Reader show that multimodality research is growing. Researchers are moving into different domains, and are honing in on various fields that can profit from a multimodal approach.

At the end of putting together such a collection of chapters from highly experienced and well-known to mid-career and young emergent researchers, it seems a good moment to think about the future of multimodality. Where will we go next?

From our positions we are seeing multimodality emerging in even more areas and we see multimodal research methods taken up by many new and emergent as well as by more experienced researchers. Certainly, this is not surprising. We have the technology to analyse multimodality and by now have various frameworks to embark on theoretically and methodologically strong multimodal research.

The world is – and always has been – multimodal. While, for a long time, language was studied quite separately from other modes; and while many areas that used a discursive approach such as discourse analysis to study a vast array of areas from health to marketing, from communication to sociology, or from anthropology to education, there now is a shift. There is a shift towards using multimodal discourse analysis, rather than relying on language, spoken or written, alone.

With this shift, multimodality is growing fast. We now see multimodality taught in undergraduate and graduate courses, see positions for Professors in multimodality, journals in the area of multimodality, and generally see an immense rise in interest across academic fields, not only including the ones named above, but also others such as business, computer science, IT, psychology and neuroscience. But even these do not name all of the areas that are beginning to view the study of multimodality as fruitful, and we will not try to provide a completed list, here, either. What we do wish to say with naming the many areas above is that multimodality is gaining momentum.

These are exciting times for those already working in multimodality, for their students, and for the many researchers who are contemplating research into multimodality.

Glossary

The definitions in this glossary have been provided by the authors who *used* the terms in their chapters. Most of these terms *were not coined by the ones who define them here*. Some of the authors included original references in these definitions, while other authors referenced the original sources in their chapters.

Some of the terms are defined by more than one author, and we included them all here, illustrating a nuanced reading and use of terms.

The terms and definitions are meant to allow the reader to understand just how the authors of the chapter use the terms. Thus, enhancing the reading experience.

At the same time, we would like to suggest the reader find the original definitions by the ones who coined the terms in the literature in order to gain *their own* understanding of particular terms.

Finding the original definitions, in fact would be a useful exercise when using the *Reader* for learning/teaching.

Affect	The term 'affect' is often used as an equivalent of the term 'emotion', but affect theory extends its meaning to refer to dynamics that are seen to be pre-personal and trans-personal. A prime example of affect in action is crowd excitement, where the manifestation and intensification of people's excitement are often difficult to anchor to specific, circumscribed actions. Affect comes into play when practitioners view themselves on video because video generates 'positive [i.e. self-reinforcing] feedback', concentrating people's attention and interest on what is seen, and its implications for them as social actors. (Definition provided by Iedema)
Anthropology	Anthropology is a discipline that has evolved its early origins in the late 1800's into a diverse interdisciplinary field combining cultural studies, linguistics and sociology. It studies the relationship between means of communication and cultural practices and culture, viewing language, gesture and other communicative means as cultural resources. (Definition provided by Jewitt)
Audience address	Audience Address refers to the means by which audiences can be engaged interpersonally in the news. Visual audience

address is established when anchors, presenters and other persons look directly at the camera and – by extension – the viewer. Verbally, the impression of a shared co-presence with the audience can be created through greetings, salutations, the use inclusive pronouns, such as 'we' and 'our', and certain spatial and temporal references, such as 'here' and 'now'. (Definition provided by Tan)

Audio-video data Audio-video data refers to audio-video recording collected during the research process. In this form, audio-video recordings as data are unedited or produced and are typically recorded by the researcher. (Definition provided by Geenen)

Authenticity Authenticity refers to multimodal strategies and conventions that contribute to the appearance of 'truth' and 'reality' on television. For example, audiences seem to credit more realism and truth-value to news images that are slightly blurry or grainy, and filmed scenes that appear rushed or hurried. Televisual authenticity encompasses the personal appearance and integrity of the news anchor or presenter. (Definition provided by Tan)

Balloon A container of verbal and non-verbal communication (Forceville et al. 2010). Balloons not only transmit narrative information but also make the reader "feel" the message, providing clues about how people behave or react. They are usually cloud-like shaped even though the author can change this depending on his specific needs. (Definition provided by Pinar)

Caption Device reserved for narration rather than dialogue that takes the form of squares of text attached above or below the panel. Captions can be used in place of thought balloons, can be in the first, second, or third person, and can either be assigned to an independent narrator or one of the comic's characters. They need not be of uniform shape, size, design or color. (Definition provided by Pinar)

Central layers of discourse	The central layers of discourse "are formed by a social actor enacting certain immediate actions" (Norris 2011: 179) and produce immediate identity elements. (Definition provided by Matelau)
Circumferencing	The broader discourses in which a particular social action operates, including the origin and direction of the action. (Definition provided by Pan)
Cognitive poetics	Developing from stylistics and drawing on the cognitive sciences, cognitive poetics is a discipline in which stylistic analysis forms part of an investigation into the cognitive processes of reading.
Comic book	Multimodal genre whose meaning is constructed out of combinations of different modes, mainly written and visual, and where each mode has a specific task and function. (Definition provided by Pinar)
Communicative space	Communicative space is a collective term defining a single semiotic unit, which comprises all physical spaces that constitute an essential part of the site of engagement within which a message is mediated (White, 2012). (Definition provided by White)
Conceptual metaphor	Understood as an underlying and structuring pattern of thought, conceptual metaphors map one domain onto another, enabling the human comprehension of an abstract concept (such as 'LIFE' or 'LOVE') by reference to a more concrete physical experience (such as the 'JOURNEY').
Connotation	Signs not only make meaning on the literal level, but they can also convey sense on a secondary, symbolic level. These kinds of meanings are called the connotations of a sign or its connotative meanings. Connotative meanings are often not fixed but can stray, which is why we say signs have a connotative potential. (Definition provided by Stöckl)
Conversation analysis	Conversation analysis (CA) is a discipline that was developed by sociologists in the USA in the 1960s to investigate the social and situated use of language in the organization of action in situ. 'Action' is a central unit of analysis, with actions seen as being connected over time to constitute sequenced or chained. (Definition provided by Jewitt)

Co-researcher	Participants are conceptualised as co-researchers insofar as when studying naturally occurring social interaction, participants co-construct and affect data collection methods and play a central role in dictating the trajectory of the research. (Definition provided by Geenen)
Corporate video	A video produced by/for a company with specific promotional purposes and targeting a specific audience. (Definition provided by Maier)
Critical discourse analysis	A detailed level of linguistic and grammatical analysis used to draw out ideologies buried in language. (Definition provided by Machin)
Cycles of discourse	The concept that discourse is across longer timescales and through cycles of change and transformation. The basic idea is that there are cycles of transformation from discourse to objects to new discourses to new objects. (Definition provided by Pan)
Diffraction	Haraway defines 'diffraction' both negatively and positively. Defined negatively, "diffraction does not produce 'the same' displaced, as reflection and refraction do". Defined positively, diffraction produces variations on existing patterns of understanding and action. (Definition provided by Iedema)
Digital humanities	The use of computational and visualization techniques to understand socio-cultural patterns and trends. (Definition provided by Kay L. O'Halloran)
Discourse	It can be defined as language in use in its narrow sense, or as social language in its broader sense (i.e., traffic discourse). (Definition provided by Al Zidjaly)
Discourse in place	Instances of language use, either written or spoken, that mark the environment in which the social action takes place. (Definition provided by Pan)
Discourse itinerary	A historical chain along which social actors appropriate various meditational means to take actions which in turn give rise to new meditational means which allow them to take subsequent actions. (Definition provided by Jones)

Discourse semantics	The mechanisms that govern the interpretation of semiotic modes in their context of occurrence. The semiotic modes are often structured to support a particular discourse interpretation. (Definition provided by Hiippala)
Embodied learning	The term emphasizes the role of the body in the learning process. It stresses that we learn through our bodily engagement in the world. Since the body is a central locus of experience and that experience transforms the individual, the body is also viewed as a place where learning that is transformative of identities, practices, awareness occurs. (Definition provided by de Saint-Georges)
Ethics application	The form or process carried out when applying for ethics approval for a research study. Generally required for studies involving people and animals, in some cases ethics approval is not required if working with publically available data. Some countries do not require ethics approval for research. (Definition provided by Pirini)
Ethics review boards	The representatives charged with assessing the likelihood of ethical execution of a research project, based on the submitted ethics application, and in some cases discussions with researchers responsible for the application. (Definition provided by Pirini)
Experiential meaning	In Functional Grammar and visual grammar these are meanings that account for the representation of any aspect of the world as it is experienced by human beings. (Definition provided by Maiorani)
Factuality	Factuality (or facticity) is an important news value that influences the selection, inclusion, depth and representation of a news event by the news media. Linguistically, factuality refers to the rhetorical devices that are used to enhance the truth-value of a news report, such as references to figures and numbers, locations, names, places, etc. In the realm of television news, factuality also involves other semiotic resources, such as visual images, sound and music. (Definition provided by Tan)

Foreground-background continuum	A graphical representation of the attention/awareness displayed by an individual or group to relevant higher-level actions. Modal density is used to differentiate between higher-level actions that are at higher and lower levels of attention/awareness. (Definition provided by Pirini)
Frozen action	Actions, which are entailed in material objects. (Definition provided by Pirini)
Geography of discourse	Scollon (2013: 188) defines the term as 'a system in which language and other semiotic systems are used together with material, concrete geographical spaces to produce semiotic-material spaces for a particular purpose'. It is used to refer to interconnections between individual actions and larger 'material-semiotic activity systems' as they are mapped on concrete geographical spaces. (Definition provided by de Saint-Georges)
Geosemiotics	The study of the social meaning of the material placement of signs and discourses and of our actions in the material world in relation to them. (Definition provided by Al Zidjaly)
Higher-level action	An action that is bracketed by an opening/closing and made up of a multiplicity of chained lower-level actions. Often, we find several higher-level actions embedded in another, and/or overarching higher-level action. (Definition provided by Pirini)
Historical body	History of personal experience in the individual body of a social actor. (Definition provided by Pan)
Horizontal identity production	The process of producing identity elements simultaneously, through multiple higher-level actions, and/or higher-level actions that produce multiple identity elements. (Definition provided by Pirini)
Hyperlink	Connections between web pages and other web pages, or between web pages and non-html documents, or between locations on a single web page. A hyperlink is the connection, not the clickable area on the page. (Definition provided by Knox and Djonov)

Hypermedia	Media which use hypertext (Definition provided by Knox and Djonov)
Hypermodality	The combination of hypermedia and multimodality (Definition provided by Knox and Djonov)
Hypertext anchor	The clickable area on a web page that activates a hyperlink (Definition provided by Knox and Djonov)
Hypertext mark-up language (html)	The computer language used to write web pages (Definition provided by Knox and Djonov)
Image-flow	A semiotic mode, which organises images into meaningful sequences. This semiotic mode has two variants: static image-flow in printed documents and dynamic image-flow in film. (Definition provided by Hiippala)
Indexicality	Refers to the context-dependency of signs (i.e., the study of the aspects of meaning that depend on the placement of signs in the material world). (Definition provided by Al Zidjaly)
Interaction Order	The forms of social interactions we produce when we come together. According to Goffman (1959), there are eleven interaction orders: single, with, file or procession, queue, contact, service encounter, conversational encounter, meeting, people-processing encounter (gate-keeping encounter), platform event (watch), celebrative occasion. (Definition provided by Al Zidjaly)
Interaction order	How people act or interact in relation to others in a social action.
	Nexus of practice: when a social action is routinely taken at a recognizable time and place, it is called a nexus of practice. (Definition provided by Pan)
Interactive meaning	In Functional Grammar and visual grammar these are meanings that account for the establishment of human relationships. (Definition provided by Maiorani)
Intermediary layers of discourse	The intermediary layers of discourse "are formed by a social actor in connection with and through their networks" (Norris 2011: 179) and these produce continuous identity elements. (Definition provided by Matelau)

Intermodal harmony	Intermodal harmony denotes a typical quality of a multimodal artefact that deliberately and intentionally links the various semiotic modes present so that a unified text emerges. Harmony between the modes must be understood as coherence, which derives from complementary connections in terms of form, meaning or function. (Definition provided by Stöckl)
Kitesurfing	Sport wherein a kite and board (and other equipment) are employed for the purpose of riding across the surface of the water and/or riding on the face of waves while often performing aerial manoeuvres or tricks. (Definition provided by Geenen)
Lower-level action	The smallest interactional meaning unit with a beginning and an end point. (Definition provided by Pirini)
Material culture	Coming from anthropology is the idea that analysis of everyday objects can reveal much about the ideas, values and identities that form our culture. (Definition provided by Machin)
Material substrate	A physical substrate, which may be manipulated for meaning-making. Historical examples include clay tablets, papyrus, manuscripts, paper and screen. (Definition provided by Hiippala)
Mediated action	The unit of analysis of mediated discourse analysis. All social actions are somehow mediated through material or psychological tools. (Definition provided by Jones)
Mediation	A property which unequivocally materialises in and through all mediated action. Refers to the real-time process wherein social actor and mediational means come together in mediated action. All social action is mediated and resultantly, mediation is a property exemplified in all social action. (Definition provided by Geenen)
Mediational interrelationship	Mediational Interrelationship highlights that the ways in which an object, article, material or tool mediates, is always and only a property of interrelationship. If one endeavours to articulate the character of a particular tool-in-use, one must always focus on the complex interrelationships which

	manifest and how the mediational means interrelate with one another. No mediational means can mediate in isolation. (Definition provided by Geenen)
Mediational means/cultural tool	The material or psychological means by which actions are accomplished. Cultural tools are a unique category of meditational means which, through the histories of their use, have come to be associated with particular social practices and social identities. (Definition provided by Jones)
Metaphor/ metonymy	Metaphor means using one sign to refer to something other than what it originally and literally stands for, e.g. low for sadness. Such transfers of meaning are based on correlations in experience between two domains, which are very different from one another. In metonymy signs can substitute for one another because they belong to one and the same concept or are contiguous to one another. Usually, metonymy is based on part-whole relations and associations, e.g. crown for government. (Definition provided by Stöckl)
Metonymy	A rhetorical figure which communicates meaning through a metaphorical making, whereby the object stands for something that is related or associated with it. (Definition provided by Stöckl)
Modal complexity	The degree of interrelationship between modes in reference to a higher-level action. An action may have high modal complexity in comparison to another higher-level action. (Definition provided by Pirini)
Modal density	The degree of complexity and intensity of modes employed in reference to a higher-level action. (Definition provided by Pirini)
Modal intensity	The degree of strength with which a particular mode is employed in reference to a higher-level action. (Definition provided by Pirini)
Mode	Semiotic system with rules and regularities attached to them as they are in use by social actors. (Definition provided by Pirini)

Mood	This is the basic linguistic structure formed by the combination of Subject and Finite that determines the mood of a clause (i.e. declarative, imperative, exclamative, interrogative). (Definition provided by Maiorani)
Motion line	Visual convention used to indicate smell or movement and to show moods and feelings. They can only be understood in context since they do not have any meanings on their own. (Definition provided by Pinar)
Multimodal analytics	A systematic study of semantic patterns in multimodal texts where complex multidimensional data structures arising from close multimodal analysis are interpreted using mathematical techniques and scientific visualizations. (Definition provided by O'Halloran)
Multimodal transcription	Multimodal transcription is the act of re-making a text for analytical and rhetorical purposes using a different set of modes. For instance, in multimodal research transcribers often turn a text originally made in speech, gesture and gaze into a text made in writing and image. (Definition provided by Bezemer)
Multimodality	The interplay of multiple semiotic modes to transmit meaning. (Definition provided by Pinar)
Nexus of practice	A nexus of practice is the point where multiple discursive and non-discursive practices come into contact and interact. The pattern that is constituted as this intersection is usually the product of a certain history and reflexive of specific social conventions for a given group. This means that a nexus of practice can simultaneously refer to a genre of activity, to the group of people practicing that activity or to the conventions that are associated with the activity. (Definition provided by de Saint-Georges)
Outer layers of discourse	The outer layers of discourse "are formed by the larger society and which are enforced by the extended networks that a social actor is part of" (Norris 2011: 179) and these produce general identity elements. (Definition provided by Matelau)

Page-flow	A semiotic mode which exploits the two-dimensional layout space for making additional meanings. This semiotic mode may combine other semiotic modes such as text-flow and image-flow in its expression. (Definition provided by Hiippala)
Participative enquiry	Participative enquiry was first defined in Reason's work as a research endeavour that seeks to involve people in research rather than subject them to it. Participative enquiry allows those of interest to the researcher a role in defining the research process, the research questions, the research procedure, and the research outcomes. (Definition provided by Iedema)
Place semiotics	A set of semiotic systems including code preference, inscription, emplacement but also anything and everything in the built environment. (Definition provided by Al Zidjaly)
Research ethics	The principles of behaviour underlying the practice of scientific research. These principles are not necessarily the same across disciplines. Principles, how they are expressed and the weighting given to them are continuously debated. (Definition provided by Pirini)
Researcher role	Researcher role refers to the position taken up by the researcher in relation to other researchers and the participants of the study. This is heavily influenced by the participants as co-researchers and can often change during the course of the research project. Researcher role refers not just to the material position and actions of the researcher while engaged in the field, but also their interpersonal positioning and affect on the research site as a whole. (Definition provided by Geenen)
Rheme	In the Theme/Rheme structure of a clause, this is what follows the Theme. (Definition provided by Maiorani)
Semantic/ pragmatic means	A pronounced lower-level action that can function both semantically and pragmatically to signal to others that the focus of the social actor performing the action is changing, and to assist the social actor to structure simultaneous and serial higher-level actions in their own mind. (Definition provided by Pirini)

(Semi-)automated communicative modes	Standardized algorithmic processes that support members in the creation and/or distribution of texts and other data. (Definition provided by Eisenlauer)
Semiotic mode	Semiotic modes are systems of signs with an internal structure (grammar). They contain sign repertoires and the rules for how they make meaning, combine to form larger structures and can be used for certain functions. Besides their coded nature, semiotic modes also involve a specific channel of perception (e.g. visual, auditory, tactile) and a medial realization using certain materials. Central semiotic resources would be language (speech/writing), picture (still/moving), music, noise, gesture and many others. All semiotic modes a culture uses in its communicative practices may be called semiosphere. (Definition provided by Stöckl)
Site of engagement	A moment in time and space at which particular meditational means, social actors and social practice converge to make a particular mediated action the focal point of attention. (Definition provided by Jones)
Social action	Any action taken by an individual in a social setting within a social network. (Definition provided by Pan)
Social actor	The agent or instigator of an action. (Definition provided by Al Zydjaly)
Social Network Sites (SNS)	Social Software-based Websites whose primary aim is establishing and maintaining online communities by asking participants to present and to communicate with other participants with the help of pre-given templates and (semi-)automated communicative modes. (Definition provided by Eisenlauer)
Social practice	A mediated action or combination of mediated actions that has/have come to be standardized or regularized within a particular community of social actor. (Definition provided by Jones)
Social semiotics	Social semiotics is a term introduced by Halliday in his book Language as a social semiotic (1978) and developed further by Robert Hodge and Gunther Kress in their book Social Semiotics (1988). Social semiotics argues against the tradi-

tional semiotic separation between language as a formal system and its use in the context of social relations and processes including power and ideology. (Definition provided by Jewitt)

State-transition diagrams Computer generated visualisations which display configurations of systemic choices in dynamic media, such as videos. (Definition provided by O'Halloran)

Stylistics The study of language in literary contexts, linking formal analysis of the work to literary interpretation. (Definition provided by Gibbons)

Syntactic parallelism Where syntactic constructions are repeated for literary effect. (Definition provided by Gibbons)

Systemic functional linguistics Systemic Functional Linguistics was developed by Linguist Michael Halliday in the early 1960's. It is a theory of language that is primarily concerned with what language does, and how it does it, with a focus on the linguistic choices present in a communicative utterance. This focus on meaning as choice provides the central theoretical framework for Systemic Functional approaches to multimodality to analyse the function and meaning of language use alongside other semiotic. (Definition provided by Jewitt)

Text-flow A foundational semiotic mode typically found in written documents. Its structure is characterised by the principle of linearity, that is, text-flow organises written language into a form of linear, unfolding discourse. Text-flow may be occasionally interrupted by various types of graphics. (Definition provided by Hiippala)

Textual meaning In Functional Grammar and visual grammar these are meanings that account for coherence in text. (Definition provided by Maiorani)

"The making of" video A promotional video intended to disclose aspects of the production process of a certain film or commercial with the implicit purpose of promoting the advertised film or the product advertised in the commercial. (Definition provided by Maier)

3-D semiotics	The analysis of the meaning potentials of shape, size, form and materials. Also here done in the tradition of Critical Disourse Analysis to reveal buried ideologies. (Definition provided by Machin)
Transcription conventions	Transcription conventions are explicit rules for transcription. They often include standard orthographic rules and linguistic conventions for representing features of speech such as intonation as well as non-standard ways of graphically representing features of action such as movement. (Definition provided by Bezemer)
Typographic configuration	Typographic configurations are patterned combinations or sets of certain typographic means and uses, which have become conventionalized for and are typical of a genre. Many everyday documents can easily be recognized not so much by what they say but how they are designed (typo-) graphically. (Definition provided by Stöckl)
Typography/ typographic resources	Typography comprises all visual aspects of writing ranging from the form of the lettering to the overall graphic design and layout of the medial space. Typography is a paraverbal semiotic mode, i.e. it accompanies the written realisation of language and is tied to the verbal message. The resources typography commands can be subdivided into micro-, meso-, macro- and paratypographic means. These are different but interlocking domains of typographic work, which relate to various elements of typography (e.g. fonts, lines, pages, documents, materials). (Definition provided by Stöckl)
User text actions	The general action of generating and distributing texts via and within a Social Software, its involved goal-directedness and its consequential effects. (Definition provided by Eisenlauer)
Vertical identity production	The process of producing identity elements influenced by, and influencing, different layers of discourse. The main layers identified in MIA are the outer layers, the intermediary layers and the inner layers. (Definition provided by Pirini)

Vertical identity production	Three layers of discourse that contribute to the construction of an individual's identity elements (Norris 2011) (Definition provided by Matelau)
Video-reflexive ethnography	Video-reflexive ethnography was defined in Iedema et al 2006 as a form of participative enquiry that seeks to involve practitioners in identifying domains of research interest, ways of capturing those domains on video, reflecting on the footage thus produced, and generating practice change proposals that have a good chance of being realised. The method arose from combining an ethnographic approach to deploying video in workplaces, with a reflexive component that enables practitioners to view and scrutinise their own ways of working. (Definition provided by Iedema)
Visual semiotics	The study of the ways in which visual images produce social meaning (Kress and van Leeuwen, 1996). (Definition provided by Al Zidjaly)
War monuments	These material forms of commemoration, comprised of figures of soldiers, religious emblems, mythical persons and other symbolic forms have been used by authorities in different ways and at different times, to naturalise and justify war. Definition provided by Machin)
Zone of identification	A routine practice in which a researcher has or can take a place as an accepted legitimate participant. Within this zone of identification, the researcher can begin to analyze the social practices of nexus in order to change the nexus of practice. (Definition provided by Pan)

Index

action
- frozen 48, 77, 80, 388
- higher-level 15–16, 77, 88, 338–343, 388, 391
- lower-level 14, 17, 77–86, 230, 390
- mediated 7, 14, 40–41, 56–60, 77–82, 247–254, 350, 390, 394

advertising
- agency 339
- commercials 107
- posters 267
- print 281

affect 196, 383
Alaska Natives 9
anthropology 130
attention/awareness 84–88, 165, 388
audience address 304, 383
authenticity 107, 259, 297–309, 384
automated modes 318

balloon 339–341, 357–369, 384
bilingual education 9
billboards 337

caption 357, 384
circumferencing 54, 58, 385
code preference 67, 70, 393
comic book 357–369, 385
communicative space 335–345, 385
communities of practice 46
configurations
- modal 108, 135
- register 32
- typographic 396

connotation 281, 385
conversation analysis 53, 61, 127, 157, 385
co-researcher 213, 386
co-researchers 234, 393
corporate video 93, 386
Critical Discourse Analysis 53, 132, 140, 386
cultural tools 40–43, 247, 252, 391
cycles of discourse 56, 58, 386

data, audio-video 213, 224, 384
dialogicality 66, 72
diffraction 196, 199, 207, 386
discourse semantics 112–116, 120, 387
discourses in place 42, 53–54, 63–75, 131, 350

embodied learning 347–355, 387
emplacement 67, 70, 393
ethics 196, 233–241
ethics application 233–241, 387
ethics review boards 233–241, 387

Facebook 23, 311–320
factuality 184, 297–308, 387
- verbal and visual 305
film 19–21, 93, 206, 214, 267, 290, 389, 396
foreground-background continuum 77

GeM model 117–120
GeM project 32
genre space 32–33, 114
geography of discourse 347, 388
geosemiotic analysis 67–76
geosemiotics 7–12, 63–77, 388

historical body (ies), 44–46, 53–59, 168, 350, 388
horizontal identity production 77, 90, 388
hyperlink 172, 388
hypermedia 172–189, 389
hypermodality 172–174, 389
hypertext anchor 172, 389
hypertext mark-up language (html) 172, 389

identity
- fluid Maori 257–262
- horizontal 77, 90, 388
- vertical 77, 255–263, 397
image-flow 112–116, 389, 393
indexicality 63–71, 128, 389
interaction order 10, 42, 53–59, 63–76, 158, 350–351, 389

interconnections 245–252, 388
intermodal harmony 281, 390
interplay 41, 94–108, 132, 273–277, 288, 299, 307–308, 360, 392
interrelations 113, 252, 315
itineraries 43–51

Kress, Gunther 20–22

layers of discourse
– central 255–262, 385
– intermediate 255–262, 389
– outer 255–262, 393
– vertical 255–262, 264
layout structure 30–32, 118–120

macrotypography 283
market 269, 278
material culture 323, 390
material substrate 112–117, 390
mediated discourse analysis V, 27, 7–12, 13, 39–51, 77, 247, 337, 347–354, 390
mediated discourse theory 53, 63
mediation VI, 1, 10, 40, 245–253, 337–340, 390
mediational interrelationship 245–251, 390
mediational means 40, 59–60, 88–89, 245–254, 342–345, 350
medium 19–21, 30, 115–117, 292, 360
mesotypography 283
microtypography 283
modal complexity 77, 83, 86, 391
modal density 17, 77–89, 335–345, 391
modal intensity 83, 77–84, 338, 391
motion line 357, 392
multimodal (inter)action analysis 13–17, 77–90, 335
multimodal analysis software 148–150
multimodal analytics 137–150, 392
multimodal genre 32–33, 111–118, 133, 359, 385
multimodal mediated theory 247
multimodal transcription 17, 81–82, 155–169, 392

narrative 7–10, 22, 306–307, 357–364, 371–378
news opening sequences 304
nexus analysis 7–11, 53–61, 63–75
nexus of practice 7–12, 55–61, 347, 389, 392
– engaging the 56
Norris, Sigrid 77–90

page-flow 112–120, 393
paratypography 283
pictorial 286–294, 360, 374
place semiotics 63–76, 393
poster 269–278, 290–291
psychological tools 78, 248, 390

references, temporal and spatial 306
research ethics 233–241, 393
researcher role 213–229, 393
resemiotisation 43–44, 148
rhetorical structure 27–30, 117–120
rhetorical structure theory 27
Rhetorical Structure Theory 26, 118

Scollon, Ron 7–12
selection 78, 117, 144, 178, 315–316
semantic/pragmatic means 77–87, 394
semiotic mode 281–283, 394
semiotic register 316
semiotic resources 23, 111–117, 129–132, 137–150, 171–183, 299, 314–318, 325–334, 394
site of engagement 40–43, 80, 220, 314, 335–342, 394
slogans 146, 270–275, 286
social action 7, 13–14, 43, 53–61, 63–75, 77–90, 247–248, 394
social actor 16, 43, 54–60, 63, 89, 133, 221, 247–253, 259, 338–344, 394
Social Media 179, 311–319
Social Network Sites 311–313, 394
social practice(s), 7, 40–44, 58, 95–98, 132, 354, 394
social semiotics 95, 127, 132–133, 137, 297, 335, 394
software bias 317

state-transition diagrams 137, 148, 395
systemic functional theory 137, 148
systemic functional linguistics 127–129, 137, 395

text generation 25–27, 311–319
text-flow 28, 30, 112–121, 395
"the making of" video 93–107
traditional/marae Maori identity 257–264
transcription conventions 82, 157, 396
trilogy 269–279
typography 23, 115, 138, 160, 281–293, 362, 369, 396

unit of analysis 12–14, 40, 53, 77, 127, 173, 247–248, 385, 390

video data 78, 195, 213, 231
video-reflexive ethnography 196–206, 397
Van Leeuwen, Theo 174–191
Vygotsky, Lev 40, 248
visual semiotics 63–76, 270–276, 397

Wertsch, James 78, 80, 247–249
war monuments 323–334, 397
workplace practices 347

zone of identification 54–57, 397

www.ingramcontent.com/pod-product-compliance
Lightning Source LLC
Chambersburg PA
CBHW051204300426
44116CB00006B/427